THE MYTH OF POPE JOAN

Detail of "The Popess," tarot card from the Visconti-Sforza deck, painted ca. 1450 by Bonifacio Bembo or Francesco Zavattari. John Pierpont Morgan Library, New York, MS M.630.3.

THE MYTH OF

POPE JOAN

ALAIN BOUREAU

TRANSLATED BY

LYDIA G. COCHRANE

THE UNIVERSITY OF CHICAGO PRESS
CHICAGO AND LONDON

Alain Boureau is director of studies at the Ecole des Hautes Etudes en Sciences Sociales, and a director at the Centre de Recherches Historiques, Paris. He is the author of nine books, including *The Lord's First Night: The Myth of the Droit de Cuissage,* also published by the University of Chicago Press.

The University of Chicago Press, Chicago 60637
The University of Chicago Press, Ltd., London
© 2001 by The University of Chicago
All rights reserved. Published 2001
Printed in the United States of America

10 09 08 07 06 05 04 03 02 01   5 4 3 2 1
ISBN (cloth): 0-226-06744-0
ISBN (paper): 0-226-06745-9

Originally published as *La papesse Jeanne,* © Aubier, Paris, 1988; © Flammarion, 1993.

Library of Congress Cataloging-in-Publication Data
Boureau, Alain.
  [Papesse Jeanne. English]
  The myth of Pope Joan / Alain Boureau ; translated by Lydia G. Cochrane.
    p.   cm.
  Includes bibliographical references and index.
    ISBN 0-226-06744-0 (alk. paper) — ISBN 0-226-06745-9 (pbk. alk. paper)
    1. Joan (Legendary Pope)   2. Popes—Legends.   3. Women in Christianity—History—Middle Ages, 600–1500.   4. Church history—Middle Ages, 600–1500.   I. Title.
  BX958.F2 B6813   2001
  262'.13—dc21   00-011154

♾ The paper used in this publication meets the minimum requirements of the American National Standard for Information Sciences—Permanence of Paper for Printed Library Materials, ANSI Z39.48-1992.

CONTENTS

ILLUSTRATIONS

I am delighted that my book is now available to English-language readers. Twelve years after its first publication in France, I have little to add to its presentation, nor have I major corrections to add. It is true, however, that the questions put to me by Lydia Cochrane, an attentive and demanding translator, gave me an opportunity to clarify some references and correct a few minor errors. The American edition has also permitted me to bring certain of the notes up to date. But all in all I have to say, with no false modesty, that my text has withstood the test of time. No review has challenged my demonstration. Still, a historian must remain skeptical where the efficacy of his or her demonstration is concerned: the deconstruction of the myth of the popess has not impeded its survival. Since 1988 a study and a novel, both of which I have added at the end of the chronological bibliography, have maintained the legend. Both of these works take my book into account, but they choose the path of reverie and the imaginary.

For an American public more sensitive to such questions than its French counterpart, I must note one aspect not sufficiently stressed in my original preface: this study has a contribution to make to Women's Studies. Whether the legend of Pope Joan was believed true or not, it in fact explored the case of a woman who transgressed the major prohibition that women not receive holy orders. That exclusion traces a strong line of demarcation between genres. My chapter on the "sisters" of the popess shows that this was an exclusion that was clearly perceived, and at times contested, not only by exceptional women but also by certain men who followed the careers of those women with admiration or awe. The case of the popess uses the experimental mode to pose the question of whether that prohibition was justified, or even efficacious.

There is another matter to which I have devoted considerable thought since the publication of this book in France, which is that of rites and ceremonies. The initial sources of this book about Pope Joan are descriptions of papal coronations. In an attempt to explain astonishing divergences in eyewitness accounts regarding what might be thought to be an objective phenomenon—given that everything in it was highly visible and public—

and in an attempt to comprehend the development of interpretations that eventually distorted the initial visions, I have tried to show that a public ritual did not always have the simplicity, or even the exclusive aim, often attributed to it. A public ritual is a common, shared action, but it also involves all the complexity and polysemy of other human actions. In other words, a ritual, even when it is strictly laid down, never has a unique function; it is reformulated, shaped by differing universes of belief and perception.

Finally, if I am still permitted this backward look at my own work, I realize to what extent I have been fascinated by the dream of exhausting a historical object and of presenting a complete description and explication of it. My attempt to cover all the sources on the popess over seven centuries and to consider the different contexts of the reception of the legend over the long term is witness to this. Another work, *The Lord's First Night* (also published by the University of Chicago Press), was motivated by the same aims. On a quite different level, my most recent book, *Théologie, science et censure au XIIIe siècle: Le cas de Jean Peckham*, reflects a similar desire for totality, though over a shorter time span. This is an orientation that may surprise an American reader accustomed to more skeptical tendencies and a more relativized historical explanation. The reader must be the judge; I am simply happy that the present translation gives me a chance to mark this difference, and also to state my hope that diversity in intellectual traditions will encourage fruitful exchange.

Alain Boureau

INTRODUCTION

In the study that I am making of our behavior and motives, fabulous testimonies, provided they are possible, serve like true ones.
Whether they have happened or no, in Paris or in Rome, to John
or Peter, they exemplify in all events, some human potentiality,
and thus their telling imparts useful information to me.

Montaigne, *Essays*, I, 21 (Frame translation)

ho would believe that there are people in Rome today who attach much importance to the story of Popess Joan?" Stendhal
wrote around 1830. His astonishment did not stop him from
treating the topic at some length. We will return to him in
chapter 8. More than a century and a half later, historians who consider
Joan often face the same condescending but titillated astonishment.
Quickly suspected of ignoring more prestigious history in order to dabble
in the dubious tinsel of scandalmongering, they are forced to defend their
austerity and seriousness, but they are not always believed. The story of
the popess continues to kindle a desire to penetrate the antechambers and
corridors of power (in this case, a sacred and obstinately male power). In
the years during which this study was in preparation three works of fiction
about Joan were published in France alone, followed by an investigation
of Pope Pius XII's female secretary-nurse titled *La Popessa*. Such works display a taste for extraordinary revelations ("Scandal in the Vatican," "The
Pope Was a Woman"), expressed more or less baldly according to the
public they seek to reach. Far from wearing thin, this sensationalism
draws from a powerful source: in today's world the papacy and the Roman
Catholic priesthood are the last bastions of the exclusion of women in
Western culture. Only in this redoubt can the ancient game of the substitution of the sexes be played and a nostalgia for the separation of the sexes
or, to the contrary, their fusion find expression.

That is all I intend to say about the fascination that the popess exerts.
Rather, I wish to proclaim my ambitions as a historian, right from the start

1

and with a rigor exacerbated by the proximity of scandalmongering chronicle. Do not expect a declaration of modesty here: the subject matter treated will take care of that. Rather than boasting of the results obtained in these few introductory pages, I shall instead stress the size of the task I have undertaken and the height of my hopes.

The first object under consideration is the tale of Pope Joan. The narrative appeared toward the end of the thirteenth century, and it soon settled down to an easily summarized common version. Around 850 a woman, born in Mainz but of English origin, disguised herself as a man so that she could follow her lover, who had taken up a life of studies and who, consequently, inhabited a totally male world. She succeeded so well in that career choice that after studying for some time in Athens, she went to Rome, where she was so warmly welcomed and admired that she entered the hierarchy of the Curia and was in due course elected pope. Her pontificate lasted a bit longer than two years and was broken off by a scandal: Joan had not renounced the pleasures of the flesh; she became pregnant, and she died after giving birth in public during a procession from St. Peter's, in the Vatican, to the Church of St. John Lateran. Different versions of this story cite various traces or proofs of this event, even a memoir written by the popess, and after that date procedures were set into place for manual verification, during the coronation ceremonies, that the new pope was male. When later papal processions from the Vatican to the Lateran reached the church of San Clemente, they supposedly veered off from the most direct route in order to avoid the spot where the birth had taken place. A statue or an inscription reportedly memorialized the deplorable incident.

Did this papacy truly exist? Certainly not. The reader who hoped to find a real person remembered in these pages will have to be satisfied with the consoling thought that Joan was as real in the minds of men of the past as an actual Joan would have been. What happened in 850 has historical reality only because of the beliefs and behaviors that it inspired; if it had actually happened but had been ignored, it would have been a fleeting news item. Imagine for a moment that Pope Pius XII was a woman in male dress. If no one had known that fact and it had been discovered by some isolated historian, it would be interesting only to someone with a deep interest in the psychological makeup of Eugenio (or Eugenia) Pacelli (1876–1958). If, on the other hand, rumors had spread in 1995 or in 2135 throughout an agitated Catholic community, their effects would indeed belong within the domain of history.

This would be a slight consolation indeed, and contestable to boot (historians are interested in the psychology of sovereigns too), if the fictive life of Joan did not offer great attractions. It is in fact a fine historical object, heavy with meaning if light on reality. Freighted with the weight of genuine disquietude, but relieved by incisions made in it by imagination and ideology, it travels briskly through zones dense with history to provide a visible signpost in the broad landscape of time. I shall insist on keeping to a resolutely historical and temporal orientation as we look in detail at Joan and her charms.

First: I shall state, with all due detachment, that the story that was so often picked up, reiterated, discussed, and reshaped in itself constitutes an important cultural phenomenon in the domains of historiography, imagery, printing and publishing, literature, and doctrine.

Second: A simple desire to describe a phenomenon is insufficient to account for the intense curiosity it aroused in history's actors and commentators (of whose company I count myself). The episode of Joan presents a major transgression that took place at the heart and at the summit of the Church, the fundamental institution of the West. It may be a commonplace to assert that Christianity constitutes the decisively original feature in all domains of Western history, but we are far from exhausting the repercussions of that observation. What happens when Peter, the rock and keystone of that central edifice, becomes Joan, and when divine election changes into human (and female) trickery?

For two or three centuries, everyone believed that the episode had truly occurred. Men of the Middle Ages faced that reality and attempted to accommodate it within their conceptions of the world; the act of narration and interpretation became part of the many single tactics and strategies surrounding the fundamental questions of ecclesiology—theories regarding the status of the Church. One such question was the validity of sacraments performed by or through an illegitimate pope; others were the challenge to papal infallibility, the principle of the continuous Roman tradition from St. Peter, and the question of the exclusion of women from the priesthood.

Appropriations of this scandal and horror, along with attempts to circumvent them and the contestations that they gave rise to, contributed much to the construction of a church that was made of both tithes and dogmas, stones and Peter, institutions and beliefs. When Catholics rejected the popess, she entered into polemics and literature, where she contributed to building the reformed and lay edifices constructed in opposition to the Church.

The episode of Joan is thus an important historical object that occupies a place between action and thought and between religion and politics and is set in the mainstream of history. Narrative and rumor act, in the sense that a chemical agent acts and prompts reactions. That conviction leads me to reject a "mythographic" approach to the topic, an approach principally interested in describing the narrative and thematic transformations of a text through time that has led to innumerable studies, in various domains, of "the image of X in the time of Y." The relatively stable narrative that interests me here does not lend itself well to that sort of exercise. Above all, however, what I reject is the nonproblematic tendency that treats a narrative as part of the decor and is satisfied with a bland contemplation of the changing colors of the times.

Third: Beyond a curiosity shared by the historian and the reader, the historian should be clear about the pleasures and the specific benefits afforded by a study and offered to that reader. The story of Joan has served me as a way to penetrate complex historical universes. The legend of the popess, authentic or not, poses the problem of belief that is the principal focus of this study. During the two or three centuries from 1250 to 1450, even to 1550, the Church believed in the existence of Joan and encouraged the faithful to do so too, even though her story was detrimental to its interests, as is clear from the later Protestant and anticlerical appropriation of that story. What mode of belief permitted both belief in the existence of Joan and belief in papal infallibility, a tenet proclaimed in clear terms as early as the fourteenth century? What does one believe when recounting the episode or reading about it in a work of fiction? Did the Lutheran who pictured Joan as the Antichrist believe in that representation in the same way as the medieval chronicler weighing the likelihood of the incident? What sort of certitude lay behind accounts of the rite to verify that a new pope was male? Radical changes in how Joan has been perceived and in the ways in which her story has been inserted into ecclesiastical discourse suggest the hypothesis of the profound historicity of modes of belief. This topic will be fully discussed.

More generally, because the story of Joan is circumscribed and of minor importance, it will at unguarded moments provide access, as if inadvertently, to a closed or complex universe. I shall hope to demonstrate that the Joan affair and its mixture of the medieval history of Rome, liturgy, and ecclesiology provide ways to grasp certain obscure aspects of the rituals of papal coronation. What is more, the history of the popess, a limited, clearly defined sample that permits an exhaustive survey of the sources, offers a case study. A brief survey of satirical versions of the episode in eighteenth-century Europe will help reconstruct one segment of the literary "Bohemia" of the Enlightenment, but it will also help to pose the question of the functions and forms of anticlericalism during the French Revolution.

In short, I intend to treat Joan as a figure emblematic of the "long

Middle Ages" of *mentalités* so dear to Jacques Le Goff—a period that I would situate between the death of St. Bernard in 1153 and that of Hegel in 1831. These dates correspond fairly exactly with the "real life" of the popess: the appearance of the first texts around 1250 leads me to suppose that the legend arose at the end of the twelfth century; the Prussian poet Achim von Arnim, Joan's last faithful supporter, died in 1831, the year of Hegel's death.

In part I ("The Sex of the Popes: A Roman Story") I will attempt to pinpoint the origin of the episode, not by interrogating the earliest texts that narrate it (which refer to an already constituted story), but rather by investigating the ritual to verify that the new pope was of male sex, a ritual soon (that is, by the end of the thirteenth century) regarded as the institutional consequence of that event. Although authors close to the papacy often present that ritual as an authentic part of the pope's coronation, it was never attested in the official prescriptive texts. Still, it designates the precise notions to which belief in Joan was anchored.

In part II ("Joan Militant") I shall investigate the reasons for the Church's support of this legend by examining uses of the narrative within ecclesiological debate in the Middle Ages. As a counterpoint to this, I shall analyze the place of the popess within perceptions of women—clerical and lay, orthodox and heretic—up to the threshold of the early modern age.

In part III ("Death and Transfiguration of the Popess") I will deal with Joan's move into anti-Roman Protestant controversy, a move that led the Roman Catholic Church to abandon Joan during the course of the sixteenth century. Finally, I shall investigate the literary functions of the popess from the late fifteenth century to our own day.

Two methods share space in this book: chapters 1 to 4 will be devoted to a search for telling indications, which will begin by reassembling and inserting them into explanatory contexts; chapters 5 to 7 will be more diagnostic.

It is a pleasure to acknowledge the many people who have aided me in this long task. As a reader I am at times irritated by this custom: a list of thanks seems to me an exercise in vanity and imposture. On the one hand, authors seem to celebrate a monument when they give a long list of people who have participated in the work; presenting as guarantors of the final result those who, out of generosity or friendship, gave the author information or guidance seems an abusive legitimation. But how else am I to thank the long-suffering friends and readers whom I pursued with my requests for information or evaluations? It is absolutely true that this book, regardless of its ultimate merits, owes much to them. I am thinking of such attentive readers as Simona Cerutti, Colette Collomb Boureau, Carlo Ginzburg, Christian Jouhaud, Giovanni Levi, Daniel Milo, Aline Rousselle, and Jacques Revel; of people who responded to my specific questions, such as Robert Darnton, Jan Macek, Agostino Paravicini-Bagliani; of others who pointed out paths to follow, such as Colette Beaune, Yvonne Cazal, Claude Gaignebet, Claudio Ingerflom, Jean-Marie Moeglin, and Pierre Tranouez. My thanks also to Maud Espérou, who managed to procure for me, and with dispatch, texts that couldn't be found in France, and to Claude Bremond, Roger Chartier, Pierre Nora, and Jacques Revel, who welcomed various states of my *papesse* into their seminars at the Ecole des Hautes Etudes en Sciences Sociales.

Finally, I owe a particular debt of gratitude to Bernard Guenée, who, on the basis of a first stammering draft of this research project and with no further guarantee than his own generous confidence, opened the door to my Joan, first to his seminar at the Ecole Pratique des Hautes Etudes; then to a session of the Académie des Inscriptions et Belles-Lettres; and eventually to the Collection Historique, in which the French edition of the present work was first published.

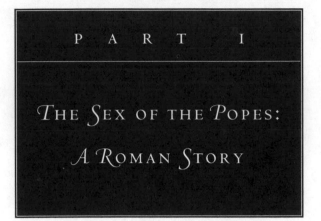

PART I

THE SEX OF THE POPES:

A ROMAN STORY

1. Woodcut from Johann Wolf, *Lectiones memorabiles,* Frankfurt. Bibliothèque Nationale, Paris.

I

The Pontificals

n 16 October 1978 the cardinals of the Roman Catholic Church, gathered in conclave, elected as pope the Polish prelate Karol Wojtyla, who took the name of John Paul II. In the *Nouvel Observateur* the essayist and philosopher Maurice Clavel heralded the event and the man in these terms:

> But let's get back to the point. First him. I see him. He has them.
> *Duas et bene pendentes,* for sure. Those shoulders, those proletarian jawbones. One of those stalwart, hearty men with an eye for the girls who—for a change—had something to offer God, like the sturdy, ecstatic medieval monks who, for that very reason, cultivated a sublime (imbeciles would say sublimated) devotion to the Blessed Virgin.[1]

Habet Duos

Maurice Clavel's populist, blustering, churlish, but emotional tone is familiar; it harks back to Léon Bloy and Georges Bernanos, but it also reflects the 1968 spirit of contestation. The figure of John Paul II, an energetic prelate of humble origin who sprang from the combative Catholic community in Poland, responded to expectations for a more dynamic Christianity after the moments of doubt and uncertainty that had been reflected in the tormented demeanor of Paul VI and the fragility of John Paul I. Clavel rejoiced in the advent of the robust, the elementary, and the virile as he hailed a leather and steel pope who promised to be a vigorous successor to parchment popes. The image that Clavel invents so feelingly for the new pope (shoulders, jawline, strength) starts with a direct attestation of virility: "He has them. *Duas et bene pendentes.*" The Latin formula elliptically cites a phrase that, according to a venerable report, proclaimed the newly elected pope to be a man: a deacon, after manual verification that the pope-elect possessed male genitals, announced: "Habet duos testiculos et bene pendentes" (He has two testicles, well hung).

Clavel's allusion resonates beyond the context of his fascination and his excitement to signal a final mode of survival of the legend of Pope Joan. The Latin phrase, which Clavel's readers probably understood well, was based on a rumor, a microscopic bit of lore, broadly shared but universally unmentioned. Several of the people with whom I spoke while researching this topic quoted the phrase, which they had heard at some time in the past and had tucked in the back of their minds. The phrase recalls the fable of a woman who, by dissimulating her sex, is supposed to have occupied the throne of St. Peter, after which the Church, anxious to avoid a repeat of such scandal, verified the sex of newly elected popes. No one today knows anything certain about the reality of this rite. The regime of belief that governs rumor makes it impossible to invalidate the rite: refutation is interpreted as denial, hence as a sort of confirmation. Thanks to the formulation of a rumor, Joan passed into eternity.

The Popess, Rumor, and Rite

From the very beginning, the rumored rite seems to have been connected with the legend of Pope Joan; it in turn lent reality and perpetual currency to that legend. As we shall see in a later chapter, the story of Joan appeared around 1250 in a handful of authors and became more widespread about 1300. In 1290 or thereabouts, Geoffroy de Courlon, a Benedictine, wrote of Joan in his chronicle of the Abbey of Saint-Pierre-le-Vif at Sens, but he closely followed the text of a Dominican, Martinus Polonus, or perhaps of the anonymous interpolator around 1280–85 who added to Martinus's *Chronica de Romanis pontificibus et imperatoribus* (Chronicle of the Popes of Rome and of the Emperors).[2] Geoffroy's use of Martinus is hardly surprising: Martinus's chronicle enjoyed an immediate, durable success, and it remained the major source for historians of Joan until the end of the Middle Ages. Geoffroy adds a note to his source, however: "It is said that this is why the Romans established the custom of verifying the sex of the elected [pope] through the opening in a stone throne."[3] At roughly the same date the Dominican Robert d'Uzès says of one of his many visions (which he dates to 1291, when he was in Orange):

> The Spirit of the Lord took hold of me in spirit and placed me in
> Rome. . . . I saw the wooden throne, very ancient and empty. . . .

Then the Spirit took me to the Palace of the Lateran. And there, it
put me down in the porch, before the porphyry seats, where it is
said that they verify that the pope is a man. Everything was covered with dust and no one seemed alive.[4]

It is worth noting that Robert seems to imply that this use of the chair was
already traditional: his allusion is brief because he supposes that the
reader knows about the rite. Around 1290 the rumor concerning the ritual
thus seems to have been well established, at least in oral form: both authors refer to a vague tradition ("it is said").

For nearly a century after, the rumored rite disappears; more accurately, no echo of it has reached our ears. All it takes to break a thread as
tenuous as this is one or two lacunae or omissions. Moreover, in the fourteenth century the papacy had left Rome for Avignon, and in spite of
scrupulous attempts to transfer liturgy to the new site, the Roman rites lost
much of their meaning and their complexity when they left the Eternal
City. In 1378, when Gregory XI brought the papacy back to Rome from
Avignon, the rumor of the ritual was revived, and around 1379 the anonymous hand who continued the chronicle of Johannes of Viktring not only
mentions Joan's papacy but also notes: "To avoid such an error, as soon as
the elected [pope] is seated on the throne of Peter, the least of the deacons
touches his genitals [as he is seated] on a chair pierced to that effect."[5]

RITES AND REGARDS

We can profit from this century-long silence to state the objectives and the
methods for pursuing an investigation that may seem as tortuous as the
route that the papal processions followed through Rome. We know that
from its inception the fable of Joan was cited as a factual proof of her existence: the liturgy of papal coronation reportedly included a rite aimed at
preventing a recurrence of the scandal of a woman pope. The rite never existed, however—at least none of the many and detailed normative texts
that outline the formalities of papal coronation mentions it. It is true that
rumor of the ritual is just as elusive as rumor of the fable of Joan's papacy,
but its secret essence suggests the hidden, invisible, inaccessible existence
of Joan, its object. There is a difference, though: the rumored ritual was a
living part of oral history, not part of the muffled tradition of books. At
every papal coronation it guided the spectators' gaze and colored their interpretation; it determined tactics of display or prohibition among liturgists and papal masters of ceremonies. Before relating the history of a
fable, it seems appropriate to sketch the history of a belief. As ceremonial

liturgy developed it became more and more public and political. It is a fact that up to the seventeenth century, spectators saw the rite of verification of the pope's male sex, thought they saw it, or thought they saw that it was being concealed. This is why I have chosen to depict Joan's place in public processions that some have seen as paying honor to her and why we will escort her through hundreds of processions recalling her memory. For the moment, we will put aside the human being behind this graceful ghost, reserving the right to inquire later into the veils and ornaments that men's dreams—gentle, vicious, or mocking—lent to Joan. She will serve as a witness, helping us to measure the meaning and the function of certain public rites. This is an immense and difficult task, and one for which we will need all of Joan's luster. Like a buoy, she is a consistent signal bobbing on the surface of the immense and imperceptible flow of the ceremonial for papal coronations. As such, she will enable us to ask what a specific ritual hides or displays, what we can observe of it from the outside, what men shaped and directed in it or history inscribed in it, and what tradition repeated of it. In short, the history of the supposed rite of verification will permit us to follow both the construction of a ceremony and its interpretation and public reception. The persistence of the belief implies that it was received in three equally revealing ways:

1. People believed, in all good faith, in the existence of the rite. In this case, we need to raise questions concerning the complexity of symbolic acts, the general comprehension of public and didactic ceremonies, the things obscured by such ceremonies, and the reasons underlying belief.

2. People pretended to believe in the existence of the rite for their own malicious reasons, playing on the weightiness of the ceremonial apparatus as a way to twist its meaning, but giving it a show of likelihood. In this case, we need to grasp the origin and the aims of this contestation, then look at the denials it prompted.

3. Some who had no intention of denouncing the ceremony constructed an imaginary reading in response to it that was parasitical, playful, or parodic. In this case, we will seek to understand the means used in such responses and the places in which they occurred.

My hope is that the slim silhouette of Joan will find a way to slip between the timelessness of the paradigm and constantly shifting contexts.

THE TWO FIRST WITNESSES: ADAM OF USK AND JACOPO D'ANGELO

Let us return to the trail of evidence where we left off. Aside from one isolated mention in the anonymous continuation of Johannes of Viktring's chronicle, written around 1379, and in spite of the wide diffusion of the fable of Joan during the fourteenth century, the next written trace of the rumored rite of verification comes in the early fifteenth century. Adam of Usk, a Welsh cleric, occupied several important posts in Rome, among them that of chaplain to Pope Boniface IX. In his *Chronicon* Adam tells of the ceremonies that accompanied the accession of Pope Innocent VII in 1404. Adam presents himself as an eyewitness to the festivities: "It gladdens my heart now to think of the part I played in such a ceremony." In reality, his only vivid description is of the public procession from St. Peter's to the Lateran for "taking possession of the Lateran," a topic to which we shall return. After the pope's coronation in St. Peter's, Adam tells us, the pope and his suite

> ride from there through Rome to the church of St John Lateran,
> the pope's own cathedral church—taking a roundabout route out
> of abhorrence of Pope Agnes, whose stone statue, with her son,
> stands on the direct route close to St Clement's—and, having ar-
> rived there, the pope dismounts and enters the church to be en-
> throned. Here he sits on a throne of porphyry through which a
> hole has been cut for this purpose, and is examined by one of the
> younger cardinals to ensure that he has male genitalia; where-
> upon, while "Te Deum laudamus" is sung, he is led to the high
> altar.[6]

It would be a mistake to take Adam's status as an eyewitness and participant in these ceremonies as pure fact; it is highly likely that his claims fall short of reality, given that he never was a member of the Curia. His rather rapid account in fact gathers together details (on the detour taken by the procession, on the effigy of the popess) that had been ceaselessly reiterated and refuted since the thirteenth century, and his report of the rite of verification is inserted somewhat vaguely and incoherently into the ceremonies at the Lateran.

The moment of verification is captured better by a contemporary of Adam's who wrote in considerable detail about the coronation ceremonies for Pope Gregory XII in 1406. Jacopo d'Angelo of Scarperia was one of the humanists active in Florentine circles who divided their time between assiduous study and the pursuit of ecclesiastical benefices. Born in Scarperia, a small town in the Tuscan hills north of Florence, Jacopo came to that city toward the end of the fourteenth century to be near the great Coluccio Salutati, in whose circle he met such young and brilliant disciples of Salutati's as Leonardo d'Arezzo and Filippo da Bergamo. Jacopo learned Greek under Emmanuel Chrysoloras, the Byzantine scholar who had transferred to Italy, and the translations from the Greek that Jacopo made after a stay in Byzantium (some of Plutarch's *Lives;* above all, Ptolemy) were probably what won him several minor posts in the Curia between 1401 and 1406. He eventually became secretary to Pope John XXIII.

In a long letter to Chrysoloras, his Byzantine Greek teacher, Jacopo describes the funeral of Innocent VII and the coronation of Gregory XII.[7] His report is important not only for its mention (and denial) of the rite of verification, but for its new approach: it is probably the first description of a papal investiture that is neither liturgical nor hagiographic. We will follow this ceremony closely: the product of two centuries of elaboration, it was still to some extent wrapped in medieval reserve, but it was beginning to be more oriented toward the public.

Jacopo wanted to impress his Byzantine correspondent with the splendor of the Roman institution, but he also wanted to demonstrate that the ceremonial was identical to Oriental rites for the consecration of popes and emperors. Hence he adopts the point of view of a bedazzled spectator more sensitive to the display of power than to liturgical norms and their theological significance. The result is that his report prefigures an entire literature of admiration that was to develop later around the monarchies of the early modern age. Jacopo's account will permit us to situate the circumstances of the rite of verification more exactly.

THE CORONATION OF GREGORY XII (1406)

The funeral of Innocent VII took place in St. Peter's at the Vatican in a solemn and public manner: the body was "mourned, washed, anointed, dressed in all the pontifical ornaments so that the spectacle of the funeral could be offered to all the people and the deceased could be publicly kissed and venerated." On the ninth day after the pope's death the Sacred College was enclosed in conclave. Once the vote had been obtained, the first phase of the ritual of installation—traditionally called *election* but actually proclamation—could begin. The newly elected pope was led into St. Peter's, where he chose his papal name.

> Then he is stripped of his former clothing and dressed in his new
> pontifical garb and is "crowned" with the miter. His feet are shod
> in gilded slippers, and he is immediately escorted to the altar,
> where he is venerated, his hands are kissed, and he prays. After
> that, the first of the pontifical deacons says in a loud voice, "I an-
> nounce to you a great joy: We have as pope Gregory XII." . . . An
> extraordinary crowd of all the human species comes running for-

ward, salutes the Holy Shepherd, venerates him, and kisses his feet.

The rite is repeated in the church next to the Basilica of St. Peter's, and the newly elected pope accepts veneration seated on a stone throne set up near the altar. During this time a curious custom takes place: Jacopo's account is the first sure mention of it, and it will be important in our later investigation: "What was formerly the private dwelling of the newly elect is openly and publicly sacked, and everything that is stolen or carried off is considered holy. Not only do the people carry off the furnishings, but also the tiles, the inner walls, the stones, even the outside walls, and they fight over all of these because they are holy." Finally, the newly elected pope, in consultation with the Sacred College, sets the day for his consecration, the second phase of the ceremonies.

On the appointed day, the pope, dressed in his pontifical robes and wearing the miter, is welcomed into the Basilica of St. Peter's by its priests and by the Sacred College, who then venerate him. Gregory blesses the throng from the sanctuary in the lower part of the basilica. Next, he puts on his ornaments of state: gilded slippers (Jacopo attributes their institution to Diocletian), the papal ring, an embroidered tunicle, a gold-embroidered chasuble, a triumphal cope, a gold-encrusted stole. For Jacopo, "These are the ornaments of the kings," following a tradition that went back to the Etruscan kings of Rome and had been transmitted by Tarquin the Elder (Tarquinius Priscus), Augustus, and Constantine. At that point the actual consecration begins. Gregory moves toward the altar of St. Peter's, holding in his hand a long reed with a bit of flaming flax stuffed in the upper end while the choir sings, three times, "Pater sancte, sic transit gloria mundi" (Holy Father, thus passes the glory of the world). When the pope reaches the high altar, where he alone can celebrate, he sits on a throne and is consecrated by the three most worthy bishops, who kiss his hands and feet. He descends to face the altar, wearing the pallium around his waist. The pallium "represents the dignity of the Supreme Pontiff. No one has the right to touch (attrectare) this pallium except with a pure and consecrated priestly hand." Then, "in imitation of your Patriarch [here Jacopo addresses Chrysoloras, his Byzantine correspondent], he goes to the high marble throne of the kings, on which the Father of Fathers (Patrum Pater) and the King of men permits himself, according to custom, to be venerated and kissed by all." After being acclaimed in various ways (and here Jacopo takes pains to stress the military and imperial character of these acclamations), the Mass of Consecration takes place. Still more benedictions follow, along with another sojourn on the raised throne. After this the coronation, the third phase of the ceremony, takes place, and it is followed by the cavalcade to the Lateran.

"Under the gaze of a throng without number, the leading members of the college of the pontiffs, after removing the miter, place on the divine head the tiara, or *citaris,* also called diadem, or *regnum.*" The tiara, with its long straight cone, "by which our Pope is declared King of kings," derives (Jacopo tells us) from the headdress of the Salian priests who were instituted by Numa Pompilius; it was subsequently transmitted to the Roman emperors, and, in the time of Constantine, to the popes. Once crowned, Gregory mounts a white horse caparisoned with a red altar cloth. The cavalcade then begins to form: first come twelve horsemen with trumpets and banners representing the twelve peoples of Etruria and carrying the signs of Roman power (the curule seat, the fasces, phalerae, and silk parasols); next come the two prefects of the navy ("so that all will understand that our Father reigns not only over the earth, but also over the sea"). After them come two horsemen brandishing long lances with cherubim set at their tips, followed by the great silver pontifical cross. The pontiff comes next. Jacopo comments that he throws fistfuls of silver coins into the crowd, as the Caesars had done. At the far end of Hadrian's Bridge the Jews of Rome, bearing the Tables of the Law, advance to meet the procession, which continues in its "triumphant course through the city," welcomed and greeted with enthusiastic applause and the thrown flowers of "an endless throng." The pope at last reaches the Lateran, the "palace particular to our sacred Pontiff." Jacopo reminds his correspondent that "the popes once used to live in it, when the air was not infected, as it is now, but was healthy and pure." He continues: "At the palace the pope dismounts his horse, and the community of the priests who serve the church lead him to a marble seat placed in the middle of the portico since time immemorial. It is called *stercoria* to remind the pope that he arises out of clay and dung *(stercus).*" The pope then dips his hand three times into a bowl and extracts gold pieces and throws them into the crowd, saying, "I want no gold for myself, nor do I want to be paid its price." After this he promises to protect and guide his people and be merciful toward them. The pope then enters into the Basilica of the Lateran and, seated on a marble chair, receives the veneration and the kisses of the priests. Next he moves from the basilica to the adjacent palace (called the Palace of Constantine). Another curule chair stands at the entrance to the palace, where Gregory stops to pray. He then mounts the stairs to the sanctuary of the chapel of San Silvestro, "before which two seats cut from porphyry are placed; and because the seats are pierced, the common people tell the senseless fable that someone touches *(attrectetur)* the pope as he sits on them to verify that he is indeed a man." While seated on the right-hand seat, he receives from the priest of San Silvestro the papal staff and the keys; while he is seated on the left-hand seat, the same priest places around his waist a red belt hung with twelve precious stones. "By the staff *(ferula)*, as if it were a royal scepter, he is given the power to judge and to govern. The keys constitute the gift made by our Redeemer to Peter." The precious stones, Jacopo tells us, evoke the priesthood of the Old Testament. Finally the pope, his ornaments removed, offers a public banquet in the Lateran Palace.

ENIGMAS OF THE RITE OF VERIFICATION

Jacopo d'Angelo's description is the first one to situate the rite of verification within the ceremony of pontifical investiture. It replaces a real, official rite that took place during the third phase of the ceremonies: the coronation and taking possession of the Lateran. As the pope sits first on one, then on the other of the two porphyry chairs with pierced seats that were placed before the chapel of San Silvestro in the Lateran palace, he dispenses wealth, then receives and gives back symbols of power (the papal staff, the keys, the belt). Even before we examine the morphology and the syntax of this official rite in chapter 2, we can hazard several remarks:

1. The verification takes place on a pierced chair. As it happens, Jacopo's description (but also all liturgical descriptions) give the seat a role of capital importance in official rites. This ceremonial obsession with a seat continues to figure in rites of power up to Saint-Simon's day. This means that our investigation should include a detailed list of the furnishings involved in papal investitures.

2. All later allusions to the rite of verification agree on the place, the moment, and the instrument used in the operation. Common sense tells us, however, that the explicit function of the rite is illogical in these circumstances. Canon law stipulated, early on, that the pope possesses full powers at the instant of his election, which would mean that this verification takes place too late. If it were to be at all effective, verification ought to take place during the conclave, whose institutional secrecy would facilitate the operation. (This was, incidentally, where and when the authors of farces about the popess written during the French Revolution situate the verification.) The rite of the pierced chairs, with its two versions, official and legendary, thus has a special density of its own that we will have to clarify.

3. The mystery of the dual rite is only a part of the larger enigma of the episode of the Lateran. In 1406, as Jacopo d'Angelo notes, the palace of the Lateran was no longer the papal residence; the liturgical and political

life of the papacy was concentrated in the Vatican. Moreover, the third phase of the investiture had become increasingly detached from the first two, and it could even take place several weeks after the pope's consecration. The ceremony of taking possession of the Lateran continued almost unchanged until it was simplified in the early sixteenth century, and it continues to our own day. The function of the ceremony remains unclear: Why repeat the specifically liturgical forms of papal investiture (the giving of the keys, the adoration of the enthroned pope, the note of stercory humiliation)? The complexity of the events that take place when the papal procession arrives at the Lateran means that we cannot consider them as simply reflecting the point of arrival of a cortege, thus analogous to a royal entry. The Lateran contains other mysteries as well: it is interesting to note the allusion to the impurity of the air in these sacred but neglected places; they are abandoned, but they are nonetheless possessed.

4. We have lingered long over the testimony of one particular spectator, Jacopo d'Angelo. This decision can be justified by the fact that he was the first writer to place the rite of verification within the overall ceremonies. Moreover, it is interesting to have a report of the ceremony set within its historical existence, halfway between when it was first instituted in full form in the late eleventh century and when it became fossilized in the seventeenth century. Jacopo's description raises the problem, however, of just what he could have seen. He probably saw more than an ordinary Roman or a foreign visitor; probably less than the canons of the Lateran. A large measure of uncertainty remains, which refers us back to the insoluble question of the visibility of ceremonies and the mode of narration proper to such accounts. The author uses the same tone to narrate what he has seen, what he knows about, and what he is interpreting. He eliminates differences as he tells of events, because the action he is representing is at once empirical, governed by set expectations, and normative. When he states, "The Pope sits down," we can read this, simultaneously, as "I have seen him sit down," "I know for a fact that he sat down," "He is supposed to sit down," and "It seems that he sat down." Jacopo's vision of the ceremony is, in a global sense, political. We might well ask what he wanted to see. Why should he mention the question of the verification of the pope's male gender and then reject the idea that it took place? We shall return to this curious denial mechanism. If we look beyond the scene at the Lateran and keep in mind that the description was aimed at Jacopo's Byzantine correspondent, we have a better grasp of Jacopo's point of view. The ecclesiological context of his description and the person to whom it was addressed seem to determine his emphasis on the magnificence of the ceremonial and its exhibition of power. In the early fifteenth century, even

as Europe was torn apart by the Great Schism, people still believed (for the last time) that the West and the East could be reunited. In 1369, the Eastern Roman emperor John V Palaeologus personally converted to Roman Catholicism; in 1438–39, the Ecumenical Council of Florence proclaimed an illusory unity. In 1406, when the groundwork was being laid for that operation of seduction, it was important to broaden the imperial dimensions of the papacy, with the pope as the sole true heir to the Roman Empire, but also to note the similarities, be they only decorative, between the rituals for the investiture of the patriarch of Constantinople and those of the universal patriarch. Jacopo was thus simply reinforcing an ancient Latin trend: since the invention of the legend of Constantine (in the late fifth century), and that of the "Donation" of Constantine (in the mid-eighth century), the pope had claimed the insignia of Roman imperial power. The staff that the pope received as he sat on the pierced chair had a political meaning, not a liturgical one; it was in fact the imperial scepter that Pope Sylvester was supposed to have received from the hands of Constantine. Tradition and circumstance met in an unchanged object, giving the illusion of continuity.

5. Beyond its immediate context, the 1406 ceremony, as seen by an external but attentive observer, contained a number of imbalances or tensions between what was public and what was secret; between the participation of the commonality and establishing a certain distance; among the various figures for power being represented (the universal Pontiff, the Bishop of Rome, the King of kings, the master of Rome); among the claimed sources of that power (Christian, Jewish, ancient Roman); and between the humiliation of the pope (the rite of the reed tipped with flaming flax, the rite of the stercory chair) and his glorification (veneration, kissing his feet, the procession, etc.). These competing traits overlapped during the three phases of the ceremony, but they failed to show any syntactical progress. Everything that had been done at St. Peter's was repeated at the Lateran: Gregory was welcomed as the Bishop of Rome by the chapter of the basilica; he was treated as supreme pontiff by the consignment of the keys of St. Peter; the staff presented to him was the rod of correction of the judge, rector, and master of the world; the gates of the palace opened for him welcomed the governor of Rome. He was venerated, as he had been at St. Peter's, and, also as at the Vatican, his humility was publicly observed. The ceremony at the Lateran reiterated the elements of the consecration without ordering them into a ritual system of transition. Should we view this as an essential, inherent hesitancy, or was it rather a proliferation of rites from the original liturgical cell?

We have a vague impression, as we read Jacopo d'Angelo's description, that he wants to rise above these tensions and depict the development of a coherent symbolism of power, but there is something that resists and nullifies that aim. It is difficult to pinpoint what it is. Is it an awareness of the weakness of a terrestrial power founded on belief in the other world? Is it a Christian obsession with the vanity of terrestrial things? Or is it perhaps the gaze, the voice, and the contact of the people? They are singularly present; they are solicited, but kept at a distance. They want contact with the sacred: they sack the pope's house and kiss his feet, but they are forbidden to touch the pallium around his waist. By means of discourse (what Jacopo calls "senseless fable"), they participate in the sacrilegious touching of the pope's genitals, and the same word, *attrectare,* is used for touching the pallium and the supposed gesture of verifying the pope's manhood. The Church cannot ignore the mystery of the Incarnation: at the risk of promiscuity, God abolished distance the day He was made man. When Thomas wanted to touch the sacred, Jesus permitted him to do so, and the pope was obliged to imitate Christ. Tolerance had its limits, however: an ancient apocryphal text, the *Gospel of James,* reports that when Mary's nurse attempted to verify her virginity manually (again, sexual touching), her arm withered.[8] Investiture had the task of gathering the Christian people together, but also of keeping them at a respectful distance, and our Roman amusements may reveal much about a power that lived by alternating contact and distance, consensus and force, both masked. The eternity shared by the divine Father and the human son, successively and simultaneously perceived by a Christian observer, becomes a metaphor for the inherent instability of a power fixed between belief and fact.

SOME FIFTEENTH-CENTURY OBSERVERS

Let us return to the history of the rite of verification after Jacopo d'Angelo's description and move forward somewhat more rapidly. Around 1435 Hermann Korner, a Dominican from Lübeck, retold the story of Joan and its institutional consequences in his *Chronica novella.*[9] The pope makes a detour to avoid the accursed spot of the pontifical childbirth, and "so as to prevent repetition of that error in the future, they take care, soon after the election of the pope, to make sure of his virility and his sex." We know that the rumored ritual was well known, even outside clerical circles, because in the mid-fifteenth century Giovanni Rucellai's *On the Beauty and Antiquities of Rome,* one of the many guides to Rome following the ancient tradition of presenting the *mirabilia urbis,* states: "Near the said Sancta Sanctorum [the chapel of San Lorenzo in the Lateran palace] there are two seats made of one piece of porphyry on which the newly created pope sits;

through an opening in the seat of the chair, someone seeks to determine whether he is a man or a woman."[10] Also in the mid-fifteenth century an English traveler, William Brewyn, reported the same oddity, which he had probably learned of from one of the picturesque guides to Rome: "In this chapel [of the Holy Savior] are two or more chairs of red marble stone, with apertures carved in them, upon which chairs, as I heard, proof is made as to whether the pope is a male or not, etc."[11]

The geographical horizon of our witnesses broadens in the mid-fifteenth century when around 1460 a Greek, Laonicos Chalcocondylas, writes about the rite in connection with the election of Pope Nicholas V in a work chronicling Turkish history. He connects the rite with memory of the popess: "For it has been established that once a woman was raised to the papacy because all were unaware of her sex. Indeed, almost all Westerners in Italy shave their beards. This is why, so as to avoid further trickery and to know the truth with no possible doubt, they touch the virile parts of the newly elected pope. And the person who touches them exclaims, 'Our Lord is a male.'" Although Chalcocondylas's report is imprecise, it has the interest of pointing out that at least for this foreign observer the bizarre ritual was an integral part of the political mysteries of a papal election. He even has the rite taking place before the enthronement of the new pope and at a time when there was concern over the political implications of the election. Chalcocondylas states:

> They choose the pope from the Colonna or Orsini families. When the necessary votes are gathered, they keep the pope-elect in the palace, and they inquire as to whether the election meets with the approval of the others [probably, with important persons who are not members of the Sacred College]. They command the chosen pope to sit on a seat pierced with an opening so that the one to whom this task is assigned can feel his testicles, which hang down through that orifice, and can state that the pope is indeed a man.[12]

The political tendency that is clear in this text's treatment of the rumored rite was more fully expanded in later humanist versions of the narrative.

Still in the mid-fifteenth century, Felix Hemmerli (Malleolus), a Swiss canon, added some interesting details in his dialogue *On the Nobility and on Rusticity.*[13] Hemmerli first relates the adventure of the popess, following the model established by Martinus Polonus, then states:

> Benedict III, who succeeded her, remembering the event, had a pierced chair installed in St. John Lateran, which can still be seen there. Two reliable clerics touched his testicles; witnesses who

presented legal evidence of his maleness. And if they found them intact, they cried aloud, while touching them, "Testiculos habet." At this the priest and the people responded, "Deo gratias." Next they proceeded joyously to the consecration of the elected pope. This custom continued for a long time.

Hemmerli's text contains several interesting new features. First, he attempts to historicize the rite by giving it a precise origin in an initiative taken by Benedict III. Consequently, the functional incoherence of the rite disappears. Verification was instituted when the papal election still took place in the Lateran, which means that the rite might precede consecration. Hemmerli's perception of the rite seems already archaeological: he bases what he relates on a collective memory that is no longer acted out in the ceremony but is instead revived by the mere conservation of a chair with a pierced seat. Finally, he is first to report the triumphal exclamation that was to accompany the rumor up to our own day.

PLATINA'S MISCHIEF

The next witness in this growing list of writers is none other than Bartolomeo Sacchi, called Platina in a Latinization of his place of birth, Piádena, near Cremona. A humanist, a member of the Roman Academy, and a talented scholar, he occupied important posts in the Roman Curia. He was first an abbreviator (member of the secretariat that prepared briefs) under Pope Paul II, who stripped him of his charge and subjected him to a thousand indignities, as we shall see. At Paul II's death in 1472 Platina was again elevated to a high curial post when Sixtus IV put him in charge of the Apostolic Vatican Library, which the pope had just founded.[14] Sixtus IV also charged Platina with writing a *Life of the Popes* that would review, harmonize, and complete the heterogeneous collection, begun in the sixth century, that went by the name of the *Liber pontificalis.* Platina set right to work: the task was urgent because the book was to be a contribution to the jubilee celebrations in 1475. He did in fact finish his labors by the end of the year 1474. Although this was an official work, Platina, a humanist critic who had been the target of Paul II's whims, did not spare the institution of the papacy. This is why the book was not printed until 1479 (in Venice, not in Rome); still, it was not subjected to ecclesiastical censure, and in fact met with considerable success, with forty-three Latin editions before the seventeenth century and twenty-one editions in Italian. In his chronological survey of the popes Platina narrates the story of Joan at the time that Martinus Polonus indicated (between Leo IV and Benedict

III), prolonging the earlier account with the institutional commentary that had become customary after Geoffroy de Courlon:

> Some write two things about this· on the one hand, that when the Pope goes to the basilica of the Lateran, he deliberately chooses a different route out of detestation of this crime; on the other hand, that in order to avoid repeating that same error, as soon as the pope is seated on the throne of Peter, perforated to that effect, he has his genitals touched by the least of the deacons. I will not deny the first custom; here is my thought as to the second: that seat was prepared in such a manner so that the one who is invested with such great domination will know that he is not God, but a man; that as such he is subjected to the necessities of nature and must defecate. This is why that seat is rightly called the stercory (or excremental) seat.[15]

For Platina the pierced chair, the major piece of evidence for the rite, thus becomes a banal toilet chair, at the price of confusing the stercory chair placed in the portico of the Basilica of St. John Lateran, known and described in official ceremonials since the twelfth century, and the porphyry chairs in the chapel of San Silvestro, which played a liturgical role only after the ceremony in the basilica had taken place. It is worth noting this bewildering ignorance of the coronation ceremonies on the part of a dignitary of the Curia. He is not alone, however, and we shall encounter constant misinterpretations of liturgy, given that the extreme complexity of the metaphors of gesture and word in it makes ritual extremely opaque. Tradition requires exegesis; its obscurity gives ceremonial objects the powerful and ambiguous, almost scriptural, status of divine creations. It is hardly surprising that error is rampant in the interpretation of ceremonies. Still, we cannot eliminate the suspicion that Platina was taking a mischievous pleasure in saving the pope from sexual impurity by plunging him into excrement!

HUMANIST JOKES AND PROTESTANT MURMURS

Platina's mischievous mockery, a harbinger of more heavy-handed Protestant jokes, is equally clear in one of his friends, the Hungarian humanist Janus Pannonius. In one of his ferociously antipapal epigrams, Pannonius too pretends to spare the papacy from a ridiculous rite:

> On an unchanged rite regarding the creation of the popes: Peter, a woman once dared to sit upon your chair, and she gave shameful

laws to the universe. She would have continued to hide [her sex] for many years if she had not made it obvious by an astonishing childbirth. For a long time thereafter Rome protected itself from such a ruse by making it customary to inspect the popes' secret corners. No one could obtain the keys that open the heavens without having his testicles examined. Why has this custom ceased in our own times? Because the pope proves ahead of time that he is indeed a male.[16]

Pannonius's final sentence is an obvious allusion to papal progeny, a theme traditional in humorous literature of the fifteenth and sixteenth centuries up to Rabelais. The joke becomes a cliché; we find it in an antipapal epigram of the late fifteenth century written by Marko Marulić of Split: "Why, Cibo, do you seek evidence that he is male or female; take his troop of children as proof: recently he engendered eight sons and as many daughters."[17]

Somewhat later a Frenchman, Jean-Jacques Boissard, repeated the witticism in his *Topographie de la ville de Rome* (1597–1602). Like the other visitors to Rome whom we have met, Boissard first speaks of the porphyry chairs with pierced seats placed at the top of the Scala Sancta at the Lateran palace. He states that the rite had continued for only a few years after Joan's pontificate. He completes the ritual formula, "Testiculos habet," with "Dignus est papali corona" (He is worthy of the papal crown). He rejects the "ridiculous story" (which he nonetheless repeats with no personal interpolations or marks of indirect discourse), adding: "Today there is no need for any such inquiry: no one is promoted to the papacy if he has not previously offered sufficient proof of his virility."[18]

The statement that the rite of verification was no longer practiced, which we find in both Pannonius and Hemmerli, by no means stopped anyone from believing that it had existed in the past, and rumors of it continued to circulate, but with some vagueness as to its currency. We find descriptions of the rite, unchanged, in the *Liber chronicarum* (or Nuremberg Chronicles: Nuremberg, 1493) of the German chronicler Hartmann Schedel;[19] in *On Memorable and Illustrious Women* by the Augustinian friar Jacopo Filippo Foresti of Bergamo;[20] in a note added by the Venetian publisher to the Italian translation of Boccaccio's *De mulieribus claris* (1506);[21] and in Joannes Stella's *Life of the Popes* (Venice, 1505).[22] Even though the popes of the early sixteenth century had eliminated the rites at the Lateran that involved the stercory chair and the porphyry seats, the humanist Giovanni Pierio Valeriano Bolzani, a protégé of Pope Leo X, published a letter to Cardinal Ippolito de' Medici, "In Favor of Beards for Priests" (1531), in which he states that if popes had been bearded the sorry scandal of Joan's pontificate would never have occurred. Valeriano Bolzani's description of the rite stresses (even exaggerates) its public and official nature:

> In sight of the entire populace, within the portico of St. John's, which faces the vast square peopled by the throng gathered there because of the rite, the new pontiff is obliged to demonstrate his virility by his abundant testicles. This confirmed and loudly proclaimed by the priest, it is immediately transcribed in the records: only then do we know that we have a legitimate pope—after the ocular attestation that proves that he indeed possesses what he should.[23]

This narrative introduces a new ambiguity: its use of the present tense refers to current, empirical reality as well as evoking a gesture customary in the past, and its ceremonial narrative style constantly mixes norm and reality, past and present.

In the sixteenth century printing and Protestantism brought on a dizzying profusion of mentions of the rumored rite. We have already noted the considerable success of the print editions of Platina's *Life of the Popes* after 1479. Schedel's *Chronicles* also met with great success. With the advent of printing, the least pamphlet could be distributed throughout Europe. Protestant propaganda relied heavily on both the fable of Joan and the rumored rite, as we shall see. Rather than presenting an endless list of Protestant pamphlets that mentioned the rite, we can use the encyclopedic work of a German Protestant, Johann Wolf, as an example. Wolf's *Lectiones memorabiles et reconditae* (Memorable and Hidden Lessons) is an enormous universal history stressing the lies and crimes of the papacy.[24] When Wolf surveys the ninth century, he does not fail to report the story of Joan; he assembles and cites seventy-nine sources that authenticate the story, sixteen of which also mention the rite of verification. A good many of these witnesses have already appeared in these pages, and we have little more to learn from Wolf's compilation, aside from one lexical invention reported by the anonymous Protestant author of *De Pontificum Romanorum emisariis*: "One hears it said that in the Papacy, the virile member is often called, by antonomasia, 'the Pontificals.'"[25]

A Lutheran at the Coronation of Innocent X (1644)

This tour following the itinerary of the rumored rite of verification ends with a final description of a papal investiture, in this case the ceremonies at the accession of Innocent X in 1644. As was the case with most of the pontifical coronations after the Middle Ages, a multitude of brief, hastily printed works was produced to publicize the occasion during the conclave, between the conclave and the coronation, and even after the ceremony.[26] One of these, *Roma triumphans*, a minutely detailed work that the Swedish jurist Lars Banck wrote about this coronation, provides us with a final mention of the rite of verification.[27] By the seventeenth century the ceremony of taking possession of the Lateran—the *possesso*—had become clearly separated from the two preceding phases. Innocent X was elected at the conclusion of a conclave lasting from 2 September to 15 September 1644; he was crowned on 4 October; he took possession of the Lateran only on 23 November. The solemn cortege that wound its way through Rome, leaving the Vatican about four in the afternoon, had grown considerably longer than it had been back in the days of Jacopo d'Angelo. In both its greater emphasis on ranks, orders, and rules of precedence and in the display of arches, decorations, and inscriptions that lined the route, it much resembled the processions that took place at royal entries (for which it had probably served as a model in the fifteenth century). The cortege reached the Lateran between nine and ten in the evening, where a dense crowd had gathered. There Innocent exchanged his litter for a sedan chair and was carried to the main portico of the Basilica of St. John, where the pavement was covered with rugs and stuffs (as it was throughout the church). The bells of all the churches and monasteries of Rome tolled. Innocent took his place there on a throne decorated with silks and gold. He was welcomed by Cardinal Colonna, the archpriest of St. John's, and by the canons of St. John's bearing silver vessels containing the gilded pontifical cross and the keys of St. Peter (one silver, one gold). The pope seized the cross, kissed it, and prayed. The Medici and Barberini cardinals then removed his triple-crowned tiara, placing on his head a miter covered with precious stones, and Cardinal Colonna, backed by the clergy of the Lateran, consigned the two keys to him with a prayer. After renewed adorations and benedictions, the pope returned to his sedan chair to enter the basilica. Banck states:

> Then the same persons [nobles and counts of St. John Lateran]
> carry him to the marble pierced chair placed not far from there so
> that, while seated on that chair, his manly parts can be touched.
> There is no doubt that things took place in this manner. Indeed, it
> is quite certain that this marble seat, pierced, is conserved in that
> same basilica of the Lateran, and I have seen it with my own eyes
> on several occasions. It is also totally certain that the newly created Pontiffs, before being admitted to the secular direction of

the Lateran, were placed on that same chair, as proven even by
Catholics such as Platina, Sabellius [Sabellico] (in his Life of John
VIII), Stella, a priest from Venice, etc. They say that after the death
of John VIII, it was judged prudent that the Supreme Pontiff be
led to a pontifical chair, and that he not be confirmed until his
manly parts had been touched in the pierced chair. I believe,
however, that the Sovereign Pontiff is placed on the chair, a seat
of humility, as a warning; he is supposed to feel his personal humility in contrast to the high and glorious episcopal seat; he is to
remember that he is like other men, subject to the same failings
of our weak nature, and that he is not God. Thus, he receives the
lesson that he must not derive any pride from the enthronement,
as it is called, that follows the rite. . . . These are the testimonies.
After that proclamation, and when it is understood that the pope
indeed has the pontificals, several signs of joy are manifested. The
pope then returns to his sedan chair, and he slowly makes his way
to the high altar.[28]

Banck presents himself as an eyewitness to the ceremony that he describes in detail, but he did not actually see the rite of verification. Although he describes it as confidently as he does the rest of the ceremony,
he contradicts himself by basing his certitude on written tradition and his
own direct observation of the pierced chairs. This still leaves us with the
mystery of a public rite always seen by others, never by the narrator. Moreover, Banck, like Platina and all those whom Platina led into error, con-
fuses the stercory chair and the chairs with pierced seats, and he does so
when the ritual of humiliation had ceased to exist for more than a century
and a half, as is clear from the magnificence of the throne set up under the
portico of the basilica that replaced the earlier stercory chair. Banck's very
precise description places the moment of verification during the pope's
entry into the basilica, between the solemn prayers of the archpriest and
the Mass itself, thus at the heart of the visual festive spectacle, as it was described by the papal master of ceremonies, Fulvio Servanzio. Banck continues: after listening to the prayers of Cardinal Colonna, Innocent,
coiffed with the miter,

gets up onto the porters' chair, on which he is led to the middle of
the basilica itself; the canons of that basilica . . . raise a baldachin
over His Holiness; once there, he descends from his chair, removes his miter, kneels, considers and venerates the chief of the
Holy Apostles, while the cardinals kneel on the bare pavement of
the side aisles. The pope is then carried in his chair to the altar of

the Holy Sacrament, after which he returns on foot to the high
altar.[29]

Banck then returns to his scrupulous description of the ceremonial. There
is an astonishing divergence in accounts of an event that took place in a
narrowly circumscribed place and time. Aside from variations in the ritual
that concerns us, there are innumerable differences of protocol (to which
one should add others found in the half-dozen or so pamphlets produced
in Rome that relate the taking possession of the Lateran in 1644 but fail to
mention the verification) that give the distinct impression that no one actually saw the ceremony take place. Even more than in the Middle Ages,
the ceremony is presented here as an infinite and obscure text that tran-
scends the immanent action of the participants and that no representation, no exegesis, could exhaust. This effect perhaps reflects an absolutism
that tends to absorb all behavior into a never-ending participation. If that
is the case, the ceremony becomes an inclusive, hypertrophied reality with
no externality, an event whose force lay in its ability to neutralize the di-
verse gaze of the pious, the ignorant, and the malicious alike. Throughout
his *Roma triumphans*, Banck, a Lutheran, displays an increasing admiration
for the obscure splendors of ceremony. When his account of the rite of verification leads him to liturgical exegesis, it loses its salaciousness. The absence of a negative charge in the ceremony (and ceremony is a machine
for producing meanings) may perhaps explain why the rumor circulated
in Rome, uncontested, for so long.

IMAGES OF THE RITE OF VERIFICATION

We should note, in connection with Wolf and Banck, that printing's power
to diffuse information and ideas was increased by the prestige of the image: the first edition of Wolf's *Lectiones* in 1600 included (perhaps for the
first time) an illustration of the rite of verification. A woodcut shows a
pope wearing the tiara and seated on a stool before a throng of bishops
and cardinals. A figure in a cardinal's hat kneels behind the pope, lifting
the pope's robe with one hand and reaching under the seat with the other.
The platform on which the stool is placed declares, in capital letters,
"HABET," the beginning of the ritual formula.[30] In a second, enlarged and
illustrated edition of 1656 that followed the first edition of his *Roma triumphans* in 1645, Banck published an image that shows the verification
scene. The caption reads, "Sedes marmorea Pontificis in Basilica Latera-
nensi" (the marble chair of the pope in the Basilica of the Lateran), and
the image shows the pope, surrounded by a dozen clerics, monks, bish-

ops, and cardinals, seated on a chair with a high back and a closed panel at the front decorated with a cherub. Two priests kneel to his right, while a kneeling cardinal to the left of the chair rests his right hand on his hat, which is lying on the ground, and passes his left hand through a small opening through the left side of the chair. A phylactery that emerges from his mouth announces: "Pontificalia habet" (He has the pontificals).[31]

A First Explanation: The Revenge
of Frustrated Intellectuals

It is clear from this long line of witnesses to the ritual of verification that there were various ways to grasp this episode as well as various attempts to rationalize it. Above all, we have seen that it was impossible, within a complex ceremony, to state clearly the futility of the rite. One question remains, however: Why did these writers positively believe (or try to persuade others to believe) in the existence of an act that no one claims to have seen directly?

There seems to be a relatively simple answer to this question after the mid-fifteenth century (but only then), if we recall that the rumor was actively spread in milieus such as the humanist circles of the Roman Curia, rather than springing from some obscure chronicler's attempts to untangle his sources. We can read into Platina's perfidious denials or the mocking epigrams of Pannonius and Marko Marulić the social reaction of a group of intellectuals harassed by Paul II and frustrated by the limited number of posts available. In the first months of his papacy in 1464 Paul II eliminated the positions of papal abbreviator that were usually held by brilliant young humanists who had purchased their charges and hoped to realize both material and social profit from them. Paul took away their positions without offering any indemnification. Platina was quick to react: he and other papal abbreviators laid siege to Paul II for twenty days in a row without being received. He then wrote a violent letter to the pope, threatening to convoke a council by appealing to the kings and princes of Christendom—a less ridiculous threat than it might seem, given that in the late fourteenth century the papacy confronted powerful antimonarchical and conciliarist currents, which the Great Schism in the West had strongly revived at the very end of the fourteenth century and the early fifteenth century, and which were brought to an end only by the acts of the Council of Constance, backed by the rulers of Christendom.[32] Paul II reacted to Platina's threats by having him imprisoned in the Castello Sant'Angelo for four months. Four years later, in 1468, the pope uncovered a plot against the papacy led by the Florentine Filippo Bonaccorsi with the support of several young humanists in the orbit of the Roman Academy. Platina was thrown in prison again. Paul II closed the Roman Academy and forbade the teaching of Latin poetry in the schools. The incident obviously had broader repercussions than in Platina's personal history, and it began to take on aspects of a social and political conflict. As Cesare D'Onofrio has demonstrated,[33] the revolt of the humanists was part of a larger pattern of the city of Rome's continual struggles for autonomy and of efforts to combat papal despotism that had been simmering for some time in Rome, surfacing first in the attempt to set up a communal government in Rome in 1144 and again with the Roman Republic of Cola di Rienzo in the fourteenth century.[34] In all three cases (twelfth century, fourteenth century, fifteenth century), the Roman party based its arguments on the traditions of ancient Rome; forbidding the teaching of the Latin poets did not arise out of an antihumanist obscurantism on the part of mid-fifteenth-century popes (Calixtus III, Pius II, Paul II); rather, it reflected a real confiscation of the patrimony of claims of the city of Rome. The career of Pius II illustrates this point. Before he became pope Enea Silvio Piccolomini was himself one of the Curia humanists. He wrote a charming and erudite little romance, *De duobus amantibus* (The Tale of the Two Lovers). As a man of the Curia (like Platina), he seemed determinedly conciliarist. As he drew closer to holding papal power, however, his antihumanist monarchism grew. I might note that during his legation in Bohemia in 1451, he was the first medieval author to refute the story of Pope Joan, a matter to which we shall return.

Platina's narration is thus neither innocent nor meaningless; rather, it signals a position in Roman social spheres situated within the Curia but desperately far from the monarchical power. The Curia humanist, endowed with a sizable symbolic capital (a perfect knowledge of the Latin language and Latin literature, at times specific competence in canon law), prefigures the "frustrated intellectual" of the seventeenth century,[35] and like his later counterpart he operated within too large a group ever to hope for a post adequate to his preparation. As if demographic surplus were not enough, the Roman situation had other constraints. Because of its millenary prestige and thanks to its aura of sanctity and the mirage of a flourishing papal bureaucracy, Rome attracted clerics from all over Europe who swarmed to the city in the hope of benefices. Unlike the city-states of medieval and Renaissance Italy, Rome offered few opportunities in the political and social realm, however: the papal monarchy, to which the states of Europe lent constant support through schisms and quarrels, left little scope for political action. The strength of the Roman nobility, which Cola di Rienzo had threatened only momentarily, clamped a further lid on opportunities in Rome. As a class (and the word is not too anachronistic in this case), the Roman or Romanized intellectuals had little recourse but spite and persiflage. This gave a special tone to their evocations of both the papacy and the ritual of verification: they did not demolish or vituperate; rather than attacking the institution they scratched away at the person and the perpetuated person.

Both the social and the political aspects of humanist criticism found quintessential expression in the *pasquinata*, or pasquinade, a well-known genre of satirical epigrams, posted anonymously, that developed in Platina's day. Although the first extant pasquinade dates from 1523, toward the end of the papacy of Adrian VI, we know from convergent indications that the Roman custom of placing libels and broadsheets on the ancient statue (an armless torso) familiarly known as "Pasquino," situated near the Piazza Navona in what is now the Piazza Pasquino, dates back to the 1460s, the very years when the Roman humanists and Pope Paul II were at odds. The Roman tradition of antipapal satire undoubtedly goes back to the first Roman Commune of the twelfth century, and it probably inherited certain themes from the ferociously antipapal, pro-Germanic sentiment of the time of the investiture controversy. It was Platina's generation, however, that combined the ancient popular satirical vein with the rediscovered art of the Latin epigram. They found the best tone and the perfect place for circulating their barbs in the antique statue of Pasquino, which henceforth replaced the Campo dei Fiori as a setting for open confrontation, but also for its repression. Internalized persiflage replaced direct attack. The rumor of the ritual of verification, as we have seen with Pannonius and Marulić, lent itself well to the ancient and often highly suggestive tradition of the epigram. Sexual allusions in fact teem in the pasquinades, one of which closely resembles the epigrams of Pannonius and Marulić quoted above:

> Let no one search for Paul's witnesses [*testes*, a time-honored play
> on words for *testiculi*];
> The daughter he engendered teaches well enough that he is
> male.[36]

It is tempting to broaden this sociocultural explanation and move it both back and forward in time, even though the moment to which it applies here shows well enough why the rumor of verification was such a success, especially given the wide influence of Platina. Looking back to the early fifteenth century, we can see that Jacopo d'Angelo's position differed little from that of Platina and his comrades: these men shared a humanist training and a long wait for a post in the Curia; they mention the ritual in similar terms. At the risk of indulging in determinism, we might state that Jacopo's refutation of the rite was an indication of his more successful, less tormented career. The fact that both Jacopo and Platina belonged to nearly analogous groups would, in this view, be apparent in the fact that they allude to the rite, "in spite of everything." If they wanted to defend the papacy against defamation, they had to recall the existence of that calumny, play with the idea, and set themselves up as symbolic champions of the institution. In contrast to them, one might cite the contemporary figure of Adam of Usk, the Welshman who also propagated the rumor, who came to Rome to seek a post that he never obtained, and who wrote his narrative about Rome when he returned, embittered, to his native land.

This is as far back as we can go, armed only with this frail explanation, in pursuit of the tradition we seek. Beyond the void of the fourteenth century the mysterious figure of Geoffroy de Courlon, the monk from Sens, evades our grasp. We know more about Robert d'Uzès, but that wandering and visionary Dominican seems made of different stuff from our ambitious, intrigue-prone young intellectuals. Robert's dramatic description of the rite is cast in a different mold than the joking allusions of the fifteenth century. We shall return to him.

This first hypothesis, which explains the rumor's longevity by a deliberate manipulation of the heavy body of liturgy on the part of a sociopolitical group in search of a carefully dosed vengeance, permits a grasp of how the Protestants could apply their much more aggressive spirit to appropriate a topic that was by then broadly diffused and use it for their own purposes. The transition from satirical allusion to the violent attack that took place in the early sixteenth century can be found in both Rome and the European milieus that one might call "evangelical," for lack of a better term.

THE "EVANGELICALS" TAKE OVER: RABELAIS

By the early sixteenth century the papacy seemed strong, and after the defeat of Bonaccorsi's conspiracy, papal absolutism no longer needed to fear the spirit of the Roman Commune. Julius II launched a genuine "territorial and military policy" and, as André Chastel remarks, "he entered Rome on Palm Sunday 1507 with a military 'triumph' the likes of which no one had ever seen."[37] Symbolic rejection of his taking possession, in both fact and ceremony, rose sharply, to judge from the increasing violence of the pasquinades. This protest met with the approval of Luther's Christian contemporaries who had remained within the Church but were horrified by the spectacle of Rome. The "evangelical" position was at the cutting edge of criticism, but it never tipped over into total condemnation. Typically, it found expression in semisatirical, semiserious fiction, as, for example, with Erasmus's *In Praise of Folly* (1511) or with the works of François Rabelais. As was true of the fifteenth-century Roman humanists, tactical positions led to the use of narrative as a technique and dictated a certain tone; also as with their Roman predecessors, such writers found it simply out of the question to believe in the legend of Joan or in the myth of the verification of papal virility. An ironic and facetious distance neutralized belief. Rabelais's allusion to the rite of verification in the *Quart livre* (1548) serves as an example of this. Pantagruel and his companions leave the island of "desolate Popefiggery," landing next on "the blessed island of Papimania." The island's inhabitants, the "Papimaniacs," welcome them effusively because they have not only seen the pope but seen three successive popes (though Panurge notes, "Yet I am none the better off for the sight"). The Papimaniacs kneel before the visitors and offer to kiss their feet, an homage that Panurge and his fellow travelers reject, because "if His Holiness the Pope were to come in person, they could find no greater homage to pay him."

> "Oh, but yes, we could," they objected. "We have already decided
> how we could honor him. We would kiss his bare arse without
> baulking at it, and his stones, sans figleaf, too. For the holy father
> has a pair of knockers; our fair *Decretals* tell us so. Otherwise he
> could not be pope, since a physical examination must precede his
> enthronement. This has been the rule ever since the scandal of
> Pope Joan. Thus, according to our subtle decretaline philosophy,
> the pope has genitals; let genitals perish from the earth and earth
> would have no more popes."[38]

Rabelais is obviously talking about our rite. Moreover, he had already done so in the *Tiers livre* (1546). Panurge, who would like to believe in marriage, conjures away the menacing thought that Jupiter reveals the fragility of matrimony by making men cuckold. He fantasizes about what he would do to Jupiter if he could:

> "I'll collar him," Panurge vowed. "Ay, I'll scotch the brangler. And
> do you know what I'll do to him? What Saturn did to his father,
> Coelius [the sky], what Rhea did to Atys, what both Seneca and
> Lactantius foretold I would do: I'll cut the fellow's knockers off so
> close that never a hair will stand to tell the tail. You remember
> how since Pope Joan was Holy Father, the cardinals have insisted

on a testicular examination of candidates. Well, I warrant you
Jupiter will never be Pope, for *testiculos non habet,* he'll have no
boulders."[39]

It would be almost as absurd to ask what degree of reality Rabelais accorded to the rite of verification as to ask whether he believed in that pagan god. Jupiter and the rite were convenient instruments for derision.
The reference to the pope is nonetheless essential: the tale of Pantagruel
and his friends visiting the equally absurd lands of Papimania and Popefiggery was aimed at producing the same effect of global satire as the
topsy-turvy world of *In Praise of Folly.* Raucous laughter works to deni-
grate the supreme institution of the papacy without claiming to topple it,
and although Lucien Febvre was right when he connected Rabelais's
"pranks" with a long tradition of "clerical jests,"[40] we need also consider
such jests as among the tactics used by the "evangelicals," in this instance
the heirs of the Roman humanists and of their appetite for symbolic
domination.

The sociocultural explanation of the rumored ritual takes into account an important transmission at the end of the fifteenth century, but it
tells us nothing about the origin of the belief that it both neutralizes and
propagates. It ignores the anguish of Robert d'Uzès and Geoffroy de Courlon; in the early Middle Ages, it can be applied only to mocking or sly narrations of the ceremony, not to the naive reconstructions of the various
Mirabilia urbis or to travel memoirs. Even Lars Banck seems more per-
plexed than polemical or biting when he mentions the rite. The tone used
to repeat the rumor counts as well: if the account had no serious, dramatic, anxious, or anguished component, the rumor would be a murmur
lost in the joyous flood of anticlerical discourse, both within the Church
and from without. This means that we need to return to our first witnesses,
in particular to Robert d'Uzès, because Geoffroy de Courlon's chronicle is
so bland that it is difficult to grasp the author's torment.

THE HORROR OF ROBERT D'UZÈS

There can be no doubt that Robert was horrified by the rumored rite. Although his mention of it seems a mere factual reference ("before the porphyry seats, where it is said they verify that the pope is a man"), it is
inserted within a collection of texts deploring the decadence of the
Church of Rome in which Robert's tone is one of sadness and affliction.
These texts are grouped into two volumes, a *Book of Visions* and a *Book of
Revelations;*[41] the genre they reflect is prophecy, as it developed in the

works of Joachim of Fiore and Jean de Roquetaillade.[42] Robert states: "It pleased the Lord Jesus Christ to reveal his will to me, the lowliest of sinners, at times during my sleep by visions in images, at times by the same visions when I was awake; at times by a discourse, external or internal, with many metaphors accompanied by their glosses."[43] God had charged his messenger *(nuntius)* with announcing to the world the imminence of the Last Days and denouncing the corruption of the Church, the papacy in particular. Robert's prophetic stance takes on its full meaning in the context in which he had his visions and wrote about them between 1291 and 1295. In 1294 Benedetto Caetani, the future Pope Boniface VIII, forced Pope Celestine V (Pietro da Morrone) to abdicate (or "resign," as it was said). Thus a politically minded, Roman, and authoritarian pope succeeded—in dubious circumstances—an ineffective, hesitant hermit, whom reformist milieus considered not only a saint (he was in fact soon canonized), but a true image of the Apostles, a man who had lived in poverty and in the inspiration of the Holy Ghost. Throughout the thirteenth century clear contrasts were drawn between true and false votaries of Christ. Robert, our Provençal Dominican visionary, creates violent images of the end of the world, the coming of the Antichrist, and the disarray of the Church (which he pictures as a rudderless boat, a deserted, empty temple, etc.). Robert locates the porphyry chairs used for the rite of verification in a deserted basilica, a sinister decor that he evokes in another of his visions: "Awake, I saw on the ground something like an infinite mass of heaped-up miters and pastoral crosiers, without bishops or prelates."[44] Whether it was a symptom or a remedy, Robert saw the verification rite within a more general evocation of the emptiness and falsity of Rome:

> Thirty-first vision on the state of the Roman Church:
> I was praying on my knees, my face raised to heaven, to the right of the altar of Saint-Jacques in Paris, and I saw before me, as if in the air, the body of a supreme pontiff dressed in a silk alb; he had turned his back to the East, and his hands were raised toward the West, as priests do during the secret of the solemn Mass, and I did not see his head, dry, parchment-like, as if made of wood. The Spirit of the Lord said to me: . . . 'Signify the state of the Roman Church.'"[45]

There is a noteworthy parallel in the expressions used in this text and in the passage that relates the rite of verification: "Sedes . . . ubi dicitur probari papa, an sit homo"; "Intuens an esset homo sine capite . . ." In this incoherent dual vision of a headless, floating pope a horror of the void combines with the horror inspired by a deceptive appearance: silk on top of dust. The papacy and the Church were performing a terrible parody that inverted right values, and no one realized it:

> Vision Twenty-seven, horrible and terrible: I saw this in sleep: I wanted to enter the church of Sainte-Marthe in Tarascon to pray, and when I entered through the main door, I saw around the altar Jews with long hair, dressed in the sacred vestments of the priests, deacons, and subdeacons, and they were serving at the altar, performing I know not what rite, and a crowd of people attended just as they attend holy offices.[46]

In another vision the Holy Ghost speaks through Robert to state: "The churches will be profaned, the holy chalices polluted; filthy men will be dressed in consecrated vestments and the sacred cloths will receive the impurities of menstruation."[47] When Robert d'Uzès evokes profanation at its worst, it involves an impure, perverse contact that inverts the sacred: Jews and menstruating women touch the holy objects of liturgy. We are far from the joking moral inversions of the humanists. In Robert, inversion is a perverse copy, a sign of the devil in action. The twelfth century, which meditated long and hard on man as the image of God, depicted the devil as the thief of that image. As William of Saint-Thierry puts it: "He had usurped the resemblance of God."[48] William uses the verb *praesumere*, the term Joan's earliest historiographers had used. Gerhoch of Reichersberg speaks, similarly, of "that presumptuous appetite for the divine resemblance."[49] Peter of Blois links diabolic usurpation with an accursed throne, a perverted reflection of the throne of St. Peter: "He [Satan]—that being of extreme perdition—did not want to remain without God, but desiring to usurp the image of divine power, he constructed a throne of pestilence for himself in the regions of Aquilon and he fell."[50] Robert mentions the rite of verification only briefly, but his mention is a precise echo of descriptions of Roman perversion and inversion; it signals (or wards off) the greatest profanation, which is a corporalization of the divine, a diabolical parody of the Incarnation. We see here a point of convergence between the rumored rite and anti-Semitic rumors that arose in the twelfth century and were also centered on perversion of the sacred through liturgical inversion and profanatory contact.[51]

A Second Explanation: Fear of the Invasive Female

In the medieval imagination the rite of verification also conjured away the persistent anxiety of female pollution of the sacred. That a woman might secretly usurp the supreme priesthood was the most exacerbated expression of a terror that more commonly found lateral outlets in fable or rites. Canon law says nothing on the question. Only quite late, in the writings of an early-sixteenth-century canonist, is there explicit mention of the exclusion of women from the papacy. In his *Treatise on the Council,* Cardinal Domenico Giacobazzi imagines the case of a papal election annulled by a council:

> What would happen if the elect is accused and convicted of being
> a woman? I think that he [the pope-elect] could be deposed by a
> council, first, because the keys of the Church cannot fall to a
> woman and [a woman] would not have the right to possess or
> conserve the pontificate; but also because she does not hold the
> right to judge, which is a male prerogative. Also because of the
> scandal [that would be] produced in the universal Church.

By this logic, verification of the pope-elect's masculinity would be justified by lack of the visible evidence present in other cases of illegitimate election: "What would occur if he were a young child *(infans)*? That problem might seem beside the point. . . . It is not likely that the cardinals would make such a senseless choice. This is why it is inappropriate to raise the question." Giacobazzi goes on to enumerate cases of incapacity, only to return anxiously to the imprescriptible fact that election definitively grants papal dignity:

> But I wonder again about the defects that one might bring against
> a pope and that make him not a true pope, even though he has
> been elected by two-thirds of the cardinals. He might be an un-
> baptized Jew, a pagan, an enemy and persecutor of our faith, or a
> woman; or another reason might prevent him in the name of di-
> vine or natural law from being pope. Can the council pronounce
> on the question in that case? It must be clearly stated that the one
> who is elected by two-thirds of the cardinals cannot be rejected;
> he is accepted because no exception can be retained.[52]

Giacobazzi's anguish at the thought of a secret invasion of the papacy seems all the stronger because he cannot cite an exclusion of women from the priesthood. Rejection had no ancient precedent, no sure theological foundation. Exclusion sprang from a profound horror of impure contact; codification came later.

THE EXCLUSION OF WOMEN FROM THE
PRIESTHOOD IN CANON LAW

The passages on the exclusion of women from the priesthood in Gratian's *Decretals* (ca. 1140),[53] the work that provides the basis of canon law, cite

no authority that justifies such an exclusion theologically. Aside from prohibitions on women's preaching (chapter 29 of distinction 23; chapter 20
of distinction 4, *De consecratione*), three passages prohibit women from
having contact with the sacred. Chapter 25 of distinction 23 states:

> It has been brought to the attention of the apostolic see that
> women dedicated to God, or nuns, touch *(contingere)* the sacred
> vessels or altar cloths and carry incense around the altar. No truly
> sensible person will doubt that such practices deserve to be cen-
> sured and eliminated. Therefore on the authority of our holy of-
> fice we direct you to eliminate them as quickly as possible. And in
> order that this pestilence *(pestis)* does not spread into other areas
> we demand that it be stopped immediately.

The same prohibition appears in chapter 41 of distinction 1, *De consecratione:*

> The Holy See decrees that the consecrated vessels may be handled
> only by holy men *(hominibus)* ordained in the Lord's service and
> by no others, in order that the Lord in his anger may not punish
> his people with calamity, in which those who have not sinned
> [against this commandment] may be also destroyed, since it of-
> ten happens that the righteous suffer for the ungodly.

Chapter 29 of distinction 2, *De consecratione*, prohibits lay people and
women from carrying the consecrated host to the sick. To be sure, the texts
collected by Gratian long predate the twelfth century: the *Decretals* were,
after all, a "Concordance of Discordant Canons" that aimed at constructing a systematic whole from a variety of sources (papal letters, synodal and
conciliar canons, etc.). Still, the exuberant quantity of religious legislation
of the early Middle Ages meant that quite different orientations might be
imposed on the synthesis being attempted, which means that we can
think of the *Decretals* as reflecting a twelfth-century state of mind. The exclusion of women, the fear of pollution by women or Jews, the supposed
installation of the rite of verification, and the story of the popess all have
their roots in a twelfth century obsessed with purity.

The decretists who so tirelessly glossed Gratian confirm the impression that woman produced a sacred horror when she approached places
and objects connected with the cult. Writing against an ancient decision of
Gregory the Great that Gratian and his earliest commentators had passed
along, Rufinus states in his *Summa decretorum* (ca. 1158), a work often
used by the canonists, that women are prohibited from entering a church
after childbirth.[54] Paucapalea, Gratian's pupil, whose *Summa* (between

1140 and 1148) was the first Bolognese commentary on his master's work, speaks of menstruation in these terms: "Only women are menstruating creatures; by touching their blood, fruits will not ripen, wine will sour, grass will die and trees lose their fruit. Iron rusts and air gets dark; when dogs drink it, they develop rabies."[55] Not long after Paucapalea, Rufinus repeated, word for word, this description of the effects of menstrual blood, which Paucapalea had borrowed from Solinus, an ancient writer on natural history.

THE GLOSSATORS JUSTIFY EXCLUSION

Justification of the exclusion of women from sacred matters came only laterally and/or late, which means that the question was embedded in a traditional and universal psychological and juridical misogyny. Bernardo Bottoni (Bernard of Parma), who wrote (in 1245) the ordinary gloss to the decretals of Gregory IX (the *Liber extra*), offers a riddle that might have come from a fabliau: "What is lighter than smoke? Wind. What is lighter than wind? Air. What is lighter than air? Woman. What is lighter than woman? Nothing."[56] The universal traits of misogyny (woman is "variable," "crafty") were reduced to theory and classified by the Justinian Code, which excludes women from civil office because of their moral, intellectual, and physical weakness *(imbecillitas et fragilitas)*. The first canonist to give a theological foundation to that "classical" antifeminism seems to have been Huguccio, quite possibly the greatest jurist of the twelfth century, who declared in his *Summa* (1188) that women's incapacity for ordination rested on an ecclesiastical decree pronounced on account of their sex *(constitutio ecclesie facta propter sexum)*.[57] Until Huguccio, commentators had followed Gratian to juxtapose prohibitions of specific acts that had been taken from ancient authorities; a simple dictum of Gratian's (that is, an opinion lacking the character of a pontifical or conciliar decision) stated that a woman could not be received as a priest or a deaconess. Huguccio turns this pronouncement into a principle. His prime argument is based on a reading of Genesis 1.27 that man—not woman—was made in the image of God. This statement reflects a hierarchical construction of the universe that was fully developed in the thirteenth century and whose reassuring legal framework (which coincided with contemporary lay constructions) lightened the burden of anguish connected with a dread of impurity. Huguccio, the most "Justinian" of the twelfth-century canonists, did not need to dwell on the impurity or the light-headedness of women. As in civil society, origin, anteriority, and hierarchic necessity rather than "nature" deprived woman of resemblance to the divine:

> It is said that man and not woman is the image of God for three
> reasons: Just as God is unique and everything derives from him,
> similarly, man alone was created at the origins. . . . Secondly, just
> as the origin of the Church, in the form of blood and water,
> sprang from the side of the sleeping Christ, Eve was formed from
> the flanks of the sleeping Adam. Thirdly, just as Christ commands
> the Church and governs it, so man commands woman.

With this quasi-feudal construction in place, Huguccio goes on to state:
"But in a fourth manner woman as well as man is the image of God inasmuch as she has access to the divine essence *(essentie divine capacem)* by
reason, by intellection, by memory, by judgment."[58] Huguccio thus arrives at stating a cold tradition of Roman legal thought and a hot antifem-
inist obsession. Fifty years earlier the two domains were still separate in
Gratian. Whereas Gratian relied on obscure "natural" prohibitions to reject the idea of female ordination, he calmly accepted Justinian's cultural
exclusion founded on tradition alone when it came to judges (and the
pope was the supreme judge): "Three things prevent someone from being
a judge; nature (the deaf, the mute, the permanently mad, the beardless,
because they lack judgment); law, as promulgated by the Senate; and customs *(moribus)* (women and slaves, not because they lack judgment, but
because it is accepted that they not enjoy civil responsibilities)."[59]

Another sign of changing ways of thinking in the late twelfth century
and the early thirteenth century appears in the second major pillar of medieval canon law, Gregory IX's new compilation of decretals known as the
Liber extra (or *Decretals;* 1234), which concentrates uniquely on limiting
the power of abbesses, in particular, abbess-canonesses, whose status in
many ways resembled that of bishops. Here we leave obsession to return
to a clear institutional context of male domination, which is an induce-
ment for placing the origin of an anguished perception of the fable of Joan
and of a desire to believe in the verification rite in the twelfth century. Late
traces of the same fears that shaped the rite of verification (and satirical
versions of that rite in the fifteenth century) and that are perceptible in
both Robert d'Uzès and Geoffroy de Courlon reflect the special position of
the "prophetic reformer." The same fears surface again at the threshold of
the early modern age in the Augustinian cardinal Egidio da Viterbo,
1469–1532, the apocalyptical author of a *History of Twenty Centuries*. After
relating the story of the popess, Egidio goes on to construct a universal history of human perdition, which he founds on three defects that result
from the feminization of the human species. The first of these was Eve's
transgression; the second, which Egidio adds with the aid of a florilegium

of prophetic quotations, was a tendency on the part of populations to "make themselves not only into women but into prostitutes." The third fault brought humanity down to the level of the animals: "We have gathered together all these words [of the prophets] as a way to discover the reason for these three defects: first the soul is coupled with a bad body, then it is weakened and feminized, and finally it slips into the maelstrom of impurity and becomes a brutish animal."[60] Members of the Roman chancery might repeat the fable or note the rite without raising an eyebrow, but in the wildernesses and forests of rumination, there were always "prophets" who perceived the threat that impurity posed to an institution rendered fragile by its lack of seriousness.

MEDIEVAL STRUCTURES OF AN OBSESSION WITH THE FEMALE

How are we to explain the origins of the twelfth-century Church's obsession with gender, an obsession that differed from rabbinic and Mediterranean misogyny and from the juridical segregation of classical Rome? The answer probably lies in the strict obligation to observe ecclesiastical celibacy instituted at the time of the Gregorian reforms of the eleventh century. Still, there is a paradox: it was when celibacy was imposed on priests that verification of the manhood of the most eminent of their number was felt to be necessary. The twelfth century, the high point of feudalism and of reform within the Church, produced a dual constraint: if the layman wanted to survive, he had to marry as closely within family ties as possible so as to guarantee the solidity of the fief, but also as far out of the family as possible in order to avoid incest, which was defined broadly in the age of Gregory VII.[61] Woman lay at the heart of this dual constraint, and she emerged from it idealized and scorned, cherished and feared. This is why the twelfth century produced both courtly literature and devotion to the Virgin, on the one hand, and a fierce misogyny, on the other. The Church, which drew nourishment from this fascination and was intent on preserving its hierarchical supremacy, gave itself a suprasexual status of male androgyny. The Church was mother (*mater ecclesia*), wife (*sponsa*, the mystic bride of Christ), and daughter, born from the flanks of Christ crucified just as Eve was born of Adam. As Roberto Zapperi shows in *The Pregnant Man*,[62] it is in the twelfth century that the first sculptural representations of a rewriting of Genesis occur in which Eve emerges from the side of a pregnant Adam rather than being created from one of his ribs, as in the Biblical text. This rewriting, moreover, is specifically connected to a parallel between the Church and Eve that also was founded on male domination, as we have seen in Huguccio's commentary on Genesis 1.17. The

Church is female on the divine side, but male in its terrestrial aspects, since it derives from both Jesus and Adam. This androgyny works only if it remains unresolved in the symbolic state. Hence the exercise of sexuality must be sacrificed through voluntary celibacy, the external mark of which is tonsuring. Because man occupies the high ground of sexual and juridical superiority, he can afford to sacrifice and to sacrifice himself; woman, who occupies the low ground, can only have access to a suprasexuality that eliminates or rejects sex. In his *Summa aurea* (Golden Summa, ca. 1250) Henricus de Segusio, the famous Cardinal Hostiensis and a great canonist, says (as a cause, not a consequence) that "women cannot be tonsured and their hair cannot be cut *(amputanda)*."[63] A woman's hair could not be cut off because her sexual being is inextricably connected with the signs that manifest it; nothing would be left of her if it were. She is cold; the ecclesiastical superman, on the other hand, presents a natural sign of gender but can also rise above that sign: he is hot. Nothing shows this reasoning better than the canonists' treatment of hermaphrodites, and their statements in this connection are of interest to us because they offer an opportunity to consider a different rite of the verification of gender. Huguccio asks whether a hermaphrodite could be ordained as a priest. He transfers what the Justinian Code has to say about the validity of a hermaphrodite's testimony, and reaches the conclusion that because a hermaphrodite's sexual nature is more hot than cold, his ordination must be accepted.[64]

How are we to understand this odd construction of a male-dominated androgyny or asexual sexuality? Obviously, the astonishing delirium of the canonists and the "prophets" should not keep us from losing sight of reality. No one, at the height of the Middle Ages, was unaware of gender differences. We have been examining a tendency fed by anxiety and a desire to adapt. St. Thomas Aquinas, a man famous for his equilibrium, provides one illustration; the illuminated "prophets" provide a quite different one. Thomas excludes woman on the basis of her inability to signify, but that limitation is tied to social values inherited from Roman juridical custom. He states, "Since a sacrament is a sign, not only the thing, but the signification of the thing, is required in all sacramental actions. . . . Accordingly, since it is not possible in the female sex to signify eminence of degree, for a woman is in the state of subjection, it follows that she cannot receive the sacrament of Order."[65] Obviously, sexual physiology did not much interest Thomas, and he would have reacted to the notion of a woman pope or a rite of gender verification with mild curiosity, at best. In Robert d'Uzès, who was younger than Thomas, we can sense echoes of the physiological categories of canon law: the ghostly popes in his visions are "beardless" and "dry," whereas the prophets of the East had abundant beards. In the Rome that Robert spews out sacred androgyny is the inverse of female lasciviousness: "The chamber of the Shepherd Jesus Christ: Joseph and Mary. And yours [the chamber of the popes] is filled with well-groomed, lascivious, shameless young people who bear arms, feed birds and dogs, steal from the poor, and enrich the prostitutes."[66]

A fairly obscure twelfth-century monk, Burchardus, abbot of Belle-vaux, deserves to be included in the lineage of prophets who were concerned about the virility required for the exercise of the priesthood. In his *Apologia de barbis* (Apologia for Beards) Burchardus presents the beard, a manly attribute susceptible of tonsure, as necessary to expression of the Church's position.[67] The extreme case that he cites—that of Galla, a bearded woman whose story he borrows from Gregory the Great—is as revealing as Huguccio's hermaphrodite. Galla's beard was the result of an excess of heat (a male trait). The only way she could get rid of it was to break her vow of chastity, which she refused to do, preferring to keep her beard as a sign of meritorious participation in holy androgyny.

Between the two extremes of Thomas Aquinas and Robert d'Uzès, the sacred universe of the Church offered a middle view of women, exemplified in an author—Martinus Polonus—who is important to us as the best-known historiographer of Joan. In the late thirteenth century this Dominican, man of the Curia, and papal chaplain wrote a convenient alphabetical index to Gratian's *Decretals* titled *Margarita Decreti* (The Pearl of the Decretals). In the entry "Femina" (Woman), he brings together a good many of the elements we have noted thus far. It reads, in its entirety:

> That woman must not be judged by the reservations attached to her sex. That even when learned and saintly, she must not preach to an assembly of men. That nuns, or any holy woman, must not touch objects on the altar or the sacred vessels. That religion does not permit a man alone to speak with a woman alone. That women's shapes are not to be discussed. That woman must neither amputate her hair nor use male attire out of a taste for luxury. That after childbirth or menstruation women must not be refused entry into church.[68]

The tone of this text is moderate, but it nonetheless bears traces of the obsessions of the twelfth century and its fears of woman and her empire.

Thus far we have dealt with two complementary ways to deal with rumor, one burlesque and vengeful, the other hallucinatory and obsessional, and we have seen two systems of representation that attempted to make sense of the rite of verification of the pope's manhood. What we need to do next is to pursue the archaeology of this rumor and to grasp the ways in which the rite was inserted into the ceremonial of papal investiture. We will need to consider the arrangement of the objects, acts, times, and people that lent substance to this rumor that was so eagerly welcomed in people's hearts—or in certain people's hearts.

2

The History of a Chair

he sex of popes was verified, or so it seems. Medieval echoes of this rumor were amplified by obsessive fears or light-hearted mockery in milieus that gave the tale strong ideological reverberations.

Before we pass on to that amplification process, we need to seize the anonymous, general murmur at its source. Thus far we have seen some frenzied or malicious interpretations of the ritual of papal accession, but any serious interpretation requires a prime object, some matter for exegesis. The rumor's longevity also depended upon the continued presence of the signs that it deciphered. Thus we will have to return to the hearth—cinders or live coals—from which the smoke of rumor emerged; we will have to retrace the history of a ritual as long as it leaves open the possibility of deviant interpretation; as long as there is a gap between what ceremony is intended to signify and what it in fact displays. The history we must trace cannot be reduced to one of a misunderstanding or a loss of information for which the various propagandists of the rite or the rumor compensated; it must also tell us how a society resists ritualization and combats the power that ritual signifies. Obviously, we will need to guard against the exaggeratedly semiotic orientation of certain overenthusiastic followers of Ernst Kantorowicz or Clifford Geertz who see all public ceremonies as an opportunity for exchange and happy ideological circulation, or as a metaphorically contractual moment between those who hold power and those who are subjected to it. We must remember that, contrary to a soothing, saccharine view of political struggle, many ceremonies (French royal entries of the fifteenth to the seventeenth centuries, for example) were open displays of raw power illustrating that the powerful had the simple choice of inspiring terror in their subjects or condescending to pity them.[1] Although after the thirteenth century the papal power tended to resemble the absolutist governments for which it provided a model, it nonetheless differed from the lay powers in its origins, as reformers who attacked the military and state powers of the popes so often remarked. The pope was the Bishop of Rome, elected by the clergy and by the Roman people; he dominated in order to serve, and his only reason for receiving wealth and wielding power was to make them available to the poor and the weak. Scripture and liturgy ceaselessly repeated this lesson. The power of the Church was in an extraordinary situation: it benefited from a divine approval that lay monarchs desperately claimed, but at the same time it was vulnerable because it divulged to its subjects the texts and beliefs on which that power was founded. The ceremonial attached to the accession of a new pope was an integral part of Catholic liturgy; as such, it was accessible, at least in theory, to all the faithful and was in fact widely known, at least in fragmentary fashion. The interaction between the pope and his Roman faithful was a result of this special situation; it was an interaction expressed by fits and starts in ceremonies that always lagged behind political and religious reality and recalled an exalted (or at least remembered) past.

It is in ceremony and within this syntax of unmatched connections that we will seek the meaning of the rite of verification, hoping to uncover the progressive and difficult implantation of the "mysteries of the state" that Kantorowicz analyzes so brilliantly.[2] Rituals of accession have been thoroughly documented and painstakingly analyzed for centuries now, and it would be an exercise in futility to pretend to chronicle them, even briefly. All that I hope to do in this history of a discordance is to scrutinize the points of agreement that directly concern accounts of the verification of the pope's manhood.

THE MORPHOLOGY OF THE RITE OF VERIFICATION

Before we reconstitute that syntax, it would be well to recapitulate the morphological elements that contributed, at one time or another, to the elaboration of the rite of verification and the legend of Pope Joan. Among these were:

• Places: the Lateran Palace, with its various basilicas and chapels. As we have seen, this was where the verification takes place. It stands opposed to another place, the Vatican (and the Basilica of St. Peter's), where Joan's procession starts. There is also an intermediate place, the spot near the church of San Clemente where the popess gives birth. One version of Martinus Polonus's text speaks of a *vicus Papisse* (street of the woman pope);[3]

• Times: From Martinus Polonus on, 855 is given as the date of Joan's papacy. The specific circumstances that argued for that date in papal historiography will be discussed in chapter 4, but the date deserves mention here inasmuch as it relates to the evolution of the accession ceremony. Precise dates do not seem particularly pertinent, given that a papal election could take place at any moment in the year after the death of the preceding pope. There are nonetheless two calendar dates that ought to be mentioned. The text that contains the first proven occurrence of the fable (Jean de Mailly's *Chronica,* ca. 1250) gives a somewhat mysterious detail: "Under him [the woman pope] the Fast of the Four Times was instituted, which was called the Fast of the Popess."[4] A second calendar indication appears in later, fifteenth-century narratives, which state that the popess gave birth during a Rogations procession, hence on 25 April, St. Mark's Day;[5]

  • Actors: The pope and his entourage; and a deacon (usually given as "the least deacon," *ultimus diaconus*) who is charged with touching the "pontificals";

  • Actions: The verification itself; the ceremony of taking possession of the Lateran; the detour taken by the procession to avoid passing near the spot where Joan gave birth. The detour appears very early, at the latest in the *Chronicle of Genoa* of Jacopo da Voragine;[6]

  • Objects: The most important objects are, of course, the pair of porphyry "pierced chairs" that, according to the rumor, facilitated the verification of papal manhood. We have seen in the preceding chapter the role played by the "stercory" chair that is connected with ritual at the Lateran and is sometimes confused with the porphyry chairs. Certain versions of the legend add other objects such as an "image" (a painted portrait or a statue) of Joan and her son, placed at the site of the childbirth, a detail first found in Jacopo da Voragine. Some later writers speak of a small shrine at that same place. The last sign of Joan's existence is a stone inscription, which is mentioned as early as Jean de Mailly's founding narrative, where it is located at her burial place. This inscription, a phrase with six initial Ps, appears at times in the form of a sarcastic quip attributed to the devil. The text of this inscription varies from one author to another, but its form remains constant: Jean de Mailly's version is "Petre, Pater Patrum, Papisse Prodito Partum" (Peter, Father of the Fathers, Publish the Parturition of the Popess).[7]

  With this collection of heterogeneous signs in mind, our next task is to discern the chief mechanisms of ritual interaction and find out what gave meaning and context to the rite of verification, hence to the legend of Joan.

THE PIERCED CHAIRS

First, let us return to the moment when the two "pierced chairs" made their appearance in official Roman ritual and examine the chairs themselves. They do indeed exist, and we can follow their uninterrupted liturgical history from 1099 to the sixteenth century, when their use in the ceremonial of papal accession was discontinued. The two seats were last used at the accession of Pope Leo X in 1513; a half-century later, in 1560, Pius IV eliminated the rite of the "stercory chair."[8] The two pierced chairs remained for some time in the Lateran Palace, but in the eighteenth century Pius VI had them sent to the Vatican Museum. The vicissitudes of history have separated them: today one is still in the Vatican Museum; Napoleon took the other to Paris after the Treaty of Tolentino, and it is now in the Louvre.

These identical chairs are made of a fine-grained marble from southern Greece of a rare color called *rosso antico* (ancient red; actually more on the orange side) that was much appreciated under the Roman Empire.[9] The stone resembles porphyry closely enough for the seats to be called *porphyreticae* or *porphyrae* in the twelfth century. Their seats are fixed to solid parallel supports 48 centimeters high, the front leading edges of which have volutes at the top and what appear to be lions' legs at the base. The back edges have volutes, top and bottom, and the outer sides of the supports are decorated with a plant design in relief. The semicylindrical back is 44.5 centimeters high; the armrests at either side are set back. In the center of the space defined by the back there is a circular hole in the seat 21.4 centimeters in diameter, which is cut out to the front edge of the seat by a nearly square opening 13.2 × 13.7 centimeters. I should note in passing that no description is neutral. The description that has just been given is constructed around the hole in the seat, but if we apply the theories and perceptive exercises of *Gestalttheorie* (or the psychology of form) to these museum pieces and concentrate on the general form of the chairs rather than on the hole in the seat, we might see chairs with deep-set seats and stepped armrests. The nuance is important.

The form of the two seats has nonetheless seemed odd enough to elicit the functional interpretations given in the preceding chapter. Scholars of today and yesterday, who may be more timid or more respectful, usually slide from interpretation to description when they attempt to determine the primary function of the chairs, whose construction does in fact go back to late antiquity. Their origin cannot be taken as a cause, however, and to use their original function to explain their later reuse is to explain nothing, although it does suggest that people of the Middle Ages were naive innocents who used ancient debris with no discernment. Most archaeologists conclude that they were bathing chairs, of a sort common in Roman baths. Frédéric de Clarac said as much in his 1841 guide to the Louvre;[10] early in our own century the notion was repeated by Walther Amelung, then in the Pauly-Wissowa encyclopedia.[11] More recently Josef Deér has argued strongly in support of that interpretation.[12] Some German scholars, Walther Amelung and Wolfgang Helbig among them,[13] do not exclude the possibility that the chairs were commodes, which means that archaeology at the most serious level comes around to agreeing with Platina's scatological jibes! If more recent scholars entertain these interpretations of the chairs' origin, however, they are totally silent regarding their later use. With one exception.

CESARE D'ONOFRIO: BIRTHING CHAIRS

The audacious, ingenious (and well-documented) construction that Cesare D'Onofrio proposed in 1989 is of interest because it explains both the origin and the later use of these chairs.[14] I find his hypothesis unconvincing, but it is solid enough to warrant examination.

For D'Onofrio, the medieval papacy made use of a pair of ancient birthing chairs to signify, metaphorically, the concept of *Mater Ecclesia*, or Mother Church. D'Onofrio relies on the interpretation of them given by a Danish physician, Ole Borch (Olaus Borrichius), who described the chairs in 1690, when they were still at the Lateran. Borch was aware of their ancient ceremonial use, but he identifies them as birthing chairs used by the empress Poppea.[15] It seems well attested that in late antiquity a parturient woman was usually placed in a birthing chair to facilitate her labor; the newborn child was received through the orifice cut into the middle of the seat. Moschion, an African physician and obstetrician, gives a description of such a chair in his sixth-century revision of a fifth-century Latin translation of the works of Soranus of Ephesus, a second-century Greek physician: "What is an obstetrical chair? You must imagine a barber's chair; [the woman] sits on it so as to have under her sexual parts a moon-shaped orifice that the baby slips through."[16] An early third-century bas-relief on the tomb of Scribonia Attica, a midwife, depicts the scene of a childbirth in which a woman is seated upright in a chair whose height, almost cylindrical form, and stepped armrests recall our porphyry chairs. A woman supports her from behind while the midwife, kneeling in front of the woman in labor, has one hand between her legs and holds out the other hand as if to receive the newborn child.[17] Birthing chairs continued to be used throughout the Middle Ages, as attested by iconography, by a treatise of

2. Photograph of the "Porphyry" chair from the Lateran, now in the Musée du Louvre. Réunion des Musées Nationaux.

Avicenna's on childbirth,[18] and by an early-fifteenth-century text in Italian of Michele Savonarola, the grandfather of the redoubtable Florentine Dominican, Girolamo Savonarola.[19] The material conditions for a metaphorical use of the chairs thus seem satisfied, but ideological conditions are also favorable, because Constantine's gift to the papacy of the Lateran Palace (and, presumably, its furnishings) supported the papal claim to a continuity between the Roman Empire and the papacy.

D'Onofrio skillfully combines the sources to show that the use of porphyry for these chairs was not by chance, but was rather a sign of imperial power. In the mid-tenth century, when Liutprand of Cremona reported his impressions of Constantinople on his return from there, he remarked that the imperial "porphyrogenetic" chair did not mean "born to the purple" (an acceptable lexical derivation), but rather "born in the building called Porphyria," a palace reconstructed in Byzantium on the model of the Lateran Palace, which Constantine had turned over to the papacy. Two centuries later, in the early twelfth century, the imperial princess Anna Comnena spoke of her own birth in that palace, stating that the "Porphyra" room, which was entirely lined in red marble (like our two chairs), was reserved for imperial childbirths.[20] D'Onofrio supposes that the imperial aura of these obstetrical chairs remained in the memory of Romans and clerics intent on retaining control over imperial symbols and on using them to the profit of the papacy. Roman ecclesiology, what is more, embraced the maternal metaphor; the expression *Mater Ecclesia* first appears in patristic literature of the second century, and it was used and glossed throughout the Middle Ages. We can agree with D'Onofrio that the custom of depicting the Virgin of the Annunciation before a backdrop of church architecture led to a blending of the iconographic themes of the Virgin and the Mother Church. The most disturbing iconographic proof of this can be found in a series of rolls of the *Exultet*, decorated with miniatures, produced in southern Italy between the tenth century and the thirteenth century.[21] Three of these miniatures show a female figure emerging from the roof of a church. These are not depictions of the Virgin, but rather female figurations of the Church, because they are quite visibly wearing a pallium, a garment reserved to popes and archbishops. The figure in the fourth picture is shown in the same stance (arms outstretched), in the same setting, and wearing the same sort of pallium, but he is a bearded prelate. By permutation, then, the pope occupies the place of the Mother Church. A final argument connects metaphor and ritual: around 1190, hence nearly a century after the porphyry chairs were introduced into this ritual, three accounts of the papal investiture ceremonies (to which we shall return) speak of an odd portion of the ritual that is difficult to explain: "In these two chairs [the porphyry chairs], the elect must seat himself as if he seemed stretched between two beds *(inter duos lectos jacere)*."[22]

Texts outlining the ceremonial of the accession of a new pope continued to repeat this notation, century after century. A reclining position totally contradicts the notion of enthronement and might indeed imitate childbirth.

CRITICISM OF THE BIRTHING CHAIR HYPOTHESIS

In spite of its seductive coherence, Cesare D'Onofrio's hypothesis fails to convince me. Four major objections stand in the way of wholehearted acceptance:

1. No liturgical or doctrinal text, in the enormous amount of commentary and description written about the ceremony, connects the porphyry chairs with the image of the *Mater Ecclesia*. The miniature of the *Exultet* rolls is a hapax legomenon, an absolutely unique case of a parallel between the pope in majesty and a female figuration of the Church.

2. D'Onofrio offers no explanation for one essential feature: the duality of the two chairs.

3. Although I have no intention of indulging in semantic nit-picking, it is a reasonable conjecture that the role of the *Mater Ecclesia* is more protective than generative. The Mother Church is pictured as a matron, a *materfamilias*, not as a woman in childbirth. To offer one example of this, the author of the 1273 ceremonial justifies the fact that the Church proclaims excommunications on Holy Thursday, even though it is a feast day, which should preclude all judiciary procedures, by stating: "One must reply that this is not to proffer a sentence, but to represent an exclusion, not by the judiciary route but by maternal warning and correction."[23] The parallel between the Church and the Virgin of the Annunciation is misleading; in the Gospels, when Mary is visited by the Holy Spirit, she prefigures the specific, unique, and irreplaceable history of the Incarnation. Mary is pregnant with Jesus and with salvation, coexistent in her. With what could the Church be pregnant? What name could be given to the newborn that emerges from under its chair? D'Onofrio adds dramatic weight to sacred demography by this reiterated pregnancy. The Mother Church, a figure already mature, well established in its wise opulence, seems instead to be a variant on the protective and dominating roles of the popes and bishops as father, mother, and pastor.

4. Sexual permutation (here, the representation of the pope as a mother) seems as impossible in any practical, individual, concrete form—any embodiment in act—as it is possible (as everything is possible) in the metaphorical drift of doctrinal meditation.[24] The paternal connotations of the pope are too ancient and too strong to permit his assimilation as female: the term *papa*, after all, goes back to the Greek of Homeric times, where it is baby talk for "father." St. Cyprian and St. Augustine apply the term *papa* to the bishop, and in the fifth century it became the common designation for the pope. The term *Pater Patrum* (Father of Fathers) appeared in the sixth century.[25] That term is all the more important because

it connects the broad familial vocabulary of Christians with the political vocabulary of the Roman Empire that the papacy so insistently made its own. Second-century jurists called the emperor *Pater Patriae* (Father of the Country). Cato and Catullus had already addressed Caesar in those terms, and in the age of Pope Gelasius (late fifth century), the title was still being used for Emperor Anastasius I. It would be highly surprising if the late eleventh century, an age permeated by nostalgia for the imperial mode, had used the opposite metaphor of a childbearing maternity. In a word, if the Church was female and mother, the pope was male and father; let us eliminate D'Onofrio's papal foetus, who does nothing but disturb that solid pair, and rescue the pope from confinement within the family by returning to the time of the first appearance of the two seats.

First Appearance: The Coronation of Paschal II (1099)

We first hear of the chairs in 1099 in connection with the accession of Paschal II. A contemporary report of his investiture in the *Liber pontificalis* reads as follows:

> The Lord Pope Urban [II], of solemn memory, having died, the Church, which was in Rome, sought to give itself a shepherd. To that end, the father cardinals and bishops, deacons, and magnates of the City [and] the first notaries and the regional scribes meet together in the church of St. Clement. Although they discuss many candidates, they easily agree upon him [Paschal II]; this choice, once known, displeased that good man; he attempted to avoid it by fleeing and hiding himself. But he could not long avoid human decision for the pleasure of one person alone: he whom the grace of the divine power had decided to designate for the salvation of the multitude. They find him; they drag him before the assembly, and they meet again. They discuss his flight: "I really had to flee, Fathers," he said, "rather than support, with an excessive presumption of soul, the weight of this burden to which I was unequal; and it was not right that the priest that I am be entangled by this honor and succumb, imprisoned in the bonds of this responsibility." "Not at all," the Fathers said, "you should not speak like that; your will should let itself be guided to where, as you will know, the divine gaze has made its decision. The people of the City have wanted you as shepherd; the clergy has elected you, the Fathers congratulate you, and, in short, the care of the entire Church rests upon you. All this is divine, and it is by divine

inspiration that, gathered together, we elect you and confirm you in the supreme pontificate." Thus, after long hesitations, he changes his name, and the first of the notaries and the regional scribes proclaims three times, "Pope Paschal, St. Peter has chosen you." Once these acclamations and other praises have been offered, the Fathers vest him with the red chlamys and coif his head with the tiara; to the accompaniment of the singing of the crowd, he permits himself to be taken to the Lateran; he is led before the north portico of the basilica of the Savior, which is called the Basilica of Constantine; he descends from his horse; he is placed on the seat that is there, then on the patriarchal seat; next, he goes up to the palace and arrives at the two curule chairs *(ad duas curules)*. There he is girdled with the *baltheum* [baltheus or subcinctorium] from which seven keys and seven seals hang; he knows by that act that, with the seven-fold grace of the Holy Spirit, he is to preside, under divine authority, over the government of the holy churches, binding and loosing with as much justice and solemnity as is required; then, placed first in one, then in the other chair, he receives the ferule in his hand. He completes the rites of election by sitting or walking *(vel sedens vel transiens)*, already as master, among the other places in the palace reserved to the Roman pontiffs.[26]

The earlier part of this text relates at some length Paschal II's reticence about accepting his election. We need not linger long over it, as it repeats a topos of pontifical election ceaselessly repeated since the election of Gregory the Great. Paschal I, whose name the new pope took, had also manifested reticence in 817. Although this attitude is always presented as individual, it is clearly ritual behavior, and proclaims that the pope-elect had not tried to obtain the papacy by intrigue. Ritual reticence also expresses a radical separation between the faithful and the pope-elect: while still an ordinary man, he is seized with fear and rejects the idea of divine transmutation by act of the Holy Spirit. The Fathers' arguments show that the divine has a share in the human activity of electing a pope. In Arnold van Gennep's analysis, separation is a necessary and integral part of the ceremonial syntax of rites of passage.[27]

The ceremony described in this passage is not liturgical, strictly speaking; the religious ceremony of consecration took place afterwards, in the Basilica of St. Peter's, Vatican. The rite of election *(modus electionis)* that resulted in papal investiture concluded with the taking possession of the Lateran, the only place specifically mentioned in the text, given that the place for voting (here, the church of San Clemente) varied. Although no Mass was celebrated during the taking possession of the Lateran, the event nonetheless had a public, religious phase that was marked off from the profane phase by the pope ascending the stairs to the Lateran Palace. The religious phase made use of two chairs: the first, undescribed (*in sede*), was located under the portico of the Basilica of the Savior (that is, the patriarchal basilica of the Lateran, also known as St. John Lateran). The second chair is called "patriarchal"; its location is not given in the text, but it was undoubtedly in the basilica itself or in a public hall next to the basilica. We shall return to these spaces when we examine later accounts of the ceremonies.

The second, public phase takes place on the upper level of the palace, and on a threshold. The pope receives the baltheus with its seven keys and seven seals that bind and loose (thus expressing the fullness of the pope's jurisdiction) just before he sits on the curule chairs. This detail is important, because, as we shall see, later versions of the ceremony attribute different meanings to the proceedings and have the keys given to the pope while he is seated on the porphyry chairs. In 1099, however, what the pope receives while seated on the curule chairs is the ferula, or staff, an imperial (and/or seigniorial), hence secular, symbol of authority used in papal investitures since the mid-tenth century. The anonymous ceremonial of the late twelfth century discovered by Bernhard Schimmelpfennig, the *Ordo* of Basel (and the Church used the term *ordo* for a text describing the rules for ceremonial and/or liturgical occasions), states that "these two chairs and the one that is called stercory were not at all patriarchal, but imperial."[28] The final part of the 1099 ritual, which has the pope sitting or walking (*vel sedens vel transiens*) refers to other places in the palace reserved to the Roman pontiffs. This suggests that the chairs stood within the pope's own, seigniorial space, apart from such shared spaces as the basilica or the public hall of the palace. The chairs connect and separate both the jurisdictional power of the pope and his seigniorial power.

THE 1099 CURULE CHAIRS

We have neglected an essential detail: the seats are called "curule." The Church deserves to be scolded for a doubly ignorant use of the term: first, a Roman curule seat or chair would never have been found in such a place; second, the Roman curule chair, a sign of the power of the consuls and the praetors, was a wooden or ivory folding chair with X-shaped legs. It bore no resemblance to our red marble seats. However, and I offer the hypothesis with due solemnity, they were indeed "curule seats." Their precise form does not matter, because the role they play here is symbolic. As we shall see, curule chairs were required here, but no examples of those fragile pieces of furniture were left in Rome. The porphyry chairs, whose glorious antiquity was certain, were used in their stead, thanks to the fact that they were identical and the fact that there were two of them (curule chairs always came in pairs). If we start from the global perception of *Gestalttheorie*, as suggested above, what we see is their narrow seats (as with curule chairs) rather than the holes in those seats; moreover, the S-shaped volutes on their base recall the curved X of the consuls' chairs. Symbolic pertinence is more important that a strict equivalence of form.

Why should it have been necessary, in 1099, to give prominence to curule chairs? An article of Stephen Kuttner's takes us on what seems an ecclesiological and political detour but is actually the right road.[29] Kuttner shows that until Innocent III, the canonical titles applied to the popes wavered between two extremes. Gregory the Great instituted the humble title of "slave of the slaves of God" *(servus servorum Dei)*, which stresses that the pontiff, the head of the Church, puts himself in the service of the bishops and the priests, the servants of God. In the age of Gregory VII (immediately before our 1099 ceremonial), the popes reversed this relationship with the prelates by attempting to proclaim themselves universal popes or patriarchs. Much was at stake here: the term "universal" meant that the other patriarchates (of Constantinople, Antioch, Alexandria, and Jerusalem) were subject to Rome, as were the offices of the prelates of the Christian church all over the world. Gregory the Great had forbidden anyone from claiming to be "universal," however, and the prohibition was strongly reinforced in the ninth-century Pseudo-Isidorian decretals, which cite Pelagius. Gregory was manifesting his personal humility, but he was also expressing a firm intent to resist any claims of universality, based on the Roman Empire, that the patriarch of Constantinople might put forth. Still in the late eighth century, during the preparations for the second Council of Nicaea, Pope Adrian I reproached Tarasios, patriarch of Constantinople, for claiming titular dominance. Later popes found the temptation to disobey this prohibition irresistible and appropriated the title of universality: as early as the seventh century, Martin I and Conon called themselves "universal"; in the eighth century the spurious *Donation of Constantine* uses the term. In the latter half of the eleventh century, the time of the Gregorian reforms that Walter Ullmann considers the apogee of hierocratic principles in the papacy,[30] popes firmly claimed universality, beginning with Alexander II in 1061 (probably acting on the advice of his archdeacon, Hildebrand, the future Pope Gregory VII). Significantly, the first oath of infeudation to the pope, given by Richard of Capua in

1073, was addressed to "my lord Gregory, universal pope." Robert Guiscard repeated the same formula in 1073 on receiving fiefs of Sicily, Apulia, and Calabria from Gregory VII. I might note in passing that the Normans contributed to the hierocratic nature of the papacy by their use of porphyry in the dynastic tombs of the Norman kings in southern Italy.[31] The expression also appears in the acts of the Synod of Rome in 1079, and the *Dictatus Papae* of Gregory VII hammer in the notion that "only the Roman pontiff can rightly be called universal." One might also cite Cardinal Deusdedit and the *Dictatus d'Avranches* (1085–87).

LUCAN, THE CURIA, AND THE PAPACY

The title of universal pope encountered strong opposition within the Roman Church itself, however. The first great canonists of the eleventh century founded their arguments against it on the fairly vague assertions of Pelagius in the False Decretals and on Gregory the Great ("Let no one title himself universal") and they firmly stated their opposition, as can be seen in the *Diversorum patrum sententiae,* in the *Polycarpus* (1109–33), or in the writings of Anselm of Lucca (1083–86). Gratian, the author of the first major collection of canon law (ca. 1140), states clearly: "The Roman pontiff is not called universal" (distinction 99). Nonetheless, the custom inaugurated by Gregory VII persisted, as Rufinus notes in his *Summa.* From then on, glossators of canon law such as Joannes Faventinus or Joannes Teutonicus note both the use of the title and its theoretical abrogation in Gratian's *Decretals.* One summa, the *Tracturus magister* (late twelfth century) argues: "This word is not conserved, so as to avoid the arrogance that the people of Constantinople brought to bear on the Roman pontiffs in the times of Emperor Maurice."[32] This allusion to Constantinople does little to conceal the Roman and political pertinence of the controversy; universality already meant pontifical absolutism. Huguccio, the great twelfth-century jurist, was one of the first champions (after Cardinal Humbert) of the oligarchical power of the cardinal bishops, whose electoral monopoly, established in 1059, threatened to become a share in papal power. Huguccio's contribution to the debate on the pope's universality took it to a more general level: "If the word ["universal"] is appropriate for several but is attributed to one alone, it seems to be taken away from the others."[33] We glimpse an antimonarchical aim in Huguccio's defense of the patriarchs. He continues: "For the one who calls himself universal *(universus vel universalis)* seems to be all *(esse omnia)* in the sense in which Caesar was all." This last phrase refers to and closely paraphrases the beginning of a line from book 3 of Lucan's *Civil War (Pharsalia)* that had become proverbial: *Omnia Caesar erat* (Caesar was all in all). A horri-fied Lucan is speaking in this passage of the senators of the Republic, forced into assembly by Caesar: "A mob of senators *(patrum)*, brought out from their hiding-places, filled the temple of Apollo on the Palatine *(pala-tia)*; the splendour of the consuls was absent from their sacred seats; the praetors, by law next in office, were not in attendance, and the empty chairs of office were removed from their places *(vacuaeque loco esse cu-rules)*. Caesar was all in all."[34]

The statement that became proverbial and was used to combat the popes' universalist and absolutist claims is immediately preceded by a ref-erence to "empty chairs of office" that are clearly curule seats. This helps us to understand the symbolic function of the curule chairs in the Lateran: when the pope sat on them, it was a symbolic denial of his "Caesarism"; they cast the cardinals into the role of "senators" *(patres)* guided by a con-sul. The porphyry seats are indeed curule chairs, symbolically charged with marking a ceremonial transaction between the monarchy of the pope and the oligarchy of the cardinals.

Huguccio's literary reference may seem to be late (the third quarter of the twelfth century) and erudite, but in fact it refers to a learned culture shared by the men of the Curia and the great theologians of the eleventh and twelfth centuries. Gerhoch of Reichersberg uses Lucan's expression to refer to the popes in his *De investigatione Antichristi*: "Thus, if, as has been said regarding Caesar, the Roman pontiff is all . . . "[35] Lucan's half-line was equally proverbial in a quite different context: in his *Verbum abbrevia-tum*, Peter Cantor lashes out at "pluralist" bishops (who held benefices in several different places): "They are worse than Julius Caesar, of whom Lu-can said, to end his enumeration of his other crimes, that Caesar was all *(omnia Caesar erat)*. Indeed, he was simultaneously consul, quaestor, etc. in the same city; those who do likewise in several cities are much worse."[36] It seems highly likely that this proverbial phrase referring to absolutism (and its translation into visible form in the empty curule chairs) circulated within the milieus of the Curia in the late eleventh century. The use of cu-rule chairs at the accession of a new pope was a metaphorical denial; the pope assumed a superiority (the role of consul) that implied hierarchy, but not tyranny. It was a reply, by a ritual act, to those who complained, like Huguccio, that "If I am all" implied "you are nothing" *(si ego omnia, tu es nichil)*. It also exactly prefigured Innocent III's more discursive, logi-cian's response to the same objection a century later:

> One speaks of the universal Church in two ways. If it is made of
> all the churches, one says the universal or catholic Church, ac-

cording to the Greek vocabulary. In that meaning [that is, because it is not all churches] the Roman Church cannot be universal; it is a part of the universal Church, but the first and principal part, like the head in the body. One calls "the Church universal" the one that governs all the churches, and in this second sense alone can the Roman Church be said to be universal.[37]

PONTIFICAL TRANSACTIONS

We need to return to ecclesiological terms of transaction, first, to justify this later use of a vocabulary of the Roman Republic, but also to see how adequately that vocabulary fit the situation in 1099.

Gregory the Great speaks of the "Society of the Christian Republic" over which the papacy exercised its principate, and Gregory calls the pope *consul Dei* (the consul of God). We can understand these titles as relating to the question of the universality of papal power, because, as we have seen, Gregory was the first to protest against the patriarch of Constantinople's claim to universal sway, a claim based on Constantinople's status as a royal city *(urbs regia)*. The Roman vocabulary reinstated Rome and its church as the head of the world *(caput mundi)*, thus enabling the pope to take to himself imperial law pertaining to the sacred *(jus in sacris)*. As the early Middle Ages advanced, the two concepts of Christian community—corporative and republican—alternated with shifting strategies, but in the eighth century, when Rome effected its total emancipation from Constantinople, the Roman vocabulary developed notably. When Pope Stephen II traveled to the court of Pepin the Short, king of the Franks, in 754, he performed the rite of unction for the king and granted him the title of *patricius Romanorum*. An astonishing phrase appears in the text of a letter that Stephen wrote to Pepin around 750 to secure confirmation of the (spurious) Donation of Constantine: "the Holy Church of God and of the Republic of the Romans" *(sancta Dei ecclesia et reipublicae Romanorum)*,[38] a designation that also appears in the biography of Stephen II in the *Liber pontificalis* and that Walter Ullmann has analyzed brilliantly.[39] The expression closely resembles the classical term, *Respublica romana*, but that was a phrase that referred to the Empire, hence to its head in Byzantium. The new title, "Republic of the Romans," includes the "Romans" within the community of the faithful—that is, Christians who live according to the Roman faith, not the Greek faith, and who follow the teachings of the Church of Rome, not those of Byzantium. Christianity became identical to Romanness, reflecting a shift initiated by Gregory the

Great after the sweeping conversions of the seventh century aimed at England and Germany, lands that were not imperial but Roman. It is clear, however, that social, political, and cultural implications accompany the strictly religious connotations of the term.

In Rome itself the Church's use of ancient words marked the stages of a conquest of the city. Between the eighth century and the ninth century, the papacy adopted many ancient political references that had pertained to lay society. Until the mid-ninth century, for instance, the term "senate" was still used in its institutional sense to designate a fairly well-defined body of patricians and consuls—an administrative and judiciary organization.[40] Roman nobles referred to themselves as *proceres* and *optimates;* the aristocratic heads of the urban militia *(exercitus)* were called *duces* or "tribunes." Ecclesiastical geography also reflects the Church's invasions of lay territory: in the eighth century, the Senate could no longer meet in the *Curia Senatus* because it had been transformed into the churches of Sant'Adriano and Santa Martina. The Church developed by absorbing the "senatorial" nobility into the clerical order. Nonetheless, the memory of the ancient republic remained sufficiently alive, in the twelfth century, for the revolution of 1144 to institute a "revival of the Senate."

THE CURIA AS SENATE

The cardinals played a role in this ideological reconstitution of ancient Rome in the eleventh century. The term "cardinal" was probably created in the sixth century;[41] it is found in the eighth century, but at that time it simply referred to the person in charge of liturgy in one of the major basilicas of Rome. Under Pope Stephen III there is mention of seven hebdomadary cardinal bishops; they were the seven suburbicarian bishops of Rome, who headed the dioceses of Ostia, Porto, Silva Candida, Palestrina, Sabina, and Tusculum and conducted weekly liturgical services at the Lateran (they were also called the Lateran bishops). Besides these seven cardinal bishops, there were twenty-eight cardinal priests who served the twenty-eight titular churches of Rome and who also conducted liturgical services at the Lateran. Finally, at a later date there were eighteen cardinal deacons in charge of the eighteen diaconal churches of Rome, to which we shall return. In this manner, a coherent body of fifty-three dignitaries slowly came into being, formed by the religious geography of Rome and its immediate environs. This body did not follow the usual diocesan structures, given that it mixed liturgical ranks; it did form something like a senate of the Roman Church, and it gave a fixed structure to the Roman clergy *(clerus)*, taken both as a group and as a part of the urban community of the faithful. The *senatus populusque* gave way to the *clerus populusque*. Even when Leo IX (1049 – 54) broadened the geographical horizon of the body of cardinals, excluding certain Roman prelates for simony in favor of Italian or transalpine prelates (the abbots of Monte Cassino, Vendôme, and Saint-Victor de Marseille), the Roman scheme of things remained, with the abbot taking on the title of a cardinal presbyter of a church of Rome. The assimilation of this clerical elite to the Senate had begun as early as the mid-eighth century, with the *Donation of Constantine*, which states:

> We decree moreover, as to the most reverend men, the clergy of
> different orders who serve that same holy Roman church, that
> they have that same eminence, distinction, power and excellence,
> by the glory of which it seems proper for our most illustrious sen-
> ate to be adorned; that is, that they be made patricians and con-
> suls, and also we have proclaimed that they be decorated with the
> other imperial dignities.[42]

Moreover, although we run the risk of sinning by anachronism if we view this clerical elite as the body of cardinals given senatorial and consular ostentation,[43] the offer attributed to Constantine quite naturally, by slippage, came to refer to the body of cardinals in the eleventh century.

But what did this senatorial metaphor actually describe? A function, or simply a rank? One response came in 1059 with the Synod of Rome under the leadership of Nicholas II. In the ancient Church, the assent of the clergy and the people was required for the election of a bishop or a pope, but developing clerical power, a fear of lay influence, and the permanent risk of shows of force led the papacy to strip the laity of any say in the papal electoral process. Pope Symmachus in 498 and Pope Stephen III in 769 attempted, although in vain, to restrict the right to vote to clergy. In 1059 Nicholas II made that right exclusive to the cardinals. The cardinal bishops designated the candidate; they then joined with the other cardinals for the formal election; finally, they asked the clergy and the people for their consent.[44] This means that in the eleventh century, the papacy installed an electoral oligarchy, following the ancient model of deliberation explicitly called for by Peter Damian, the great ideologue of the Gregorian reform, who was himself the cardinal bishop of Ostia: "The Roman Church, which is the seat of the apostles, must imitate the ancient curia of the Romans."[45] For Peter Damian, the cardinals were the "spiritual senators of the universal Church." In the same age, Cardinal Deusdedit pushed the comparison even farther: just as the Senate came from the patrician class, so "the Roman clerics take the place of the ancient patricians."[46] Still, if apparent convergence, expressing a common intent to give a

strong, concrete organization to *societas christiana* as an autonomous political body, gave rise to the Roman Curia, that still leaves open the question of how the pope and the cardinals shared power. The cardinals cited
the republican model of a Senate that kept a strict control over the consulate, but the papacy thought in terms of the imperial model of a Senate
whose responsibility was to support the *principatus*, the sovereignty of the
emperor. Peter Damian explicitly says as much: "The terrestrial Senate
gave counsel, governed, and concentrated the efforts of its common operation so as to submit the multitude of the peoples to Roman sovereignty."
These are the notions that underlay the geographical enlargement of the
corps of cardinals begun by Leo IX and pursued by Gregory VII: the many
cardinals who came from north of the Alps signified the universality of
Christian society. The cardinals countered that representative and intermediary function with their own oligarchical vision of the leadership of
the Roman Church. Cardinal Humbert, whose brilliant career followed
Huguccio's a century later, claimed that the Roman Church was composed
of the pope and the cardinals;[47] the cardinals also based their arguments
on imperial Roman law, claiming that they should become part of the
body of the pope just as the senators had been a part of the body of the
emperor.

The electoral decree of 1059 gave an ambiguous status to the seven
cardinal bishops responsible for designating the pope: when they directed
the choice of the clergy and the people, they played the role that a cathedral chapter played in relation to the ordinary bishop; when they confirmed that election, they were acting as fellow provincial bishops of the
pope-elect; when they consecrated him (a liturgical responsibility attributed from ancient times to the bishop Hostiensis, the bishop of Ostia, assisted by the bishops of Porto and Albano), they took on, collectively, the
function of the metropolitan. As Jean Gaudemet says, "Since the apostolic
see was superior to all the other churches in the world and, consequently,
could have no metropolitan above it, it was the cardinal bishops who
probably fulfilled the functions of metropolitan and who bore the elected
bishop to the highest apostolic summit."[48] This accumulation of identities gave the group of the seven cardinal bishops a strong corporative personality that fell outside church hierarchies but was lodged at the heart of
the institution of the papacy, which they perpetually engendered.

THE POLITICAL FUNCTION OF THE 1099 RITE

In the late eleventh century the cardinals' rising power received a new
boost. The schism prompted by Guibert of Ravenna (proclaimed as

Clement III, antipope to Gregory VII, in 1080) increased the oligarchical claims of the Sacred College. The antipope moved to ensure the cardinals' support by granting them privileges that they never relinquished, even when the schism failed: their precedence over all bishops, the right to judge any bishop, the need to have three dozen witnesses if a cardinal was to be convicted of a crime, a right of subscription of pontifical acts, and an almost total replacement of synods by meetings of cardinals to be called "consistories," a term first mentioned under Paschal II, the pope of the curule chairs. Cardinal Hugo Candidus went quite far in this direction, claiming that without the signatures of the cardinals, the pope's declarations (or decretals) were worthless, a view that reduced the pope to being merely the voice of the Church.

Some of the cardinals defected to Guibert (John of Porto, for example, in 1084), and by the time of Guibert's synod in 1098 a second Sacred College had been created.[49] The election of Paschal II, himself the cardinal priest of San Clemente, thus occurred in an atmosphere of ferocious competition for power in which all participants had a stake.

The invention of the rite of the curule seats fits right in with this highly important debate in the final years of the eleventh century, when the cardinals and the Curia were constantly gaining power. As Paschal II took possession of the Lateran his first step (inside the basilica) was to assert his full religious power as universal patriarch by occupying the "patriarchal" throne; when next he mounted the steps to the Lateran Palace, he linked his full jurisdictional authority to the seven judiciary powers by donning the baltheus with its seven seals and seven keys. Who were those seven judiciary powers? Certainly not the seven judges known as "ordinaries" or "judges of the clergy" (the *primicerius*, the *secondicerius*, the *acarius*, the *sacellarius*, the *protoscrinarius*, the *primus defensor*, and the *nomenclator*), who were simple officials of the Lateran, at times even laymen, and whose original functions had faded away in the tenth century, leaving terms that merely designated rank.[50] We should probably see the custom as a ceremonial opening up of pontifical power to the seven cardinal bishops; a translation into ritual of the cardinals' subscription to the pontifical acts (papal decretals were judiciary documents). If not, how are we to understand the number seven, vaguely connected with the seven gifts of the Holy Spirit, but explicitly connected, in the text of the *Liber pontificalis*, to the direction *(regimen)* of the churches? Moreover, the first occurrence of the rite in which the baltheus figures was in 1099. Earlier rites involving keys (without the seals) present them in threes; a later rite with a different significance has twelve keys hanging from the papal belt.[51] In the third phase of the ceremonial the pope acts as the only consul (the imperial position) when he seizes the ferule. At the same time he proclaims—given that the curule chairs are not empty—his own personal, organic relationship with the corps of the Fathers. This occurs in the narrow threshold located beyond the public, liturgical space of the basilica; it happens between the judiciary and ecclesiastical space of the palace, which the pope shared with the Curia, and the space reserved for the papal, lordly dwelling.

THE FRAGILITY AND OBSCURITY OF RITUAL MEANING

We can begin to understand the fragility of this subtle rite, a gestural metaphor for a delicate transaction, addressed to a few men of the Curia. It was inevitable that although the rite retained its form, because it was part of the ceremonial liturgy, its meaning would become completely opaque. Twenty-five years later, on the occasion of the accession of Honorius II in 1124, we find a second mention of curule chairs, but the redactor of the *Liber pontificalis* calls them "the chairs in the form of a sigma" *(in simis)*: all he sees is their shape. The *ordines* of the late twelfth century (the *Ordo* of Basel and those of Albinus and Cencio), do not even mention the shape of the chairs; they and subsequent texts speak only of the material they are made of, which is one step even further from their meaning. Henceforth the chairs are known as two "porphyry chairs." This shift from form to material may reflect a desire to avoid the scatological or titillating interpretations of the rite of the twelfth century. The *sima* (Sidonius Apollinaris calls it a *sigma*)[52] referred to a bathing chair with a deep indentation, so named because of its semicircular shape (in uncial writing the Greek sigma was shaped like a C). The frank imprudence of this 1124 name for the chairs may have encouraged interpretations inappropriate to the pontifical dignity, hence the rectification.

Misunderstanding of this ritual, which reached its height in the rumored verification of papal manhood presented in chapter 1, sprang from an institutional structure that operated on two levels: the transaction that was given physical form thanks to the chairs took place among a limited number of individuals, but because the ceremony was liturgical its narration was played before the entire community of the faithful. If this is true, what is the point of a ritual act if its meaning is obscure to most of the people in attendance? For the men of the Curia, habituated by their liturgical and juridical formation to a certain "realism" in the terms used for verbal expressions and acts, the rite reflected legislative behavior. The pope established the law; it was the task of the faithful to know the law. Ritual acts and words were law; as such they were just like decretals, which were laws created by the pope regarding particular circumstances, addressed to an individual or a group in the form of a letter, but whose value was nonetheless universal (as demonstrated by the fact that they were collected together).

This continuity between ceremonial acts and the redaction of decretals is clearly demonstrated in Pope Adrian IV's treatment of Emperor Frederick Barbarossa around 1155.[53] After a long period of conflict between the papacy and the empire that had started in the age of Gregory VII, Adrian wanted to make it clear that the emperor was subject to papal authority. His first move in that direction was to attempt to have Frederick act as *strator*, holding the bridles of the papal horse before his imperial coronation in Rome. In Adrian's mind, this act would ratify the principle of the translation of the empire from Byzantium to Germany, thus making Frederick the successor of Constantine, who, according to the text of the Donation of Constantine, had demonstrated his respect for the papacy by serving as *strator* for Pope Sylvester I. Frederick flatly, even violently, refused because he interpreted the act as an overly explicit sign of feudal submission. Adrian IV did not insist. Ten days later, however, when the moment came for the imperial coronation in St. Peter's, he pursued his efforts to legislate by means of visible acts, modifying a ritual that had remained unchanged since 1014. The imperial unction would not take place during the Mass, but before it. In this way it would no longer seem to confer a holy order. Moreover, the anointment would be performed by the cardinals; it would not take place at the high altar (whose use was reserved to the pope), but before the altar of San Maurizio. Another change seemed to enhance the emperor's prestige but in fact lessened the importance of his coronation: the pope gave the imperial insignia, not before the altar of San Maurizio, as had been customary, but before the high altar and during Mass. By this means the principal theme of the ceremony became the pontifical donation of the insignia, which presented the papacy as the source of lay power. Frederick did not protest, probably because he failed to comprehend the nature of these complex, simultaneous changes. As far as the papacy was concerned, however, the changes became law, and Innocent III incorporated them into the last set of rules for imperial coronations of the Middle Ages. Frederick Barbarossa did not fully grasp the pope's intentions until 1157, when he was in Besançon and received a letter from Adrian that mentioned the *beneficium*—the good deed—that had been accorded to Frederick at his coronation. Rainald of Dassel, Frederick's counselor (and later archbishop of Cologne), translated the word *beneficium* (the emperor did not understand Latin) with the Germanic equivalent of "fief." Once again Frederick flew into a rage. The anecdote illustrates the point that ritual could function as legislation, just like papal decretals, but it also shows that obscure rites could generate misunderstandings.

THE THRONE OF ST. PETER

Such failures to understand or see clearly in 1099 would not have become so important if they had not accompanied and expressed a major redistribution of civic and religious space in Rome. Even though only a few people grasped the significance of the curule chairs, the overall scenario of the ritual confirmed for one and all the constitution of an abstract place of power—a court, a Curia—where Rome had previously known only a concrete, accessible space of episcopal domination. A rapid survey of these successive and overlapping spaces, moving from chair to chair, *vel sedens vel transiens,* and following the papal custom of concentrating meanings, will help to clarify the change.

Until the eighth century, the religious and civil life of Rome was spread over a wide network of places. Since the age of Constantine the Lateran, with its palace and its basilica of the Savior, had served as the episcopal residence of the popes; the Basilica of St. Peter's in the Vatican gave material form to papal primacy by the presence of the body of St. Peter; the various churches of Rome (basilicas, titular churches, diaconal churches) were integrated into a communitarian, episcopal space by the liturgy of the stations of the cross. The Lateran was hardly distinguishable from any other episcopal residence, and like its counterparts it withstood attack in times of rival candidacies or schisms. Papal specificity emerged out of this local network only slowly, crystalizing around another chair of central importance, the throne of St. Peter, whose history is now well known thanks to the works of Michele Maccarrone and Nikolaus Gussone.[54]

That "chair" *(cathedra)* at first had only a symbolic meaning; St. Cyprian (third century) used the term to express St. Peter's preeminence over the other bishops: "God is one and Christ is one: there is one Church and one chair founded, by the Lord's authority, upon Peter."[55] The notion of the "apostolic seat" or "see" *(sedes apostolica)* was defined in the fourth century, before it encountered the concrete object that is the episcopal throne. That throne is essentially a liturgical custom: the throne and the altar were the basic elements for defining sacramental space. Two other types of seats appeared in the basilica of the early Middle Ages, and in all cathedrals as well. These were the portable seat for apostolic confession *(sella gestatoria apostolica confessionis),* first mentioned in the sixth century, and another folding chair placed in the sacristy and reserved for the judiciary functions of the pope as bishop. The hierarchy inferred by the use of such seats was limited to the religious sphere, however, as shown by a canon of the Council of Carthage in 395: "Let the bishop, in the church, be seated higher than the priests; but in the palace, let him know that he is the colleague of the priests."[56]

Sacred space began to be specified under Gregory the Great, who instituted the custom of papal consecration in St. Peter's. He seems also to have instituted the use of a fixed stone chair. The spatial arrangements he chose were coherent with his choice of title. Gregory shunned signs of pride, but he took care to proclaim the superiority of Rome by having twenty-four seats placed around the papal throne in the apse of St. Peter's. That number of course recalls the eschatological assembly of the Apocalypse; by its presentation of the Christological heritage, it expresses the primacy of Rome over Constantinople at the very place that justified that primacy, near the tomb of St. Peter. This was the first separation put into effect within Roman space. The Vatican, which was situated outside the city walls, transcended the urban network; thanks to the throne of St. Peter, it gave form to the notion of the apostolic see, or seat.

THE EMINENCE OF THE LATERAN

Just as Rome's appropriation of the patriarchal, universal title developed out of a defensive tactic that seemed to play down that title, so the personal eminence that the bishop of Rome enjoyed at the Lateran reached its full expression when the pontiff himself, in the Vatican, was overshadowed by the transpersonal notion of the apostolic see. The role of the Lateran was strengthened in the eighth century, when Rome definitively won autonomy from the Eastern Roman Empire at Constantinople. What had been known as the *episcopium* of the Lateran (that is, the residence of the bishop) became, in the last decade of the seventh century, the *patriarchium Lateranense* (the patriarchate of the Lateran). At roughly the same time (685), the *Liber pontificalis* contains a first mention of the ceremony of "introduction" to the Lateran immediately after a new pope was elected. "According to the ancient tradition, the elect is introduced by the assembly into the church of the Savior, which is called Constantinian, then into the episcopal residence."[57] The change signals a new regime of papal power. The ceremony seems to have taken as its model the taking possession (*introductio* in juridical terms) of a titular church on the part of a priest who has just received consecration at St. Peter's. In both instances a juridical and liturgical right is confirmed by acclamations, the use of a seat, a Mass, and a banquet. During the eighth century, an even stronger distinction was made between the power of jurisdiction *(potestas juridictionis)* and the power of ordination *(potestas ordinationis)* of the popes, hence between the Lateran and the Vatican. Constantine's basilica lost all of its liturgical role in the installation of a pope, to the profit of the palace, which in the ninth century (and thanks to imperial influence) was called the "sacred palace of the Lateran" *(sacrum palatium Lateranense)*. A court (or curia) began to form there, and it soon became the center of Roman life. A pontifical decree of 769 attempting to set down rules for papal elections gives a good indication of this change: "And after the pope has been elected and led to the patriarchate, then everyone hurries to salute him as universal lord *(omnium dominum)*."[58] The notions of the universal patriarchate and absolute domination (whose ritual modes we have seen in the 1099 curule chairs) soon became centered in the Lateran Palace. Although the decree of 769 was only partially applied, it marks the setting up of a hierarchy in Roman sacred space because it excluded laymen from both papal elections and the taking possession of the Lateran. As long as that taking possession occurred entirely within the basilica, it addressed the community of the faithful; in the palace only dignitaries were admitted. Roman space was no longer a network; it had become concentric circles constructed around the pope. Around the eighth century, the bishops of the suburbicarian churches and the titular churches shifted from their more communitarian disposition to focus on the Lateran, thanks to the system of hebdomadary incardination in which bishops, priests, and deacons took weekly turns providing liturgical services in the basilica of the Savior. This organization reflected the corporative model of the Church as a whole, which was directed both from the top and from below (or from without). The five patriarchal basilicas (first mentioned at a somewhat later date) were under the basilica of the Lateran, which was chief among them and regulated liturgical functions from both above and outside of their patriarchal structure. The basilica of the Lateran seems indeed to have been "the head and the summit of the churches," as the Donation of Constantine said. At the same time, however, the pope no longer received his religious investiture there: the papacy was proclaimed at a physically higher spot, from atop the stairs to the Lateran Palace, or at St. Peter's, outside the Roman network. At that point Rome's new liturgical space was a representation of the successive, overlapping stages of the pontifical monarchy: the five patriarchal basilicas (the Lateran, the Vatican, San Paolo, Santa Maria Maggiore, San Lorenzo in Verano) stood for the five patriarchates of Christianity; the titular cardinalcies (bishops and churches) represented the Roman people, who were present at the Lateran thanks to the cardinals' liturgical duties. The pope participated in this construction, but he stood apart from it at the top. As provincial bishop on the same footing as the seven cardinal bishops, a patriarch among the patriarchs, his place was ever higher in the ascending spiral symbolized by the taking possession of the Lateran. The bishop and the patriarch made way for the pontiff, whose palace, standing higher than the other buildings of the Lateran and towering over the basilica, displayed his supremacy.

FROM THRONE TO CORONATION

Here, too, a chair expresses expanded power. A pontifical seat at the Lateran is first mentioned in a description of the investiture ceremonies for Pope Philip in 767, when the pope-elect was "introduced" into the patriarchate rather than the basilica:

> They led Philip [and leading is no longer an "introduction"] into the basilica of the Savior, according to custom; there, after hearing the orisons of a bishop, he distributed the peace to all, after which they introduced him into the patriarchate of the Lateran. There he sat upon the pontifical seat *(in sellam pontificalem)* and once again distributed the peace, according to custom, [then] went up to the palace and offered a banquet, as pontiffs do.[59]

In 827 mention of a pontifical throne at the Lateran occurs, reflecting an increasingly imperial style: Valentinus, "elected to the pontifical seat, was led to the patriarchate and placed on the pontifical throne; he received the unanimous ovation of the senate of the Romans."[60] The ancient image in which the notion of senate still vaguely applied to lay aristocrats seems essential here. Ninth-century papal accessions varied only slightly from this model. After 847 (Leo IV), the pope-elect was led to the "palace" of the Lateran, which became the "sacred palace" in 885 (accession of Stephen V). From then on, the throne was designated as *solium*, a more secular term than *thronos*. In 855, on the occasion of the invasion of the Lateran by Anastasius Bibliothecarius, the adversary of Benedict III, the narrator of the *Liber pontificalis* furthers the sacralization of the Lateran throne by expressing his indignation that Anastasius had sat upon a seat "that he should not have touched with his hands."[61] The throne became an object as sacred as the pallium or the high altar of St. Peter's, both reserved to the person of the canonically elected pope.

At the same time, St. Peter's chair (that is, the marble throne situated in the apse of the Basilica of St. Peter's) took on new importance. From the late ninth century on, a liturgical enthronement took place on the Sunday of a papal consecration, replacing the combined ordination and consecration with a specific ceremony held when the pope-elect was already a bishop, hence had already been consecrated. This was the case in 882 with Pope Marinus (already bishop of Caere) and again in 891 with Pope Formosus (bishop of Porto). Until that time, canon law forbade "translation," or moving from one bishopric to another. The novelty was not easily accepted, as seen in the posthumous fate of Formosus, whose body was exhumed and thrown into the Tiber, but the custom of electing a bishop to the papacy nonetheless became widespread in the eleventh century.

This multiplication of thrones and seats tended to symbolize, in the eyes of the faithful, the increasing dominance of papal jurisdiction over shared responsibility for liturgy. The installation of the patriarchal throne in the Lateran (the second seat in the ceremony in 1099) was physical evidence of a separate papal space. The pope-elect passed from the first, public zone inside the basilica of the Lateran to a second zone reserved to the patriarchate. During the eleventh century the palace became a third, even more secret, almost personal zone. The curule chairs stood at its threshold.

On the Threshold of the Palace

The Lateran became increasingly closed during the tenth and eleventh centuries. We can, without forcing the comparison, transpose to the Lateran Palace the process of *incastellamento* that Pierre Toubert has so brilliantly analyzed for feudal Latium in the tenth century,[62] where zones of seigniorial domination sprang up around castles (*castra, castelli*), that were organized quite differently from the vassalic feudal structures of the late eleventh century. After a phase of renewed agricultural development in the ninth century (which also concerned the papacy, as proprietor of an increasing number of agricultural *domuscultae* in Latium), growth in the tenth century was channeled into such *castra*. As a result, the network of rural churches in Latium became concentrated in much the same way as agricultural holdings and the parish system in the city of Rome. Scattered village churches *(plebes)* and baptismal churches and demesnial oratories and chapels created in the eighth and ninth centuries came to be dismantled, leaving only the seigniorial churches (*ecclesiae castri*). In the same way and at the same time, the Lateran Palace became the bureaucratic center for the administration of the patrimony of St. Peter, following the pattern of the seigniorial forms of the *castrum*. Beginning with John XIII (970), the annual payment of the *cens* and of Peter's pence took place there; following the lordly and imperial model of the palace in Pavia,[63] the Lateran had a chancery, archives, and a court of law. The term "chancellor" *(cancellarius)* appears under John XVIII in 1005; under Benedict

VIII there is mention of an "archivist and notary of our sacred palace and of our holy Roman church." That expression shows in what direction the political life of the Lateran Palace was trending during the eleventh century. After a "quasi-municipal" phase (as Pierre Toubert calls it) of urban and demesnial administration, a dual movement of feudalization and curialization instituted a supra-Roman pontifical administration. Ecclesiastical infeudation took place at exactly the same time that lay feudal and vassalic structures were put into place in Latium (the second half of the eleventh century). The feudal vows of the Normans in Sicily (1070–80) have already been mentioned; after that date, papal ambitions to acquire vassals (both metaphorical and actual) reached out in the direction of Croatia and Dalmatia (after 1076), then toward Provence, Brittany, Denmark, and Hungary. The Gregorian reforms put the bishops of Christendom under direct submission to Rome, and although that is not the same thing as feudal subjection, it used the same vocabulary (swearing "loyalty") and produced similar effects. The Curia of the Lateran became totally distinct from the city and episcopal administration; it was constructed like a feudal or monarchic court with a new financial organization in which the *cubicularius* and the *vestararius* inherited from the Roman Empire were replaced by a chamberlain, called *camerarius domini papae* under Urban II and *camerarius curiae Romanae* under Urban's successor, Paschal II. The functions of *dapifer* (lord high steward), *pincerna* (cupbearer), and *capellanus* (chaplain) also appeared at that time.

A new power sat on the curule seats in 1099, a power doubly alienated from the Roman community. On the one hand, the Roman power of the popes took refuge, withdrawing into itself in the inaccessible Lateran Palace, the throne, the center, and the summit of Rome and a haughty *castrum* that emptied the city of its local life. On the other hand, the Roman people lost mastery of a communitarian symbolic language, whose ancient liturgical simplicity was now inserted into the sinuous, obscure, juridical discourse, in both act and word, of state negotiations.

In the uncertain interstices of that language of Peter, however, the city of Rome still managed to communicate a muffled derision. Festive substitution made it possible for joyously subversive commentaries to push their way into the legislative escort to ceremonial acts. For a brief Carnival moment, the Roman Joan was to push Peter off his apostolic seat, especially when that seat took the burlesque form of a bathing chair. Let us lend an ear to the exchange between Peter and Joan in those decisive years of the twelfth century.

3

The Popes between Two Stools

t is difficult to document Rome's reactions to the papacy's growing hold over the city before the communal movement of 1144, because there are almost no narrative sources for the early Middle Ages. Nonetheless, two fragmentary traces left in texts written in Curia circles show the sort of festive response that Romans were capable of making to papal confiscation of the city's civic and symbolic life. A ritual performed outside the Lateran Palace dramatized a carnivalesque inversion of values and roles. As that ritual developed through time, it elicited a variety of interpretations, both malicious and naive, of the purpose of the oddly formed curule chairs, mixed with rumors regarding the mores of the popes.

The Cornomannia according to John Hymmonides

The first mention of this parodic ritual is in a brief text by John Hymmonides, also known as John the Deacon of Rome, the author of a much-admired life of Gregory the Great and deacon of the Lateran during the second half of the ninth century. John's text, which Arthur Lapôtre analyzed in detail in a scholarly but witty article at the turn of the twentieth century,[1] updates a parody in the form of a poem attributed to St. Cyprian (third century), "Cyprian's Supper." The piece describes a burlesque meal at which the guests are the principal personages of sacred history, depicting their attitudes and gastronomic preferences by means of Scriptural references, plays on words, and subtle allusions. The parody's venerable age and its boldness provide a good illustration of the talent of medieval clerics for laughing at themselves: strong, all-embracing institutions can indulge in partial, periodic self-criticism.

For our purposes, however, the circumstances surrounding the revision of "Cyprian's Supper" are more interesting than the text itself. According to Father Lapôtre's solidly argued deductions, the "Supper" had its first hearing at the festivities offered by Charles the Bald on the occasion of his imperial coronation by Pope John VIII, Christmas 875. The text of the "Supper," as adapted by Rabanus Maurus, the great Carolingian theologian, is supposed to have come to Rome with Charles's baggage. Rome was pleased by the poem, even though Rabanus Maurus's emendations had made the work so subtle that its satire was blunted and its meaning obscured. Someone with a more pliant mind and a deeper familiarity with classical culture was needed. John Hymmonides set to work, and his version was ready in time for the festivity that concerns us here, the Cornomannia.

In preface to his "Supper" John tells us that the festivity took place on Saturday *in albis,* the Saturday after Easter, in the presence of the pope, and that it mocked the prior of the *scola cantorum* of the Lateran, who appeared in it perched on an ass and crowned with horns:

> The Roman pope was amused during the *albis*
> When the prior of the *scola* came, crowned with horns,
> Like a Silenius on his ass, mocked by the singers,
> Who thus illuminated the mystery of the priestly play.[2]

That particular year (876) the old prior added the dangerous words of the new "Supper" to his customary mockery.

The Testimony of Canon Benedictus

A later source, the *Polyptych of Canon Benedictus,* provides a clearer view of this rite at the Lateran. This text, written by Benedictus, a canon of St. Peter's, is essential to an understanding of papal Rome around 1140. The collection includes liturgical fragments, a list of pontifical holdings (which explains the work's title), and a limited number of descriptions of the marvels of Rome. The Cornomannia that was performed in the presence of the pope and the Roman people before the Lateran was a genuine rite of inversion of ecclesiastical dignities. The relevant passage reads:

> Saturday *in Albis* the *laudes Cornomannie* must be sung to the Lord
> pope in the following manner. All the archpriests of the eighteen
> diaconates, after lunch on the said day, ring the bells, and every-
> one rushes to his parish church. The sacristan *(mansionarius),*

dressed in an alb or a rochet with a horned crown of flowers on his head, holds in his hand the *phinobolum* connected with his office: this is a hollowed concave stick a half-cubit long, covered with small bells at the middle and upper parts. The archpriest, wearing the pluvial, goes with the clergy and the people to the Lateran, where there, everyone awaits the pope under the fulling shed on the square before the palace. When the lord pope knows that everyone is there, he descends from the palace toward the place where it has been determined that he will attend the lauds of the Cornomannia. Then all the archpriests, with their clergy and the people, form a circle and begin to sing, "Eya preces de loco, Deus ad bonam horam," and the Latin and Greek verses that follow. The sacristan dances around and around in the middle of the circle, shaking his *phinobolum* and bowing his horned head. Once the lauds are done, an archpriest leaves the circle and mounts backwards on an ass that has been prepared by the Curia; a *cubicularius* places a bowl containing twenty small coins on the head of the ass, and the said archpriest, turning around backwards three times, grabs as many coins as he can in three tries and keeps them for himself. Next, the other archpriests, with their clerics, place crowns at his feet. The archpriest of Santa Maria in via Lata gives a crown and a small fox with no leash, who flees; and the pope gives the archpriest a bezant and a half. The archpriest of Santa Maria in Aquiro gives a crown and a cock and receives a bezant and a quarter. The archpriest of Sant' Eustachio gives a crown and a deer and receives a bezant and a quarter. Each of the archpriests of the other diaconates receives one bezant. After they have been blessed, they all return [to their churches]. When they have left, the sacristan, still dressed as he was, goes with a priest and two companions carrying holy water, cakes, and laurel branches to visit the houses of his parish, dancing as before and shaking his *phinobolum*. The priest salutes the household, asperges them with holy water, places the laurel branches on the hearth, and gives cakes to the children of the house. During this time, the sacristan sings the following lines in a barbarous fashion: "Iaritan. Iaritan. Iarariasti. Raphayn. Iercoyn, Iarariasti," and so on. At that point, the master of the house gives them a gift of a denier or more. This took place until the time of Pope Gregory VII, but after the increase in war expenses he gave up the custom.[3]

A Counter-Liturgy

Benedictus's description is precious to us because it presents an authentic rite of inversion and compensation that created a fleeting equilibrium between the papal powers, on the one hand, and the clergy and the people of Rome, on the other. This joyful inversion concerned postures (the archpriest is installed backward on the ass), but especially roles: the last becomes the first and the first last; the sacristan dons the liturgical vestments of the archpriest (alb and rochet) and directs the festive "liturgy." This immediately calls to mind the Feast of Fools that took place in late December and was directly patterned after the ancient feast of disguises, the Saturnalia. One event in the Feast of Fools, which was celebrated in Rome until the end of the Middle Ages, was the election of a bishop and an archbishop.[4] It is possible that when the Cornomannia disappeared in the late eleventh century, a spontaneous remnant of it radicalized the scenes of clerical inversion to present a woman disguised as a pope. A clearly parodic current aimed at the person of the pope had always lurked behind the good humor of the Cornomannia.

The Saturday after Easter was exactly symmetrical to Palm Sunday. The palm branches of Palm Sunday set the scene for the *adventus,* Christ's entry into Jerusalem, riding on an ass, and the palms may have been reflected and parodied in the laurel branches of the Cornomannia (although laurel was a familiar harbinger of spring in many European festive occasions). In the early Middle Ages the *adventus* was welcomed with ceremonies of a powerful sacredness, giving rise to a genuine liturgy whose most ancient extant *ordo* was written down at the Abbey of Farfa in the tenth century. In the Roman ceremony the people assembled sing lauds, as they did in 1120 for the entry into Rome of Calixtus II: "He was welcomed by the lauds of the young people and children carrying branches of a variety of trees."[5] Canon Benedictus gives the text of the lauds addressed to Alexander II: "Open the gates for us. We come to the lord Alexander. We come to salute him and honor him and raise lauds before him, like those who come to Caesar. Lord, open your window. See who has come. Sun, come; moon, come; celestial cloud heavy with manna, come, and to our most holy lord pope Alexander come with palm branches. God, give him life; Christ, give him life."[6] The allusion to Caesar here is a clear indication that rivalry and emulation were on display at the pope's entry into Rome on Palm Sunday: "The singing of lauds in fact made up an important part of the ceremonial in use in Rome . . . for the reception of the emperor."[7] The custom is mentioned in the annals of the abbeys at Lorsch and Fulda *(Annales lauris-*

senses; Annales fuldenses), in a panegyric of Emperor Berengar, in the chronicle written by Benedictus of Mont-Soracte, and in the works of Carolingian poets such as Notker of St.-Gall and Walafrid Strabo. The popes took over this classical and Christian rite that cast them in the role of both emperor and Christ. In 1211 Honorius III supported custom with theory by decreeing that the reception of the *adventus* was reserved to anointed persons, which meant kings, emperors, popes, and bishops. The pope's role as the *adventus* to whom lauds were addressed was transferred in the Cornomannia to two personages who operated on two different levels. On the level of farce, the sacristan played the pontifical role in its clerical dimension: wearing liturgical vestments and crowned with horns (and the term "horns" is often used to refer to the two points of the bishop's or the pope's miter), he places himself at the center of the chorus singing the lauds, and he holds in his hand the *phinobolum* that recalls the fool's belled stick, but also the bishop's crosier or the pope's ferule. I might note that later texts state that spring flowers strewn in the pope's path were called *philobolia*.[8] On the level of satire, the archpriest also mimes the pope, but in a dimension that recalls parallels to Christ and the emperor. This is a transposition more than an inversion, given that the archpriest is not a minor personage exalted in derision. Like the pope (and the popes first used a white horse for their *adventus*, then a mule), he arrives in solemnity perched on a mount. The archpriest seizes money in a bowl; the pope does the same when, seated on the stercory chair during the accession ceremony, he picks up three handfuls of coins and throws them to the people, stating that he will not keep them for himself. His refusal is inverted by the archpriest, who keeps the money, but in both instances, the verb *habere* is used. Like the pope, the archpriest is crowned, but his position, seated backward on an ass, also figures a disorder perhaps aimed at a papacy capable of inverting the Christlike humility of the *adventus* and turning it into imperial pride. The allusion comes close to being a threat, if we remember that after his capture in 1122 Maurice Bourdin, antipope to Calixtus II, was placed backward on a camel and paraded through the streets of Rome. Earlier, in 967, the prefect Peter, antipope to Pope John XIII, had been humiliated by being paraded through Rome seated backward on an ass, his beard shaved off and his head crowned with a waterskin stuck with feathers. The cavalcade ended at the square in front of the Lateran, where Peter was hung by his hair from the equestrian statue of Marcus Aurelius that then stood across from the palace. Bishop John of Calabria suffered similar indignities in 998 for similar reasons. Closer in date to our Cornomannia and in a context of genuine threat to the popes, in 1184 antipapal rebels blinded some of Pope Lucius III's clerics and pa-

raded them seated backward on asses.[9] The ceremony of the Cornomannia was an encounter between joyous reversal and a threatening allusion
to satanic and schismatic reversal. Joan is not far off.

INVERSION: THE CLERICS' REVENGE

The parody was all the more delectable because the official ritual that it
parodied was already an inversion, in a serious vein, of the Gospel account of the entry into Jerusalem: Jesus, the absolute Lord, enters into the
City mounted on the humblest of creatures (the ass). Jesus himself stated
that the first shall be last. In the Cornomannia and the carnivalesque rites
that it spawned, inversion freighted with irony bent literal meaning to the
purposes of wit. Parody reworked rite after its first, serious performance: it
was as if the Christian people, the true subject of the liturgy, granted itself
a right to censure or criticize. The Cornomannia took place after the quasi-
imperial *adventus* of Palm Sunday and after the solemnities of Easter
Week, in much the same way that the Feast of Fools (the Feast of the Asses)
on 1 January took place after the celebration of the Nativity. All levels of
ritual commentary on the rite might be brought into play, from bawdy humor to calls for greater rigor: the ass of the Feast of Asses or the Cornomannia was honored in an almost pagan derision of Christian humility, as an
ironic reminder of the evangelical spirit, or as a satirical denunciation of
devout literalism. In 825 Claudius of Turin delivered a vigorous attack on
the Church's fondness for fetishes, suggesting ironically that old clothes,
boats, and asses ought to be venerated because Jesus had lived among
them.[10]

It would be a mistake to underestimate the subversiveness lurking
within feasts of inversion that the clergy, both local and curial, could never
wholly control. The frontiers between burlesque play, parody, and subversion wavered, as we have seen. Leaving aside for the moment the role-
playing that took place in the Cornomannia, we can note that Bonizo of
Sutri reports that in the age of Gregory VII the sacristans of St. Peter's
dressed up as priest cardinals to extort alms from pilgrims: "All of these,
their beards shaved off and coiffed with miters, called themselves priests
and cardinals."[11] Burlesque disappears here, leaving imposture based on
greed: such rites of derision could shift their focus and become available
for more radical enterprises. The detail of the sacristans shaving off their
beards to mime the priesthood points the way to the sexual neutralization
analyzed in chapter 1. Here too the woman pope lurks, seeking a role to
play.

Within the span of one calendar moment, the Cornomannia extracted compensation from or wreaked a form of vengeance on the dominant power. In the ninth century, as John Hymmonides tells us, that revenge took the anodyne form of young people, the pupils of the *scola cantorum,* mocking their former master, the subdeacon who was prior of the *scola.* The house-to-house visits after the Cornomannia in Canon Benedictus's version of events recall the many festivities between Lent and May in which the population at large submitted to the rule of youth. Benedictus himself says of the lauds of the "children" at the mid-Lenten festivities, "At mid-Lent the schoolchildren take lances with banners and little bells; first they sing lauds before the church, and then they go from house to house singing and receive eggs in return for their lauds. They have done this since ancient times."[12]

The custom of the clergy and the people having their moment seems to have been stronger in Rome than elsewhere, even though, as Jacques Heers has shown, most burlesque festivities in the Middle Ages were clerical in origin.[13] The sacristan's parodic royalty provides a clear example of a fleeting revenge of that sort. I might note (and we shall return to the topic) that here we come upon a faint trace of the popess. One item in our survey of evidence of Joan in ritual pertains to the Four Times, or quatember days, fast days whose origin Jean de Mailly attributes to the popess. In the Roman liturgy priests were ordained on a Saturday (also the day of the Cornomannia) during one of these Four Times. Moreover, the Cornomannia, which served as a counterpoint to the quatember days, as we shall see, can be interpreted as a holiday for parishes and the ordinary clergy and a playful exaltation of the priesthood. John Hymmonides claims that this feast explained the "mystery" of "the priestly role" (and in the Middle Ages "mystery" was a doublet of "ministry"). In this view, the Cornomannia would use the semiserious mode of carnival inversion to express the primacy of ordination over the high jurisdiction of the papacy. This would make Joan the patroness of the proceedings. We need to examine the parish dimension of such festive occasions.

INVERSION: THE COMMUNITY GETS EVEN: DIACONATES

During the Cornomannia, the Roman clergy worked against the curial, patriarchal structure to return to its earlier communitarian stature. No supra-Roman intermediary stood between the pope and his faithful or between the clergy and the people. The crowd that assembled at the Lateran arrived in eighteen parish groups. The "deaconries" represented in these eighteen parishes have a complex history, which Ottorino Bertolini has done much to clarify.[14] Deaconries were a purely Christian and urban institution, first mentioned in the late sixth century, under Gregory the Great. The term is unrelated to both the liturgical rank of deacon (which also has a very long history) and the administrative function of the regional diaconate, a form of papal inspectorate put in place in Rome in the third century. The deaconry was Eastern and monastic in origin; it was apparently imported to Rome by Greek monks who served in the agency for papal distributions of foodstuffs. The earlier term for imperial distributions, *annone,* disappeared when Rome no longer had a resident emperor. The establishment of districts for works of charity occurred in the eighth century; in the early Middle Ages these charitable institutions grew little by little. Disregarding existent administrative and religious geographical divisions, they centered on a church or a monastery and were clustered in the more thickly populated sections of Rome. The first *ordines romani* draw a distinction between the diaconal churches and titular churches and the "other" churches. Diaconal churches seem to have enjoyed a degree of autonomy from papal control: whereas the titular churches, scattered nobly about the hills of Rome according to the city's ancient geographical divisions, were administered by a priest (later, a cardinal priest) and by "major-domos of the Roman Church" *(majores domus Ecclesiae Romanae),* the deaconries were headed by a priest (the "dispenser") and a lay "father" *(pater),* who may have been designated by the community. These characteristics made the deaconries the truly popular parishes of Rome. They were still a lively institution in the twelfth century (or the eleventh century, because Benedictus based his report on late-eleventh-century sources), as we can see by the Cornomannia and by the strange and probably emblematic animals offered to the crowned archpriest playing the part of the pope. Canon Benedictus's narration prominently mentions three of these deaconries (Sant'Eustachio, Santa Maria in Aquiro, and Santa Maria in Via Lata). The two first were extremely old deaconries; the date of founding of the third is more uncertain. Taken together, these three deaconries represented the most central and the most popular of the eighteen groups that converged on the Lateran, which means that the arrival of the diaconal communities forged a symbolic reconstitution of the organic bond between the pope and his people (a bond become ambiguous thanks to the popes' clever and tenacious efforts to establish a hierarchy). In the eleventh century, in fact, the popes took back the popular districts of Rome in an effort to integrate them into the concentric pattern established by the Lateran. The subcollege of the cardinal deacons, the last such group to be formed (after those of the cardinal bishops and the cardinal priests) justified its title by tracing its origins back to the Roman deaconries, although no local liturgical functions were attached to their title and the diaconal churches remained under the direction of an archpriest and priests. This subtle shift in function can be seen in a late-eleventh-century *Description of the Sanctuary of the Holy Church of the Lateran.*[15] This text states: "There must be present here the archdeacon of Rome, with the six deacons of the palace who must read the Gospel in the palace and in the church of the Lateran, and the twelve other regional deacons who usually read the Gospel in the stations fixed in the churches of Rome. These eighteen deacons possess as many churches within the walls of the city, and nonetheless they are canons of the patriarchal churches of the Lateran." This statement makes the eighteen titularies of diaconates dignitaries of the patriarchal churches, where they enjoy the rank of canon and exercise a liturgical function (reading the Gospel). The passage in the text that follows enumerates the other liturgical personnel required by the Lateran: subdeacons, acolytes, lectors, exorcists, and porters. They, along with the priest (and of course the deacons), formed the seven liturgical, ecclesiastical ranks.

Papal arithmetic was attempting a clever operation here: $(1 + 6) + 12 = 18$! Bypassing the old popular diaconal districts, the papacy transformed the seven old (third-century) regional deacons, who corresponded to the seven ancient administrative regions and who exercised a central (rather than a local) function, into a group of six palatine deacons with an archdeacon over them. The archdeacon was an ancient ecclesiastical function promoted in the tenth century—hence recently—to the high rank of vice-pope, responsible for filling any vacancy on the throne of St. Peter. The twelve other deacons ($18 - 6 = 12$) headed diaconates that corresponded to the new administrative and military (not religious) division of Rome into twelve regions instituted during the second half of the tenth century, when the papacy tightened its seigniorial and imperial hold over Rome. At that time these twelve deacons took the names of regional diaconates whose title holders became the six or seven palatine deacons. The arithmetical uncertainty ($6 + 1 = 6$? 7?) is yet another reflection of the pontifical model of corporative domination analyzed in chapter 2. The festivities in the square in front of the Lateran Palace begin to look more like a Day of Dupes than a Feast of Fools!

The ambiguity inherent in the diaconate may perhaps explain the role of the "least of the deacons" *(ultimus diaconus)* in the rumored rite to verify the pope's manhood. The term "least of the deacons" reflects an inversion in the spirit of carnival or the Cornomannia, because in the official ritual of papal investiture the archdeacon, acting as first deacon or prior *(primus = prior)* of the cardinal deacons, gives the pallium to the newly elected pope. We have already observed that the same word *(attrectare)*

was used to indicate the least deacon's touch of verification and in the prohibition on touching the pallium. It is also possible, however, that in the
people's memories the "least of the deacons" retained something of the
popular and the familiar by being confused with the *pater* of the popular
deaconry. The mocking, table-turning inversion took place in the gap between the remote "father of fathers" and this ancient, approachable father.

PARODY IN THE LITURGICAL CALENDAR

From the ninth century to the eleventh century the Cornomannia, in spite
of papal manipulations, was the keystone of a fragile edifice symmetrical
to the solid architecture of the Lateran. Canon Benedictus makes this clear
in his descriptions of feast days in Rome as they followed the calendar
from January to Carnival, the mid-Lenten break, the Cornomannia,
etcetera. What we see is a lighthearted counter-liturgy that was intimately
connected with the Easter cycle and was focused on the Lateran. To return
to the mysterious and fragile link between the Four Times and the festive
figure of Joan: the origin of the Four Times is uncertain, but it is clear that
their place in the calendar was disputed heatedly between the ninth century and the eleventh century, when Gallican and Roman usages stood
firmly opposed to one another. The Frankish position was first stated at
the Council of Mainz (the city of Joan's birth!) in 813, and it was constantly reasserted thereafter (by Amalarius in a letter to Hilduin of 825, by
Rabanus Maurus, by Reginon of Prüm, and by Burchard of Worms) until
the Council of Seligenstadt in 1022. For such writers the four "times" occurred during the first week of the first month, March (when the calendar
year then began); in the second week of the fourth month (June); in the
third week of the seventh month (September); and in the fourth week of
the tenth month (December). The Roman usage, which was ancient but
had been stated explicitly by Gregory VII at the Paschal synod of 1078 and
confirmed by Urban II in 1095 and by the Councils of Quedlinburg
(1085) and Constance (1094), placed the two first "times" at the beginning of Lent *(in initio quadragesimali)* and during the week of Pentecost,
thus at the beginning and the end of the Easter cycle.[16] In the Roman calendar there were thus three moments when celebrations of Christ and of
the papacy coincided, for priestly ordination and Roman festivity. This
triple cycle began with Carnival (which Canon Benedictus, as we shall
see, was the first to describe), immediately preceding Lent and the first of
the Four Times. Next came the festive mid-Lent break, Palm Sunday (the
moment of the pontifical *adventus*), Easter, the Saturday *in albis* of the
Cornomannia, Ascension Day (which was preceded by Rogations, the oc-

casion for the procession that was Joan's undoing), and then Pentecost (a time for baptisms at the Lateran and the second of the Four Times). This entire cycle turned around Easter, a moment of glory at the Lateran, of breaking the Lenten fast, and of theatricals: until the twelfth century, on Holy Thursday the pope, surrounded by twelve cardinals, performed the Last Supper, with the role of Judas being taken by the archdeacon. Benedictus says little about the community celebration at Easter, but a more detailed evocation is available in the highly important *ordo* written in the late twelfth century by Cencio Savelli, at the time papal chamberlain and later pope as Honorius III. Cencio states:

> Once Vespers have been celebrated triply in the basilica of the Savior, at the Fountains [San Giovanni in Fonte, the baptistry at the Lateran], and at the [church of the] Holy Cross, everyone returns to the portico of San Venanzio [next to the baptistry]; there the pope sits with the bishops, the cardinals, and the other orders, with others, both lay and cleric, on the ground on rugs. Then the archdeacon and other wine stewards pour him claret wine, for him and for all who are there. During this time, the *primicerius* arrives with the singers, and they sing a certain Greek prose piece.[17]

The conjunction between the liturgical times for ordination and festive moments continued up to the end of the year. The third of the Four Times (at the end of September) coincided with the feast of St. Michael the Archangel (Michaelmas) and with the Roman *Ottobrate*, which came eight months after mid-Lent. Canon Benedictus speaks enigmatically and fleetingly of this feast, but we know that it was Roman and military in character and involved a celebration of the papal crown and the papal horse.[18] The fourth of the Four Times came at the end of December, after Christmas, coinciding with the Feast of Fools. Benedictus notes the celebration of "communal games of the calends of January" (that is, the end of December). These games were quite certainly an adaptation of the ancient Saturnalia, a time for disguises. Already (or perhaps still) in the eighth century, Boniface complained to Pope Zacharias of survivals of dances "in the style of the pagans" *(paganorum consuetudine)* that took place day and night near St. Peter's. Benedictus's description seems more anodyne, but he notes curious reminiscences of earlier customs:

> On the vigil of the Calends the young people leave, bearing a shield. One of them is grotesquely masked *(larvatus)* and has a club hung around his neck. Playing a pipe and drum, they visit

the houses, standing in a circle around the shield; the tabor drums, the masked piper plays. When their playing has finished, they receive a gift from the master of the house, according to his pleasure. That day they eat all sorts of vegetables. In the morning two young men go out bearing olive branches and salt and enter into the houses. They salute the household: "May joy and merriment be in this dwelling." They throw handfuls of branches and salt in the fire and say: "[May you have] so many sons, piglets, lambs" and wish them all sorts of good things, and before the sun has risen, they eat lima beans with honey or something sweet so that the whole year will be sweet for them, without conflict or travail.[19]

The coincidence between the dates of the Four Times (moments attributed to the woman pope; times dedicated to priests) and Roman seasonal festivities is too striking to be pure chance. The ancient elaboration of this paraliturgy was an attempt to hold fast to communitarian rhythms that were in turn dovetailed into the Paschal cycle, hence pontifical. The sovereign of the Four Times and of the cheerful compensatory inversion might well have been a popess.

THE ROMAN CARNIVAL AND ROOM FOR COMPROMISE

The series of seasonal festivities in Rome also engendered a space in which compromise was possible (or did the two stand in a parasitical relationship, the one feeding off the other?). The papal space moved out in concentric circles from the Lateran, but it also had an east-west extension (a fundamental orientation in Christianity) that stretched out from the Lateran to the Vatican and was most visible in the Via Sacra (popularly known as the Street of the Pope), the route of papal enthronement and coronation processions from and to St. Peter's. Communitarian space, as we have seen, was irresistibly drawn into the sphere of the Lateran between the ninth and eleventh centuries, but in his description of Carnival Canon Benedictus tells us that it also had a north-south axis:

On the Carnival game. On the Sunday of giving up meat horsemen and foot soldiers start out after lunch; they have something to drink. Then the foot soldiers put down their shields and go the Testaccio; the prefect and the horsemen go to the Lateran. The lord pope descends from the palace and rides on horseback, with the prefect and the horsemen, to the Testaccio. There, at that place where the city originated, our bodily pleasures come to an end that day. Games take place under the gaze of the pontiff [who makes sure] that no contestation arises among the contestants. A bear is killed—that is, the devil who tempts our flesh is killed; bulls are killed, thus killing our beloved pride; a rooster is killed, thus killing the lust of our loins so we will live thereafter chastely and soberly in the combat for our souls and that at Easter we will be fully worthy of receiving the body of our Lord.[20]

The Monte Testaccio lies not far from the Tiber, to the south, outside the ancient walls, which means that it was separated from the medieval city (which was much smaller than in later centuries). In spite of Benedictus's interesting remark that Rome originated there, nothing in ancient classical geography corresponds to it: the hill was in fact built up slowly and at a later date on the site of the *emporium* (warehouse area for the Tiber port) by the accumulation of trash of various sorts, in particular, broken pots and amphora shards *(testae)*, hence the name "Testaccio." The name itself first appears only at the end of the eighth century, in an inscription in the church of Santa Maria in Cosmedin, one of the eighteen diaconal churches, that speaks of a donation to the deaconry of a vineyard on that hill. Aside from Canon Benedictus's *Polyptych*, no text mentions festivities at the Testaccio before 1256, when a charter for a lease mentions the "Mons de Palio," the hill of the race (a word that persists in our own day, notably in Siena's famous Palio).[21] The Testaccio occupied the same place in the community's festivities that the Vatican did in the pontifical system: in both instances a place outside the city was venerated as a founding site—the Testaccio as the mythical place of origin of Rome, the Vatican as the site of the tomb of St. Peter, the founder of the Church. Both places were the point of arrival for major commemorative marches as well. The myth of Rome's founding at the Testaccio, which occurs in Roman memoirs and is attested by Benedictus, is curiously attached to Joan in a sixteenth-century text cited (in 1600) by Johann Wolf, who attributes it to Gergithius and Pierus (authors otherwise unknown). Coins struck with a helmeted female head on them either evoked the ancient name of Rome, "Cephalon" (a pseudo-Greek translation of Testaccio), or alluded to "Joan VII, pope."[22]

The festive parade to the Testaccio (on horseback, like the cavalcade from the Vatican to the Lateran) thus took place north to south. That direction is confirmed by another festive space for Carnival celebrations, attested somewhat later but implied by Benedictus in what is probably a play on words, *in agone animae* (in the combat of the soul). In the thirteenth century, the Roman Carnival was called the "Feast of the Agone and

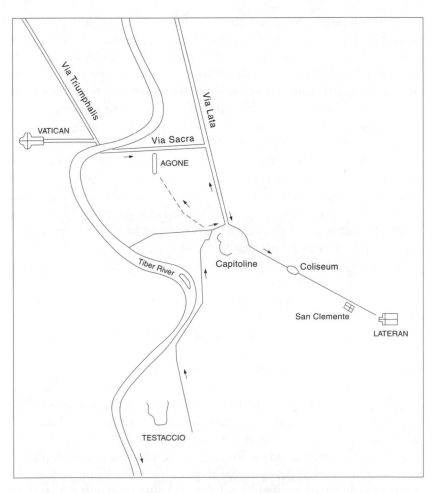

3. Schematic view of the two festive axes in medieval Rome: the pontifical axis from the Vatican to the Lateran and the Carnival axis from the Testaccio to the Agone and the via Lata.

the Testaccio."[23] "Agone" referred to the stadium of Domitian, a circuit for public games and competitions (Agonale), now the site of Piazza Navona, a name derived, by corruption, from "in agone," via "nagone," "navone," to "navona." Bull races at the Agone took place on the Thursday before Lent, which began on Sunday with ceremonies at the Testaccio. The route between the Testaccio and the Agone cuts right across the Via Sacra, the pope's route, precisely at the square near the Agone that contains the statue of Pasquino.

Carnival celebrations were later discouraged, or even forbidden, and in the fifteenth century Paul II instituted a new route for Carnival processions, by then cast in a strictly pontifical framework, that lay farther to the north but still followed a north-south axis, moving along the Via Lata (now the Corso) from the Porta Flaminia to what is now Piazza San Marco. The two axes met, symbolically, at the Capitoline Hill (the Campidoglio), the hill of Roman memory and the center of the antipapal Commune in the twelfth century. The light steps of the popess follow the same route because the Rogations procession (or the procession of the Minor Litany) took the same north-south path along the Via Lata from San Lorenzo in Lucina north to the Porta Flaminia, arriving at the right bank of the Tiber and continuing on to the Vatican over the Ponte Milvio. Like Carnival, Rogations combined the two cultural axes of Rome; Joan, a Church figure but also a popular figure of the Four Times and Rogation Days, stands at the balancing point of a fragile symbolic equilibrium between the pope and Rome.

More accurately, Joan's place was prepared at that point of equilibrium. Joan very probably did not occupy it until the late twelfth century, when the symbolic rupture between the pontiff and his people had quashed the parasite festive ritual, thus lending it the more secret and more savage form of murmur and scandal. Ceremonial dialogue reached its height between the ninth century and the eleventh century precisely because the *incastellamento* of the Lateran fixed the visible face of power in both space and time, thus prompting a reaction that crystalized the scattered culture of Roman customs. Although older sources regarding the founding of such ritual usages do exist, the Roman community festivities that we have been discussing were reduced to a system only when the power structure that opposed them began to gain a hold over Rome. What is called popular culture often reflects a struggle to resist more than it does a survival: nothing survives.

Admittedly, when we focus on phases of tension between the dominators and the dominated, we probably exaggerate the weight of ceremonial dialogue between the papacy and the community. The Cornomannia probably did not set the collective imagination on fire; rather, it seems to have been an act of pontifical goodwill for which the papacy set the limits and which it controlled. An aside in Canon Benedictus's account notes that the Curia prepared the ass ridden by the archpriest. Festivities of the sort could be classified as folklore or seen as a reminder of the "good old days" divided (unevenly) between a mistaken nostalgia and a condescending amusement. The simulated division in this rite is quite different from the 1099 transaction symbolized by the curule seats. In the Cornomannia a rite delegated the task of relegating a resolved tension to what we now call the cultural or the social sphere; with the curule chairs actions took place, promises were made, and negotiations were engaged upon in a rite that took over from words, decisions, and the law.

Nevertheless, this parasitical culture (or this culture that drifted toward more radical forms) must have appeared to Gregory VII as dangerous when he prohibited celebration of the Cornomannia, as Benedictus states. Like many folklorists, the good canon was reporting memories when he wrote around 1140: the texts that he cites go back to Gregory VII's predecessor, Alexander II (1069–73), whose name is mentioned several times in the lauds reproduced in the *Polyptych*. Explicit dialogue thus disappeared when papal domination took a more abstract but less discernible turn; when it surrounded itself with the "mysteries of state" after the shift from a phase of infeudation under Gregory VII to a phase of state creation under Innocent III.

THE END OF COMPROMISE: THE ABSTRACT SPACE OF PAPAL DOMINATION

The imperial model and the move to "incastellation" that had enhanced the function of the Lateran became totally outmoded with the papacy's aspiration to universal domination in the twelfth century. Throughout Europe a feudal and vassalic form of domination arose, founded on omnipresence and mobility, while in Rome the papacy shifted from a palatine administration to a curial bureaucracy. Function became more important than place. According to an adage borrowed from Roman law, the pope "carried the archives in his heart."[24] A rejection of retrenchment and a new interest in spatial organization implied an increasingly important role for St. Peter's, the place that embodied the transpersonal notion of the "pontifical see." During the tenth century and in the early eleventh century, liturgy and choral services had degenerated considerably in the Vatican,[25] in striking contrast to the rising importance of the Lateran. The revival of St. Peter's was linked to the movement for reform of the second half of the eleventh century: in 1053 Leo IX, the first reform-minded pope, placed an archpriest at the head of the basilica chapter. Next, the hebdomadary incardination that had been practiced in the Lateran for three centuries was moved to St. Peter's. Seven cardinal priests became cardinals of St. Peter's and rules were drawn up for their relative rank before the altar of the basilica. In 1123, on the occasion of the First Lateran Council, Calixtus II consecrated the high altar of St. Peter's with full solemnity. Around 1140 a canon of St. Peter's whom we know well (he is the same Benedictus) established the offices of the liturgical year particular to that basilica in his *Ordo Ecclesiasticus totius anni,* a work continued somewhat later by Petrus Mallius. The Feast of the Throne of St. Peter (22 February) was instituted in the early twelfth century.

The increasing role of St. Peter's in the twelfth century is important to our topic: by partially withdrawing from within the city of Rome the papacy threw the urban networks that had formed around the Lateran into disarray; shifting the center of gravity of the sacred away from the Lateran and creating two poles of attraction in the two basilicas brought on the decline of Lateran rituals. The shift of emphasis gave new vigor to liturgical consecration at St. Peter's, and it reduced the civic space common to the pope and the city of Rome.

Three *ordines* written in the late twelfth century within a few years of one another and with closely similar contents describe the advent of a new pope. They are the *Ordo* of Basel, probably written by a canon of St. Peter's; the *Ordo* of Cardinal Albinus (1189), contained in the *Gesta pauperis scolaris Albini* (Acts of the Poor Student Albinus); and the *Ordo* of Cencio (1192), a fragment from his *Liber Censuum.*[26] I shall refer primarily to the text of the *Ordo* of Basel, for which the best edition is available, but will note important variants in Albinus and Cencio.

The composition of the *Ordo* shows that an extremely important change had occurred since 1099: although the descriptions of the papal election, the taking possession of the Lateran, and the consecration at the Lateran that form the first two parts of the work follow the eleventh-century model (and, for the consecration, the medieval model) but with fuller detail, part 3, "How everyone takes his place walking for the coronation of the pope," describes a new ceremony, the coronation, or rather, the coronation procession. This may seem hardly an innovation, given that popes had been crowned ever since Nicholas II's coronation in 1059,[27] but until the twelfth century the new pope received the crown discreetly at the end of the Mass of Consecration, without any particular demonstrations. In 1099 Paschal II returned to the Lateran with his crown, but as if from an ordinary evening ceremony. Only in the twelfth century were custom and theory set down for a genuine coronation procession moving from St. Peter's to the Lateran:

> Once the Mass is celebrated, the lord pope descends with all the
> orders of the Roman Curia toward the designated place, where
> the papal horse has been appropriately caparisoned, and where
> the archdeacon receives from the hands of the first marshall the
> *regnum* (crown), also called *frigium,* with which he crowns the

> lord pope. And thus, passing right through the city by the Via
> Sacra, called the Street of the Pope, he descends, crowned, toward
> the palace of the Lateran.[28]

All along the way the priests of the various churches honor the pope; the Jews of Rome greet him in the Parioni neighborhood; the papal chamberlain and members of the Curia throw handfuls of coins to the crowd to encourage it to stand back a bit. At the Lateran Palace the pope hears Lauds said by the cardinal priests of San Lorenzo and the judges before being conducted to his chamber. The third part of the *Ordo* of Basel describes the composition of the cavalcade: soldiers, acolytes, marshals and chaplains, standard-bearers, foreign bishops and naval prefects, lawyers and archivists, regional subdeacons and subdeacons of the basilica, the *primicerius* and prior of the subdeacons, deacon cardinals and archdeacons, and, finally, the pope, accompanied by a regional subdeacon and followed, at a distance, by the prefect. The personnel of this urban procession, the only truly public moment of the ceremony, was exclusively curial (except for the prefect, who kept his distance). Even police duties were entrusted to the archdeacon and the prior of the basilica.

By means of the coronation procession the Curia made the public, Roman route of this urban event its own, excluding the community from a liturgical parade that had been a living, cyclical means for marking its territory. Various ceremonies in which the pope moved through the city during the fourteenth and fifteenth centuries show that the change was an important one. Ostentation took precedence over the places where the procession began and ended, the Vatican and the Lateran. When John XXII was crowned in Lyon in 1316, he considered it imperative to specify a point of departure (in his case the cathedral of Saint-Jean, where the consecration took place) and a point of arrival (the Dominican friary at Place Bellecour) so as to follow to the letter the rules solemnly governing the coronation procession.[29]

JOAN AS THE ULTIMATE REVENGE

Faced with this new dispossession, the Carnival spirit could no longer be channeled into the institution of the Cornomannia, which had been abolished. Instead, it became a parasitical, parodic interpretation of the coronation procession that gave a burlesque twist to certain details. As we have seen, most historians of the popess take as an indication of a commemoration of Joan's existence the fact that after her supposed papacy processions made a detour near the church of San Clemente to avoid the place where she gave birth. Cesare D'Onofrio has untangled this mystery, and I shall follow his version of events.

As it moved from the Lateran to the Vatican (the inverted direction of movement is necessary to give the episode coherence) the papal procession first went toward the Coliseum along what is now the Via San Giovanni in Laterano; near the church of San Clemente it veered slightly to the left (it was not until the sixteenth century that Via San Giovanni was cut through the ruins of the *Ludus magnus*, where Roman gladiators had trained, and made to continue in a straight line). Following a narrow street (now the Via dei Querceti) for a few paces, the procession then turned right at the Via dei Santi Quattro Coronati and continued on to the Coliseum. Canon Benedictus gives a clear account of this route around 1140.[30] Beginning in the mid-twelfth century, however, when the pontifical party arrived at San Clemente it turned the other way, toward the right, taking what is now Via Labicana to reach the Coliseum. This change may have been in response to increased numbers of people in the procession, but at the time it was interpreted as a deliberate detour. Rumor gave a coherent meaning to several details: one was that the narrow Via dei Querceti created a bottleneck that accelerated Joan's labor. As a result the street was called the *vicus papisse*. A chapel standing at the corner of the Via dei Querceti and bearing a fresco of the Virgin and Child came to be seen as a shrine to the memory of Joan and her infant.[31]

TWELFTH CENTURY: ORDERING THE CORONATION RITES

To return to the official ritual: when the coronation procession became a second taking possession of the Lateran, it emptied the first ceremony of its role in papal accessions. The pope-elect now held power as soon as the cardinals had voted. Liturgy and ceremony were fully displayed only after the consecration. One point of difference between the *Ordo* of Basel and the *ordines* of Albinus and Cencio makes it clear that the situation was bizarre: the author of the *Ordo* (probably a canon of St. Peter's) insists, almost violently, that the pope-elect cannot sit on the patriarchal throne before his consecration: "It is false to say, as is found written elsewhere, that the elect must be led to the major seat or to the altar of the basilica of Constantine, because he must not sit on the chair of St. Peter until he is consecrated and provided with the pallium."[32] The canon may well have been manifesting Vatican chauvinism, but the fact remains that the need for the seats at the Lateran had diminished and they bore less meaning. All three *ordines* give a metaphorical, less charged interpretation of the ceremony at the Lateran; henceforth it "represented" or "signified" rather than trans-

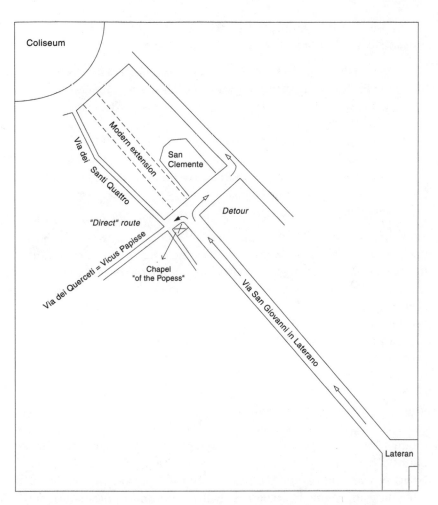

4. The pontifical itinerary from the Lateran to the Coliseum. The black arrow indicates the route followed up to the twelfth century (the "direct route"). Contemporary street names have been used.

formed the pope's status. In 1099 the three seats at the Lateran offered the new pope an increasingly strong grip on power. The first seat, the chair situated at the entrance to the church, gave material form to the possession of a sanctuary (in this case, the episcopal church of Rome); the second chair, the one in the *triclinium* of the basilica, stood for the patriarchate. The third seating ceremony, the one that involved the curule chairs, gave the pope an imperial, seigniorial mastery over the Curia, tempered by the ancient memory of the Roman senate.

In these twelfth-century *ordines* the first chair is called the *sedia sterco-raria* (stercory chair or seat of mire):

> Two of the magnates [Albinus and Cencio specify that these are
> cardinals] lead the elect to the seat of marble that is called the seat
> of mire *(stercoria)* in order to give truth to the verses: "He raises
> up the lowly from the dust; from the dunghill he lifts up the poor
> to seat them with princes, with the princes of his own people."
> When he rises up from this seat, the elect receives from the cham-
> berlain three handfuls of coins, which he throws to the people,
> saying, "This silver and this gold are not given to me for my en-
> joyment; what I have, I give to you."[33]

The original meaning of the ritual described here may be perceptible for the first time: it was designed to manifest the religious transformation of the new pope as dominator, thus prolonging the rite of selecting a papal name that immediately preceded it: by divine act, the poor human became the occupant of the throne of glory. Transposed into feudal terms, the rite also says that the pope-elect takes possession of the Church by giving to the people, who had elected him (in the theological sense if not in practice), the symbolic offering that the tenant gives the proprietor or the suzerain. The pope takes money from the hands of the chamberlain (the official responsible for papal finances) and proclaims that he has possession of it *(habeo)*, but not ownership of it *(non est mihi)*. In the *ordines* in question, however, this meaning is lost. The *Ordo* of Basel (unlike those of Albinus and Cencio) does not mention the seat's placement at the threshold of the basilica. This absence, joined to the probably popular term, "stercory seat," moves the biblical phrase used to gloss the rite into another thematic mode that retains only the preliminary humiliation of the pope-elect as a first step in his glorification, which is now liturgical rather than political.

The second and patriarchal chair is deliberately omitted in the *Ordo* of Basel, as we have seen. The Lateran is no longer a place specific to the pope, and the patriarchal throne of the Lateran Palace simply duplicates the throne of St. Peter.

The curule chairs that in 1124 became "seats in the shape of a sigma" now transmit only a vaguely theological meaning limited to the confines of the palatine basilica of San Silvestro. The *Ordo* states:

> And when the elected Lord has come to the basilica of Sylvester,
> the judges leave him, and he sits on the first porphyry chair, on
> the right hand, where the subdeacon, prior of the basilica [Albi-

nus and Cencio specify that this is the basilica of San Lorenzo in the Lateran Palace], gives the ferule to the elect as a sign of correction and of magistracy. He also gives him the keys to the basilica and to the sacred palace of the Lateran, because the Lord has specially given to St. Peter the power to open and to close, to bind and to loose. And, with the ferule and the keys in hand, he goes to the other similar seat and returns both the ferule and the keys to the prior. On this seat he is girdled by the same prior with a red belt from which there hangs a purse containing twelve seals made of precious stones and some musk. . . . And while in these two seats the elect must sit as if seeming to lie down between two beds *(inter duos lectos jacere),* so that he extends himself between the primacy of Peter and the assiduous predication of the action of Paul. The belt expresses continence and chastity; the purse is the *gazofilactum* by which Christ's poor and widows are nourished. The twelve seals signify the power of the apostles. The musk is placed there so that the people will smell its perfume, as the apostle says: "To God, we are a pleasing odor."[34]

At the end of the twelfth century ritual enters into the system of representation and leaves the domain of action. We have already noted this shift in connection with the careful organization of the coronation cavalcade, the prototype for royal entries. The writers of ceremonials took their painstaking competence in liturgy and applied it to institutional presentation. The procession does nothing: it shows. In the ceremony at the Lateran as well, objects and gestures represent a general theological content; rite becomes a particular illustration of dogma, ceasing to be an act of transformation or negotiation. The most impenetrable of the mysteries of state is that the state hides nothing and says nothing, but represents itself perpetually. The problem is that rumor, be it malicious or naive, joking or serious, attempts to find the action in rite. If those chairs are there and if the pope is placed on them, it cannot be for nothing. But in fact it was for nothing; the chairs or thrones have become monuments. Rite has been transformed into ornamental celebration. In 1099 the ferule and the seven keys made a statement about ruling: before the pope took his consul's seat he brandished imperial domination (in the ferule) and collegiality (the seven keys and the seven seals that multiplied the jurisdictional power to bind and loose sevenfold). At the end of the twelfth century the keys— now twelve—were part of a symbolic bric-a-brac in which everything signified and nothing stated; by then the ferule had lost all precise contextual meaning and simply designated pontifical magistracy. The keys no longer bore any specific meaning; the other objects referred to virtues (purity, chastity, charity) and operated like simple attributes within the panoply of papal qualities. Interpretation welcomed the indefinite gratuity of metaphors: the duality of the twin curule chairs recalled Peter and Paul, the only readily available pair in pontifical imagery. Those chairs, which figure so prominently in the history of Joan, deserve one last look.

The pope sits on them, the twelfth-century texts tell us (in a formula that remained unchanged until the sixteenth century), as if stretched out between two beds. How are we to understand this astonishing use of two curule chairs, a use that clearly contributed much to the rumors about the pierced chairs? I have already rejected Cesare D'Onofrio's hypothesis that the pope was miming a metaphorical birth to illustrate the concept of *Mater Ecclesia*.[35] Let me add to my more general refutation that this indication of the pope's position appeared a century after the first mention of the curule chairs and has no antecedent. This means that it must be understood within the context of the twelfth century. Moreover, the pope does not lean back in each of the chairs, but as if between two beds. In spite of the respect due to Monsignor Maccarrone's immense erudition, his appeal to the French expression "être assis entre deux chaises" (a rough equivalent in English, to fall between two stools), is no more satisfactory.[36] Lexical proximity is of little help in seeking genuine meaning.

TWELFTH CENTURY: NEW MEANINGS FOR THE CURULE CHAIRS

1. The Theological Metaphor

It is clear from the exegetical practice of writing about ceremonials in the twelfth century that the new pope could not have reclined between the two chairs. The ceremonials no longer describe an act, as in 1099, but rather a symbolic decor. An *ordo* redacted in 1273 under the close supervision of Gregory X follows the lead of its twelfth-century counterparts by introducing liturgical colors into ritual. When twelfth-century liturgists were confronted with two seats with no apparent function, they read into them (what is more, they say as much) a representation of Peter and Paul, the two apostles of the Vatican. This surprising shift of ritual in the direction of theological metaphor must be seen as part of the development of the passion for "similitudes" analyzed by David D'Avray in connection with the technique of the sermon as a unifying principle in the thought of the central Middle Ages.[37] Cardinal Lothar of Segni (later pope as Innocent III) wrote in 1198—thus soon after the redaction of the three twelfth-century *ordines*—a symbolic commentary on the Mass, *De missarum mysteriis,*[38] which interprets the liturgy of divine worship in much the same way that Albinus, Cencio, and the author of the *Ordo* of Basel strove to interpret the rite of accession. Hence ceremony, both ritual and liturgical, entered into the world of texts and scholarship; to borrow Cyrille Vogel's expression,[39] a second liturgical alienation occurred in twelfth-century Christianity.

2. The Ecclesiastical Metaphor: The Threshold of the Apostles

We must take seriously the exegesis proposed by the authors of the various *ordines:* the two porphyry chairs represent the "primacy of Peter" and "the assiduous preaching of Paul." It was in fact in the late twelfth century that it was first believed that Paul's body lay in the Vatican. According to a legend made famous in the thirteenth century by Jean Beleth (Joannes Belethus) in his *Explicatio divinorum officiorum* (1265) and immediately repeated by Jacopo da Voragine in *The Golden Legend* (ca. 1265), a movement had arisen soon after the conversion of Constantine (312) to build a church in honor of each of the two apostles, whose bodies had been buried together. Because their bones were mingled it was impossible to tell whose were whose, but a celestial voice explained that the bigger bones were Peter's. St. Sylvester had the bones weighed so they could be identified. In 1192 (once again, roughly at the time the three *ordines* were being redacted), a canon named Romanus was the first to speak, in his additions to the description of the basilica at the Vatican by Petrus Mallius, of the place "where their precious bones, as is said, were weighed."[40] At the end of the fourteenth century an inscription on a porphyry memorial in the crypt of the Vatican indicated the spot where the weighing had taken place. As the Lateran became a Roman, urban pendant of the Vatican, people drew an analogy between the joint tomb of Peter and Paul and the twin seats and applied it to the two patriarchal seats. The physically impossible position that the new pope was supposed to assume in the ritual, lying between the chairs, became a metaphor for the entrance to the basilica of San Silvestro, the "threshold of the apostles" *(limen apostolorum).* Certain popes of the early Middle Ages were buried at the threshold of a Lateran church or the basilica; the pope, seated analytically on two identical chairs at an entrance to a basilica became, synthetically, a living metaphor for the threshold.

As a designation of the apostles' threshold, the two seats formed a link in the long metaphorical chain of altars, chairs, tombs, etcetera, that symbolized the apostolic see. Early in the thirteenth century Innocent III was to give concrete form to the "between two chairs" figured in the papal pos-

ture by constructing a palace at the Vatican, but at the same time main-
taining the eminent position of the Lateran by making the basilica of San
Salvatore a pontifical "cathedral." This move established a rigorous symmetry between the Lateran and the Vatican: the Vatican obtained a palace,
which was what had given the Lateran its prestige; the Lateran recovered
the liturgical majesty that had given the Basilica of St. Peter's its prominence in the eleventh century. Putting aside Innocent III's immediate motivations (formerly a canon of the Vatican, he enjoyed living there), an
important change had taken place. The symmetry between the Vatican
and the Lateran restored nothing, nor did it establish any equilibrium:
rather, it introduced abstract uniformity into papal space, henceforth
made of identical cells that took on life and meaning only with the presence of the pope. Roman power was no longer localized and no longer territorial. This is why the twelfth-century *ordines* could imagine coronations
and consecrations held outside Rome. To be sure, the thirteenth-century
popes (before Avignon) spent only a third of their time in Rome,[41] but the
notion that a coronation could take place elsewhere than in Rome cannot
be explained uniquely by the tribulations of the papacy in the twelfth century (the episode of the Roman Commune and various schisms): the true
site of papal power lay with the pope and the Curia as they moved through
space, bearing the archives in their hearts. Paschal II, *vel sedens vel transiens*,
was marking his territory. Eugenius III and Innocent III took care to signal
their passage. They opened the way to the great curial monarchies of the
later Middle Ages.

We can measure how marginalized the ceremony at the Lateran (and
the Roman community) had become from the *ordo* redacted in 1273 for
Gregory X that has already been mentioned. The ceremony itself need not
detain us, as the text is a faithful and literal transcription of the *ordines* of
the twelfth century. Rather, it is the overall composition of the solemniza-
tion of papal accession that is interesting. The odd placement of taking
possession of the Lateran between the pope's election and his coronation
disappears: the 1273 ceremonial first describes the election, then the
pope-elect's ordination as deacon or priest (if necessary), then his consecration at St. Peter's (or a substitute ceremony if he was already a bishop).
The Mass of Accession follows. Next the ceremonial describes the cavalcade through Rome and the arrival at the Lateran. Coming after the new
pope's consecration, taking possession of the Lateran has only a fossil
value; its primary function seems to have been to give the newly crowned
pope a destination for the solemn cavalcade. The Lateran has become a
papal succursal. Even when the pope was elected and crowned outside

Rome, he went first to St. Peter's for a *Te Deum* before going on to the Lateran. Rome was no longer within Rome.

3. The Juridical Metaphor: The Pope's Body

The pope's posture on the porphyry chairs seems to me to have a clear mortuary meaning. The pope must sit as if stretched out between two beds *(inter duos lectos jacere)*. The expression *jactere in lecto* was a fairly common way of indicating the funerary position of a pope's corpse: the phrase *lectulos in quo jacebat* was used to refer to the dead Leo IX.[42] Moreover, the reference to Peter and Paul, as we have seen, probably implied an allusion to their intertwined bodies and their dual tomb. Finally, the tomblike aspect of the two porphyry seats seems even clearer in the testament of Roger II of Sicily (1145), which gives directions for the king's burial in the cathedral of Cefalù: "We have decided that at my death, there will be established in the said church two fine sarcophagi of porphyry to serve as a perpetual monument. In one of the two I shall repose near the choir of the canons, who will chant prayers on the day after my death; and we establish the other for the illustrious memory of my name and for the glory of the church itself."[43] Cardinal Lothar summarizes the itinerary of the twelfth-century ritual at the Lateran in a text contemporary to the *ordines:* "The one who just a moment ago was seated *(sedebat)* gloriously on the throne [the moment of the stercory chair], now lies *(jacet)* in the tomb [the moment of the porphyry chairs]."[44]

Thus the pope mimed his own death, but by immortalizing himself: by stretching out between the two tombs of Peter and Paul he superimposes himself on the threshold of the apostles; he is a living rock resting on Peter, the Rock. He performs a genuine dramatization of papal immortality, lodged at the heart of an extremely important debate on the pope's body.

An article by Reinhard Elze calls attention to some curious and extremely ancient funerary rites.[45] When a pope died, the Roman people sacked his house and even stripped his body. Traces exist of this strange custom, intermittently practiced from the first centuries of Christianity, but evidence of its codification and its origin is elusive. Still, the repetition of such acts and the Church's passive attitude before an expected, hence clearly avoidable, pillage make the event seem a rite. How else are we to understand how (according to Jacques de Vitry) the body of Innocent III, the most powerful pope of the Middle Ages, could have been completely stripped, not only of ornaments but of clothing as it was laid out for the mortuary vigil in 1216.[46] To be sure, from the Council of Chalcedon (451) to the Renaissance, the Church condemned such carryings-on time after time, but the chronicles and the *Liber pontificalis* regularly report scenes of pillage as the "custom of the Romans" *(mos Romanorum)*. Only the German popes of the Gregorian age, who were strangers to Roman tradition, seem to have escaped this violent rite. The only explicit, official interpretation of the rite is in a canon of the Council of Rome given under Gregory the Great in 595:[47] The Church claimed credit for organizing mysteries that surpassed it, attributing the pillage to an excessive devotion directed toward the bodies of the popes, considered to be relics.

PILLAGE AND POWER

In reality the rite of pillage reflects a clash between two sorts of logic, one juridical and religious, the other political.

The juridical and religious logic was connected with the right to spoils *(spolii jus)* defined somewhat later (in the fifteenth century), but implicitly invoked when one prelate, a bishop in particular, succeeded another. The departing prelate's ecclesiastical goods did not belong to him, but to the community that had elected him—or at least this was so before the Church became enmeshed in the trammels of common feudalism, or before it became an autonomous juridical entity. In a study of the right of spoliation F. de Saint-Palais d'Aussac distinguishes three phases in this process.[48] In Christian antiquity, a bishop's spoils and possessions belonged to the clergy; during the early Middle Ages, they were passed on to the feudal (or prefeudal) lord; beginning with the thirteenth century, the papacy (or, in certain cases, the national church) claimed a bishop's belongings. This juridical framework still does not explain the pillage, which was a brutal attack on a prelate's furnishings and his corpse totally out of proportion to the spoils obtained. In other words, ritual pillage seems to have taken a turn more symbolic and political than real or juridical.

The people and/or the clergy (and, as we have seen, in the Roman context these two categories were inseparable) used violence to show that one power had ceased and died, and another power would have to seek a new consensus. Clerical power, which was elective, both in theory and by theology, made more forceful demands than did lay powers strongly anchored in an affirmation of dynastic continuity.[49] This situation reached a critical point in the central Middle Ages, when such powers became strong enough to elaborate a theory of the transpersonality of political power. These tensions were resolved in the fourteenth and fifteenth centuries within the framework of the state, as Ernst Kantorowicz and Ralph E.

Giesey have observed.[50] The new status quo was expressed in statements such as: "The king never dies," "The king is dead; Long live the king," and *Dignitas non moritur*. Helmut Beumann and Carlrichard Brühl allow us a clear perception of the political problem connected with the practice of pillage as early as the eleventh century.[51] According to the *Gesta Chuonradi II imperatoris*,[52] when Emperor Henry II died in 1025, the inhabitants of Pavia pillaged and sacked the royal palace in that capital of the Germanic emperors' kingdom of Italy. In justification of their acts they announced to Henry's successor, Conrad II: "We have maintained our loyalty to and our veneration of the emperor until the end of his life; at his death, we had no more king, and it is wrong to reproach us with the destruction of the dwelling of our king." Conrad's remarkable response prefigures the efforts of later state jurists: "I know that you have not destroyed the dwelling of your king, because you no longer had one at that moment; but you had no right to destroy the royal dwelling. If the king has perished, the kingdom has remained, just as a ship remains when its pilot dies."

When monarchies detached the body of the king from its perishable envelope, they made it participate in the immortality of the kingdom. This is of course the theory of the king's two bodies, as analyzed by Kantorowicz. For the papacy, however, resolving the problem was more difficult, because—paradoxically—the extremely old corporative theory of the Church had already provided for continuity of power with no need for the transpersonal mutation of the ruler. The force of lay theory resided, precisely, in having the genesis of the state concomitant with the metamorphosis of the sovereign, as illustrated by the case of the mad king Charles VI of France.[53] Every pope in the hierocratic system put into place after Pope Leo the Great was the direct heir of St. Peter; transmission by election refounded the apostolic see with each new pope; the incertitude brought on by an interregnum was not simply the result of the lack of a dynastic principle, but derived from the corporative theory itself. This is why Augustinus Triumphus, a jurist of the late Middle Ages, could declare that "the king does not die; the pope dies."[54] Thus it is understandable that the clergy and the people rushed into the void created by an interregnum and showed by pillage that power was nullified and had been returned to the Christian people. Another group had strong interests to defend in this debate: the cardinals, as a group, embodied the perpetuity of the apostolic see (the apostolic see does not die; the pope dies). In the case of a vacancy on the papal throne, the Sacred College assumes full pontifical powers, which is why the popes and the college engaged in a muffled struggle over the amount of time that should elapse between the pope's death and the election of a successor. Constraint in the form of the conclave, with severe penalties to be meted out to the cardinals in cases of delay, arose in 1274 with Gregory X's decretal, *Ubi periculum*.[55]

THE POPE DIES

These circumstances and these debates, along with broad changes in people's ways of thinking, explain the obsession with death that invaded the papal court in the twelfth and thirteenth centuries. To take one example, the prologue of the *ordo* redacted for Gregory X in 1273 justifies its description of the pope's accession thus:

> The fact that "all power is short-lived" touches the Roman pontiffs, who hold primacy in the hierarchy here below; they end their lives in little time, and after quitting the prison of the flesh, they pass on to the freedom of the country of their elders. And as a hierarchy this considerable must not be headless like a monster, the holy fathers have providentially decided that once the body of the deceased leader has been delivered over for ecclesiastical burial, someone else will substitute, in the canonical manner, for the deceased head and preside "over the charge and the honor."[56]

Agostino Paravicini-Bagliani has shown that the Roman Curia in the central Middle Ages expressed this obsession with death on several levels.[57] On the one hand, cardinals' wills show that they took great interest in funerary rites; on the other hand, the scholars of the Curia (what Paravicini-Bagliani calls "the Viterbo circle") directed their studies (in alchemy, medicine, and physics) toward prolonging life.

The twelfth-century *ordines*, faithfully copied in the thirteenth century, attempted to use ritual to construct an image of the corporeal immortality of the popes. The stercory chair promises the pope glory, but it also recalls that he is dust. This first, public venue (in front of the basilica of Constantine) seems a concession to an expected reduction to nullity, formally backing up the mortuary theology of the Church (which was, in this case, in sharp contradiction with papal ambitions!). The pope then takes the initiative in the symbolic exchange that transposes the pillage.[58] It is while seated on the stercory chair that the pope throws out three fistfuls of coins, saying, "This money is not mine." The permutation of roles here (taking or pillaging as against distributing or conceding) is important, because it places the newly elected pontiff in a Christlike position and works to annul, before the fact, the funerary rite of pillage that reduces the person and the body of the pope to nothing. Might it be that looting the house of the prelate elected to the papacy, which Jacopo d'Angelo re-

ports in 1406 (see chapter 1), replaced despoiling the pope's goods at his
death (at least in the Curia's dispositions)? When the new pope permitted
the sack of his former dwelling as a man (and, if he was a cardinal, the cell
he occupied during the conclave),[59] he inverted the meaning of the rite: in
terms that recall St. Paul, he proclaimed that he was putting off the old
man, thus acceding to a higher personhood. The second phase of the ritual, the one involving the porphyry chairs, shows that the body of the living pope, which had just been removed from common corporeality, is
already mixed with the ashes of the apostles, the solid soil and threshold
of the Church. In the enthronement ceremony at the Lateran the pope's
body slips in between the bodies of Peter and Paul. "Tu es Petrus." The
pope's body enters into the monumental construction of the Church. Because he sits on the apostolic seat, the pope does not die.

A century after the curule seats first appeared in papal ceremonial they
completely changed both their meaning and their function, but they too
spoke of papal supremacy. Whether this rite was understood or not (and
comprehension certainly must have varied enormously and been only
partial), the secret importance of the ceremony and the odd actions that
were involved in this staging of pontifical power could only have reinforced burlesque or savage responses.

We will leave our pierced chairs once and for all after glancing at the
year in which they disappeared, 1513. A few weeks before Julius II died,
and before the last utilization of the chairs by his successor, Leo X, Julius
accorded an audience to his master of ceremonies, Paride Grassi. That glorious Renaissance pope, sensing that death was near, spoke to Grassi
about his lugubrious anxieties: "He said that he remembered having seen
many popes abandoned, at the moment of their death, by their relatives
and by all those who accompanied them, to the point of being left lying
(*jacuerint*) indecently, already naked, their shameful parts uncovered *(de-
tectis pudibundis)*: So much majesty ceased in shame."[60] Despite all the
ruses of ceremonial representation, the rite of response patiently continued to whisper that the pope was nude. The sex of the popes, savagely laid
bare, jokingly praised, or touched in imagination, was always celebrated
in a Rome that obstinately refused to angelicize power and its vain triumphs over death. The pope is a man; the pope dies.

CONCLUSION: THE BIRTH OF JOAN; FROM REVENGE TO RUMOR

To summarize: beginning in the mid-twelfth century, the Roman community saw itself deprived of intra-urban contact with its pastor; from the
time (the ninth century to the eleventh century) when the territory of

Rome, richly provided with both official ceremonies and parodic counter-rites, was concentrated around the Lateran, the people and the clergy retained their ability to decipher ceremonies and took pleasure in doing so. A sweeping change in the rite of accession to the papal throne in the twelfth century left behind it only empty shells devoid of meaning in which only a few theologians could hear vague murmurs of a vast exegetic sea. The curule chairs that had been placed at the Lateran toward the end of the eleventh century as a means for opening negotiations with power were mere relics or monuments a century later. Since they could not be moved, they took on the meaning that was given to them. The theological ingenuity of liturgists and writers of *ordines* was bent to this task; at the other end of the scale simple clerics and laymen in quest of a bygone function applied their malice (or their candor) to other interpretations. A search for compensatory rituals taken from the rich reservoirs of Carnival inversions (and serious inversions as well) led the search for functional meaning. A burlesque counter-knowledge turned the tables on the dominant, closed knowledge. Even reading written script was eventually beyond the ordinary competence of a Roman cleric: beginning in the late tenth century the new "curial minuscule," which was read much more fluently in the papal chancery than in Rome itself, replaced the old curial script derived from Roman cursive.[61] Moreover, the solemn and ornamental return of ancient epigraphic models in the outdoor spaces of twelfth-century Italian cities (pontifical Rome in particular) contrasted with writing styles used in the communities' intellectual endeavors, as Armando Petrucci has demonstrated.[62] A mocking decipherment of the inscription with the six capital Ps gave it the function of commemorating Joan, thus providing a fine example of revenge taken on an alienation of meaning!

A modern example will help us grasp the full malice of this mechanism of burlesque decipherment of acts and words. In the 1930s, when the French still thought anticlericalism humorous, a well-known comic mimed, to perfection, the liturgical gestures of a parish priest saying Mass, whereas in reality he was looking for his hat. By all reports, the comic was right on target. A similar mechanism was at work in Rome in the twelfth century when people feigned wonder at an incomprehensible inscription, an odd turn of a tiny Roman street, a small construction placed at the corner of that turn, and an obscure ceremony that required the pope to be placed on two identical, deeply hollowed-out chairs. Remembering the clean-shaven sacristans disguised as priests, the bishops of the fools, and the Carnival popes, people amused themselves by seeking a woman everywhere. They found one: Joan, triumphant, borne aloft by the merry lore of the clerics and the Roman people.

As long as she remained among her Roman friends, Joan babbled away, doing no harm. It took a century before she too entered into the texts. When she did, she set off an interminable discourse, which is what we must turn to now.

PART II

JOAN MILITANT

5. Illustration for Martin Schrott, *Von der erschrocklichen Zurstorung des Bapstums*, 1550, fol. A 5v. Germanisches Nationalmuseum, Nuremberg.

4

Joan the Catholic

To be verified: There is supposed to have been a certain pope, or, rather, a popess, for it was a woman; disguised as a man, he became, thanks to the honesty of his character, a notary of the Curia, then cardinal, and finally pope. One day when he was riding on horseback, he gave birth to a child, and immediately Roman justice tied his feet together and had him dragged, attached to the tail of a horse; he was stoned by the people over half a league and was buried where he died; at that place was inscribed: "Petre, Pater Patrum, Papisse Prodito Partum" (Peter, Father of the Fathers, Publish the Parturition of the Popess). Under his papacy the Fast of the Four Times, called the Fast of the Popess, was instituted.[1]

First Version: An Item in a Chronicle

his first known version of the story of Joan comes from a brief *Universal Chronicle* written in a monastery in Metz around 1255.

At the risk of anachronism, we might call this entry in the Metz chronicle a news item. The author seizes on a bizarre, astonishing encounter between an individual and a milieu that ought to be mutually exclusive. "Hoax in Rome: A Woman Becomes Pope." An intruder creates an anecdote, but fails to make the institution totter; the event changes the course of the history of the papacy, only slightly, but enough to cause scandal, which calls for an investigation. The change is limited to a rectification and the invention of a new term: "a pope, or, rather, a popess *(vel potius papissa)*, for it was a woman." Papal history absorbs the anecdote, enfolding its singularity within regularity. The acts of a woman are reported as if the subject were male (or, more accurately, neuter animated, which amounts to the masculine): *factus; tractus; lapidatus.* The real subject exists only in the revelation of the hoax ("one day when he was riding on horseback"); the real subject has no name and no individual history, given that he/she exists only as long as the scandal lasts. We do not know the reason for the cross-dressing ("disguised as a man . . . he became a notary of the Curia"). We know nothing about how the pregnancy originated: childbirth is not given as the result of immoral behavior, but simply permits the strange event to come to light. The story of the popess, in short, is a Church story: in a typical rise justified by the "honesty of his character," a desirable quality in a cleric, he/she becomes a papal notary, then a cardinal. When the transgression is discovered, it is immediately pursued by "Roman justice" and punishment is completed by the Roman people and noted in an inscription attesting to the serenity of the Church: "Peter, Father of the Fathers, Publish the Parturition of the Popess." The institution continued to function during this singular papacy, however: "Under his papacy the Fast of the Four Times . . . was instituted." As in a news item, the individual, the pinch of salt in the narration and the grain of sand in the machine, does not really trouble the institution. When the story appeared in Metz around 1255, it surprised and piqued people's curiosity, but it did not produce meaning. Meaning was born later, from a different narrative.

Joan had entered into a new existence, however: far from Rome and its festivals and rites, she left the limbo of rumor, both jocose and tearful, to create a sensation in texts all over Europe.

The Enigma of Joan

Thus far the enigma of Joan has resided in a silence; henceforth there was a surprising amount of chatter about her. Between 1250 and 1450 dozens of clerical texts transmitted the story related in the Metz chronicle. These texts never cast doubt on the popess's existence; no author tries to dissimulate her, twist her story, or omit her. The popes themselves lent credence to the fable by following the processional detour commemorating the event. Until the Reformation (or at least until the Hussite revolution), the Church believed and presented as worthy of belief an event that seemed to compromise its reputation and that it would later present as a vile, base, Protestant, or anticlerical invention.

That paradox (which will require explanation) will perhaps protect us from the determinist temptation to ask "who benefits" from the story. The implicit notion of "ideological profit" is a variant of a vapid theory of reflection that often governs cultural history, and recent scholarship has been all too quick to reduce the motivation for writing a life of Joan to a desire to harm the papacy. The facts prove that this view is anachronistic: until around 1450 Joan belonged to no party and was used by all parties.

The abundance of versions, however, offers the danger of a false objectivity. It is tempting to become fascinated by the series itself, to hold it up as a pseudoreality, and to treat the Joan narrative as a "legend" or a "motif," those ersatz substitutes for the phenomenon in the narrative order. The existence of the series is contested, however, both de facto and de jure. By fact: an omission may conceal the loss of a manuscript; a particular density of mentions may result from the hazards of conservation. By right: the texts about Joan are, first and foremost, words. In medieval clerical discourse Joan's story is told gravely, seriously, dramatically; it does not shift key as a simple literary or historiographical theme might do.

The way seems narrow, then, between an ad hoc analysis of specific occurrences and a historiographical description of an anecdote often repeated and varied. Nonetheless, in her place between the happenstance of the event and the constraint of cultural usages, Joan embraces a large portion of truth and reality concerning the Middle Ages. This means that we will have to approach her person prudently, considering first her attractions and her ambience, her forms and forces, as she moved along the path that the Church of the Middle Ages laid out for her.

A CHRONICLE IN SEARCH OF AN AUTHOR

The inaugural text is our first stop. Thanks to the powers of deduction of Ludwig Weiland (in 1874) and Antoine Dondaine (in 1946), the Metz *Universal Chronicle* found an author: Jean de Mailly, a Dominican.[2] Another Dominican, Etienne de Bourbon (Stephanus de Borbone), repeated the story of Joan several years later in a collection of anecdotal exempla left uncompleted at his death in 1260. In his prologue Etienne cites among his general sources "the chronicle of Jean de Mailly of the Order of Preachers."[3] In the body of the text the source of the anecdote is simply given as "a chronicle." Etienne uses no other contemporary chronicle, however, which means that the story of the popess could only have come from the work of this "Jean de Mailly." The most obvious candidate is a preacher of that name who completed the first Dominican universal collection of legends, the *Abrégé des gestes et miracles des saints* (ca. 1243).[4] These two works, the legendary and the chronicle, contain at least two episodes rarely given elsewhere, the apparition of St. Michael at Monte Gargano and Pope Cyriacus's renunciation of the papacy so that he could follow St. Ursula and her eleven thousand virgins. Moreover, both texts confuse Gerbert of Aurillac (Pope Sylvester II) with Guibert of Ravenna (antipope Clement III).

Unfortunately, our knowledge of Jean de Mailly is limited to these two attributions. One biographical inference is perhaps justifiable: because a Burgundian sanctorale is included in the legendary, the "Mailly" attached to Jean's name may be a village of that name near Auxerre. The Dominican house at Auxerre was founded late (in 1241), which would explain Jean's choice of Metz.

These wisps of Lorraine and Burgundy mist make the rapid mention of the popess in the chronicle even more enigmatic. The autograph copy of this work (Bibliothèque National, Paris, Latin 14 593) presents what seem to be a draft and a clean copy, written one after the other by the same hand. Jean de Mailly enters this vague, already ancient news item at the bottom of a folio of the draft dedicated to the late eleventh century, adding a touching note that shows the historian at work: *Require* (To be verified).

Apparently, what we see here is rumor pushing its way into a text: a medieval author, especially if he is relating an event unknown to him or that he is unsure of, seldom fails to note his source, oral or written, provided that it offers the least guarantee or credibility, or at least to note a vague *legitur* (we read somewhere). The lack of any sign of a source in Jean de Mailly's report of the Joan episode is a clear sign of a rumor "to be verified." How, and why, did Jean de Mailly pick up that rumor? We will probably never know. Nothing in the text permits us to assign any intention to Jean, and the mention of "bad" popes in his chronicle (Gerbert, Leo VIII) was a common occurrence in both earlier and later texts, as we shall see.

THE DOMINICAN NETWORK

The near anonymity of Jean de Mailly, whom we know only by his works, shows the power of the Order of Preachers' system for the diffusion of Christian narratives and dogmas throughout Europe. It is amusing to note that Jean, an unknown preacher, was both the first to report the story of Joan and the first in a long line of Dominicans who compiled collections of legends, a genre that produced and popularized a steady stream of saints' lives. After Jean de Mailly's anthology (1234) there came the *Epilogue on the Lives of the Saints* of Bartholomew of Trent (1245),[5] the *Miroir historial* of Vincent of Beauvais (ca. 1260), and the famous *Golden Legend* of Jacopo da Voragine (ca. 1265), a medieval best-seller with over a thousand known extant manuscripts.[6] The Preachers' passion for popularizing and compiling soon led them to include the legend of the popess in their chronicles (for example, in Martinus Polonus's *Chronicle of the Popes and the Emperors* and Jacopo da Voragine's *Chronicle of Genoa*) and in anthologies of exempla (such as those of Etienne de Bourbon and Arnoldus of Liège). The rapid pace of Dominican narrative production can perhaps be explained more by a cultural logic than by any political or religious orientation: thirteenth-century Dominicans offered constant and loyal support to the papacy.

The story of Joan might have been told elsewhere (and indeed it was, as we shall see). Its entry into the Dominican corpus made its circulation inevitable: whereas a monastic manuscript was copied only by chance or by individual decision, a Dominican text traveled rapidly. The Order of Preachers was in fact famous for its far-reaching network, for the mobility of its members, and for its production of easily transported intellectual tools. By definition, a preacher moved from one friary to another; whether a simple preacher or a preacher general, he covered the vast area of a Dominican province (the province of France covered the entire northern half of the country from Lyon to Metz). Etienne de Bourbon had probably read Jean de Mailly in the friary at Metz. If a brother became a reader or a prior, which were more stable responsibilities, the Order would still move him regularly from house to house.[7] Regular and frequent provincial chapters and general assemblies brought together large crowds of Dominicans. Moreover, itinerant preaching encouraged the production of easily transportable manuscripts: the legendaries of Jean de Mailly and Bartholomew of Trent were circulated in closely written, small-format manuscripts. This explains how the legendary of the obscure Jean de Mailly could have enjoyed an honorable career (to date, at least ten manuscripts have been located) and could have been copied, in part, as far away from Lorraine as Italy. Bartholomew of Trent's legendary, which was used by Jacopo da Voragine, survives in thirty manuscripts.

Thus, if the first vehicles for the legend of Joan seem fairly modest (the *Metz Universal Chronicle* and Etienne de Bourbon's *Traité des sept dons du Saint Esprit*), they nonetheless paved the way for the inclusion of the anecdote in the most widely propagated historical memoir of the Middle Ages, the *Chronicle* of Martinus Polonus. In fewer than twenty-five years (1255–79), Joan's fortune had been made.

TELLING ALL

If speculation about Jean de Mailly's motivations as the receiver and transcriber of a rumor seems an exercise in vanity, it should be noted that a mental attitude widespread in Dominican circles (and beyond) excluded censoriousness. A solid confidence in the powers of faith and knowledge permitted a compiler to consider any assertion and any narrative. Still, Jean de Mailly's notation, *Require* (to be verified), has to be taken seriously: if Jean had lived long enough to complete his text, he would undoubtedly have reviewed his chronicle with a critical eye and added some indication of the credibility of this item. Admittedly, such a critical review would have been made with the methods of the times. It would have been founded primarily on the authorities, and only secondarily on a more general chronological concordance. Still, critical review permitted repetition of any statement, provided that the acceptable critical apparatus of evaluation had been applied. When Jacopo da Voragine relates the legend of St. George (for the first time in the West), he prefaces his narration with a warning: "At the council of Nicaea his legend was included among the apocryphal writings because there is no sure record of his martyrdom."[8] Any anecdote, any "news item," any legend could be related without danger, because the narrator had available ways to modalize, neutralize, and suspend the question of truth. The intellectual revolution of the twelfth century gave the Church the means for this universal absorption of meaning: biblical exegesis, techniques of meditation, and a mastery of allegorical and figural decipherment made it possible to transform everything into Christian truth.

THE CHURCH CONQUERS THE REALM OF THE IMAGINATION

If everything can be told, everything must be told. The Church in the thirteenth century, at the height of its cultural monopoly, held a position of total, global power, and it claimed that it could account for everything. That desire to say everything perhaps explains the paradox of the reduction to folklore of thirteenth-century religious culture described by Jacques Le Goff.[9] Jacopo da Voragine gives an explicit description of this process of commandeering extraneous meaning *ad majorem Dei gloriam*. In his chapter in the *Golden Legend* on the purification of the Virgin, Jacopo explicitly presents the Church's tactic when he deals with the ancestral custom of carrying lighted candles on Candlemas, the Feast of the Presentation in the Temple and the Purification of the Virgin, 2 February:

> The Church established this usage for four reasons. The first is to
> do away with an erroneous custom. On the calends of February
> the Romans honored Februa, the mother of Mars the god of war,
> by lighting the city with candles and torches throughout the night

of that day. This they did every fifth year (that span of years being called a *lustrum*) in order to obtain victory over their enemies from the son whose mother they so solemnly celebrated. . . . Since it is hard to relinquish such customs and the Christians, converted from paganism, had difficulty giving them up, Pope Sergius transmuted them, decreeing that the faithful should honor the holy mother of the Lord on this day by lighting up the whole world with lamps and candles. Thus the Roman celebration survived but with an altered meaning.[10]

The clerical talent for absorbing and assimilating customs explains why medieval texts are so seldom watered down, unlike the texts of the post-Tridentine era. Another Dominican, Hermann Korner of Lübeck, who has already been mentioned in connection with the rite of verification of the pope's manhood, relates the story of Joan (as do many of his confrères), following the common version of Martinus Polonus. Korner expresses surprise, however, at not finding any trace of Joan in the chronicle of yet another Dominican, Henry of Herford (ca. 1350), which he used as a secondary source. Korner implicitly blames his fellow Dominican's timidity for his rejection of the precedent: "However, Henry of Herford makes no mention of that woman who so fraudulently invaded the papacy, perhaps out of fear of scandalizing the laity who know how to read by making it known that such an error was produced in the Church of God, which professed to be guided by the Holy Spirit but is directed by clerics and priests."[11] Henry's timidity, which was not widely shared, given that few universal chronicles omitted Joan, nonetheless testifies to an interesting awareness of the dangers of literacy. Individual reading of the Bible was cause for fear that was much more intense and more frequently expressed,[12] precisely because legendary or historical narration was usually completely smothered by clerical interpretation, whereas with individual reading there was always a risk that the divine Word might pierce through the ecclesiastical ornamentation surrounding it.

Platina gave a particular meaning (and a slightly perverse slant) to his decision to relate the life of the popess in the chronicle that he wrote at the command of Sixtus IV (1472), but he perpetuated the thirteenth-century intention of "telling all." For Platina it was communitarian concern that made telling all important:

These events [the verification of the pope's virility] that I have indicated are commonly related, even though the guarantees for them are uncertain and obscure. I have decided to give them, nakedly and briefly, so as not to seem to omit too obstinately and

tenaciously what almost everyone affirms, at the risk of erring
with the commonality in this matter, although it appeared that
these events that I have reported belong to the class of what can
in all likelihood occur.[13]

Beginning in the twelfth century, legendary themes were gradually as-
similated into the lore of the Church, but this process reached its height
with Dominican compilations of the thirteenth century. Nothing illustrates this Dominican conquest of people's imaginations better than a
comparison between the legendaries of Jean de Mailly and Bartholomew
of Trent. As Antoine Dondaine convincingly demonstrates,[14] Jean de
Mailly wrote a first version of his *Abrégé* for the sheer pleasure of argument
when he was a cleric but not yet a Dominican (probably around 1230).
He was at the time loathe to state that the legends he was relating were untrue. He says about certain marvelous aspects of the lives of Cyricus and
Julitta: "If we report these things, it is in order to refute the apocryphal
writings by means of authoritative works, for if they were true the historians would surely not have kept silent about them."[15]

Jean de Mailly is equally firm regarding another apocryphal episode
(mentioned above): when he deals with the Nativity of Christ, Jean drew
upon an ancient tradition derived from a Greek apocryphal text of the
second century, the Gospel of James, translated into Latin in the sixth century under the name of "Pseudo-Matthew." According to this text, two
midwives, Zebel and Salome, assisted the Virgin Mary at the birth of Jesus.
Zebel immediately proclaimed Mary's miraculous virginity, but Salome
was skeptical, and when she attempted to verify Mary's virginal state manually, she paid for her incredulity with a withered arm. St. Jerome, one of
the highest patristic authorities in the West, had strongly condemned this
version of the Nativity, citing the Gospel of St. Luke, according to which
Mary herself, unaided, brought forth and swaddled the divine newborn.
The suspect version of the story nonetheless circulated in the West, as attested in iconography, but it was never dignified with a text version (except
for a metric adaptation by Abbess Hrothsvitha in the tenth century).

Jean de Mailly was sufficiently confident of his mastery of veracity to
relate this episode, then reject it: "Neither were there midwives to assist
her, no matter what certain books or old wives' tales say."[16]

Several years later Bartholomew of Trent, who was better versed in the
Dominicans' techniques of integration, offered a clever compromise version in which Joseph calls in the midwives only because it was customary
to do so: "Although Joseph was not unaware that it was the Lord who was
to be born of the Virgin, nonetheless he followed the custom of his land

and sent for midwives."[17] The minute Bartholomew could justify Joseph's move without impinging on the dogma of the Incarnation (which was the nub of Jerome's criticism), he was free to relate the episode, which served as the paradigm for many miracles in medieval hagiography in which skeptics are punished. Jacopo da Voragine makes constant use of such clever devices, which permit reconciliation of the irreconcilable and bring together scattered traditions for the greater profit of the Christian story. In the thirteenth century the legendary narrative thus seems to have been the essential element in an ideological mastery that presented, simultaneously, a symbolic object, its valorization, its use, and its subjection to control. Everything could be said within the Church, because nothing should be said outside of it.

Moreover, the permanence of narration seemed a doctrinal duty. The profound originality of Christianity lies in the Incarnation: God manifested himself on earth, among humankind and in the middle of its history, not at the time of origins. He returned; He announced a Last Judgment at the end of terrestrial time, the end of the history of the world. The sacred thus is related and must be related, for it manifests itself (or can do so) suddenly, in proximity to humankind. The grand evangelical model is first a narrative: legend, the historical anecdote, or a banal news item can arrive like a meteor, bearing the sacred. Thus in March 1429, when Joan of Arc went to Chinon to proclaim her divine mission, a commission of clerics presided by the archbishop of Reims examined her closely. They concluded, very prudently, that events would have to confirm the divinity of Joan's inspiration. She pointed out, however, that it would be impious to let pass an opportunity to witness a celestial manifestation: "For to doubt of it or neglect it with no appearance of evil would be repugnant to the Holy Spirit and would make oneself unworthy of the aid of God, as Gamaliel said to a council of Jews [the Sanhedrin] regarding the Apostles."[18] The Incarnation gives an ontological foundation to narrative: because narrative has an essence of the sacred at its disposal, it brings together and reveals what informs the being of the terrestrial world. Everything must be said in the Church, because everything may possibly bear significance.

This means that in the thirteenth century the Church methodically aspired to universal narration. Churchmen took over the oral tradition regarding the popess, possibly discernible in Rome beginning in the mid-twelfth century, within a centripetal whirl (vorago, which it is tempting to see as an imaginary etymology for "Voragine").

When the history of the popess fell within the Dominican network, it had an excellent chance of being infused with meaning, developed, and circulated. The medium created the message, thanks to an exemplary combination of chance (who knows? someone in Metz made a note of a rumor; a traveler passed that way; a pilgrim related the latest news from Rome) and necessity (the Dominican system converted all raw data into reproducible discourse).

CHANCE AND NECESSITY: ENIKEL AND VAN MAERLANT

Necessity seems to have played a major role in establishing Joan, precisely because the beginning of her story among the Dominicans was not its origin. The anecdote had quite certainly been related elsewhere and earlier (between 1150 and 1250), but within the realm of contingency and without the mediations necessary for it to spread. Perhaps as forgotten texts continue to be discovered, would-be popesses will be found in chronicles predating Jean de Mailly's. It is true that the "Johannists" (those who have believed in the real existence of the popess) have tried in vain to move the date of the tale's narration closer to the events it narrates by finding pertinent texts written before 1250. Some read the story of Joan into the *Liber pontificalis*, but only before the critical edition of Louis Duchesne, who clearly demonstrated, with facsimiles to back up his argument, that the twelfth-century manuscript that the Johannists had used as a source (Vaticanus latinus 3762) mentions the story of the popess only in a fourteenth-century marginal note that repeats the Martinus Polonus version word for word. Nor was Marianus Scotus (1086) aware of Joan: the edition of Scotus prepared by Johann Pistorius in 1583, which has misled even such scholars as Cesare D'Onofrio, is in fact based on a fourteenth-century manuscript. The same editorial mechanism pertains regarding Sigebert von Gembloux (1112), Otto of Freising (1158), Richard of Poitiers (1174), Geoffroy of Viterbo (1191), and Gervase of Tilbury (1211), but they may have copied the mention from one another.[19]

Still, the dam constructed by scholars and philologists since the late nineteenth century does not exclude the possibility that narrative streams may have flowed into the current of the Joan story upstream, without reaching the Dominican pool. For example, there is a mention written slightly later than Jean de Mailly's (around 1280), but certainly not dependent on Jean's version, in a lengthy rhymed chronicle in Old High German by one Jansen Enikel, a Vienna burgher. The episode, told in a rough, uncertain style, runs thus:

> There was in Rome a woman who had a beautiful body and who disguised herself as a man. No one could guess that she was a woman. One day, she was elected pope, for she was held to be a

hero agreeable to God. She was very versatile, for, a woman, she wanted to be a man; and thus, she became pope. What she did that was extraordinary while she was pope I cannot say, so I must remain silent on the question. But about her there is one thing that I must say: she was not spared, and what they did to her, that I know well, for she had to suffer a misunderstanding aimed at her honor and was obliged to leave Rome. She harmed people by the horrible misdeed that her body did.[20]

With Jansen Enikel we are within a hair's breadth of rumor: the narrator knows nothing and says as much several times ("des kan ich niht gar gesagen / dâ von sô muoz ich stille dagen"). Briefly stated, a woman succeeded in becoming pope by cross-dressing, and the adventure ended badly. At roughly the same time (1283) but at the other end of Europe, another burgher, Jacob van Maerlant, reported a similar anecdote in a rhymed chronicle written in Flemish, the *Speigel historiael*.[21] Van Maerlant, too, knows almost nothing, but he states that he has heard about a commemorative statue (whose existence is confirmed by the oral tradition) and that he sought in vain to authenticate the story of the popess in the pontifical chronicles. Enikel and van Maerlant note and repeat the rumor, but they are incapable of drawing any conclusions from the anecdote. They lack the Dominicans' mechanisms for creating meaning.

Second: From News Item to Exemplum: Etienne de Bourbon

Around 1260, only a few years after Jean de Mailly's account, Etienne de Bourbon pressed Joan into his service. He took the anecdote, handily extracted from the Metz *Chronicle*, moralized it, and set it up as an exemplum.

We know a bit more about Etienne de Bourbon than about Jean de Mailly, but not much. He was born in Belleville-sur-Saône, not far from Lyon, around 1190–95. He attended the chapter school at Mâcon, then the University of Paris, and he entered the Dominican house in Lyon in 1223, hence in the very early years of the Order of Preachers. For some thirty years he led the itinerant life of a preacher general, traveling in the vast Dominican province of France from Savoy to Lorraine. We find him at Vézelay in 1226, preaching the crusade against the Albigensians; he later became diocesan inquisitor (a post usually filled by a Dominican) at Clermont, then at Lyon. At the end of a long and laborious life he retired to the Dominican house in Lyon, where he died around 1261.[22] Etienne was primarily a preacher. The only work he left behind (unfinished) had a practical purpose: in his retirement in Lyon, between 1250 and 1261, he wrote a thick treatise on sermon topics, *Tractatus de diversis materiis praedicabilibus*, a work more commonly known as *Traité des sept dons du Saint-Esprit* because its contents were divided into seven books, each one devoted to one of the seven virtues that the Spirit breathes into the faithful. The book offered preachers an organized summa of citations from authorities *(auctoritates)*, scholastic arguments *(rationes)*, and exempla, the three major components of the medieval sermon. An exemplum was a brief narrative used within a sermon to illustrate a doctrinal or moral truth.[23] The prodigious preaching campaigns of the thirteenth century, especially on the part of the mendicant orders, created a demand for large numbers of exempla, and a skilled and active practitioner like Etienne de Bourbon would quite understandably dip into all the available written sources as well as into real life and reported experiences. It was natural that the anecdote that a fellow Dominican in Metz had noted down should find a place in Etienne's anthology.

The story is lodged in one small niche of one subdivision of Etienne's weighty, hierarchically constructed treatise: we find it in book 5, "On the Gift of Counsel"; title, "On Prudence"; division, "On the precautions to be taken in the election of prelates"; chapter, "That the election must be pure"; paragraph 10, "Which shows that the election must be sheltered from all usurpation." The text states:

> An astonishing stroke of audacity, or, rather, insanity, took place around the year 1100, according to what is said in the chronicles. A well-educated woman, learned in the art of writing, dressed in men's clothing and was taken for a man. She came to Rome, where she was well received for her energy and her culture; she was named a notary of the Curia, then, with the devil's help, cardinal, and finally pope. Pregnant, she gave birth during a cavalcade. Roman justice having learned of these events, her feet were bound and she was attached to the hoofs of a horse, which dragged her out of the City, and she was stoned by the people for half a league. She was buried at the very place of her death, and on the stone that covered her body were written these words: "Beware, Father of the Fathers, of Publishing the Parturition of the Popess." See to what a detestable end such bold audacity leads![24]

The narrative no longer relates an event in papal history (as it did with Jean de Mailly), but rather a crime of a scope that augments its gravity and broadens its import. The moral lesson to be drawn from the event is forcefully presented in introduction to the narrative and in conclusion to it: "An astonishing stroke of audacity, or, rather insanity. . . . See to what a detestable end such bold audacity leads!" This time a genuine subject stands at the center of the story. Etienne calls her "a woman," using the word *mulier*, in contrast to the *femina* used by Jean de Mailly, a term that designates a social and moral category in the literature of exempla, an often misogynous genre. Moreover, the female subject governs a narration in the feminine: *facta est notarius . . . distracta*. Here the popess is clearly responsible for her acts, as seen by her premeditation and the fact that they begin before her arrival in Rome. The Curia and the papacy are simply echo chambers here, seemingly not engaged in the event. Nothing is said of the popess's official acts. Above all, Etienne differs from Jean de Mailly by deliberately situating both the preparation of the crime and its punishment outside of Rome: "She came to Rome"; she was "dragged out of the city *(extra Urbem)*." This is clearly Etienne's interpretation, given that he does not modify the facts as reported in Jean de Mailly: in both narratives the popess is dragged "for half a league" from the place where the scandalous birth took place. What is more, in his desire to preserve the papacy, Etienne reverses the thrust of the formula with the six Ps, giving: "Beware . . . of publishing" rather than "Publish." We shall return to the question. The popess's female deceptiveness and the devil's aid exonerate the Curia: "She was well received for her energy and her culture; she was named a notary of the Curia, then, with the devil's help, cardinal, and finally pope." The means used (deception and an appeal to the devil) and the motivation for the crime (insane presumption) win our heroine a place in the literature of exempla within the category of unscrupulous women.

JACOPO DA VORAGINE PROVIDES A MORAL

The traits of the exemplum also appear in the version of the Joan story given by Jacopo da Voragine, a Dominican and archbishop of Genoa, in his *Chronicle of Genoa* (completed around 1297). The story of Joan, as it is inserted in this chronicle, speaks to our interests because it reflects a free, undetermined use of the episode before it became fixed in the historical and juridical mold imposed on it by writers who had read Martinus Polonus.

Jacopo da Voragine was born in Liguria around 1230, probably in Varazze, on the Italian Riviera west of Genoa. He entered the Order of Preachers at a very early age, where he carved out a career much more brilliant than those of Jean de Mailly and Etienne de Bourbon: he was in turn a preacher general, reader, and prior before moving on to the highest administrative ranks of the Order as provincial prior for the province of Lombardy (1267–77 and 1281–86) and even as master general of the Order when that post was temporarily vacant. Around 1265, just before taking on those high functions, he wrote the famous *Golden Legend* that won him lasting fame. He never abandoned his literary activities, however, and he composed several collections of model sermons in 1270 and 1290. In 1292, when he was archbishop of Genoa, he undertook the task of writing a brief history of his city "for the instruction of his readers and for the edification of his auditors," but also to give its due to a city that the historians had unjustly neglected: "We are astonished that so little has been said about this city of Genoa, so illustrious, so noble, and so powerful."[25] The rhetoric of prefaces was not the only reason for the dual aim that Jacopo set himself; the composition of the work sets it apart from the common sort of city annals. The first five parts treat the city as a collective religious subject, created (parts 1 and 2), named (part 3), converted (part 4), and striving constantly toward moral perfection (part 5). Parts 6 through 9 present a short treatise on Christian political morality. It is not until the final three parts that Jacopo discusses the history of Genoa, following the chronological succession of bishops and archbishops. A grasp of the doctrinal construction of the *Chronicle of Genoa* helps for an understanding of the exemplum that Jacopo makes of the story of Joan.

Joan's story is told in part 9 of Jacopo's *Chronicle* ("Genoa in the Age of the Bishops"), chapter 8, when he writes about the eighth bishop, Sigebert. Jacopo did his utmost to present the bishops of Genoa in an unbroken line of succession, but for the early times he had only a list of names with no knowledge of contemporary events in the city. This led him to insert episodes pertaining to the age that he had found in universal chronicles but that had no bearing on Genoa. Thus the chapter on Sigebert includes the story of the woman pope; a passage on Pope Sergius IV, who initiated the custom of a pope taking a papal name (perhaps because the name he was known by, Os Porci, had unfortunate connotations as "pig bones" or "pig head"); the episode of a false accusation made against Theodulf, the bishop of Orléans in the reign of Louis the Pious; and an account of a prodigy (a rain of blood on Brescia). The last three episodes had already been included in the brief universal chronicle that Jacopo placed in the chapter on Pope Pelagius in the *Golden Legend*, which indicates that in 1265, despite his fondness for collecting stories and legends, he was unaware of Joan.

The narratives in the *Chronicle* aim at the same comprehensiveness

that Jacopo gave to the *Golden Legend*,[26] offering in turn historical instruction (on the institution of papal names; on Theodulf's creation of the
liturgical response when he used liturgical dialogue to communicate with
the outside world from his prison cell); eschatological instruction (the
prodigy of Brescia); or moral instruction (the story of the popess). Joan's
story is followed by a moral commentary as long as the narrative itself. I
will not reproduce the text itself, as it offers little that does not appear in
Martinus Polonus's version (given below). It has not been proven that Jacopo da Voragine based his text on Martinus's, and he uses none of Martinus's phraseology (which was copied incessantly in the fourteenth and
fifteenth centuries), but both authors place Joan's papacy around the
same time (864, which may be a faulty reading for 854), and both note
the existence of a lover before her election to the papacy and speak of a ritual detour taken by later Roman processions. Finally, it seems improbable
that in 1297 a reader as subject to cultural bulimia as Jacopo da Voragine
could have been unaware of Martinus's versions of the story, which were
rapidly known after 1280. Nonetheless, details that all later readers of
Martinus mentioned (the popess's identity as "John the Englishman," the
fact that she was born in Mainz, the length of her papacy), are not given in
Jacopo's version. Perhaps it was Jacopo da Voragine's moralistic perspective and his penchant for exempla that made him prefer a more generic
description: "a woman *(quedam mulier)*." Two new details surface, however: Jacopo da Voragine was the first (after Jacob van Maerlant, who was
not part of the Dominican network) to speak of "a marble effigy that signals this event." He also states that when the popess felt the onset of labor,
she entered "into a little house situated on the street; she gave birth there,
died of the pains of childbirth, and was buried there." This detail confirms
the topographical hypothesis of Cesare D'Onofrio, who, as we have seen,
identified the places whose odd configuration may have given rise to the
legendary event. D'Onofrio, who does not mention Jacopo da Voragine's
Chronicle of Genoa, bases his conclusions on a much later mention in the
Itinerary of the City of Rome (1517) of Mariano da Firenze, a Franciscan.[27]
No other medieval version of the story contains this detail, which fits well
with the Roman legends discussed in part I. The clerical inscription of the
episode may have briefly crystalized oral traditions that had spread from
Rome, but the force of the canonical narrative obliterated the Roman cir-
cumstances of the event from memory.

Jacopo da Voragine adds to his narrative a weighty moral commentary
close in inspiration to that of Etienne de Bourbon, but with a more
scholastic insistence on demonstration. He hammers in his point:

That woman *(ista mulier)* undertook with presumption, pursued with falsity and stupidity, and ended in shame. That is indeed the nature of women *(natura mulieris)*, who, before an action to be undertaken, have presumption and audacity at the start, stupidity in the middle, and meet with shame at the end. Woman, therefore, begins to act with presumption and audacity, but fails to take into consideration the end of the action and what accompanies it; she thinks she has already done great things; if she can begin something grand, she is no longer able, after the beginning and during the course of the action, to pursue with sagacity what has been begun, and this is because of a lack of discernment. Thus she must end in shame and ignominy what has been undertaken with presumption and audacity and pursued with stupidity. And thus it appears clearly that woman begins with presumption, continues with silliness, and ends with ignominy.[28]

We can note that beyond a solid misogyny common to men of the age and a wholly scholastic delight in tripartite structures, Jacopo da Voragine seems to have a curiously Machiavellian view of the popess's acts. He seems almost to regret her lack of firmness: she might have gotten away with it. Should we interpret this as an early emergence of the fascination with the adventure of transgression that appears in Boccaccio half a century later? This question will be discussed in the next chapter.

THE POPESS IN THE ALPHABET: ARNOLDUS OF LIÈGE

The story of Joan might have become a permanent fixture in the genre of moral tales, but that literary mode did not last long, whereas the corpus of exempla continued to grow until the fifteenth century, thanks to copyings and borrowings, and Etienne de Bourbon's anthology continued to meet with success and was reproduced in other broadly circulated collections. The only other instance of Joan's story as an exemplum occurs in the *Alphabet of Tales (Alphabetum narrationum)* that another Dominican, Arnoldus of Liège, wrote around 1307.[29] This large collection of 819 exempla was highly successful (there are 98 extant manuscripts), probably thanks to its alphabetical classification of themes and its ingenious system of cross-references. It was translated into English and Catalan, and I might note in passing that although the English translation was quite literal, a Catalan adaptation, *Recull de eximplis e miracles, gestes et faules e altres ligendes ordenades per ABC,*[30] adds a detail not found in the canonical version by Martinus that Arnoldus summarizes: during the procession, Joan arrives before an image of the Virgin Mary, who asks her if she would prefer to expiate her sin throughout eternity or in this world; Joan chooses immediate purgation and dies in childbirth.

MARTINUS'S METHOD

Another way of relating the episode of the popess arose very early (around 1260) but embryonically in the *Chronica minor* of an anonymous Franciscan in Erfurt, which states: "There was yet another pseudopope *(pseudopapa)* whose name and dates in office are unknown. It was a woman, according to what the Romans say."[31] The term *pseudopapa* returns us to the institution of the papacy, whereas Jean de Mailly used the more picturesque term *papissa* and Etienne de Bourbon and Jacopo da Voragine omitted any reference to the papacy (except in the formula with the six Ps). The version of Joan's story by Martinus Polonus integrates it even more markedly into the history of the papacy (in contrast to pure anecdote).

Born Martin Strebsky in Troppau, in Bohemia, Martinus entered the Dominican house in Prague, which depended from the vast province of Poland, which means that "Polonus" was more administrative in origin than geographical. Martinus had a brilliant career, to the point of becoming chaplain and penitentiary to Pope Clement IV in 1265. He was retained in these functions under Clement's successors; in 1278 Nicholas III named him bishop of Gnesen (now Gniezno) in Poland, consecrating him personally. Gnesen was an important diocese, whose bishop became primate of Poland in the fifteenth century, but Martinus never took up his episcopal duties because he died in Bologna as he was making his way there. His works include a slim alphabetical index to Gratian's *Decretals*, in the purest Dominican tradition of aids for the divulgation of Christian doctrine, and the *Margarita Decreti*, which contained the article on "woman" mentioned in chapter 1. In a similar spirit, he wrote a brief universal chronicle, the *Chronicle of Roman Popes and Emperors*, several hundred manuscript copies of which are extant, as well as translations into English, Armenian, Czech, Spanish, French, German, Greek, and Italian. The success of this chronicle was perhaps due to its concision, as well as to a clever page layout that permitted rapid consultation: in the copies made from the original manuscript, each page was made up of fifty lines and covered fifty years of history.

Joan's story does not appear in the earliest extant manuscripts of Martinus's *Chronicle*. According to Ludwig Weiland,[32] Martinus wrote three versions of his chronicle, first under Clement IV (1265–68), then in 1268, and finally around 1277. The note on the popess was presumably inserted into the third version. It is also possible that the addition was made by another hand in a posthumous version circulated after Martinus's death or by someone who continued his chronicle. In any event, the episode figures in all the manuscripts that appeared after 1280 under Martinus's name and bearing his authority. This short text deserves to be read in its entirety; by fixing the form of the Joan story, giving it broad circulation, and granting it reliability, it closed a phase in her history. Martinus states:

> After that Leo [Pope Leo IV], John, English of nation, born in Mainz, reigned for two years, seven months, and four days. He died in Rome and the papacy was vacant for a month. According to what is said, he was a woman; in her adolescence she was taken to Athens, dressed as a man by the man who was her lover; she made so much progress in the various branches of knowledge that no one equal to her could be found; it was for that reason that she next taught the trivium [the literary arts] in Rome and had high officials as her disciples and auditors. And because her conduct and her learning were held in high repute in the City, she was elected pope by unanimous vote. But during the course of her papacy her companion made her pregnant. But she/he was unaware of the time of her delivery, and, while making her way toward the Lateran coming from St. Peter's, seized with the pains of childbirth between the Coliseum and the church of St. Clement, she gave birth, then died right at the precise spot where she was buried. And as the lord pope always takes a detour on this route, it is generally believed that he does so out of detestation of that event. He has not been inscribed in the catalogue of holy pontiffs by reason of the nonconformity that the female sex involves in this matter.[33]

The story begins to take on the colors of truth, because Martinus indicates a date and a rank in papal succession. He wards off scholarly contestation by explaining that no list of popes contains Joan's name. Moreover, he gives the episode a certain coherence: Joan's actions are motivated by love; her meteoric career is due to her extraordinary talent. When gifted with an identity (name, date, acts), Joan finally begins to live as an individual.

We can never know where Martinus found the indispensable details that give Joan a durable life in the realm of the imagination. Her romance might just as easily have been constructed on the basis of the raw event, as reported by Jean de Mailly, with the addition of responses to questions of why and how the popess acted as she did.

In Martinus, Joan begins her career with general teaching (the trivium), rather than as a notary. This correction may be based on likelihood. The notary's position was no longer as prestigious after the invention of the *cursus*, the pontifical style of redaction, as it had been in the eleventh and twelfth centuries. In the autobiography of Guido Faba, as deciphered by Ernst Kantorowicz, the notary (in Faba's case, a civil notary) is compared to a tanner because he works with dog feces (to whiten parchment) and an awl (to sew and stretch his working materials).[34] Martinus was the first to give an emotional reason (following a lover) for Joan's decision to dress as a man.

It seems more difficult to trace the formation of Joan's identity. Martinus calls her John, not Joan. The name "John" was chosen by many popes of the ninth and tenth centuries, from John VIII (882) to John XVII (1003). Thanks to the tumultuous vicissitudes of the papacy (depositions and returns to the papal throne) the numbering of popes who shared the same name became confused. The bad reputation of John XI and John XII, the "pornocracy" popes, may have influenced Martinus's choice (or that of his unknown source).

Martinus's odd indication of Joan's origins ("English of nation, born in Mainz") is even harder to explain. I shall propose a few summary associations, but without suggesting they be given the dignity of causes: spare us from the demon of endless analogy!

Anglicus, the Englishman. The only English pope in history was Adrian IV (1154–59), whom we have already met in the context of his conflict with Frederick Barbarossa. If we admit that the Joan legend circulated for the most part in Germanic lands (which would include the Empire, plus Lorraine and Burgundy, which were culturally oriented toward the Germanic sphere), we can imagine—though the hypothesis is admittedly feeble—that the intense Germanic production of antipapal materials in the eleventh and twelfth centuries might have charged that English pope with a thousand sins and oddities. The sudden appearance of a pope from a distant nordic realm surprised Christianity: a *Cronica pontificum et imperatorum sancti Bartholomaei in insula romani* (Chronicle of St. Bartholomew, ca. 1256) includes an account of Adrian's life and meteoric career that may have some relation to Joan. The *Chronicle* states: "His English father, come to Avignon, earned his living there with his own hands, and at his death his son, who was still young, was placed as a servant in the hospital of Saint-Ruf; then he became a canon, then abbot, and finally pope."[35] Legend transposes the facts of a life that was in fact a truly astonishing example of social promotion. Nicholas Breakspear, the son of a humble cleric, wanted to enter the monastery of Saint-Alban; while waiting to be received there, he went to Paris, where he lived on charity before putting himself in the service of the chapter of Saint-Ruf in Avignon, where he became a canon, then a prior, before he caught the notice of Eugenius III (when Breakspear and his canons had been brought to Rome by a suit) and the pope made him bishop of Albano. Even if the life of Adrian IV has only a remote connection with Martinus's elaboration of the Joan story, it sheds light on one important aspect of that story: the papacy, the supreme power on earth, might be offered to anyone, grace and merit aiding. In a strongly hierarchical world, the assumption of someone who would normally be excluded—a pauper or a woman—gives one pause.

There is only one vowel separating "Anglicus" (the Englishman) from "Angelicus" (the angelic): even less, given that medieval scribes regularly abbreviated an interconsonantal "e." Plays on words involving the two terms had an ancient and noble pedigree, beginning with Gregory the Great, who was supposed to have exclaimed, on catching sight of the handsome blond slaves for sale in Rome, that they should be called angels rather than Angles. The strong impression they made on him is reputed to have kindled in him a desire to convert the people of the British Isles.[36]

While we are taking a break from causality, let us indulge in a few paragraphs of free association. The idea of the imminent arrival of an angelic pope *(angelicus papa)* was in fact a notion that circulated in people's minds in the late thirteenth century, as we shall see in connection with Joachimite and Franciscan expectations. We shall also see traces of it in heretical circles in Milan, but that, too, is for a later chapter. For the moment it is enough to remark that clerics were used to wordplay and appreciated it. We might imagine a clerical discourse that evokes Joan as a response to Joachimite prophecy and insists that nothing in it announces an angelic pope, but rather an English pope who is female. An ironic *reductio ad absurdum* of the sort had proven its worth in euhemerism: in his *Sacred History* (third century B.C.E.), Euhemerus rationalized Greek myths by showing that the gods were men, deified by fear or admiration. Christian apologetics made constant use of derisive euhemerism in their struggle against paganism and heresy.

The plot thickens in Mainz, as does the mystery. From the whirl of analogies we might also pull out St. Ursula and the eleven thousand virgins in the Rhineland, escorted by Pope Cyriacus, who (according to the twelfth-century visionary, Elizabeth of Schönau) was dropped from the list of popes (like Joan) because he had abandoned the papal throne.

There is also Hildegard of Bingen, who was active in the twelfth century not far from Mainz. We shall return to Hildegard, a woman of inspired knowledge and high, almost pontifical, spiritual stature, in the next chapter. None of these connections is convincing.

And what if Martinus had moved from one association to another with no intention of signifying anything? In that case, we can image the learned Dominican leafing through the chronicles of his times, trying to find in accounts that related to the end of the reign of Pope Leo IV (854) passages that marked or masked the presence of Joan. He might have found, for example, in the *Book of the Times (Liber de temporibus)* of Alberto Milioli, a notary in Reggio Emilia, that in 854, in a parish in Mainz, an evil spirit possessed priests and citizens. Chased away by aspersions of holy water, the spirit took refuge "under the cape of a priest, as if it were his familiar" (*familiaris* is the word Martinus applies to Joan's clerical lover).[37]

Where did Martinus get the date 854? Jean de Mailly made a note of the rumor concerning the popess at the bottom of a folio regarding the late eleventh century, perhaps only because he found free space there, intending to verify the story and date it more accurately when he could. Etienne de Bourbon may have taken the date given in Jean's notation ("around 1100") without close chronological inspection, given that the exemplum is a form that does not imply temporality. If we allow Martinus a similarly cavalier attitude toward methodology, we might imagine that in his page layout he might have had eight lines to use up for the reign of Leo IV, a pope little known to history about whom he knew nothing. His painstaking calculations, what is more, leave a gap of more than two years. But this reductive and lazy hypothesis fails to take into account the chronological intuition of the Franciscan from Erfurt, who wrote before Martinus, and who places the history of the pseudopope in the ninth century, without adding further precisions. Are we to imagine that Joan, a figure of disorder, might have been placed in the interdynastic gap between the Carolingian and Ottonian emperors as a sign of disintegration and an appeal to a return to Germanic order?

Enough of this series of analogies, which are endless and perhaps senseless. To continue on this path is to risk finding all the reasons in the world to situate John, the Englishman from Mainz, in 854, thanks to a cancerous proliferation of microcausal cells that coagulate without any articulation among them. Contextual causality, that peril to historiography, begins here. Its ravages are obvious to anyone who cares to peruse school textbooks for the "causes" of the French Revolution in 1789 or of World War I in 1914: everything converges, hence nothing is explained. The event disappears under layers of a context that exists only by reason of the event.

This means that we need to return to more rational certitudes by examining the reality of Martinus Polonus's text and the historical uses to which it was put. Martinus was not content to give the popess an identity and a coherence: he also assigned a function to the story of her life that (once again) neutralized its venom.

THIRD: FROM EXEMPLUM TO JURIDICAL-HISTORICAL CASE: MARTINUS POLONUS (CA. 1279)

Martinus treats the episode of the woman pope as a historical case, as we can see by its subtle interplay of genders. As pseudopope (mentioned with no ordinal number in Petrine succession), the subject of the passage governs the masculine *(Iohannes Anglicus, mortus est)*; when Martinus speaks of Joan as an individual, it governs the feminine *(ducta, sepulta)*. In short, the narrative presents a case of nonlegitimacy within pontifical history, signaled here by the feminine subject and elsewhere by other means. This juridical and historical orientation of the text can be seen just as clearly in Martinus's exoneration of the Curia. Etienne de Bourbon was intent on protecting the purity of the Roman site; here Martinus seems instead to emphasize early premeditation: Joan is seduced as an adolescent *(in aetate puellari)*, and far from Rome (her lover takes her from Mainz to Athens); after her election to the papacy, the father of her child is the same lover, not a Roman. The election itself seems perfectly regular and sincere: "Because her conduct and her learning were held in high repute . . . she was elected pope by unanimous vote *(concorditer)*." The final portion of Martinus's entry no longer centers on morality (as in Etienne de Bourbon and Jean de Mailly), but on the question of papal legitimacy. After noting the detour taken by the papal processions (a positive and institutional reading), Martinus concludes that the reign was invalid (a reading in applied canon law): "He has not been inscribed in the catalogue of holy pontiffs by reason of the nonconformity that the female sex involves in this matter *(propter mulierus sexus quantum ad hoc deformitatem)*." Martinus's vocabulary is patently juridical. He resolves a case: an ineligible individual, even when elected legally, does not benefit from any legitimacy. The conclusion was to bear a great deal of weight a century later, with the Great Schism.

Geoffroy de Courlon, one of the first chroniclers to follow Martinus Polonus, relates the episode of the popess in comparable terms in his chronicle of the Abbey of Saint-Pierre-le-Vif in Sens (completed ca. 1290). The heading he gives to the episode is characteristic of the juridical-historical approach: "Deception directed at the Roman Church" *(Deceptio*

Ecclesiae Romanae).[38] Geoffroy's version of the case is the first to mention the use of the pierced chair to verify the manhood of the pope as a preventive measure made necessary by such a break in trust (see chapter 1).

Thus at the turn of the fourteenth century, the narrative mode of the case history shifted the story of Joan toward a juridical and historical usage that, in contrast to its use as an exemplum, confined it within the world of the Church, or at least did so as long as debate on papal authority remained internal to the Church of Rome.

SHOULD WE BELIEVE IN JOAN?

The story of Joan, as told within Church discourse, could stop here: from Martinus Polonus to 1450, the canonical narrative was repeated, paraphrased, and summarized, with no notable changes, in innumerable chronicles. The existence of the popess was never questioned; the nearly juridical presentation of Joan's case threw her into the controversies of the fourteenth and fifteenth centuries with no contestation of her strange papacy. This general acceptance seems simple and clear; it derived from a solid cultural logic. The disquieting and obscure event reported to the laity by Jansen Enikel and Jacob van Maerlant had no hope of taking on meaning or prestige; within the Dominican network, however, where nothing was lost and everything bore meaning, the anecdote grew and multiplied. All the story needed was to pass through the hands of a great transformer, and in 1280 he was Martinus Polonus. Twenty years earlier, he would have been Jacopo da Voragine. To cite just one example: the legend of St. Christopher, the Christ-Bearer, which had arrived in mysterious ways from the far reaches of Mozarabic liturgy in Spain, appeared in the *Golden Legend;* it then invaded the entire West and continued to be believed until our own times, when Pope John XXIII brutally struck St. Christopher from the calendar of saints. This process of diffusion, as we have seen, cannot be reduced to automatic reproduction: in the Dominican laboratory, the story, pruned of disturbing elements, had undergone a first transformation into an exemplum. Martinus's text removed the story from a possibly dangerous contact with the faithful (as an exemplum set with a sermon) and gave it a place in ecclesiastical history, a genre primarily reserved to clergy. In short, a collective subject, the Dominican Order, served as *auctor* (in Latin, originator and warrant as well as author) of the episode, and once it had been cast into a form that lent itself to broad diffusion, eminent secondary and locally identified figures (Jean de Mailly, Etienne de Bourbon, Jacopo da Voragine, Martinus Polonus) fixed the form of the anecdote, addressing another collective subject, the Church. Around 1450 interest in the story declined as those two collective subjects gradually weakened under such pre-Reformation assaults as the Hussite revolution.

An inescapable and essential question remains, however: did people of the Middle Ages—that is, churchmen between 1280 and 1450—believe the story of Joan? Thus far, our analysis provides only ambiguous answers.

On the one hand: the question of belief does not arise. Jean de Mailly registers a rumor and defers the question of truth with *Require*, "to be verified." Etienne de Bourbon places the story within a moral world in which signification is more important than truth. Along with anecdotes that he presents as true, he includes several of Aesop's fables, and when he retells the story of the lion, the wolf, and the fox, he is well aware that the fable is not true referentially but metaphorically.[39] It is of course probable that the story of Joan's presumption may have had more reality for Etienne than the tale of the lion taking advantage of the other animals, but in the long view of veracity in the exemplum, his belief or that of his reader is not pertinent. In Martinus's treatment of the story, as we have seen, the jurisprudential aspect of the narrative neutralizes the question of belief.

On the other hand: ecclesiastical history claims to relate what is true, and the precision of the details given by Martinus (Joan's name, date, place within papal succession; her place of birth; the location of the spot where the scandal took place; the reasons for her absence on lists of popes) all engender a "reality effect." We return here to the binary choices we have attempted to avoid: in 854, Joan/John either reigned or did not reign. Until 1450, no one claimed that she had not reigned. Neutralizing belief in her existence simply reflects an attempt to acclimatize her; it is a trick played with belief.

In reality the question is more complex. We will undoubtedly never know what people believed between 1280 and 1350; it is difficult enough to discern what they were given to believe. Do we ourselves know what we believe? When we are confronted with direct or indirect knowledge ("The cat is on the mat," or "Water boils at 100 degrees Celsius"), what weight should be assigned to belief, tastes and aesthetic certitudes, moral and social conventions, or habits of thought and language, which are so easily shaken and so easily reconstituted? Something as viscous as tar flows in to close the gaps in reality, often taking the place of the living mortar of belief.

Nonetheless, let us try to define the question of belief in the Middle Ages.

Medieval Belief: A Long but Necessary Excursus

Assigning strict veracity to history (in this case, Martinus Polonus's chronicle of the popes and emperors) seems anachronistic. History, like anecdote or legend, tells one truth that is plausible, optional, and open to permutations. To take a simple example from within papal history: Sylvester II (Gerbert of Aurillac), who was pope at the turn of the first millennium, has a well-established, historical existence. Medieval chronicles (regardless of exact chronology; their moment of redaction is not pertinent) regularly present two opposing versions of his life. In the first, Sylvester was a good pope, learned, and attentive to the possessions of the Church. He shaped the careers of two great sovereigns (Robert the Pious, king of France, and Otto III of Germany), teaching them to respect the Holy Mother Church. In the second view, Sylvester was a diabolical pope who made a pact with Satan, gave his soul to the Evil One in exchange for mastery of the malefic arts, and did his utmost to weaken the venerable structure of the Church. His punishment shows the defeat of the devil: the impious Gerbert had been told that he would die in Jerusalem, so he took care not to go in holy pilgrimage to that city, but he died suffocated under the rubble of the Roman church of San Giovanni di Gerusalemma when it collapsed, struck by divine providence.

Both of these versions speak of facts, not judgments or evaluations: we are indeed in the realm of the binary nature of truth and falsehood. Polemics do not enter into these divided opinions, as they did in the case of Pope Gregory VII (Hildebrand, called Brandellus or Merdellus), whom his imperial adversaries charged with all possible sins. Moreover, the choice between one version and the other happens almost by chance, even when each chronicler has both versions available to him. Nothing proves this better than the chronicle of the popes written by the Dominican Leone da Orvieto (ca. 1315). Leone himself states that his principal source was Martinus Polonus; his chapter on Joan copies Martinus word for word; his continuation of Martinus's chronicle (1278–1315) seems fairly critical of the papacy since, as we shall see, his chapter on Boniface VIII is downright ferocious. Thus he has every reason to copy or summarize Martinus's version of the life of an evil Sylvester II. He chooses to praise him, however, with no further explanation. We will never penetrate the mind of Leone da Orvieto, a fairly obscure Dominican whom we know only from a few brief remarks on his career in the Order of Preachers and this one work, which has come down to us in only one, probably autograph manuscript.[40] It seems certain, however, that Leone, like many others, saw history as a reservoir of narratives that did not involve truth, imposed or proved.

The narrative tradition (both historical and legendary) is not a closed and delimited corpus of the true, or even of the probable: it offers an indeterminate raw material that takes on the color of truth through a series of operations that produce significance and of contracts that lend veracity.

The simplest form of those operations, as we have seen, links a writer and a reader or auditor who receives elements to be evaluated. Jacopo da Voragine did not hesitate to relate a fabulous or apocryphal episode, and he pointed them out to the reader as such. A century later (around 1340) Pietro Calo da Barletta (also a Dominican) gives a version of the birth of St. Stephen that does not figure in the canonical texts. He adds: "I wanted to mention this apocryphal story here, leaving it up to the reader to judge."[41]

The compiler creates an index of truth for himself by placing a narrative on a dual scale of evaluation, in relation to its source (the scale of guarantee) and in relation to the use that he makes of the text (the scale of implication).

The apex of the scale of guarantee is the revealed. Revelation is limited to Scripture, but the question of apocryphal texts sets up uncertain boundaries to this domain. Next come what might be called the authorized. These texts are the writings of the Fathers of the Church, whose authority is incontestable. Here, too, the outside limits of the category are difficult to ascertain. A time-honored custom, confirmed by Jacques-Paul Migne, has patrology stop with St. Bernard, but if one defines patrology by the absolute refusal to contest an author, the last Father of the Church would be the Venerable Bede. The next level is the authenticated. In this case, the authenticity of an episode proceeds from a contract of belief renegotiated in each instance. This means that it is the narrator himself who offers the guarantee and who invokes either his own credibility (stating, "I have seen," "I have remarked") or the credibility of a live witness or a text that he interrogates. When Guibert de Nogent, in *De vita sua* (1115), authenticates the legend of the British king who took the name Quilius on his conversion, he confirms an oral tradition *(historia)* by citing inscriptions in the church in Nogent.[42] The moral and religious value of the witness is worth at least as much as confirmation by texts. An early-fourteenth-century English Franciscan, John Lathbury, expresses this idea in connection with his account of a miracle of the Virgin, declaring that he had heard of it from a "certain trustworthy man to whose word I hold *(adhereo)* as I would to his book *(quaterno)*." Elsewhere John says about another legend: "A venerable knight, whose holy life gave credence to his words, devoutly related this to me."[43] It is significant that in both of these instances the anecdote related was in fact extremely old (but did John

Lathbury know that?). The medium was more important than the tradition. There is another essential clause in the contract of belief that deserves mention: signification, too, gives authenticity. The intention of the knight, who speaks "devoutly" (devote), is as important as his holy life. Similarly, in the history of King Quilius, a pagan who, alone and unassisted (as Guibert claims to be), found faith even before he knew of Christ's Passion, Guibert's projection of himself into the narrative provides a signification that lends it authenticity. We must respect Guibert's ambivalence when he states that the texts of the inscriptions merit belief (roborant fidem). Simultaneously, they confirm the reader's confidence (fidem) in their existence and fortify his faith (fidem). What is being authenticated in this contract between the witness and the compiler (or the redacter) is chosen out of the immense, unstable mass of what is alleged (dicitur; fertur), which is the same position that Pietro Calo and Jacopo da Voragine take when they establish a contract with the reader. What is alleged—given without guarantee, but nonetheless given—is not excluded from the field of legend, unlike the fabulous. The alleged governs an obscure zone of strong belief, the zone of history that is basically true (that is, that lies beyond formal veracity, at the bottom of things, where everything must be taken as true). At this point, history approaches rumor, the oral and unstable form of the alleged, where guarantees are insinuated ("Of course, naturally," the speaker says, with a wink), which makes them all the more forceful. Here the contract privileges the reader who understands subtleties. The legend of Judas in the twelfth century, for example, clearly demonstrates how close a connection there is among rumor, the alleged, and the authenticated. When the Church wanted to dissipate a rumor, it made use of a counter-authentification. This was what occurred in 1247 when Pope Innocent IV sent the bishops of the Rhineland a letter stating that the rumor about Jews who had supposedly performed a ritual cutting up of the heart of a Christian child was totally untrue.[44]

A second, parallel scale ranks narratives according to the nature of their use. At the top of the scale is liturgy or paraliturgy (for example, texts for monastic collations or reading at table), and the list continues, in descending order, with devotional reading (matter for oral reading judged worthy of being put into writing, thus that enjoyed great prestige); sermons (and here the freer oral form must be distinguished from notes on sermons and rewritten sermons); celebrations of an institution (including ecclesiastical chronicles); and, finally, controversy or moral discussion (including the nontheological exempla). The lower degrees on the scale of narrative usage neutralize the question of the authenticity and signification of legend. The history of the popess belongs in the lowest categories of this double scale of truth, in alleged historical narrative. It is not contested because it is not presented as incontestable. Narrative, in medieval clerical discourse, was evaluated by its effects and its causes. In turn true, significant, or illustrative, it might be compared with the case in psychoanalysis, where the narrative, ceaselessly reiterated and reinterpreted, bears a truth that is neither literal or original (in the sense of going back to origins), but rather is secondary and constructed. The transitive and transitional narrative acts more than it represents.

This plasticity of truth is not an inconsistency that might lead to a generalized relativism. It came, as has been said, from the particular conditions of Revelation within Christianity: the truth is not crystalized in a text, given that God came to earth in order to revise the ancient contract. That is both the drama and the grandeur of the Christian Incarnation. Truth became mingled with history and with time, without preceding them or dominating them. At the time of Christ, truth became meteoric, and one cannot determine exactly what are its fragments and its luminous traces. It was only in the sixth century that the Gelasian Decree attempted to separate the corpus of revealed, canonical texts from apocryphal ones. To be sure, a mystical and spiritual tradition guided the popes and the doctors of the Church in the wake of that meteor, but nothing seemed sure in that domain, as shown by the debate over papal infallibility, which started in the thirteenth century and concluded only in 1870! I may perhaps be reproached for slipping from narrative truth to doctrinal truth here, but the two domains are not easy to distinguish in a universe whose founding text is the narrative of a life.

The Incarnation multiplied the possible sources of truth. The uncertainty and the tolerance of the medieval Church (a florilegium, narrative and doctrinal, of the orthodox doctors of the Church would confirm this apparently provocative phrase) were the result of an overproduction of truth. Scholars have all too often confused the ardor (at times violent or literally incandescent) of conviction with doctrinal closed-mindedness; the mind truly closed to the spirit of truth is found instead in the indifference that followed post-Tridentine dogmatism.

Medieval belief thus should be represented as a series of contracts drawn up between a subject (individual or collective) and a guarantor who can be of infinite extension (God the author). Scripture is the only indispensable part of this contract, which can also include the Fathers, Tradition, the papacy, and the Holy Spirit (which blows where it wants).

The truth of Joan is thus not a deposed truth, but one ceaselessly included, adjusted, and modulated, though not rejected. It moves through a clerical discourse that is indefinitely flexible and conjunctive, full of restrictive terms (most of the narrators relate the story to the accompaniment of "according to what is said": *dicitur; fatentur*), and segmented—that is, fragmented and recomposed according to the meaning that the writer wants to give it. Nothing shows that characteristic better than the second version of the story attributed to Martinus Polonus, in which the popess does not die of her treatment by Roman justice, but is deposed and repents; her son becomes bishop of Ostia. After her pious death, miracles occur at her tomb. Here Joan's story is grafted into the great hagiographic tradition of repentant female sinners.[45] This sort of clerical discourse could embrace everything, assimilate everything. In Hegelian terms, it was a discourse without negativity, an obverse with no reverse, as long as it did not encounter the contrary discourse of a strong rival institution—that is, until it clashed with the Reformation.

The thirteenth century found even greater possibilities for a new manifestation of the truth as it went through alternating movements of expansion and contraction. Beginning in the late twelfth century the Spirit had been breathing harder. This is not the place to draw up the vast and impressive inventory of the various prophetical movements of the central Middle Ages that André Vauchez dubbed "informal powers,"[46] but mention must be made of the enormous repercussions of the prophetical work of Joachim of Fiore (ca. 1140–1202), a Calabrian Cistercian with whom medieval minds were obsessed. Joachim announced that the Last Times and the final revelation would arrive in the year 1260. After the book of the Father (the Old Testament) and the book of the Son (the New Testament), the book of the Holy Spirit would have to be written, and it was that Eternal Gospel that a Franciscan, Gerardo da Borgo San Donnino, thought he was redacting in 1254. In the prophetic tradition, Christian truth spread by successive, dovetailed advances. The popess was to find her place in that tradition, as we shall see.

The domain of guaranteed truth could also contract, however. From the twelfth century on, as Marie-Dominique Chenu has shown, theology was considered a science.[47] Where the prophetic spirit added, the science of theology pared away. It even threatened the venerable text of Revelation, as Bernard Guenée remarks in connection with Roger Bacon and Pierre d'Ailly. Roger Bacon (1210–92), a Franciscan, "gave numerous proofs that in Jerome's Latin translation of the Bible, the Vulgate, which the Church adopted as its official version of Holy Scripture, the illustrious doctor had made mistakes or had not said everything or had added to the text."[48] Roger Bacon's minimal contract bound him only to the Author of the Hebrew or Greek text, excluding the venerable translator. It would obviously be absurd to make the illustrious and subtle-minded Bacon into a reforming fundamentalist: his great learning honored the doctors of the Church, but it also commanded him to anchor his belief to new connections. Bernard Guenée has noted the response that Pierre d'Ailly (1351–1420), a prudent and orthodox theologian, gave to Bacon a century later in his *Epistola ad novos Hebraeos* (Letter to the New Hebrews):

> The obligation to believe a human authority is not absolute. Salvation does not hinge on such a belief: "Nulla auctoritas humana firmiter est credenda de necessitate salutis." . . . It was absolutely necessary, in order to be saved, to believe in the authority of the Christian Church *(auctoritas ecclesiae christianae a quolibet firmiter credenda est de necessitate salutis)*.[49]

Pierre d'Ailly's position permitted him to rescue Jerome, whose translation of the Bible was guaranteed by the Church, but it did little to define the realm of truth: Where, in what texts, did the authority of the Church reside? (In the ancient councils? In the present councils? In the pope? The Curia? The Fathers?) The question was not vain; it was to rend the Church asunder in the fourteenth century.

Pierre d'Ailly's formulation confirms the concept of a systematic scale of veracity in the Middle Ages, discussed above. Jerome's truth, Pierre d'Ailly tells us, is probable in itself, but absolute within the Church system of verity. Belief in the Middle Ages was not brought to bear analytically on one object or another, which is why acceptance of Joan can be found in systems of truth as mutually exclusive as those of William of Ockham, John Wycliffe, Jan Hus, and Dietrich of Nieheim. Moreover, Pierre d'Ailly defines firm belief as a necessary component of salvation: there is no salvation without just and good belief. The originality of that concept lay in its combination of the possible and the necessary. By twisting a fine phrase of Daniel Milo's, one might posit that medieval religious belief became established when "the possible aspires to the necessary in order to escape the aleatory."[50]

THE FORTUNES OF JOAN

This long excursus into the domain of medieval belief helps us to understand the immense success of the story of Joan, which Martinus Polonus situated at a low level of the scale of belief, but among a segmented body of materials (ecclesiastical history) that were ceaselessly manipulated to serve as the foundation for systems of salvation. This gave Martinus's version of the Joan story a very wide circulation within Church discourse until around 1450, a threshold that corresponds, as we shall see, with a profound break in the organization of Catholicism. Joan will help us grasp that turning point. Still, old mental habits remained strong, and the life of the popess continued to be repeated here and there within the Catholic Church until the late sixteenth century, even in the face of a growing number of refutations and even when the various Reformations had co-opted the story and used it to attack Rome. Around 1550 the Dominican Bartolomé Carranza (†1576) mentions Joan in his *Summa omnium conciliorum* (Summa of All the Councils). Although his comments clearly devalue the story—he states: "The thing is currently told, but under the guarantee of uncertain and obscure authors"[51] (a phrase that he borrows from Platina but transfers from the rite of verification to the life of Joan)—he nonetheless repeats it. In 1576 Jean Rioche, a Franciscan from the friary of Saint-Brieuc in Brittany, not only repeats the episode but gives it credence: "Although Platina and the *Somme des Conciles* [Carranza's work] affirm that one should scarcely believe in it, the universal Church nonetheless gives witness to this event."[52]

ACCOMMODATIONS

It would be tedious to analyze all the occurrences of the life of Joan in clerical writings between 1280 and 1450 (or 1500), given that they make up a repetitive corpus of indefinite size. A rapid glance at the major lines of diffusion of Martinus Polonus's text will have to do.

Some chroniclers were content to give a literal copy of the canonical text. This was the practice of the Dominican Leone da Orvieto (ca. 1315), the English Benedictine Ranulf Higden in his *Polychronicon* (ca. 1330),[53] the anonymous authors of interpolations to the *Liber pontificalis* (early fourteenth century), and the chronicle of Richard of Poitiers.[54]

Such authors quite often limit themselves to condensing Martinus's narrative into a rapid mention of Joan. This was the procedure of the fourteenth-century interpolators who copied the ancient chronicles (Marianus Scotus, Sigebert von Gembloux, Otto of Freising, Geoffroy of Viterbo, Gervase of Tilbury, etc.). Vast numbers of summaries of this sort can be found up to the sixteenth century (the *Chronicle* of the monastery of Hirsau by the German Benedictine Johannes Trithemius, 1462–1516, or the *Enneades* of the Venetian Marco Antonio Coccio, known as Sabellico, 1436–1506).

There were also a large number of vernacular adaptations of Martinus, particularly in Germanic lands. These are arid stuff, however, for which the reader is referred to the chronological bibliography of works regarding Joan.

Finally, there were other chroniclers who paraphrased Martinus without changing the broad outlines of his narrative. The paraphrasers produced only a few significant variants that deserve mention, and we shall pass over copyists' distortions and errors, although at times these could be sizable. For example, Jacopo d'Acqui (ca. 1370) has Joan reigning for nineteen years. Neither will we mention stylistic improvements: Platina's 1472 version adds nothing to Martinus, but he writes in an elegant humanistic Latin.

Some of Martinus's readers attempted to rationalize Joan's identity, given the geographically contradictory indications that Joan was both English and from Mainz. In the list of popes that Bernard Gui, an illustrious Dominican, appended to his great *Flores chronicarum* (probably ca. 1315), he copied Martinus but substituted *Teutonicus* (the German) for *Anglicus* (the Englishman). This rationalization met with little success, however, thanks to the authority of Martinus's text (or perhaps because writers thought it risky to Germanize the popess!).[55] Later, many authors resolved the contradiction by respecting Martinus's terminology but eliminating one geographical indication or the other: Joan was English for Tolomeo da Lucca, Antoninus of Florence, and Jean Rioche; she was from Mainz in the *Eulogium historiarum* and for Dietrich of Nieheim.

The precise date ascribed to Joan in Martinus called for her inclusion, with name and number, among the popes, but Martinus himself stated that the popess did not figure in the catalog of popes (which was what explained her absence in earlier documents). Martinus calls her "Johannes" (John), a name that corresponds to the institutional, masculine-neuter nature of the personage. Catholic tradition retained that name, and it was feminized as "Johanna" or "Johanessa" only in the lay and romanesque versions of her story that we will turn to in chapter 5. The only writers who were exceptions to this rule were Wycliffe, who speaks of "Anna," and Jan Hus, who calls the popess "Agnes." These exceptions reflect a pre-Reformation rejection of the Catholic model. We shall return to the topic. Let me note in passing a comment made by Robert-Henri Bautier: "If there are texts that call [the popess] Anna or Agnes, this should be seen in relation to the deformation that occurred, under similar conditions, concerning Anne of Kiev, queen of France: for certain chroniclers of the eleventh century 'Anna' became 'Agnès,' and for others 'Johanna.'"[56] For Catholic chroniclers, however, Joan remained Johannes, the woman pope.

Joan was soon promoted to full nominal status: Tolomeo da Lucca, a Dominican, a late disciple and continuator of St. Thomas Aquinas, and a respected scholar, wrote of her in his *Ecclesiastical History* (ca. 1312), giving her the title of "John VIII" and placing her 107th in the papal succession.

He gives a close paraphrase of the narrative of his fellow Dominican, Martinus.[57] Bartolomé Carranza and Jean Rioche retained "John VIII," but another tradition preferred "John VII" for the popess. She is presented thus in the *Eulogium historiarum* (1366), an anonymous English chronicle, and in Platina's *History of the Popes* (1472). Placing Joan among the "Johns" did not pose any great historiographical problem: all that was needed was to conflate two previous Johns (stating that the return of an exiled pope had created the confusion), or to eliminate a doubtful or schismatic John. Even now, although contemporary scholarship is categorical about the Johns, it hesitates over the Stephens, giving dual numbers such as "Stephen III/IV." Joan's integration into the list of popes was not universally recognized, and there were many authors who refused to assign her a name or a number. For instance, in his *Chronik* (1340) Johannes of Winterthur, a Franciscan, lists 197 popes who preceded Gregory X, "Linus and Cletus excepted, as well as a woman who is not counted."[58]

This effort to achieve historical coherence was accompanied by a search for confirmation through supporting references. Martinus showed the way (if the pun may be pardoned) by presenting the detour taken by papal processions through Rome as a lasting trace of Joan. Chroniclers constantly repeated this information, and it was confirmed in ritual until the reconfiguration of the streets that lead to the Lateran. When Urban V attempted (unsuccessfully) to return the papacy to Rome from Avignon in 1368, he quite naturally refused to take the detour, not so much to deny Joan's reality, but rather to deny the need to commemorate her in Rome, which he wanted to reestablish in its primitive purity after the many years in Avignon. The *Life of Urban* states:

> From there [the Lateran], he returned to the palace [of the Vatican] peacefully and tranquilly, riding through the city and following the most direct route, without changing direction here and there, even in relation to that mad woman who is said to have occupied the papacy one day and to have given birth to her runt in that same street; such a detour, it is said, was sometimes taken by some of his predecessors.[59]

In reality, Martinus's text did as much to establish the detour as did physical disposition of the streets around San Clemente. The papal Master of Ceremonies, Johann Burchard, states in his journal that in 1486 he attempted to eliminate the commemorative detour for a procession led by Innocent VIII. He had the support of the bishop of Pienza, but he met with a vehement, angry reaction from Rinaldo Orsini, the archbishop of Florence.[60]

Martinus's readers complemented his account by noting the existence of the marble statue (Jacopo da Voragine around 1295, Siegfried of Balhusen around 1304, etc.); Dietrich of Nieheim noted that the statue was still standing in his day *(adhuc)*, and Martin Luther claimed (in his *Tischreden*) that he saw it during his trip to Rome in 1510. Dietrich of Nieheim offers an additional referential proof, stating in his *Chronicle of the German Emperors* that the story of Joan was a gloss on the Greek school of Rome, where St. Augustine and Joan were supposed to have taught.[61]

THE SIX Ps AND NEGLECT OF THE FRANCISCAN TRADITION

Supporting references disappear fairly quickly from the literature on Joan. This absence deserves careful examination, because it will put us on the track of a total reinterpretation of the clerical history of Joan.

First Jean de Mailly, then Etienne de Bourbon, who had read Jean, mentioned a stone that bore an inscription with six initial Ps commemorating the popess's childbirth. Martinus, who had in turn read Etienne, did not choose to include this memorial in his narrative, which means that the detail had every chance of disappearing, given that Martinus "replaced" and perfected Etienne's version within the Dominican network. As we have seen, the detail reappeared around 1260 in a Franciscan version of the popess's story (hence independent of the Dominican tradition) in an anonymous chronicle written in Erfurt:

> There was still another pseudopope, whose name and dates of
> rule are unknown. In fact it was a woman, according to what the
> Romans say, of great beauty and considerable learning and, be-
> neath a deceitful appearance, of perfect conduct. She hid under a
> male habit until she had been elected pope. And during her pa-
> pacy she conceived, and when she was pregnant, the demon re-
> vealed the fact to everyone publicly in a consistory by launching
> at the pope the phrase: *Papa, Pater Patrum, Papisse Pandito Partum*
> (Pope, Father of the Fathers, Publish the Parturition of the
> Popess).[62]

Although this version of the episode was roughly as fully elaborated as Jean de Mailly's account, its chances for wide diffusion were less. The Dominicans, whose network circulated the versions of Etienne de Bourbon and Martinus Polonus (1260, 1280), soon outstripped the Franciscans, who were less well equipped for the diffusion of texts.

The only known repetition of the Erfurt version of the story of Joan occurred in the *Compendium historiarum* of Siegfried of Balhusen (or of

Meissen), who copied the Erfurt passage around 1304, adding a mention of the marble statue that gives fuller detail than in Jacopo da Voragine: "Since then, they show in Rome, on a square in the city, a figure *(symulacrum)* in pontifical robes sculpted on a marble slab, with an image of a child."[63] Siegfried, a fairly obscure author, was a priest, not a Franciscan, and he probably borrowed from the Erfurt text because he was unaware of Martinus Polonus's chronicle. Moreover, Erfurt, in Thuringia, was not far from his natal Meissen, and the two areas had both been part of the margravate of the Wettin family in the thirteenth century, which may have had something to do with his choice of source.

The Dominicans did not totally obliterate the Franciscan tradition, however. In 1290 a Franciscan chronicle, the *Flores temporum* (Flowers of the Times), widely circulated in Germany and continued by several hands,[64] reproduced Martinus's narrative almost textually. Ten years earlier, the *Flores* might have played the same role as Martinus in circulating the Joan story; after Martinus, writers felt obliged to follow the tradition that had become canonical. The anonymous author of the *Flores* adds to his borrowed passage on Joan a quotation of the phrase with six Ps, following the Erfurt version but completing and refining it. He repeats the passage, including the devil's challenge, but he gives it a different setting: "She was made pregnant by the lover of whom we have spoken; she then interrogated the demoniacal one, begging him to say when it would please the demon to withdraw from her. The devil answered in these words: 'Pope, father of the fathers, publish the parturition of the popess / And I will tell you when I will withdraw from your body.'"[65]

Beyond the problem of textual filiation, this episode is interesting because it brings us back to the mysterious six Ps that accompanied Joan from her first appearance in the world of texts. We need to pause over it for a moment, calling on the definition of the three levels of the existence of a text proposed by Jean Molino and Jean-Jacques Nattiez:[66] the neutral level (the level of the immanent existence of the text); the level of poetics (the level of the fabrication of the text); and the aesthetic level (the level of the reception of the text).

THE FORMULARY TEXT

In itself, the phrase with six Ps is presented as a mnemonic device: the listener retains the forceful phonic pattern and the overall theme associated with it (a pope gave birth). We are close to the model analyzed by Albert Bates Lord and Jean Rychner in connection with the oral epic narrative, in which a rhythmic and phonic matrix is transmitted without establishing any lexical or semantic detail.[67] Our authors are sensitive to rhythm; what is more: they speak of lines of verse, verses (in the biblical sense), or versification *(versiculus; versus; versifice)*. Thus two concomitant texts (ca. 1255; 1260) that appeared in Metz and in Erfurt find different ways *(Petre/Papa; Prodito/Pandito)* to render the same phonetic and thematic pattern, which had probably been transmitted orally from Rome to the far reaches of Europe. The formula then became associated with a cry of alarm: *Require* (to be verified); *Fuit et alius pseudopapa* (there was yet another pseudopope). But the continuators went beyond the stage of astonishment to moralization: Etienne de Bourbon, by charging the phrase with conjuring away danger rather than denouncing misdeeds, and the *Flores*, by revealing an implicit pact made with the devil. At a third stage (with Martinus), the formula disappears. When the story is integrated into history, its terrifying auditory recall is no longer needed. The cry becomes text; memory attaches to chronology rather than to a phonic and thematic structure.

FABRICATING THE FORMULA

Let us attempt (following Nattiez's level of poetics) to return to the source of the fabrication of the six-P phrase that appeared here and there in Lorraine and Thuringia. There is no direct documentary evidence of how it first arose. Ignaz von Döllinger applied his ingeniously philological mind to the problem and proposed a possible reconstitution of the process. His point of departure is a model attested in a medieval chronicle, which states that an inscription was found in Rome that read "R.R.R.F.F.F," deciphered by modern scholarship as *Ruderibus Rejectis Rufus Festus Fieri Fecit* (After having swept away some ruins, Rufus Festus had [this construction] built). The medieval inhabitants of Rome, sensitive to prophetic signs, interpreted the initials as a terrible pronouncement of the ancient Sibyl: *Roma Ruet Romuli Ferro Flammaque Fameque* (Rome will collapse by the sword of Romulus [and by] flame and famine). This model, applied to the six-P inscription, suggests a possible primitive text from late antiquity: a worshiper of Mithra commemorated a donation with a stone inscription: *Propria Pecunia Posuit* (with his own money has offered) *Patri Patrum* (to the Father of Fathers [a title for the officiant of the mysteries of Mithra]) *P* (the initial of the unknown donor's name).[68]

Döllinger's reconstruction seems fairly convincing, although we might reproach him with designating as the "author" of the formula regarding the event in 1250 (?) a subject (the people of Rome?) incapable of reading an authentic text and being fooled by it. Döllinger is anticipating Cesare D'Onofrio here. When D'Onofrio speaks of the rite of verification, he supposes the existence of both a primitive "text" (in which the pope is the mother of the community of the faithful) and an ignorant and literal-minded decipherer who draws the conclusion that the pope has given birth. The philological spirit implies a general entropy of meaning, which can only degenerate.

The explanation proposed in the preceding chapter is perhaps not very different from Döllinger's. It suggested a satirical reading of an ancient inscription that was infused with the spirit of a carnivalesque challenge to the papacy when it dealt with a solemn reuse of ancient materials and inscriptions, vehicles of an overwhelming opacity. That same explanation also leads to rejecting a timeless binary scheme (primitive and authentic text; naive decipherment) in favor of the model proposed by Christian Jouhaud of contemporary, partial, and hierarchical but convergent readings that include an initial text, learned reuse, authoritarian nonscholarly reuse, satirical scholarly decipherment, satirical nonscholarly decipherment, and erroneous reading.[69] Such concurrent readings would operate together to construct a symbolic system figured by the popess.

If we look at the narrative content of the formula rather than its form as an epigraph, we can hope to return it to other possible places of production. We have seen that Franciscan versions place the formula in the mouth of the devil: in the Erfurt chronicle as in later chronicles (the *Chronicle of Saint-Gilles* and Engelhusen's *Chronicon*),[70] the phrase was a cry of triumph from the devil. This is even clearer in the *Chronicle* of the Abbey of Kempten, in Bavaria, where the formula is translated into German without any attempt to respect the phonetic repetition of the six Ps: "O du papst der du solt senn ein Vater unter allen andern Vatern nie du wirst offenbahren in deiner Geburt dass . . ." (O you, Pope, who should be a father above all other fathers, you will reveal by your childbirth), and the text continues: "that you are a popess, and that thus I am going to carry you away with your soul and your body and take you home with me and into my society."[71]

The supernatural interpretation of the event attaches to the Virgin in the chronicle of Heinrich von München. Here Joan, passing before the church of San Clemente, addresses an *Ave Maria* to an effigy of the Virgin Mary painted on the outside wall of the church. The painting responds, telling Joan that because she has put herself above women, her body and its fruit will be accursed: "Du pist gesegen ueber allens weib de sprach daz pild so sei dein Leib verfluocht under allen weiben die suend solt du niht mer treiben."[72] Heinrich von München, an author who is unfortunately unknown, uses the Franciscan *Flores* (as can be seen from the duration of Joan's papacy, three years, five months, and two days, as in the *Flores*), but he introduces a new source for the sanction against Joan (the Virgin) and a new definition of her crime (raising herself above the female condition). This sort of supernatural punishment, signaled by a miraculous utterance, may mark the emergence within clerical discourse of fragments of "popular" culture. The fact that the Franciscans gave a more "popular," less "Roman" treatment of the narrative than the Dominicans had done might thus reflect the genuinely popular orientation of the Order founded by St. Francis. This hypothesis finds confirmation in the development of the narrative itself: in the 1290 *Flores* the six-P formula draws meaning from an implicit pact between Joan and Satan in which Joan wins salvation in exchange for public exposure of her misdeed. In this interpretation the childbirth simultaneously signifies the devil's triumph (in public exposure of her fault) and his loss of a hold on Joan. In the Catalan version of the *Alphabet of Tales* of Arnoldus of Liège (and the Franciscans had an enormous influence in Catalonia), the image of the Virgin gives Joan a choice between immediate punishment (public exposure of her sin, followed by death) and celestial punishment (eternal damnation). The universe of tales contains countless examples of this schema of a choice between immediate but temporary suffering and delayed but irrevocable damnation, which was a narrative transcription of choices to be made among the major categories of existential investments.[73] This would explain the exceptional success of the Joan narrative in southern Germany: in theory, this episode in Church history coincided with and absorbed a current form of popular narration that centered on the theme of the unlimited ambition of women (Heinrich von München) and that used the device of a choice between immediate danger and a promising future.

Although we cannot totally exclude this hypothesis, it has limitations. Like philology, folklore postulates a collective and intemporal subject (the people, who are no longer ignorant and serve as narrator) by a simple reversal of the mechanism of diffusion in which it is the Church that becomes the unwitting and distorting mirror of an authentic primitive text.

The odd particularity of the Franciscan tradition, however, incites us to move from the production of the formula to its reception and to give up the uncertain quest for the "original" meaning of the formula in favor of its adventitious, historically identifiable meaning. This means that the detour of a methodical analysis of the six-P formula has brought us back to the principle of ideological profit that we rejected at the beginning of this chapter. We are constrained to do so by the limitations of a strictly immanent and cultural analysis of the diffusion of the Joan narrative. That sort of analysis told us how, by means of what narrative modes, and by what combination of chance and necessity *a* legend could spread within clerical discourse, but it fails to tell us why this legend spread.

THE FRANCISCANS AND THE PSEUDOPOPE

A rereading of what the Franciscan chronicle from Erfurt tells us about Joan shows that its author had no more information available to him than Jean de Mailly had at the same period (1255–60), but also that the Erfurt chronicler lacked Jean's dominating curiosity and his insistence on verification *(Require)*. The Franciscan author is moved by fear: the devil, who pronounces the six-P formula, has appeared within the Curia and speaks to the pope. The phonic structure of the formula signals the satanic nature of its message, recalling the repeated Rs that, according to St. Louis, rasp the throat of the Christian and "stand for the devil's rakes."[74] The Erfurt chronicler, unlike Jean de Mailly, confidently proclaims, "There was yet another pseudopope." This is an astonishing statement: for Martinus Polonus, Joan was not a pseudopope, but a pope illegitimately elected; it was up to the jurists to determine her status. Indeed, even at the end of the Middle Ages it was a delicate problem that Cardinal Domenico Giacobazzi found it impossible to resolve, as we have seen. The chroniclers who followed Tolomeo da Lucca in calling the popess John VII or John VIII decided that Joan had been a real pope.

For a Franciscan in 1260 the term "pseudopope" had a weighty and specific meaning. It needs to be clarified, even at the cost of yet another detour (but Joan is the Roman patron of detours!).

In the early thirteenth century Francis had no intention of creating a new institution; rather, he wanted to convert the whole of society to the authentic message of the poor Christ. His *Testament* demanded that his initial intent be respected: he required of the Friars Minor absolute obedience to the Rule, which meant strict observance of poverty and rejection of all privilege. Until his fall from papal grace in 1239, Brother Elias of Cortona also insisted on respect of the spirit of Francis's *Testament*. From Gregory IX to John XXII, however, the papacy repeatedly attempted to integrate this anomic Order into the Church structure by encouraging tendencies within the Order that favored compromise (like-minded friars were called Conventual Franciscans). It is important to appreciate fully the broad attraction that the "fundamentalist" segment of the Franciscans (at first called *zelanti*; later known as Spiritual Franciscans) exerted over Christendom. By affirming its loyalty to Francis and to the poverty of Christ, that "zealous" fraction crystalized the immense eschatological and reformist aspirations of the faithful. Papal policy from 1230 to 1330 seems to have fluctuated regarding the Franciscans, not only because policy varied with the spiritual choices of each pope, but also because political and ecclesiological shifts within the Church brought to prominence configurations that also changed constantly. The Franciscan purists, the *zelanti*, represented a threat to the institution of the Church because they encouraged a simmering urban heresy. On the other hand, the Franciscan Order, by its discipline, by its centralization, and by its direct dependence on Rome (reinforced by the bull *Ordinem vestrum* of Innocent IV in 1245 and the bull *Quanto Studiosius* of Alexander IV in 1247) offered the Church a precious ally in its struggle against the centrifugal claims of national churches, the bishops, the university masters, and the cardinals of the Curia. It is understandable that the popes' shifting policies aroused genuine perplexity among the Spirituals, who were inclined to see changeable papal policies as dictated either by the Holy Spirit or by the Evil One. Defending their "state" (which amounted to a defense of Francis's *Testament*) became an obsession with them, because they were totally persuaded that they were defending the salvation of the Church and that their "state" embodied Christian perfection. One Spiritual Franciscan declared in a eulogy of "the perfection of the state of the Friars Minor" that "this state" was "more arduous, more perfect, and more essential to the existence and perfection of the church" than that of the bishops; it was "more perfect and more meritorious" than even the papal "state."[75]

Between 1254 and 1260 (when Joan's story was elaborated in clerical discourse), the tension between the papacy and the mendicant Orders was at its height. The papacy had constantly supported the Orders' independence from the bishops concerning preaching and hearing confession (which were considerable sources of prestige, authority, and revenues), but pressure from the bishops obliged Innocent IV to restrict that liberty in a bull, *Etsi animarum* (1254). Innocent died only a few days after the promulgation of the bull, which some Franciscans viewed as proof of heaven's wrath or of satanic influence over the pontiff. Innocent IV's successor, Alexander IV, annulled the bull, but the Franciscans continued to live under a threat. The Council of Lyon (1274) suppressed all the new Orders except the Franciscans and the Dominicans, with the Carmelites and the Augustinians obtaining only a provisory continuance. The papacy continued to be a genuine threat.

During that same year, 1254, the mendicant Orders (that is, the Franciscans and the Dominicans) were attacked from another quarter: the secular masters of the University of Paris, who chafed at the favorable position accorded to mendicant masters who enjoyed the freedom of regular clergy, privileges as university scholars, and the prestige attached to the great doctors of the age, Thomas Aquinas, Bonaventura, and Albertus Magnus.

The details of that skirmish would not concern us if William of Saint-Amour, the Paris master who headed the attack, had not singled out the Spiritual Franciscan Gerardo da Borgo San Donnino, the author (in 1254, decidedly a year of coincidences for the Friars Minor) of an *Introduction to the Eternal Gospel.* This work was a systematic rearrangement of the prophecies of Joachim of Fiore predicting the end of time in the year 1260. The Middle Ages had known many other eschatological deadlines, both before and after the thirteenth century,[76] but no prophetic author had made as strong an impression on the faithful as Joachim. His work, which the Franciscans circulated massively, completed, and commented on, was part of a complex and coherent exegetical system that Joachim based in his vast theological culture. His perception of the immanence of the Last Times took on a special meaning in an age whose best minds were imbued with the principles of a historical economy of salvation that had been put in place, as Father Chenu has shown, in the twelfth century.[77] Brian Tierney notes that around 1250 historical ecclesiology became an integral part of theology.[78] Gerardo da Borgo San Donnino's treatise presented the Franciscans as the apostles of the imminent reign of the Holy Spirit; the writings and the Rule of Francis constituted a third Testament, the Testament of the Holy Spirit; Francis took on the role of the Angel of the sixth seal of the Apocalypse.

William of Saint-Amour responded to Gerardo's treatise in 1254, the very year of its publication. His *De periculis novissimorum temporum* (On the Dangers of Urgent Times) mocked the Franciscans' fears and eschatological enthusiasm, presenting these as the real dangers of the age. The attacks of the masters of Paris came to naught in 1257, thanks to Alexander IV's energetic support of the Franciscans and his reinforcement of their position at the University with the bull *Quasi lignum vitae,* but the decisive year of 1254 had shown the Spirituals that the external Church could be headed by a malevolent pope (Innocent IV) just as easily as by a spiritual one (Alexander IV). That distinction fitted in with Joachimite-Franciscan prophecies that declared that the arrival of the Last Times would be preceded by the reigns of a pseudopope and an angelic pope. Somewhat later, Peter of John Olivi (1248–98), with Angelo Clareno and Ubertino da Casale, among the prime movers of the Spiritual movement, connected the eschatological announcement with current ecclesiology: A mystical Antichrist would appear, and when he did, "a prince of the house of Frederick" would "establish as pseudopope a certain false religious who will plot against the evangelical rule" and impose a false *(dolosam)* dispensation.[79] "Dispensation" refers to the Franciscans' vow of absolute poverty, constantly eroded by the popes since the bull *Quam elongati* promulgated by Gregory IX in 1231.

The Erfurt chronicle (ca. 1260) thus appears to transcribe a genuine fear that a pseudopope might usurp the Holy See. The narrator does not doubt the existence of the female pseudopope, questioning only the accuracy of her date of reign, which affected eschatological computation. The brief note in the Franciscan text insists on an opposition between appearances and reality (*latuit*, "he hid," as opposed to *publice*, "publicly"; *in ypocrisi magne vite*, "and under the deceptive appearance of perfect conduct"). The six-P formula crystalizes that opposition; it commands the pope (*papa*, the neuter, institutional form) to reveal the childbirth of the popess (*papessa*, the same individual, but a satanic, female reality). In this terror-stricken version, the devil denounces more than he mocks; he splits the pseudopope into two, a pope and a popess, as a way to contaminate the one by the other. The version of the *Flores temporum*, interpreted above as folklore, also (and especially) develops the message of the triumph of Satan within the Church: the diabolical possession of Joan's body is part of the devil's plan; the Evil One has invaded her body in order to publicize his triumph.

This interpretation differs notably from the Dominican version: the stone inscription (which is not satanic) is addressed to St. Peter, who is taken as a motherlike, eternal figure; like a rock he cannot be shaken by one deplorable incident. The inscription urgently invites to vigilance, as Etienne de Bourbon makes clear. The formulaic text, written on stone and in Peter (following the play on the words *petra* and *Petros* that Jesus himself initiated) asserts the solidity of the papacy, come what may.

Still, in spite of the strength of the Dominicans' network of preachers and their efforts to neutralize the story of Joan, they failed to obliterate one capital aspect of the secret life of the popess, and Joan's adventure, as it was told around 1260, served as a dress rehearsal for the great shadow play of the Franciscans, which was promised a great future and lasted until the 1330s.

THE ANGELIC POPE AND THE PSEUDOPOPE: THINGS COALESCE IN 1294

An extremely important event occurred in 1294, giving a new meaning to Joan's case after Martinus Polonus's juristic interpretation, but also giving a new shape to the pairing of the pseudopope and the angelic pope.

In 1294 the Holy See had remained vacant for twenty-seven months.

The cardinals, gathered in conclave, were unable to agree on a pope from among their number, so they elected the eighty-five-year-old Pietro da Morrone, a Benedictine from the Abruzzi, the founder of a hermit colony, and a man who had lived in retirement from the world for eight years. Christendom, after years of debate about poverty, put at its head Celestine V, the man who best embodied a return to the letter of Christ's message, but also the least skilled administrator imaginable. The crafty, somewhat devious Cardinal Benedetto Caetani swiftly obtained the pope's abdication, and on 13 December of the same year he himself succeeded Celestine, taking the name Boniface VIII. The event aroused intense anxiety within Christianity: could a pope, designated by the Holy Spirit, abdicate? What was one to do about a pope who proved inadequate to the task but had been elected following all the proper canonical procedures (also the case with Joan)? Celestine V soon came to be called "the angelic pope," which ineluctably led to Boniface VIII being identified as the "pseudo-pope" of prophecy who used trickery to dislodge the angelic pope. Jacopone da Todi did in fact call Boniface *pseudopresul*.[80]

The tumultuous succession of two such opposite popes provided a concrete paradigm (the prelate *vs.* the hermit; authority *vs.* humility, etc.) that forced many to take sides. To be sure, there were also many of the faithful who did not participate in this search for the "bad" pope (be he Celestine or Boniface). Jacopo da Voragine, in his *Chronicle of Genoa*, a work written not long after the event, takes an institutional position, recognizing both the merits and the inadequacies of Celestine V.[81] Bohemond, bishop of Trier, illustrates that same position in his episcopal *Gesta* by comparing the paired popes, Celestine and Boniface, first to Mary and Martha, then to Rachel and Leah. Pairs of biblical women were often cited in the Middle Ages to demonstrate that industrious activity (Martha, Leah), which was ungrateful but necessary, formed the essential complement to illuminated but inactive meditation.[82] We cannot but admire, in passing, Bohemond's subtle and intricate use of the biblical narrative. In Genesis, Jacob wants to marry the beautiful Rachel, not her sister Leah, but Laban, the father of the two sisters, substitutes Leah for Rachel by trickery. Thus the role of Boniface-Leah (the fertile servant without grace) is justified, but the comparison also suggests that trickery was used to harm Celestine-Rachel. On the one hand, the substitution of one woman for another was part of the divine plan; on the other hand, it did not prevent Jacob from eventually marrying Rachel, a union that proved belatedly fertile and brought new hopes. Bohemond's dizzying "dialogic" virtuosity should dissuade us from any pronouncements on the claimed sterility of the commonplace in the Middle Ages.[83]

The Franciscan idea of the pseudopope had made sufficient headway in the Church to induce commentators to classify popes into the good and the bad. Arnoldus of Liège, in the compact style of an author of exempla, notes *bonus papa* (good pope) in preface to an episode in the life of Gregory the Great. Evaluating the popes had become part of ecclesiastical mores.

By an odd twist of history, however, the most eminent of the Spiritual Franciscans, Peter of John Olivi, supported Boniface VIII as a true pope.[84] This support, which ran counter to the Spirituals' principles, can probably be explained by a radical conception of papal infallibility, to which we shall return. Olivi might also have been moved by tactical considerations, because at the beginning of his pontificate Boniface VIII had championed the Spirituals' cause; in 1290, before he himself became pope, Nicholas IV, the Franciscan pope, had delegated the then Cardinal Caetani to defend the cause of the friars in Paris. Most of the Dominicans were ranged against Boniface VIII, however. Influential Preachers such as Jean Quidort (Jean de Paris), the author of a formidable treatise attacking Boniface VIII and the hierocratic claims that he pressed against the king of France, Philip IV (Philippe le Bel),[85] were more apt to back limitations on the growing power of a papacy that they needed less than the Franciscans did. The Dominicans of the house of Saint-Jacques in Paris supported Philip in his fulminations against Boniface. The nearly spiritualist (or at least reformist) tendencies of certain Dominicans (tendencies that were less pronounced than among the Franciscans, however) had not been the target of papal attacks, and this group displayed a certain sensitivity toward the austere image of the hermit-pope from the Abruzzi. Robert d'Uzès, one of the first witnesses to the rite of the verification of the pope's manhood, connected his terrible visions to the events of 1294. In his thirty-second vision, "On the carrying off and despoilment of a sovereign pope," he gives an interpretation of somber scenes of violence and adds, "After that, and after several days had passed, we learned that the lord pope Celestine had renounced the papacy and had once again become a hermit; several days later, we learned that Benedetto had been elected pope."[86]

The possible parallel between Joan and Boniface, two clever usurpers, appears in Leone da Orvieto as well. We know little about Leone apart from his modest career in the Order of Preachers as reader and subprior at Orvieto from 1287 to 1295, visitor of the Dominican houses of Tuscany in 1304, and prior at Tivoli, Cortona, and Arezzo (where he died in 1315). He probably took little part in the struggles in Italy between Boniface and the Colonna cardinals, but in his *Chronicle of the Times and Acts of the Ro-*

man Pontiffs, into which he copied Martinus's entry on Joan, he relates the papacy of Celestine thus:

> He attempted to reduce the cardinals to their former status; all the cardinals were to ride simple donkeys. That is why one of the cardinals, who was named master Benedetto Caetani, a man artful in all domains and filled with malice, sent children up to the roof of the house in which the pope was sleeping. They called to the pope and said to him that he was in a dangerous state, about to lose his soul, and that the only way he could save it was by abdicating. The pontiff, hearing these voices, thought they came from angels, and after having consulted with the cardinals, he abdicated, and master Benedetto Caetani, the inventor of this trick, was elected to the supreme papacy.[87]

This anecdote combines the angelic, innocent character of the good Pope Celestine and the ambitious, deceitful ruse of the man who, thanks to angelic disguise, obtained the papacy.

Beyond the antagonism between the Franciscans and the Dominicans, and beyond the struggles between priesthood and royalty, the pressure put on Celestine V and the imprisonment of Boniface VIII at Anagni in 1303 that brought his papacy to a violent end seriously shook the papacy. On both sides, the Bonifacian and the Celestinian, the argument of guaranteeing the salvation of the Church was used to justify putting an end to a papacy. Whether Joan was seen as the prototype of a pope illegitimately installed through ambitious trickery or as an example of a pope harmful to the good administration of the Church, she served all causes. The gap through which Joan slipped was to broaden into a full-fledged schism some seventy-five years later.

JOAN, PATRONESS OF PAPAL INFALLIBILITY

Joan's career does not stop here, and by a prodigious paradox, the popess contributed to creating the notion of papal infallibility. Brian Tierney has brilliantly analyzed the mechanism of that ideological construction, and we shall follow him, but still keeping an eye on Joan.[88]

The Spiritual Franciscans believed, above all else, in Francis's insistence on absolute poverty, the key to their eschatological role. Beginning in 1231, they had been obliged to resist accommodations gradually imposed on them by the papacy and by the Conventual branch of the Order. St. Bonaventura (1221–74) attempted to reconcile the *zelanti* and the

Conventuals by writing a watered-down *Life of Francis*, freely glossing his Rule and persuading the chapter at Narbonne (1260) to approve the *usus pauper*, or moderate use of possessions. This compromise position proved impossible to maintain after Bonaventura's death in 1274, when the Conventuals challenged the doctrine of poverty itself.

In reaction, Nicholas III (1277–80) promulgated the bull *Exiit qui seminat* (1279), which imposed a return to both the spirit and the letter of Francis's *Testament*. The Spirituals were deeply grateful to him, perceiving his act as the result of divine inspiration. Peter of John Olivi attempted to place Nicholas's text within an untouchable, sacred tradition by asserting that the pope, as the heir of Jesus and of Peter, could not err in matters of faith. Thus Olivi brought a radical solution to the old, ceaselessly debated problem of defining the limits of matters of faith: Should the Christian consider that matters of faith resided only in Scripture, or in Scripture and Tradition? In the latter case, what should be included in Tradition? Was it made up of the writings of the Fathers and/or the early conciliar texts? And/or papal doctrine? The Spiritual Franciscans resolutely added the doctrinal work of the popes to this list, thus producing the first affirmation of papal infallibility. The bull *Exiit qui seminat* was not merely a praiseworthy text; it was absolutely sanctified by infallibility. But if this were the case, how could one condemn the positions of the successors of Nicholas III who challenged (or who might challenge) either the bull or the status of the Order? The way out of this dilemma was to return to the eschatology of the 1250s: any pope hostile to that status declared himself a pseudopope, *ipso dicto*. By divine right, the universal Church and its leader, the pope, could never be mistaken. In fact, however, a pseudopope, a pseudocouncil, a pseudo-Curia, or a pseudo-Church could obliterate the sanctified life of the true Church, which, according to Peter of John Olivi, could never disappear, though it could be reduced to a handful of the faithful, even to a few women and children.

This startling theological and ecclesiological construction (which should not be taken as a mere trick of argumentation) clearly appears, and in relation to Joan, in the work of William of Ockham. Ockham, arguably the greatest philosopher of the fourteenth century, was born at the end of the thirteenth century in Surrey. He entered the Franciscan Order at an early age and studied at Oxford in 1312 and again in 1318. His commentary at Oxford on Peter Lombard's *Sentences* (1318–20) caused him difficulties that gave his career a new direction: the Curia called him to Avignon to explain himself on some theological positions that seemed suspect. He went there in 1324, and stayed for four years. There he met Michael of Cesena, the general of the Franciscan Order, who had also been summoned on suspicion of heresy. The question of poverty had, in fact, reemerged in dramatic fashion. Although Clement V (1305–14) supported Ubertino da Casale, he had attempted to update Bonaventura's gestures of reconciliation by justifying a moderate use of possessions in his bull *Exivi de paradisio* (1312). John XXII, elected in 1316, was a strict canonist with mystical tendencies who at first seemed moderately favorable to the Spirituals, but he soon became irritated by their extremism, and in 1317 he demanded, in the bull *Quorumdam exigit*, that they submit to the Conventuals. Four Spiritual Franciscans were burned in 1318. Ubertino da Casale left the order, and Angelo Clareno and his disciples, the *fraticelli*, took refuge in the mountains of central Italy. Resistance continued, however, and the general administrator of the Order, Michael of Cesena, who had started out as a Conventual, passed over to the Spirituals. John XXII decided to have done with this cycle of compromise and condemnation, and he put an end to the debate in 1322 with the bull *Quia nonnumquam*, in which he demonstrated that Christ and the apostles had had personal possessions. The Franciscans, gathered in a chapter general at Perugia that same year, explicitly contradicted John XXII, who, like a good administrator, replied with the bull *Ad conditorum canonum* (1322), in which he eliminated the juridical fiction of papal ownership of the Franciscans' possessions. Henceforth the Order was, de facto, the possessor of such goods. The pope then delivered a statement on the theological basis of the debate with the bull *Cum inter nonnulos* (1323). Michael of Cesena, who had come to Avignon to explain his conduct, accused the pope of heresy and fled from there with William of Ockham on 26 March 1328. The two Franciscans then went to Munich to the court of Louis of Bavaria, where they met Marsilius of Padua, a resolute opponent of the Avignon pope. While he was in Munich Ockham write a series of libels against John XXII, and he died in that city in 1350.[89]

In 1332 Ockham wrote the *Opus nonaginta dierum* (or Work of Ninety Days, so called because it took him ninety days to write it). This treatise is an immense commentary (more than a thousand printed pages in modern editions) on the bull *Quia vir reprobus* (1329), aimed at Michael of Cesena and his companions. In the 124th and last chapter of his treatise, Ockham finally arrives at a discussion of the bull that declared the Spirituals to be heretics. Ockham turns the accusation back against the pope, painstakingly defining the crime of heresy as explicit, manifest, and repeated error. The pope's faults corresponded precisely to all those criteria. Thus it was necessary to appeal to Christianity at large and to avoid any contact with the pope, because any Christian who considered John XXII to be pope would himself be open to the accusation of heresy. William states:

And concerning what precedes, the accusers [*impugnatores,* the as-
sailants, that is, the true Christians; the Spirituals] conclude that
the accused [*impugnatus;* John XXII, who is never referred to in
other terms throughout the treatise] must be avoided *(vitandus)* for
the necessity of salvation, by all those who know that he is a
heretic. But those who do not know that he is a heretic, even if they
suffer from a crass and lazy ignorance, are in no way excused from
the gravest moral sin. Those who are unaware that he is a heretic, if
they suffer from a reasonable and invincible ignorance by reason
of ignorance of that fact, seem excused from communicating with
the accused and from obeying him. As to the question of avoiding
him or not, it is the same for the accused and for the woman who
was thought to have been a man and who was raised to the papacy.
Indeed, those who, afterward, knew that she was a woman should
not in any fashion hold her to be pope. But those who did not
know, and who suffered from an invincible ignorance, who presented her as pope, were excused by their ignorance for holding her
as a pope. The same is true of the accused, for he has no more true
authority than had that woman who, as the chronicles say, was
venerated as pope by the universal Church for two years, seven
months, and three days.[90]

Ockham thus enrolled Joan as a prototype for John XXII and as an image of a pseudopope capable of deluding people. John's lack of existence
in the Church (the true Church) was just as real and just as concealed as
Joan's existence. But this factual illusion, this confusion in meanings, by
no means leads to any certitude that the universal Church and the pope
(the true pope) could ever be mistaken:

And what if someone should say that such a thing [the real inexis-
tence of John XXII] could not happen because the universal
Church cannot err, the accusers respond that in the domain of
faith and custom, the Church cannot be mistaken, but in the
domain of fact, the Church militant can err and can be mistaken.
It was in this manner that it erred in venerating a woman as
pope.[91]

Ockham goes on to give other examples: Anastasius II, Sylvester II,
and in all twenty-seven popes had criminally deceived the Church. Joan
was his first and principal reference because, in her case, de facto ignorance could be proven very clearly, with no need to refer to any scale of
crimes or faults.

Ockham returned to the question ten years later, in his *Octo quaestiones de potestate Pape* (Eight Questions on the Power of the Pope; 1340–42). In chapter 17 of this work he shows that it is legitimate to bring the pope before justice and to appeal his decisions if he is guilty of heresy, because at that point the "pope" would no longer be part of the body of the Church: "Thus no heretic is the true head of the Church, even if it is thought that he is; similarly, the woman who was thought to be the pontiff for two years was not the true head of the Church, even though everyone thought that she was."[92]

Franciscan argumentation bore fruit well beyond the realm of spiritual subversion. The founding concept that gave structure to infallibility and imposture (and that can be found in a totally different context in czarist Russia of the sixteenth to the eighteenth centuries, brilliantly analyzed by Claudio Sergio Ingerflom)[93] found an immediate, pro-papal, and absolutist application in Guido Terreni, a Carmelite. A century later, in spite of the great shock of the Schism, two pillars of the monarchical papacy of the fifteenth century, Torquemada and Antoninus of Florence, picked up the Franciscan argument and used Joan to illustrate their point.

The famous Dominican cardinal, Tomás de Torquemada (1420–98) uses terms in his *Summa de Ecclesia* (Summa on the Church) that closely resemble the ones that Ockham had used in his *Eight Questions:* "Since it is established that one day a woman was held to be pope by the generality of the Catholics, it is not incredible that one day a heretic could be held to be pope, even though he is not the true pope *(verus papa).*"[94]

A bit earlier, at the beginning of the fifteenth century, St. Antoninus, the Dominican archbishop of Florence, had related the story of the popess in his *Chronica,* closely following the version of Martinus Polonus. Commenting on the popess according to the Ockhamite distinction between fact and faith, a distinction that had become of capital importance in the diffusion of the story of Joan, Antoninus states:

> But if the story is true, it bears no prejudice for salvation, for the Church in those times was not deprived of its head, which is Christ; He held it in the river of grace, and the ultimate effects of the sacraments that she [the popess] conferred were not lacking to those who accepted them devoutly from her, that is to say, from grace. To be sure, this woman, no more than other women, was not capable of bearing the mark of any sacred order, nor of conferring the eucharist; certainly she could not, de facto, perform ordination, nor absolve sins, therefore the faithful received nothing from her. Nonetheless, Christ compensated for grace in

the sacraments for those who received them worthily, and ignorance of the facts *(ignorantia facti)* excused them from sin.[95]

This distinction between fact and faith could lead to a separation between a work (which was inspired by the Holy Spirit) and its author (an
individual usurper who was physically present, but whose role was fulfilled by the Holy Spirit or by Christ). Thus Leone da Orvieto, after depicting Boniface VIII as a usurper and noting that he was malevolent, wily, full
of pride, avarice, and greed, could still declare that "he made the sixth
book of the *Decretals,* which contains many good and useful things."[96]
This suggests that Jean de Mailly's remark concerning the Fast of the Four
Times (a custom initiated by the popess and maintained in Catholic
liturgy) is perhaps a good illustration of this duality. Other authors attributed prefaces to the Mass to Joan: Martin Lefranc, the prevost of Lausanne
around 1450 and secretary to Popes Felix V (that is, the antipope, Amadeus VIII of Savoy) and Nicholas V, mentions Joan's liturgical activities
with approval in his poem *Le champion des dames.* Martin says:

> So let us leave the sins, saying
> That she was a learned clergywoman
> When before the most prideful
> Of Rome [she] had issue and entry.
> Moreover, there can be shown to you
> Many a preface that [she] dictated,
> Well ordered and in saintly fashion,
> Where in matters of faith she did not hesitate.[97]

JOAN AT THE FRONTIERS

Ockham and the Spirituals made no distinction between orthodoxy and
heresy, but instead offered the specter of continual evaluation. The most
ardent supporters of the papacy reduced errors of fact to a few isolated incidents, but for the Spirituals, such errors became increasingly frequent
with the approach of the Last Times. In the long run, all it took to turn
impostures into history, and to arrive at the heretical conclusion that the
apparent Church was a permanent lie and an obliteration of the true
Church, was to link those impostures. There was only a step from the
Bavarian schism to heretical secession, a step that Wycliffe took, dragging
the unfortunate Joan with him as a hostage.

Thirty years after Ockham, John Wycliffe (1330–84) had a destiny
similar to Ockham's, though with the essential difference that Wycliffe did
not enter the Franciscan Order. Both were trained at Oxford; both received

protection from an antipapal monarch (the king of England); both were condemned. Their ecclesiologies present traits in common: both were founded on an opposition between the apparent Church (Wycliffe called it the "visible" Church) and the real Church. But whereas for Ockham that opposition occurred within time and could be reduced to the period when the Church was headed by a pope like Nicholas III, for Wycliffe the two Churches were a perennial, hard reality. Above all, predestination made the role of the institution completely secondary. Where Ockham's nominalism permitted him to build a fine Catholic construction in which various planes of Church reality could be shifted to cover one another, integrating all Christian dogmas into them, Wycliffe's rough and summary realism led him, unhesitatingly, to separation, secession, a rejection of transubstantiation, and the harsh Reformation tautology that the Elect are the Elect. From Wycliffe on, the popess, whom he calls "Anna," stood as proof of the continuing decadence of the Roman Church. In 1382, in a brief work titled *Cruciata*, written to protest the crusade launched by Urban VI at the beginning of the Great Schism, Wycliffe relates the episode of the popess as a way of denying the Curia any spiritual power: "In the apocryphal chronicles it is commonly reported that the assembly of the cardinals was deceived concerning the sex of a pope when they elected as pope Anna, who was pregnant; whatever the case, it is certain that the assembled cardinals could be mistaken, to the point of electing as pope a demon who hated the memory of Christ and troubled the Church."[98] Wycliffe concludes, after citing the precedent of Judas, that only a man's acts authorize a "probable supposition" about his spiritual power. Ockham's Joan floated on the buoy of "fact," and Ockham, a fortunate Franciscan swimmer borne along by the current of the grace of Christ and the Church, could simply avoid her, as he "avoided" John XXII. Wycliffe's Anna attached her satanic ballast to the Church and sank it.

Jan Hus (1369–1415) further radicalized Wycliffe's position, completing the job of compromising our popess. He used the story of Joan, whom he calls Agnes, on several occasions. The last and most dramatic of these occurred in his defense, during his trial at Constance in 1415, according to the moving account of his disciple, Peter of Mladoňovice.[99] On 8 June 1415 the court examined the authenticity of certain propositions drawn from Hus's treatise *De Ecclesia*; according to the fourteenth article of accusation bearing on chapter 13 of that work, Hus was accused of claiming that the pope was simply the head of a particular church, unless he was predestined by God. Hus confirmed this stand, and supported it with this argument: "This is clear because otherwise the Christian faith would be perverted and a Christian would have to believe a lie. For the church was deceived in the case of Agnes." On the same day, when the first article of his treatise against Stanislas of Znojmo was being examined, Hus repeated his argument. Next he added, in response to questions about the fourth article:

> Nor is the doctor able to give a reason why the Church at the time of Agnes had been without a head for two years and five months, living on the part of many members in Christ's grace. Why cannot it in the same way be without a head for many years, when Christ without such monstrous heads, through His true disciples scattered over the circumference of the earth, would rule His Church better?

Hus made similar statements during the hearing of 18 June. On 6 July 1415, Jan Hus was burned at the stake.

The dangerous development of the Franciscan machinery, which contributed both to the installation of the notion of papal infallibility and to radical contestation of the sacred legitimacy of Rome, brings us to the crucial moment of the Great Schism (1378–1415). This was, however, when Joan played her role as a Catholic for the last time, a more modest role than she had played in the great Franciscan drama, for Joan the Catholic was content with the juridical (rather than ecclesiological) role that Martinus Polonus had created for her. At that time, when opposing camps of jurists competed to display their demonstrative virtuosity, the case of Joan had become valuable only as an illustration. In 1399, when the University of Paris suggested to the Oxford masters that they withdraw their obedience from the pope, basing their arguments on the cases of Anastasius II and Calixtus II, the Oxford masters replied that the law says what should be, not what is.[100] Let us follow Joan in this last stage in her clerical career.

JOAN IN THE SCHISM

On 7 April 1378, Bartolomeo Prignano was elected pope and took the name Urban VI. The conclave, divided, had long hesitated. The Roman people grew impatient; worried that the papal court might depart for Avignon, they demanded an Italian pope. They became threatening, and riots broke out. The conclave was terrified, to the point that the cardinals disguised the aged Cardinal Tebaldeschi as pope to gain time. Urban VI, elected in a climate of division and haste and in the absence of the powerful French cardinal, Jean de la Grange, displayed a rigor that soon alienated the Curia, which yearned to be rid of him and demanded that he step down. Urban refused. After Jean de la Grange had returned to Rome, he had Robert of Geneva elected pope under the name Clement VII. Since Clement was unable to occupy the Roman see, he moved to Avignon, thus bringing about the Great Schism. The Christian nations were divided between obedience to Urban or Clement, Rome or Avignon, but the shock seems to have been profound within Christian consciences as well. From 1378 to 1415, all Christendom endlessly debated questions of papal legitimacy and power. Joan was used in support of a variety of arguments: a popess served all the imaginable solutions to resolve an unbearable schism. Three ways, three means were suggested for achieving that end.

The first of these was the *via facti*, or the way of fact. At first, each faction thought that it could crush the other. That name for their war (the "fact" involved) by implication cited Joan's adventure in its Ockhamite version: an illegitimate pope was a matter of fact, not a matter of faith or mores. Before Martinus Polonus had Joan die in childbirth, Jean de Mailly and Etienne de Bourbon had presented her lapidation, without benefit of judgment by the people or the Church of Rome, as normal procedure.

The second way to resolve the schism was the *via cessionis*, cession, or persuading one or both popes to resign. In 1394 the court of France, which had imposed obedience to Pope Clement VII on the University of Paris, was persuaded by the University to seek a resolution of the crisis by withdrawing its support of the Avignon popes (Clement and his successor, Benedict XIII). This *subtractio obedience* (and Bernard Guenée suggests that the full import of the Latin term would be better rendered as a "refusal" of obedience)[101] resulted, on the practical level, in the deposition of popes who could not be persuaded to abdicate. This option claimed to be juridical.

The story of the woman pope bore two warnings: first, an election stained with illegality could be annulled; second, it was in the interest of the Church to take the lead and authorize deposition in case of scandal. The first argument had been raised as early as 1378, when the French cardinals stated that the election of Urban VI was invalid since it had been imposed by pressure from the Roman people and voted under the grip of fear (*timor* was a canonical case for annulling a decision).

Some years later (and before France abandoned the Avignon popes), Philippe de Mézières invoked Joan in *Le songe du Vieil Pèlerin* (ca. 1386) to support just that sort of argument. Philippe, formerly a councilor of Charles V and chancellor of Cyprus, devoted the last years of his life to piety and to writing that great work, which preached a general reform of Christianity, a revival of the crusades, and putting an end to the Schism. In book 1 of his *Songe*, the "Old Pilgrim," Ardent Desire, sets off under the escort of Good Hope to find Queen Truth in the farthest reaches of the

Egyptian desert so as to persuade her to return and remain among humanity. The queen agrees to test Christendom by traveling through the world to search for a place worthy of her lasting presence. This immense and vain quest carries her and her escort from the Indies to the Low Countries. Rome offers the travelers the spectacle of a parade of men with the heads of animals. Truth cannot imagine remaining very long in the company of Ambition, Simony, and Avarice, the divinities honored in Rome. Soon after, they arrive in Avignon just as a consistory is being held in which Pride, Avarice, and Lust play major roles. In describing the hold she enjoys over the papal court, Lust tells Truth: "Lady Queen, as lieutenant to your Father [God] in this court of Rome I caused to reign a woman, who was of England."[102] Somewhat later Ardent Desire seizes on this allusion to suggest a plan for resolving the schism, "in order to put an end to the great doubts and perils of the said division and to the subtle arguments of the Italians and others of the adverse party." The cardinals could, in fact, undo a papal election in cases of deception or physical pressure. Ardent Desire explains:

> They have such power that if in electing the sovereign shepherd
> they have been deceived in any fashion, for they are men, by ig-
> norance, as they were by the woman who was pope, or out of rea-
> sonable fear and manifest oppression, as it happened in our case,
> or by simony and several other cases written about in decrees and
> divine Scripture, the said cardinals have full power to renegotiate
> their difficulty, without the authority of others, and to make a
> new election or elections valid according to both divine and posi-
> tive law.[103]

In a different context, far from the affairs of France and Avignon, the same sort of argument was put forth in favor of rejecting another supernumerary pope. Dietrich of Nieheim, who occupied a high post in the Church and who relates the story of Joan in his *History of the Acts of the Roman Emperors*,[104] discusses the right to undo a papal election. Addressing his remarks to John XXIII (1410–15), who had succeeded Alexander V as a "third pope," and who had been elected to remedy the untenable situation of obedience to two popes but had refused to abdicate when the operation failed, Dietrich states:

> And if the lord pope says "There was at Pisa a true council, holy
> and just; what was decided there is holy and just, and the two
> who were rejected there [Gregory XII, the Roman pope, and Bene-
> dict XIII, the Avignon pope] must not be heard." (Response):

> "The council can be holy and just, but the election that results
> from it can be null for many reasons, for a defect in the person or
> in the form, if the elect is incapable, insufficient in his learning, or
> even criminal."[105]

Dietrich's final phrase corresponds exactly to Martinus Polonus's juridical disqualification of Joan. Moreover, one of Martinus's versions of the story of Joan states that she was deposed. The *Eulogium historiarum* (ca. 1366) confirmed that juridical outcome *(ipsa deposita est)*.[106] Even in this legal debate, the Franciscan version of Joan retained its grip: when in 1399 the masters of the University of Cambridge refused to withdraw their allegiance to the Roman pope, they spoke of Urban VI in the ecclesiological language of the Spirituals rather than in the juridical vocabulary of the canonists. Walter Ullmann remarks: "One could not easily presume that such eminent men [the cardinals] would have suggested *toti christianismo* a false *(falsum)* vicar of Christ."[107]

Jean Gerson (1363–1429), a major figure in the French Church of the late fourteenth century, developed a second justification for a pope's withdrawal that took into consideration the primacy of the peace of the Church in cases of scandal. On the Feast of the Circumcision in 1403, Gerson preached at Tarascon before Benedict XIII, Clement VII's successor, who had been sequestered at Avignon since 1398 by the French court, under the influence of the University of Paris and its two great Doctors, Gerson himself and Pierre d'Ailly. In his sermon Gerson made another attempt to move the pope to abdicate:

> Second consideration. All power, in the ecclesiastical hierarchy, is
> oriented toward a salutary peace. . . . It appears that the salutary
> peace can be broken by the persistence of an ecclesiastical power,
> in the case of John, for example, whereas the destitution of that
> power would bring back peace: in that case, rejecting that power
> is to use [power] well; its maintenance becomes an abuse. More-
> over, there is no power that is not subject to the law, divine and
> natural, that is not liable to sin, to suppression of suspension,
> and to abdication.[108]

The "John" mentioned by Gerson has traditionally been seen as our popess, but the identification is not certain. Gerson might also have been thinking of John XII, deposed by Otto I of Germany in 964, although that identification is not totally persuasive either. Whatever the case, the brevity of the allusion reflects at least a passing thought of Joan.[109]

Later in his sermon, Gerson's reference to Joan illustrates an error of fact, not of doctrine, thus an error that should be resolved by a simple "retreat": "Moreover, these circumstance that bring dissension in the present schism consist essentially in questions of fact, in which not only one individual or another may err without risk to his salvation, but also the Church has been or can be (as is said) deceived, as when, long ago, it honored a woman as pope."[110]

But Joan, with her typical agility, also served as an argument against the antihierarchical fideism of Gerson, who contributed to weakening the papacy (even if he did not hold the "pre-Gallican" opinions of the French prelate Simon de Cramaud in his 1396 treatise, *Sur la soustraction d'obédience*).[111] Jean Roques, a Franciscan who had come to the Council of Constance as vicar of the minister general of the Franciscans of the Observance (the latter-day heirs of the Spirituals), argued against Gerson's position in the session of 24 October 1415, where he praised the idea of the absolute necessity of the ecclesiastical hierarchy, independent of the personal qualities of the popes. Here Joan no longer represented error or deceit, but another, more considerable evil, the suspension of order. Jean Roques states: "First, the hierarchical status of the Church loses all certitude and all surety if there is no pope; and that status was also uncertain when John of Mainz reigned as pope."[112]

A third way to resolve the schism was the *via conventionis*, or by the convocation of a general council. From the outset of the Great Schism, theologians on both sides had urged that the schism be resolved in that manner (Vincent Ferrer and Nicolas Eymeric among the supporters of Clement VII; Konrad von Gelnhausen and Heinrich von Langenstein in support of Urban VI). Around 1408 a number of cardinals and prelates, weary of the schism, formed a third, conciliar party, and in 1415 they succeeded in calling the Council of Constance. The idea of a council was not new in the fifteenth century, but the schism gave it a high priority among theories concerning limitations on the power of the popes, replacing the oligarchical ideology that had been developed in the eleventh to the thirteenth centuries by the great canonists who gravitated to the Sacred College of Cardinals. William of Ockham was by no means a conciliarist, but his ecclesiological dialectic influenced theorists of the council of the time of the Schism. These theorists made a distinction between *potestas habitualis* (habitual, subsistent power) and *potestas actualis* (actual power); the community of the faithful or the Church held the first; the pope could only dispose of "actual" power, which meant the Church, represented by the council, could dispossess him of that power. We return here to Ockham's distinction between fact (and *factum* is close to *actus*, the act to which papal power is reduced) and faith; between the individual who had been invested (and, at times, "transvested") and the sacred institution. In a new irony of history, the operative scheme here was an exact inverse of the theory of the sovereign's two bodies (which, as a theory, hence indefinitely reversible, is not a thing, but rather a vocabulary ceaselessly made into discourse). Joan, a woman and a pope, was an excellent figure for the duality of that power, and Dietrich of Nieheim, the most resolute conciliarist of his time, was also the most prolix of the biographers of the popess and the one most convinced of her existence.

JOAN AND THE DOGS OF GOD

Between 1250 and 1450 Joan was a faithful servant of the Church, which she served and followed, with her agile dialectics, through the sinuous twists and turns of a Catholic discourse gripped in the claws of time and necessity. The Dominicans (Jean de Mailly, Etienne de Bourbon, Martinus Polonus, Jacopo da Voragine, Arnoldus of Liège, Bernard Gui, Tolomeo da Lucca, and others) had been fond of the popess, the mother of paradoxes and reversals, but it was their rivals, the Franciscans, mere stammerers in promoting Joan in comparison to the skilled Dominican preachers, who armed Joan with a trenchant argument and gave her the poignancy of a suspicion. One might even stretch the hypothesis to another domain and see a dramatic Franciscan orchestration of Dominican themes.

On the other hand, this opposition between the two mendicant Orders might require revision, correcting some of what has been said above about the efficiency of the Dominican network. Cultural continuity probably masks some gaps. There is no common measure between the transcription of a rumor in a cloistered community in Metz or Lyon and its inscription in a history of the popes written by a papal chaplain. We have neglected an important detail: the pope who protected Martinus Polonus, personally ordaining him bishop in 1278 (the probable moment of the third[?] redaction of his *Chronicle*, the version that contains the story of Joan), was Nicholas III, whom the Franciscans considered the most authentic of the popes, as we have seen.

At the same time that the pope laid down rules for authenticity (in the bull *Exiit qui seminat*) the Dominican wrote his narrative on imposture that provided the matrix for many other accounts. This chronological proximity weakens the image of the Dominicans as sage mediators, particularly if we look at the conjunction of events in 1278. Martinus, who occupied a position close to the angelic pope, was telling that angelic pope how close supreme dignity was to its total subversion. He was playing the role of the pope's fool, evoking a possible inversion (Ockham would say, of fact: "The pope is a woman") in order to exalt a necessary inversion (Ockham would say, of faith: folly in Christ; Peter of John Olivi said that if the Church should fail, a woman might also be the final depository of grace). Martin recalls to mind the figure of the fool Ramón in the romance *Blanquerna* of the Franciscan Ramon Llull (1233–1315): "A man with shaven head and clothed in the garb of a fool" arrives at the papal court, accompanied by a sparrowhawk and leading a dog. He announces that "in praise of God and to reprove the vices of the Court of Rome Ramón the Sage has taken the office of fool." Ramón's dog (and the dog was the traditional attribute of God's fools)[113] reminds us that the Franciscans were not alone in playing the fool or being *joculatores Dei:* the Dominicans carefully conserved the etymology of the name that they gave themselves in honor of their founder, St. Dominic, *Domini Canis,* or "the dog of God."

The crucial event in this chronicle of Joan the Catholic becomes opaque at this point: was the 1278 narrative a product of the cultural necessity of Dominican transmission, hence quantitatively established, or does it instead arise from an ideological choice of a "spiritual" history (both Dominican and Franciscan) that is significant qualitatively? The serial presentation of the various Joan narratives given at the beginning of this chapter privileges the first hypothesis, whereas the contextualization of the moments of conjunction in 1254, 1278, 1294, and 1378 that wound its way through this narrative sequence leads instead to the second hypothesis. We are right back to the dilemma with which we began, and we have not resolved it. Yet the meaning of Joan depends on resolution.

Only with the end of Joan's Catholic career, after 1450, could these recurrent cycles of appearances and hypotheses come to a stopping point. Nonetheless, before the popess's expulsion from the tense but captivating clerical discourse in which Joan, a woman of passion, was quite at home, she found a way to slip out of the Church and insist that she was a woman, not just a pseudopope.

5

THE POPESS AND HER SISTERS

rom 1450 on Joan passed through the hands of hundreds of thousands of people who had intimate experience of her and enjoyed it thoroughly. In her cosmic development, outside the confines of Rome and the clerical scriptorium, the popess entered into a game, quite literally, by becoming a figure in the tarot, a card game invented in Ferrara, Milan, or somewhere between in the mid-fifteenth century. From there the popess invaded the world: it has been estimated that more than a million tarot decks were manufactured in France during the seventeenth century, and to this day the venerable firm of Grimaud continues to print Joan's portrait on playing cards.

When she became a tarot figure, the popess returned to her initial carnivalesque existence, but as her horizon expanded it changed hue, no longer reflecting the Roman purple but taking on a varied, contrasting motley. Carnival replaces and inverts things; the card game lays out and combines them. When Joan became a figure on a card, it was the last step in her passage into the realm of allegory.

JOAN AS ALLEGORY

In tarot the popess, fourth in rank in a series of allegorical cards called "triumphs" that supplement the four suits, is a trump card. She is distributed; she makes decisive contributions to the game. She represents female domination, feigned or constructed, winning or losing, and she combines with the other figures in an unpredictable, ceaselessly varied, and endlessly renewed series of actions as the cards are dealt and tricks are taken. Tarot, which in itself is allegorical, involves a certain construction of the female role in relation to learning, ambition, love, and the sacred, a role played out in the space of the phantasmagoric or literary game as an occasion and opportunity for an existential allegory.

The date at the head of this chapter, 1450, is not meant to suggest that clerical discourse about the popess stopped at that date and gave way to games. The allegorical reading of Joan ran parallel to the ecclesiological reading, never replacing it even though the two elements gradually tended to separate. Around 1360 Giovanni Boccaccio made slight transformations in the "real" popess of the Church and turned her toward literature. He added a few more details than the ecclesiastical chroniclers had given, and although his narrative might seem just an amplification of the original story, in reality Boccaccio's treatment of the life of Joan was different and more "literary" in ways that will be discussed below. For the moment, let me simply note that as the Church popess became a "lay" popess, she changed, first, in the themes that she represented, and second, in the way in which people believed in her history.

Joan took her place in a system of role oppositions (sexual, social, moral) when she left the gallery of papal portraits, where she figured only as a different, abnormal pope. In Boccaccio's hands she became part of a series of 106 "illustrious women"; similarly, in the tarot she took her place among the "triumphs"—trump cards—that pictured conditions or scenes symbolizing a range of human experience lying well beyond clerical circles.

As for the second difference, neither literature nor the card game claims to tell the truth (or even a truth) in the same way as the chronicle. Rather, they signify, or at least they do so until the game disintegrates into a stereotypic "genre" or falls victim to automatically applied rules.

How did this change occur? One simple but false answer needs to be eliminated at the start. One might think that all it took was to "embroider" on the original story, as when a vague memory of a Carolingian count killed by the Basques became the *Song of Roland*. But Roland was not born of this silky transition, nor was that how Joan found her "lay" conversion. The domain that welcomed both Roland and Joan (something like "literature" or "fiction") had no existence of its own in the Middle Ages. The medieval playful imagination neither copied reality nor broke with it. To speak of Boccaccio or tarot cards does not totally explain the historical popess; rather, it extracts her essence and multiplies her meanings.

Once the popess was removed from her ecclesiological context, she developed individual characteristics: her disguised femininity, her learning, her sexuality, her ambition, at first fulfilled, then dashed. She became a free, ambivalent figure (even when her meaning was narrowly determined by a specific situation), and a symbolic type who invited varying levels of belief.

Joan became a powerful, troubling image; allegorical production led to the exact sort of iconic creation that the clerical tradition lacked. Before the flow of Lutheran materials on the popess that will concern us in chapter 6, the tarot images and the miniatures in manuscripts of Boccaccio's *De claris mulieribus* were the two sources for figurative representations of Joan. Rather than risk losing our way in the maze of contingent lay narratives (or, more simply, nonecclesiological narratives) about Joan, these two sources of images will serve us as points of departure and instances of the emergence of allegorical readings of the story of the popess.

Access to Joan becomes difficult. Up to this point the logic of rituals or texts has guided us on a historical route marked with successive milestones, even if an occasional detour seemed surer than the direct road. Once we leave the solidity of the Church we will have to move from one image to another with no guarantee that we are on the right path, also shifting our time frame from the slow process that produces the symbolic type to the instantaneous event that produces the figure. Beginning with the tarot, we will shuffle the cards, lay them out, and see what configurations they reveal, but we will also attempt to discern the rules of the game. The procedure is uncertain, but it seems preferable to the arbitrary approximations of a cartomancy that glosses the figures one by one.

THE INVENTION OF THE TAROT

The first question to examine (ignoring chronology for the moment) is the advent of the popess among the figures in the tarot deck. This task is made easier by the scholarly but amusing tome devoted to the tarot that Michael Dummett, the great Oxford logician, wrote as an exercise in learned relaxation.[1]

Card games, first attested around 1375, came fairly late to Western Europe. They are said to have originated in Islamic lands, though this is still unsure and disputed. When the West took over the cards on which such games depend, it also adopted two of their essential characteristics: hierarchy among the "honor" cards (the King, the Lady, the Valet) and the principle of taking "tricks," each participant playing in turn. Tarot seems to have been invented around 1430–50 as a special variant of ordinary card games. Dummett has demonstrated that until the eighteenth century (specifically, until Antoine Court de Gébelin, a Geneva Calvinist), tarot had no occultist or astrological component. Like ordinary card games, the tarot deck is made up of four suits (or colors), each with ten cards, numbered in descending order from the ten to the ace, and four "honor cards" or "court cards," the King, Queen, Knight, and Valet (in later terms, the Jack) instead of the three in the usual games. What sets the tarot apart, and where Joan fits in, is its series of twenty-two supplementary cards that operate as permanent trumps (rather than having one suit chosen as trumps at each deal or by convention, as in other card games). The twenty-two extra cards are called "triumphs" (contemporaries called them "tarots"; later astrological derivations of the tarot called them "arcanes"). These twenty-two triumphs (more precisely, twenty-one triumphs and the Fool) depicted human or allegorical figures whose identities have changed through time but whose essential structure has remained the same. They make up three groups: the ranks (the Pope, Popess, Emperor, Empress, and the Mountebank or Merchant); moral allegories (the Lovers or Love, the Chariot, the Wheel of Fortune, the Hermit or the Old Man, the Hanged Man, Justice, Temperance, and Fortitude); and cosmological symbols (Death, the Devil, the House of God or the Tower, the Star, the Sun, the Moon, the World, and Judgment or the Angel). Although these figures are arranged hierarchically, they do not seem to have been ranked among themselves, one to twenty-one, and legends came to be attached to them only in the seventeenth century. For anyone skeptical about stability in any game after its creation, there is a late-fifteenth-century text written in Ferrara, tarot's probable place of birth, that lists the triumphs in Italian and in numerical order.[2]

JOAN IN THE TAROT

The sequence of triumphs ends with the Pope, the Popess, the Emperor, the Empress, and the Mountebank. From a technical viewpoint, the triumphs were an extreme example of a structural tendency within card games to introduce hierarchical disequilibrium (trump cards) into an equilibrium established by chance within a system of symmetrical suits and by distributing the same number of cards to each player. The choice of one triumph figure or another and its place in the hierarchy were just as arbitrary as Montesquieu's face on a French two-hundred-franc note: he might easily have been replaced by Diderot, or have been assigned a value of ten francs or five hundred francs. Still, we are discussing the popess, not Montesquieu, and the presence of Joan calls for an examination of the themes portrayed in the triumph cards.

In the fifteenth century, the triumphs did not form any visible system, and no use of them (before the eighteenth century) induces us to see them as an ordered whole. Nonetheless, the figures on them do not seem totally arbitrary. Similarly, if Montesquieu is agreed to be worth two hundred francs, the choice of his image was the result of an implicit but complex norm: he was chosen from among the "great men" of France; the fact that he connotes gravity and the French civic tradition may have entered into the choice of his image over Diderot's for an infrequent, slow-paced use in a two-hundred-franc note rather than on a postage stamp, for example. The choice made in the fifteenth century of the twenty-one figures of the tarot triumphs also responded to vague criteria of selection. These included a dialectic of order (social, moral, cosmic) and its transgression (dealing out the cards introduced gaps in order and inversions). This notion rejoins the theme of the wheel of fortune that was always present in this civilized and melancholy "autumn of the Middle Ages."[3] Tarot cards also reflect the taste for symbolic images that developed at that time, along with a passion for "devices," talking images that signified, whereas the classical heraldry signaled and classified.[4] The elastic envelope of "context" might also contain the humanist tendency to mix cultural references to Christian and classical allegories or real and imaginary persons. Finally, in the early fifteenth century didactic games using images became extremely popular. The adolescent Filippo Maria Visconti, later duke of Milan, had a game called "The Gods and their Attributes"; other such games were "Our Lord and the Apostles," "The Seven Virtues," "The Triumphs of Petrarch," and "The Planets." When Pope Pius II and cardinals Nicholas of Cusa and Bessarion met in Mantua around 1459, they devised a game called "Government of the World."[5]

The famous "Mantegna Tarots" (which are neither tarots nor by the hand of Mantegna) are close to the tarots that interest us here, both thematically and chronologically. They are fifty vignettes laid out in five series of ten, designated by letters from E to A in reverse alphabetical order, also placed in reverse numerical order from 1 to 50. The figures seem to be more systematically arranged than in the tarot proper: they begin with E, the hierarchical ranks, and continue with D, the Muses; C, the arts and sciences; B, moral and cosmic principles; and end with A, the planets and the celestial spheres. Nearly all the tarot triumphs reappear or are approximated in these images. The series of the triumphs does not have a meaning; it has meaning (to paraphrase Merleau-Ponty's dictum on history). That indeterminate quality may be just what the series was intended to express as a metaphor for the world.

The popess takes her place within a human micro-hierarchy, abstracted and reduced to a sketchy version of the three orders of medieval society, warriors, priests, and producers (the Mountebank or *Bateleur* is often called the Merchant or the Artisan). A pope would be understandable, but a popess? Her presence cannot be explained by the convenience of pairs, because the Mountebank has no female equivalent. An abbess (a quasi-episcopal rank in the Middle Ages) might have been a more respectable choice. The popess can be explained by two contradictory reasons, one cultural, the other contextual.

The feminization of the pope may result from a malicious inversion of the sort that occurs in a game (the popess is the only tarot figure that is not reflected in the more serious vignettes of the "Mantegna" series). Inversion runs rampant throughout the tarot game: the suits equivalent to latter-day hearts and diamonds reverse the usual point values, with 1 high and 10 low, rather than following the usual system of point values of 10 high to aces low after the face cards. The Mountebank, the weakest of the trump cards, earns extra points when he takes the last trick, indicating that the seller (the Merchant) pays. In Germany people declared *ultimo pagat*, punning on "Bagatto," one name for the Mountebank. A popess in this happy lot of playful reversals should come as no surprise. The extreme conservatism of gaming traditions, which have retained their fifteenth-century rules and figures to our own day, helped to retain the popess. She disappeared, however, in the Besançon tarot, where a taste for classical culture replaced her with Juno, and she is omitted (along with some other figures) in fantastic or occult versions of the tarot produced in the nineteenth century.

The context in which the first tarots were produced gives a particular meaning to the choice of themes made in Ferrara around 1430–50.

THE VISCONTI-SFORZA TAROT

The three earliest sets of tarot cards that have been conserved are magnificent illuminated cards painted on a tooled gold and silver background made for the Visconti and Sforza families. The oldest of these, and probably the prototype, is in the Cary collection of the Beinecke Rare Book Library at Yale University. It was commissioned by Filippo Maria Visconti (†1447), as seen in the coats of arms and the device, *A bon droyt*, depicted on the cards.[6] The seventh triumph, the Lover, also shows the coat of arms of Savoy, which might indicate that Filippo Maria's marriage with Maria of Savoy was the occasion for the ducal commission and the invention. A recent study on the question attributes the cards to the painter Francisco Zavattari.[7] Unfortunately, we do not have all of these cards, and the popess is among the missing. She does appear in a second set of tarot cards, some of which are in the John Pierpont Morgan Library in New York, some at the

Accademia Carrara in Bergamo, and some in the Colleoni Collection, a private collection in Bergamo. This set was painted around 1451–53 by Bonifacio Bembo (according to Roberto Longhi) or Francesco Zavattari (according to Giuliana Algeri);[8] close inspection of the coats of arms and devices has pointed to Francesco Sforza, after his marriage with Bianca Maria Visconti and after he became duke of Milan in 1450, as commissioner.

The popess appears in this Visconti-Sforza tarot seated on a throne, holding in her right hand the pontifical staff topped with a stylized cross and, in her left hand, a closed book resting on her knee. The papal triple tiara is on her head, and she wear a simple brown robe belted with a knotted cord and a cloak of the same color. Her face, slightly turned to her left, shows a surprisingly sweet gravity. Nothing about her suggests derision or inversion. The quasi-Franciscan robe, an odd note among her pontifical trappings, has led Gertrude Moakley, in a painstaking iconographic study, to the interesting hypotheses that some of the human figures in this tarot were modeled after members of the Sforza and Visconti families.[9] According to Moakley, the popess recalls Manfreda da Pirovano, a first cousin of Matteo Visconti, the imperial vicar in Milan in the early fourteenth century.

Popess Manfreda

Manfreda was a member of the Umiliati, a lay, urban religious movement that was very active in Lombardy. Although recognized and encouraged by the Church, the Umiliati always operated at the edge of heresy. They wore a plain brown robe as a sign of humility, in imitation of the Franciscans. But why should Manfreda be promoted to the rank of pope? The explanation may lie in her astonishing career as a heretic, for she was burned not long after 1300 as a disciple of the heresiarch Guglielma.

Some time between 1260 and 1271, a woman named Guglielma (or Guillelma, Guillemetta, Guillemine, Wilhelmina) arrived in Milan, supposedly from Bohemia, with a young child.[10] Her disciple, Andrea Saramita, stated during his trial by the Inquisition (he was burned at the stake along with Manfreda) that Guglielma was the daughter of Przemil, the king of Bohemia, and Queen Constance. Her messianic message predicted the end of time, to be preceded by her own coming as the incarnation of the Holy Ghost.

Guglielma's message met with a sympathetic hearing in aristocratic milieus in Milan and among the Umiliati, to the point that her followers adopted the latter's brown homespun robes. It was rumored that Guglielma bore the stigmata and possessed the power to heal. After her death in 1282, her body was translated to the cemetery of the Cistercian house at Chiaravalle (a disposition that hints at the ambiguity of her situation). The Cistercians built a chapel over her tomb with an altar and an image of her. A cult began to develop: on the anniversaries of the day of her death and the translation of her body and at Pentecost (the Feast of the Holy Ghost) lamps were lit, hymns sung, and litanies recited. The Inquisition became concerned about this heterodox cult, and in 1300 it opened a trial at which thirty disciples were charged, which gives an idea of the success of the sect. The trial records also mention a banquet given by the Cistercians at Chiaravalle that was attended by 129 of the faithful, some of whom were recruited from among the best families of Milan. One was Francesco Garbagnate, later a professor of law at Padua and a member of a family allied to the Visconti. The Inquisition had Guglielma's bones burned and sent her three most prominent followers to the stake, Manfreda da Pirovano, Andrea Saramita, and Giacobba dei Bassani, also a member of the Umiliati.

The 1300 trial helps us to define fairly precisely the pontifical status of Manfreda, especially if we complete the trial records with the bull *Dudum ad nostri apostalatus,* promulgated on 23 March 1324 by John XXII (a pope often paired with our popess), and with information given by Odorico Rinaldi in his *Annales ecclesiastici.* John XXII's act came well after the trial, probably because the sect was still showing signs of life under the ashes, and because the pope wanted to grasp an opportunity to attack his Ghibelline enemies in and around Milan. He accused Matteo Visconti of having protected his cousin Manfreda, and he declared both Galeazzo, Matteo's son, and Francesco Garbagnate, their ally, under suspicion of heresy. This makes it quite understandable, incidentally, that the fifteenth-century Visconti-Sforzas, always resolutely antipapal, might have had tender memories of Manfreda.

"Manfreda asserted that the Holy Ghost had been incarnate in the person of a certain Guglielma, and that the said Guglielma had enjoyed divine assumption."[11] Here Guglielma's body is merged with the body of Christ and then, in a dual, successive incarnation of the Word, with the Holy Ghost. Guglielma, dead and resuscitated, had appeared before her ascension, designating Manfreda as her vicar, hence as true pope. Indeed, Guglielma had abolished the pope and the cardinals; Boniface VIII had no rights "because he had not been created justly" (here again, Popess Manfreda followed the steps of Joan).

This new incarnation offered a radically feminized Christianity. Manfreda named women cardinals, among them her servant Taria. The popess officiated at all divine services in Guglielma's chapel and in the church of Santa Maria Maddalena in Milan, where she preached, distributed the host at communion, and permitted the congregation to kiss her hands and feet. She also wrote (or had someone write) a new Gospel: "Like the disciples of Christ, they wrote Gospels, epistles, and prophecies. . . . Andrea [Saramita], changing the wording, wrote his gospels, epistles, and prophecies thus: 'In those times, the Holy Ghost said to his disciples. . . .'"[12]

This historical chassé-croisé is worthy of admiration: the adventure of Joan, which was very probably imaginary, engendered a belief in its veracity, while the real, historically documented episode of popess Manfreda survived only in a card game.

This affair would have an importance limited to the aristocracy of Milan in the fourteenth and fifteenth centuries if it did not strike deeper chords. Guglielma's experience in Milan created an echo that reverberated from that city, in lands and terms that recall Joan. In the *Annals of Colmar* for the year 1301 there is a notation that the heresiarch passed through Bingen: "The previous year, there came from England [our Joan-sensitive ears prick up] a very beautiful and very eloquent virgin, who said that she was the Holy Spirit incarnated for the redemption of women, and she baptized women in the name of the Father, the Son, and Herself. After her death, she was taken to Milan and burned there. Brother Johannes of Wissenbourg, of the Order of the Preaching Friars, told certain people that he had seen her ashes."[13]

This meeting point between the ecclesiastical history of Joan and the mystical episode of Manfreda and Guglielma has repercussions that reach beyond their common theme (the coming of a popess) and that merit examination, although we need not pause too long over questions of a reciprocal influence that is extremely difficult to trace. It seems probable that the anonymous author of the Colmar Annals had heard of Joan when he reports the "passage" of Guglielma through Bingen; conversely, the adventure of the Milanese popesses must have played an important part in Joan's rehabilitation in fiction, to be investigated below.

On a deeper level, the fifteenth-century Ferrarese triumph card caps the divinely inspired career of a popess. Here the signs are reversed, and imposture gives way to authenticity. We can leave the tarot triumph to its posterity in the world of games, for it tells us, on the aesthetic plane, about the pride of being a Visconti. Cousin Manfreda took her place in a glorious gallery of eminent men. She represented celestial inspiration, just as other figures represented the triumph of the arts, arms, or laws. The popess's later career in the ordinary tarot pack reduced her to the flat two dimensions of a playing card.

A CHANGE OF SCALE

A historian can choose a more radical view of the heretics in Milan that moves them closer to Joan. If Guglielma was indeed the daughter of the king of Bohemia, was born in 1210, and arrived in Milan around 1260, we can reconstitute her itinerary. She would have made her way around the Alps somewhere around 1250, bearing her part-divine, part-pontifical identity through Thuringia, the Rhine Valley, Alsace, Lorraine, and Burgundy. This route, if we admit the transposition, would explain the early strength of the legend of the popess in Thuringia, its emergence in texts in Metz and in Burgundy around 1260, the mention of it in the Colmar Annals, and Joan's putative birthplace in Metz. Prague was perhaps remote enough to be taken for England.

A new configuration begins to take shape. The female pope may have sprung from a triple matrix: Roman parody in the twelfth and thirteenth centuries, a Dominican and Franciscan construction of a spurious papacy (1260 – 80), and a transposition of a female heresy of the pneuma (Holy Spirit) (1250 – 1300). This triple extraction makes it impossible to decide on any one origin; in an ironic form of the revenge of events over hypotheses, each choice is muddled by interferences from the other possible origins.

That very uncertainty suggests that we investigate the third explanation. On a very different level from that of its ecclesiological import, the history of Joan also tells of female aspiration to a central role in the Christian world. This obliges us, however, to modify the starting point of our quest. Thus far, the first two hypotheses could be supported by vestiges that can be analyzed and used to document a reconstruction (on the basis of chairs and rites, or of Dominican and Franciscan texts). Here there are no traces. If we begin with Guglielma, we will have to leap over two centuries before finding even a feeble echo of the Milanese popess. Only a few late texts give a "feminist" version of the story of Joan, and we hardly need be reminded of male cultural domination of the Church in the Middle Ages: ecclesiological texts may have stifled any laudatory mention of a female incarnation of God or a holy woman pope.

For a moment, let us abandon the search for evidence, ignore strict methodology, and examine the events of 1300 as part of a picture of female aspiration to religious supremacy. In other words, let us change historical scale and allow Joan to become a detail in a fresco in which she takes on meaning (or a meaning).[14] We will lose something in rigor, but perhaps not in truth. Shifting back and forth between the pertinence of evidence and the contingency of the general picture may enable us to vary the focus of our picture and gain a stereoscopic view of Joan.

The lighting in this picture necessarily remains indirect, because the conversion of a male order into a virtual female order involves the suppression of a tendency deeply rooted in Christianity from its earliest days. We can acknowledge, following Jack Goody, the violence that Christianity did to a profoundly male and agnatic Roman society.[15] The prohibition of adoption and concubinage feminized the juridical structures of society by making the mother the legal parent of origin rather than the father. We should of course also mention the powerful presence of the Virgin, the only human being who truly participates in the divine. The canonists repeatedly evoked the Pentecost, when the Mother of God, like an original popess, directed the Church, both de facto and de juris. An intense marian devotion (free of the platitudes of later religious bric-a-brac) accompanied the extraordinary renaissance of learning in the twelfth century, and throughout the Middle Ages marian theology, centered around the gradual emergence of the dogma of the Immaculate Conception of the Virgin, tended to construct a parthenogenetic genealogy of the divine that ran counter to a return to the principle of male transmission.

I have no intention of using a facile paradox to establish a Church "feminism" contradicted by too many facts: I am simply noting the force of a maternal metaphor and of an imaginary matriarchate underlying the image that the Church projects of itself.

It is fair to speak of the suppression of that metaphor because male order knew how to resist, as demonstrated by St. Paul's interpretation of the Gospel or by the rejection of the female that we saw in chapter 1. What I hope to do in the present chapter is thus to present instances of the difficult emergence of a spiritual matriarchate, within the Church and outside the Church, and to depict the background from which Joan managed to detach herself as a figure of the return of the Mother of Christian Mothers.

The way to penetrate this vast tableau is by examining what was at stake in the years from 1280 to 1300 in Rome and in Milan. When they are removed from ecclesiological discourse, Joan the imposter and Manfreda the inspired represent two opposed and fundamental figures, the witch and the prophetess.

THE POPESS AS WITCH

In the Franciscan versions of her story, Joan acted as an agent of the devil, using the perverse imitation of the sacred characteristic of Satan's works.

Peter of John Olivi and William of Ockham theorized this diabolic menace and gave it an institutional and historical form.

Pope Boniface VIII (whom we have already met as a double for Joan, and who was himself accused of sorcery by Nogaret, chief adviser to Philippe le Bel)[16] was the first interpreter of the story of Guglielma. Speaking of Guglielmite practices in the bull *Nuper ad audientiam* (1 August 1296) he states: "The women have little night-time meetings *(conventicula)* and they assert that prayers are more efficacious when they are offered by people who are totally nude in their whole body; the women denude themselves, as do the men of this accursed sect."[17]

Soon after the trial a legend (probably of clerical origin) repeated in a chronicle by Antonio de Retanate (1302), now lost but cited by the Milanese chronicler Bernardino Corio, presented the sect's meetings in the "synagogue" of Andrea Saramita as sexual orgies. Between 1371 and 1375, the preacher Gabrio de Zamorei of Parma reiterated this version in a sermon, "De Fide."[18] This pontifical and clerical interpretation of the episode seems of capital importance. It recalls the prototypical forms of the nocturnal sabbath (a point made by Norman Cohn but that Carlo Ginzburg contests in an important debate to which we shall return).[19] For Cohn, the witches' sabbath, an essential element in the vast persecutions of the fifteenth and sixteenth centuries, arose out of a progressive diabolization of heretics. He sees the prototype of this diabolization in Western Europe in Adhémar de Chabannes and his treatment of eleventh-century heretics who had formed a group around certain canons in Orléans. As with many extremist sects, they preached a rigid piety and strict asceticism, rejecting certain essential dogmas that they considered to be accessory, including the virginity of Mary, the Eucharist, baptism, and the intercession of saints. Like Guglielma's followers, they claimed to be inhabited and guided by the Holy Spirit. They were burned at the stake in 1022. The episode would have remained among the formless and repetitive marginalia of heresy if Adhémar de Chabannes had not written about their diabolical practices.[20] According to him, after making a pact with the devil, they ate the ashes of a dead child and indulged in all manner of vices, all the while preserving all outward appearance of true faith. Around 1090 Paul, a monk at Chartres, added the theme of sexual promiscuity to descriptions of cannibalistic practices.[21] Somewhat later (around 1115), Guibert de Nogent applied the same description to peasant sects in the region of Soissons, artfully complicating the picture. According to him, the heretics cannibalized the fruit of their incestuous debauchery, using the ashes of their infants to make the Host for their Eucharist.[22]

For Carlo Ginzburg, the tradition of profanatory gatherings is insufficient to explain the presence of the aggressive witch or sorceress endowed with supernatural powers who appeared in the Alps and the Apennines around 1350.[23] He suggests that this specific form of witchcraft was the result of a "historic compromise" between a clerical image (of a hostile, diabolic, profanatory sect) and an image drawn from folklore of *benandanti*, individuals capable of visiting the realm of the dead and bringing prosperity to the community on their return.[24]

Boniface VIII's bull may permit us to reconcile Cohn's and Ginzburg's viewpoints by adding a third term to the two agents of the sabbath, as portrayed by Ginzburg. Boniface only hints at the nocturnal scene, but it becomes an integral part of a feminized tradition that moves from Adhémar to Paul to Guibert, where Guglielma and her sisters take the initiative, directing the lustful goings-on. Moreover, the pact with the devil takes on a much broader scope: where the canons of Orléans and the people of the region around Soissons got only a bit of money or some illusions in exchange for profanation, Guglielma constructed a universal Church founded on the reversal of gender roles, which, to my mind, is fundamental in female sorcery. As is known, until the thirteenth century the Church did not believe that witches were real and treated them as imaginary creatures drawn from popular superstition. Whether by coincidence or cause, from the moment that people believed (at the urging of the Dominicans and Franciscans) that Satan was attacking the Church through a woman (Joan), the diabolical *usurpatrice* took on reality in both Rome and Milan. One of the earliest instances of judiciary treatment of an "objective" sabbath (that is, one that had really taken place, according to the judges) occurred between 1384 and 1390, and in Milan. Two women admitted to having paid homage, twice a week, to "Signora Oriente" (whom they also called Diana or Herodias) when they went to the "society" or the "game."[25] The members of Guglielma's sect (and the worshipers of Signora Oriente) declared themselves to be inspired. Like the *benandanti* of Friuli and their ancestors throughout Europe, they loudly denied any collusion with the devil and claimed to offer authentic means of salvation. This may easily be a third agent of the sabbath, which operated in radical and "feminist" milieus of urban Christianity (and I use the term "feminist" in full awareness of the anachronism, which is more lexical than real, however) situated at the edges of the female and prophetic mystique that began to develop in the late twelfth century in Flanders, northern Italy, and the Rhineland. We shall return to this topic.

That the Church began to believe in witches is a familiar topic that has been thoroughly described. We need repeat only that Joan's story, which took on renewed importance in the years around 1278, 1294, and 1330–

35, gave that fear a concrete form, analyzed in chapter 1, of female subversion of the sacred. The thirteenth century discovered, and under dramatic conditions, that the female attack it so dreaded was aimed at the summit of terrestrial holiness, the papacy. The threat of an invasion of power may have helped to create the forceful and objective figure of the witch. Joan of Arc, a cousin of the popess in a later age, provides confirmation of this notion.

THE TWO FIGURES OF JOAN OF ARC

I do not intend to insist on any overly facile parallel between the two Joans (once again, the siren of analogy calls to the unwary): two women came from nowhere, used fascinating speech and male dress to reach the summit of power, then died because of it. More important to our purposes is the dual image projected by Joan of Arc.

The available documents are obviously very biased, given that both sets of trial records—those of Joan's condemnation in 1431 and those of her rehabilitation in 1456—reflect the passage of time and the very different positions of the persons to whom they were submitted, the first to the king of England and France, Henry VI, and the second to the king of France, Charles VII.[26] As one deposition follows another, we can sense the genuine anxiety that Joan of Arc caused (or, rather, that her figure caused, given that the real Joan remains just as inaccessible to us as the popess). Fear of the witch permeates all the tactics and servilities of the 1431 trial. It is worth remembering that the trial was conducted exclusively by the Church under the authority of Pierre Cauchon, the bishop of Beauvais, assisted by the vice-inquisitor of France, Jean Le Maistre, a Dominican. We can see two levels in the perception of Joan, linked to two chronological phases. During the interrogation (9 January 1431–15 March 1431) and when Jean d'Estivet, the *promoteur* (prosecutor) was drawing up the seventy articles of accusation (17–31 March 1431), the "objective" tendency dominated—that is, Joan's accusers seem to have really believed she was a witch. Later, when the court (in essence, Pierre Cauchon, but with the aid of theologians), determined its position and submitted it to the University of Paris for a definitive redaction of the twelve articles of accusation, witchcraft disappears from the list, and the charges speak of idolatry (through superstition), schism (rejection of the Church), apostasy, and heresy. When Master Pierre Maurice, doctor in theology, commented on the conclusions of the University of Paris masters, the term *présomption* (a term often encountered in the clerical versions of the history of the popess) returns continually: "Nothing but superstition, divination, presumptuous affirmation and vain boasting."[27]

The two Joans share the same exoteric accusation of presumption: a woman claims, against the law and the canons, to be stronger than the Church. This is one of the few points on which the court took care to explain its thinking to Joan of Arc, drawing a distinction between the Church Triumphant (God, the saints, the blessed) and the Church Militant: "our Holy Father the Pope, vicar of God on earth, the Cardinals, the prelates of the Church, and the clergy, and all the good Christians and Catholics: and this Church in good assembly cannot err and is governed by the Holy Spirit."[28] Joan declared that she obeyed God alone.

Behind this judiciary and ecclesiological logic, which was quite sufficient to satisfy the English (this was necessary to proclaiming Joan guilty), we can sense terror and an esoteric understanding of Joan (or both Joans) as an aggressive imposter and a satanic substitute for the Church. The imposter takes the place of the legitimate occupant, while the schismatic or the heretic claims to occupy another (better, more authentic, or more salutary) place. The imposter is the legitimate occupant inverted; the heretic is his double. I have attempted elsewhere to use a similar schema to explain the genesis of anti-Semitism in the twelfth century, a time when the Jew tended to replace the Christian in sexual and economic contexts in legendary narratives and rumors, and a time when Christians had less scope in those domains because of Church constraints over matrimony and lending money at interest.[29] The twin figures of the popess (in the Franciscan version) and the witch (in the "objective" view) varied the schema without changing its structure.

That schema led to a sort of autonomous belief that I shall call phantasmagoric, in contrast to the belief aiming at veracity discussed in the previous chapter. There are no gradations of phantasmagoric belief; it depends on no suspension of disbelief. It ceaselessly links the real and its signs to a type, an image (the Jew, the Witch, the Imposter) in which it invariably finds confirmation. Nothing illustrates the way this works better than the seventy articles against Joan redacted by Jean d'Estivet, which take no account whatsoever of her denials and construct a perfect portrait of the witch. Joan clearly states on 27 February 1431 that she had never possessed any mandragora (a root reputedly much used in witchcraft, whose magic powers came from the sperm of a hanged man) and that she did not believe in its powers. In spite of that denial, Jean d'Estivet wrote (in a passage that Pierre Cauchon did not retain): "Article VII. The said Jeanne was wont to bear a mandrake in her bosom, hoping thereby to have good fortune in riches and things of this world; which mandrake, she affirmed, possessed this virtue and potency."[30]

To be sure, Jean d'Estivet was acting as a prosecutor, thus he tended to load his charges against the accused. Pierre Cauchon's task, and in accessory fashion that of the University of Paris, was the very different one of finding acceptable, calm, and rational terms according to which Joan could be tried. Still, an obsession with witchcraft went beyond any assignment of judiciary roles: the real dividing line here ran between a rationality attentive to gradations (the position of the Church, represented by Pierre Cauchon, who has recently and rightly been rehabilitated by François Neveux)[31] and a horrified, brutal fascination (as with Guibert de Nogent in the twelfth century or Robert d'Uzès in the thirteenth century). Even the duke of Bedford displayed a phantasmagoric fear of Joan of Arc when he stated that Joan's success during the siege of Orléans was "produced in large part by the English soldiers' enlacement by false beliefs and by the insane fear they had of a disciple and hound of the Enemy [Satan] called *La Pucelle*, who used false enchantments and sorcery."[32] The anonymous university man who wrote the *Journal d'un bourgeois de Paris* commented on Joan's defeat before Paris on 8 September 1429, after she had launched an attack on the Feast of the Nativity of the Virgin Mary (when fighting infringed on religious custom): he refers to Joan as "a creature in the form of a woman, whom they call the Maid (la Pucelle)—what it was God only knows."[33] On 30 May 1431, after the executioner had tied Joan to the stake, he lifted her robe to display to everyone that "that creature" was indeed a woman.

The sticking power of the phantasmagoric scheme of belief may explain the obsessive quality of her interrogation. Almost daily Joan was questioned about the male clothing she continued to wear; every day her interrogators demanded that she reveal her secrets. The judges, baffled by the mystery of cross-dressing and by the hidden force that sustained Joan, interrogated her in minute detail about signs that they attempted to find in her banner (were the inscriptions at the top or at the bottom?), in her rings, and in the letters she wrote. Joan's defense corroborated their suspicions, for example, when she said that at times she followed the "Jesus-Maria" that began her letters with a cross, which signified that she intended the opposite of the missive's literal content. The innocent code system of an improvised woman soldier became a proof and a manifestation of overall blasphemous inversion.

A connection between the image of the warrior witch and the image of the popess (Joan-Manfreda) occurs at two points in Joan of Arc's trial. On 1 March 1431 the court asked her "what she said concerning our lord the

Pope and whom she believed to be the true pope."[34] Although the trauma of the schism had subsided by 1415–17, the judges' question shows to what extent that trauma still affected Catholics, prolonging the Franciscans' attacks of the years 1278–1335. The papacy was vacant at the time of Joan's first trial: Martin V had died on 20 February 1431, and Eugenius IV was not elected until 3 March, but that vacancy does not explain the court's concern. It is true, however, that the election of Martin V (in 1417) at the Council of Constance, although universally recognized, had not stopped a few irreducible prelates from electing "Clement VIII" as successor to the antipope Benedict XIII; a third candidate to the papacy was elected and took the name Benedict XIV. These claimants no longer tore the West asunder, however. In this domain as well, Joan gave grounds for suspicions. The comte d'Armagnac, the leader of King Charles VII's party, had plotted with King John II of Castile in support of "Clement VIII," and he sought the approval of Joan of Arc. Joan had the imprudence (or the vanity) to say that she would think about it, thus posing as a virtual guarantor, in the name of God, of papal authenticity. Joan states: "I am for the present too occupied with acts of war. But when you [the comte d'Armagnac] hear that I am in Paris, send a messenger to me, and I will let you know truly which [pope] you should believe, and this I will have known by the counsel of my guide in rectitude and sovereign lord."[35] There is further, and more serious, evidence of this Manfredan desire to be Church in the place of the Church that inhabited Joan, according to the phantasmagoric vision of her as witch warrior. According to Article XI of Jean d'Estivet's requisitory (another article that Pierre Cauchon did not retain), Robert de Baudricourt reported that Joan had boasted that when her mission was done, she would have three sons, one of which would become pope, the second emperor, and the third king. "Hearing which the said captain said to her, 'Now then, I should like to give you one if they're going to be such powerful men, because I should be better off.' To which she answered, 'No, gentle Robert, no, this is not the time; the Holy Spirit will find a way.'"[36] In 1431, Joan of Arc, the pope-bearing virgin fecundated by the Holy Spirit, throws a retrospective light on the fear that ran through Milan in 1300.

JOAN AS WITCH

Thus even the virginity of Joan of Arc, like the apparent chastity of the popess, hid its inverse, a determination to proliferate by debauchery and people the world with little demons. With Joan of Arc, this theme appears only in the interstices of the trial, in an obscure story of a suit for breach of promise of marriage, in suspicions that Joan had lodged with "la Rousse" (the redhead) in a bordello in Neufchâteau, or in Jean d'Estivet's insults ("That excommunicated whore"). There is eloquent testimony, however, to the image of Joan of Arc as a false virgin scattering satanic bastards in what may have been William Shakespeare's first play, *Henry VI, Part One*. The play is thought to have been written around 1592, a century and a half after Joan's trial, and its portrayal of the figure who put an end to the ambitions of the English in France is clearly insular. The text nonetheless attests to the persistence of the phantasmagoric image of a woman dressed as a man in order to turn the world upside down, and Shakespeare's drama, written at the height of the witchcraft craze and closely based on the chronicles of Holinshed, Hall, Fabyan, Grafton, and Stow, clearly displays what terror a false virgin and her subversive and dissolute excesses could arouse in men.

La Pucelle (as Shakespeare always calls her) presents herself to Charles, the dauphin, as a shepherd's daughter illuminated by the grace of the Virgin.[37] This classic version of the story of Joan of Arc immediately takes on disquieting, seductive, and provocative shadings. La Pucelle declares her joy in the beauty that the Virgin (?) instantaneously granted her:

> And, whereas I was black and swart before,
> With those clear rays which she infus'd on me
> That beauty am I bless'd with which you see.
>
> *(Henry VI, Part One,* 1.2.84–86)

She immediately proposes to the dauphin that she prove the validity of her mission by single combat, and when she vanquishes him, he speaks in amorous terms when he submits:

> Impatiently I burn with thy desire;
> My heart and hands thou hast at once subdu'd.
>
> (1.2.108–9)

Joan inverts the order of things: the dauphin offers to be the servant of the shepherdess; La Pucelle rejects him in terms that recall the "testimony" of Robert de Baudricourt on his own high hopes. Joan states:

> I must not yield to any rites of love,
>
> . . . .
>
> When I have chased all thy foes from hence,
> Then will I think upon a recompense.
>
> (1.2.113–16)

Like the popess, Joan of Arc reverses the direction of asceticism, moving from the celestial to the terrestrial through exaltation of the flesh. La Pucelle pursues her career by using trickery, and she attempts to retake Rouen by disguising her soldiers as merchants. For Lord Talbot, commander of the English forces, Joan's tactics are "treason," "treachery," and "hellish mischief," and the work of a sorceress:

> Pucelle, that witch, that damned sorceress.
>
> (3.2.38)

When her ruse fails, Joan returns to her favorite weapon, sexual seduction, and she charms the duke of Burgundy, an ally of the English. The duke immediately declares himself vanquished:

> Either she hath bewitch'd me with her words,
> Or nature makes me suddenly relent.
>
> (3.3.58–59)

When the warlike valor of the English carries the day, Joan desperately calls on the powers of darkness:

> The Regent conquers, and the Frenchmen fly.
> Now help, ye charming spells and periapts;
> And ye choice spirits that admonish me
> And give me signs of future accidents.
>
> (5.3.1–4)

The fiends appear, to Joan's great satisfaction:

> This speedy and quick appearance argues proof
> Of your accustom'd diligence to me.
>
> (5.3.8–9)

The fiends remain silent, however, without accepting the satanic eucharist she offers:

> Cannot my body nor blood-sacrifice
> Entreat you to your wonted furtherance?
>
> (5.3.20–21)

The English capture La Pucelle, who publicly displays her carnal nature as she rails aggressively (like a witch) at the duke of York. She appears before the duke again, followed by her shepherd father, who offers to go to his death with her. Joan violently rejects his paternity:

> Decrepit miser! base ignoble wretch!
> I am descended of a gentler blood.
> Thou art no father nor no friend of mine.
>
> (5.4.7–9)

This rejection leads La Pucelle to assert a sainthood founded on both lineage and election:

> First, let me tell you whom you have condemn'd:
> Not me begotten of a shepherd swain,
> But issued from the progeny of kings;
> Virtuous and holy; chosen from above,
> By inspiration of celestial grace,
> To work exceeding miracles on earth.

$$(5.4.36-40)$$

This proclamation fails to persuade the duke of York or the earl of Warwick, so La Pucelle, as changeable as all witches, declares that she is pregnant:

> Will nothing turn your unrelenting hearts?
> Then, Joan, discover thine infirmity,
> That warrenteth by law to be thy privilege.
> I am with child, ye bloody homicides!

$$(5.4.59-63)$$

Warwick immediately thinks, with horror, that the father is Charles VII, but Joan disabuses him by first naming the duc d'Alençon, whose name inspires equal horror ("That notorious Machiavel!"), then Reignier (René d'Anjou), king of Naples. This list of possible paramours scandalizes the two Englishmen even more. They send Joan off to the stake, and she exits cursing them. Thus Joan of Arc, like Manfreda-Guglielma, was a variation on the type of the witch, an inverted copy of the Virgin, and a force for the destruction of natural and divine order.

Nothing shows better than this fleshly version of Joan of Arc the tendency of a phantasmagoric belief to tip back and forth between positive and negative or good and evil. The image of the witch, a false virgin who unleashes desire, stands opposed to the image of the prophetess, the saintly leader, and the "virginal" virgin who inspires chastity in others. Dunois, Joan of Arc's companion in arms, testified in Orléans in 1456 at Joan's rehabilitation trial that he believed in La Pucelle's divine inspiration because of three miracles. First, she had recognized him without ever having seen him before. Unlike the sorceress, who produces bastards, she gave legitimacy to Dunois, "the Bastard of Orléans," by making him a part of the divine plan of action. In this first case, the miracle arose out of Joan's innate knowledge. Second, when Joan herself was wounded, she recovered immediately (the gift of force). Third, and for Dunois the most miraculous manifestation, Joan made the soldiers chaste: "He and others, when they were in the society of La Pucelle, had no will or desire to have commerce or society with a woman, which seemed to him something almost divine."[38] The duc d'Alençon, whom Shakespeare casts as a possible father for Joan's child, reiterates the miraculous impression created by this chaste intimacy, saying that he slept several times next to her on the straw. Moreover, "he sometimes saw Joan as she was preparing [for battle], and sometimes he saw her breasts, which were beautiful, but he never had carnal desire for her."[39]

We must take care not to reduce this ambivalence of the image to opposing customs (English and French, clerical and lay, etc.). One archetype (in the literal sense, not the astrological and Jungian sense), that of the "reversing" woman who introduces sexual and political reversals and is gifted with an astonishing, dominating knowledge, can be divided between the two types of the sorceress and the prophetess that give direction to the archetypal themes. In the case of Joan of Arc, a national polarization obliterates any oscillation or competition between the two interpretations. Still, the Cistercians' early support of Guglielma shows the reality of that ambivalence, and it can be seen in many other witchcraft cases as well. People found the Christian prophetess just as fascinating as her reverse image, the sorceress.

THE CHRISTIAN PROPHETESS

The beneficent type of the prophetess played a role in the biographical development of Joan the popess. We can see traces of this type in the tarot figure (except in the Visconti sets, the popess's attribute is a book) and in the episode of Manfreda in Milan, which had an influence on Joan. Moreover, Joan owed her career to an almost miraculous learning (Martinus Polonus noted that no man could equal her) that in itself was not an imposture, even though it was turned away from its holy function to serve the ends of ambition and deceit. Still, the way that such learning was acquired separates the popess and the prophetess: Joan learned what she knew; the prophetess's knowledge is a divine gift.

The type of the prophetess is important to an understanding of Joan because "allegory" (the type, the image) is integral to an articulated symbolic language of binary oppositions. Clerical readings of the episode of Pope Joan tended to place the popess in the category of evildoers: the only exceptions are Jean de Mailly, who speaks of the Fast of the Four Times as a beneficent act, and Martin Lefranc, who mentions prefaces to the Mass.

The falsity imputed to Joan can only be grasped in reference to what she was counterfeiting.

In antiquity, female prophetism was honored throughout Mediterranean lands, among the Jews and the so-called "Oriental" religions as well as among Greeks and Romans. There were such famous prophetic figures as the Pythia of Delphi and the Sibyls, the oldest of whom officiated at Erythrae, in Asia Minor. Late-Roman scholarship (Varro, Lactantius) lists ten Sibyls, scattered from Persia to Italy. Sibylline oracles played an important role in Rome from the time (as Pliny and Dionysius Halicarnassus tell us) when Tarquin the Elder bought three books of oracles from the Cumaean Sibyl. A college of priests was specifically charged with caring for these books and arranging for their consultation, which was last done at the request of Julian the Apostate in A.D. 363. Stilicho destroyed the sibylline books around 408.[40]

Christianity had no difficulty absorbing pagan or Jewish female prophetism; the Sibyls were honored until the end of the Middle Ages, and certain great female mystics were venerated for their divine inspiration. The transition was an easy one for reasons that I will list briefly, then discuss more fully.

1. Both its inspiration and its textual form made the Greek model of female prophecy readily adaptable to Christianity. The prophetess, like St. John the Evangelist, the author of the Book of Revelation, received a divine breath *(pneuma)* and produced an enigmatic but fixed text that lent itself to being glossed;

2. Christianity, a religion of revised revelation, had a tendency to include ancient traditions and insert them into new doctrine, as has been observed in connection with narrative traditions: Christ did not come to abolish but to accomplish;

3. In these early stages, the sociological composition of the Christian religion was markedly female. The hagiographic commonplace of the Christian wife or daughter of a pagan notable who chooses Christ had a basis in reality. In times of persecution, the virgin martyr was the epitome of Christianity;

4. Christ's message of a celestial inversion of earthly hierarchies privileged women, children, and the poor;

5. The Virgin Mary, an ordinary woman and a human among humans, offered the highest form of mediation between heaven and earth; she was the receptacle of the Incarnation and the knowledge (the Annunciation) that prepared it. After the Passion and the Ascension, she (and John) guaranteed the authenticity of the commemorative tradition of the New Testament.

The Pythia: A Bad Prophetess

Comparison between the way that Christianity treated the Sibyl and the Pythia, twin figures in ancient Greek prophecy, returns us to the great ambivalence that underlies the production of metaphorical types. The two were caught in a convention that, from earliest times, separated the prophetess from the witch (and I shall retain the anachronism to designate this still-virtual personage of a powerfully demoniac female with a deceptively mild appearance).

Giulia Sissa has provided an admirable analysis of the Pythia in her study of female virginity in ancient Greece,[41] where she shows that in the oracle at Delphi a virgin was seen as receiving the word of Apollo (perceived as chaste fecundation) into her intact but receptive body. We see here the banal metaphor of "divine inspiration" (breath, *pneuma*), but added to it (or substituted for it) is the notion of a divine emanation that issues forth out of the ground like the gynecological fumigations that Greek medicine believed set the female reproductive organs back in their proper places.

It is understandable that this view of the Delphic oracle was too close to the marian theme in Christianity (virginity, divine fecundation, supernatural knowledge) not to give rise to demonologic suspicions. Indeed, two Fathers of the Church, Origen and John Chrysostom, declared themselves scandalized by the Pythia's manner of prophesying and refused to explain her acts euhemeristically (pagan miracles were the result of human trickery), as was often done in Christian apologetics from antiquity to the central Middle Ages. The Pythia was a manifestation of an obscene demonic possession (as was the "objective" sorceress). Origen said of her attitude as she sat on her three-legged stool offering herself to the telluric *pneuma*: "In this was there not proof of the impure and vicious nature of this spirit? It insinuated itself into the soul of the prophetess not by way of scattered and imperceptible pores, much purer than the female organs, but because the chaste man was not allowed to look much less to touch." The femaleness of the medium was proof of the satanic quality of the message:

> If Apollo of Delphi were the god the Greeks believe him to be,
> whom would he have chosen as prophet if not a wise man or,
> lacking such, a man progressing toward knowledge? Why did he
> not choose a man to prophesy rather than a woman? And assuming he preferred the female sex, perhaps because he had neither
> power nor pleasure other than in the bosom of women, why did
> he not choose a virgin rather than another woman as interpreter
> of his will?[42]

John Chrysostom's version of the same process, as Sissa presents it, is even more striking: "The Pythia is seated on Apollo's tripod, her legs spread. An evil spirit *(pneuma poneron)* rises from below, enters her vagina, and fills her with madness. Her hair is disheveled, and foam flows from her mouth: she is like a bacchante. And it is in such a state that she speaks." John adds, "I know that you were ashamed and blushed to hear this story," and Sissa comments, "Thus the church father apologizes, knowing the effect upon his listeners of visualizing the spread thighs, the open mouth, and the wild hair: the possessed woman accuses her master."[43]

Sissa sees this interpretation of the Pythia of Delphi as constituting an important break: Origen is indignant that the priests did not choose a virgin, given that virginity seemed essential to the oracular statement. Two different notions of virginity were involved, however. As Sissa has discovered, the Greeks did not believe in physical virginity or in the existence of the hymen. Thus the Pythia could open herself to the divine *pneuma*. Her virginity guaranteed her ability to accept and close, hence a capacity for the reception and retention of secrets, in a very Greek analogy between speech and sexuality. For the Fathers of the Church, the possibility of sexual communication was proof, to the contrary, of imposture and demonism.

The personage of the Pythia and the surprising connections between virginity, child-bearing, and prophecy that she embodied were probably soon forgotten outside of Greek patristics, but Christian thought continued to be troubled by a virgin who produces a child. The Romans and the Germans, with their rough and ready juridical approach, had some difficulty imagining that a virgin could give birth to the Good News, to the point that in the ninth century certain German heretics professed that Mary had given birth to Christ through her ear. The Church got around such concerns by continually extending the divinity of Mary, who was proclaimed born unstained by original sin by Pius IX in 1854. The redoubtable Oskar Panizza pushed the logic of that dogma to a joking extreme by offering to define "The Immaculate Conception of the popes" (1892).[44]

The prophetic sacrality of Mary, virgin mother, was a source of anxiety and disequilibrium that sought a counterweight. That role, which the Pythia fulfilled, was passed on not only to witches but to the popess, a false virgin, a mother through debauchery, whose knowledge hid a truth rather than revealing it. The parallel may seem forced, but the Romans who presented an image of the Virgin and Child as a portrait of Joan were making a joking use of this same parallel. In the fourteenth century, Dietrich of Nieheim referred to Joan's child as her *primogenitus,* an evangelical term traditionally applied to the Son of the Virgin.

THE RETURN OF THE SIBYL

The Pythia crystalized an obsession with learned demoniac virginity, but the Sibyls were fully welcome in the Christian universe, as the works of Bernard McGinn have shown.[45] The difference in treatment probably resides in the textual, rather than the sexual, status of sibylline revelation, which was due more to the hazards of tradition than to Greek prophetical practice. The appearance of the Cumaean Sibyl in the sixth book of Virgil's *Aeneid* offered a guarantee of authenticity, because both ancient and medieval Christianity considered Virgil to be a pagan precursor of the Good News, even though another tradition saw him as a quasi-prophet, hence a satanic necromancer. Obviously, the great phantasmagoric figures are always ambivalent.[46] Above all, several books of sibylline oracles that were taken as clear announcements of the coming of Christ had escaped Stilicho's destruction. The prescience of these oracles is not as surprising as it might seem: current scholarship tells us that although these texts incorporated ancient fragments, they were produced by Jewish and Christian authors writing between B.C.E. 150 and A.D. 300. Jewish and Christian apologists were making use of a prestigious tradition of the Greek or Roman world for missionary purposes. Hence the first Fathers of the Church (Justin, Athenagoras, Hippolytus, Tertullian, Clement of Alexandria, Theophilus of Antioch, Eusebius) larded their writings with sibylline excerpts. The Sibyl was implanted in the Western tradition by the necessary and sufficient route of Augustine, a man normally wary of prophecy of all sorts.

The sibylline tradition continued uninterrupted in the West, with powerful assistance from Christian encyclopedists from Isidore of Seville in the seventh century through Rabarus Maurus in the ninth century to Vincent of Beauvais in the thirteenth century. Interest in the Sibyls peaked in the thirteenth century (a moment, as we have seen, of recuperation and reorganization of the historical and legendary heritage) and their success came at the price of watering them down to permit the integration of female prophecy into Christian learning. Belief in the Sibyls was more of the veracity sort than the phantasmagoric sort. The Sibyl was used as a measure or standard of evaluation: Peter Lombard speaks of the Sibyl in his *Sentences* to wonder how much faith was needed for salvation and whether a vague prescience of the advent of Christ was sufficient for election. Thomas Aquinas pronounced on the question in the affirmative, stating that the Sibyls had indeed been gifted with true revelation.[47] Questions of the sort found a place in attempts to determine how the afterworld (paradise, hell, purgatory, and limbo) was organized. As Jacques Le Goff has demonstrated, these were urgent matters in the late twelfth century.[48]

The Sibyls became so well integrated into Christian lore that at times they were disposed architecturally as a pendant to male prophets. Iconography was at first concentrated on the Erythraean Sibyl, who was mentioned by Augustine and was usually paired with David, the prophet par excellence. In a famous text on the *Dies Irae,* Thomas of Celano, St. Francis's companion, wrote:

> Day of wrath, that day
> That will reduce the world to ashes
> As attested by David and the Sybil *(Teste David cum Sibylla).*[49]

In later ages galleries of Sibyls were created in which they were matched up with the prophets of Israel, a custom that culminated in Michelangelo's magnificent frescoes for the Sistine Chapel. One late-fifteenth-century writer, Filippo Barbieri, stretched the number of Sibyls from the ten cited by Lactantius to twelve so as to set up a better comparison with the prophets and the apostles. This triangular disposition (pagan antiquity, Old Testament, New Testament) replaced the medieval typology limited to the two Testaments.

The integration of sibylline wisdom, unlike the amorous madness of the Greek prophetess, permitted the assimilation of local and folk traditions into Christian lore. In Rome, for example, it was said that one Christmas Eve the Tiburtine Sibyl had shown Augustus the Virgin and Child in *ara coeli* (the altar of the sky). This foundation legend of the Roman church of Santa Maria d'Aracoeli, on the Capitoline, was attested as early as the eighth century; it was legitimated by Innocent III in his second sermon on the Nativity and was later repeated, first by Bartholemew of Trent, then by Jacopo da Voragine.[50] The pagan companions of the ancient Romans took on the role, in relation to the Virgin, that John the Baptist played in relation to Christ. The image of the prophetess, the inspired woman, was so strong, however, that inevitably it gave rise to other versions outside the edifice of the Church or on its threshold.

THE FOLLIES OF THE WISE VIRGIN

Among the Sibyl's attributes were two characteristics that had disqualified both popesses and the Pythias: ambition and powers of enchantment. A late instance of these qualities was the fifteenth-century appearance of the Sibyl of the Apennines, who was imprisoned in a grotto near Lago Pilato in the province of Picenum (Piceno). This Sibyl, who seems to have been the same as the Cumaean Sibyl, was imprisoned there until the Last Judgment for having claimed (presumptuously, like a popess) that she, not Mary, would give birth to the Son of God. The Sibyl of the Apennines became a temptress and a prophetess in Andrea da Barberino's romance *Guerrin Meschino* (early fifteenth century). Somewhat later, in the *Paradis de la Reine Sibylle* of Antoine de la Sale (1430), she became the queen of a subterranean realm who seduced knights.[51]

Finally, the Sibyls, who functioned as simple mirrors of revelation in the clerical tradition from Augustine to Thomas of Celano, regained active prophetic powers beginning in the eleventh century. Two distinct bodies of works, of uncertain origin, attest to this new role.

The prophecies of the Tiburtine Sibyl were widely known, and they found their way into manuscripts in the eleventh century. In this tradition the Sibyl recovers biographical details that a purely clerical tradition had omitted. The daughter of Priam and Hecuba, she is young and beautiful (an important detail, as the clerical tradition had made her aged). This mitigated the youthful seductiveness that Origen had objected to in the Pythia of Delphi, who, by a curious paradox, had given the Church the model of an aged Sibyl. According to Diodorus Siculus, in ancient times the Pythia had been a young virgin, until Echecrates the Thessalian, who had come to Delphi to consult the oracle, fell in love with her for her beauty (much like Dauphin Charles before Joan of Arc in Shakespeare), carried her off, and raped her. Diodorus tells us: "Following this scandal the Delphians decreed that henceforth the prophetess would no longer be a virgin, but a woman above the age of fifty. Yet she wears the clothing of a young maiden as a reminder of the prophetess of old."[52] In the Greek world, this "decorporation" of the prophetess may perhaps refer to an origin of oracular inspiration common to Daphne, the Pythia, and Cassandra: Apollo pursues a beautiful young virgin who rejects him, but to whom he gives, in exchange for a noncarnal possession, oracular powers and immortality (but not perpetual youth). Thus from paganism to Christianity there are connected themes—dangerous virginal seduction and the exchange of knowledge for youth—woven tightly about the prophetess. Just as the Church soon imposed minimal age limits (something that, for social reasons, it did not do in the Middle Ages) for the few religious orders open to women (deaconess, canoness, or abbess), it also took care to present the Sibyls as aged, like the white-haired, bearded figures of the prophets of Israel. The seduction of youth combined with learning continued to exert a pull, however, as evidenced by Michelangelo's Delphic Sibyl.

The Tiburtine Sibyl thus appeared, in all her beauty, before the Roman Senate of Trajan's time to explain the vision of nine suns that a hundred senators had seen in a dream. They exclaim: "Teacher and Mistress *(Magistra et Domina)*" (irresistibly recalling the attribute of the Church as *Mater et Magistra*, but with the added connotation of domination), "since your body is great and exceedingly beautiful in a way we have never seen in any woman but you, we ask you to interpret what the dream we all saw in a single night portends for the future."[53] The Sibyl tells the senators that the nine suns stand for nine generations preceding the End. The passages regarding the two last generations, cryptically written and ceaselessly rewritten and glossed, found a place among the great prophetic texts of the Middle Ages.

In the thirteenth century a second group of texts known as the *Prophecy of the Erythraean Sibyl (Vaticinium Sibyllae Erythraeae)* returned to the Sibyls, recasting their prophecies, a form common among Franciscan Joachimite circles around 1250. The adapter of this collection of texts may have been John of Parma, the minister general of the Franciscans. The principal prophetic authors of the thirteenth to the fourteenth centuries (Arnau de Villanova, Angelo Clareno, Jean de Roquetaillade) all glossed this text. Once again, the people we find clustered around the "free" Sibyl are the ones at the fringes of the Church who were interested in Joan.

FOUR CONFIGURATIONS

Let us try to impose some sort of order among the female images enumerated thus far. We will need to begin with Origen's somewhat naive astonishment and apply it to a consideration of the odd figure of the Virgin Mary. Why did God not confide his message uniquely in wise men? What is a woman doing in Revelation? More simply, why should there be women? Nicole Loraux has shown that Hesiod, perhaps reflecting the eternal male, put that question to the episode of the creation of woman.[54] The Church offered one answer by enclosing Mary within her maternal role and the Sibyls (and in their wake, female saints and devout women) within their function of mirroring revelation. The terrible pressure to which the Church subjected eleventh- and twelfth-century society in sexual matters (priestly celibacy, the prohibition of consanguineous marriages) engendered tensions that broke that male dam. What issued forth was the type of the Mistress *(Domina)*, an omnipresent female figure, strong but protective, close but inaccessible. This was the Virgin of twelfth-century monastic culture, the Lady of courtly literature, the Sibyl of eschatological expectation, and the Inspired Woman of the mystical groups. This type crystalized hopes and fears, but it might easily tip over into its contrary, the Sorceress, the Foolish Virgin, the Seductress. The popess played her role in this game: as she emerged out of clerical discourse, she illustrated the imposture of the false virgin and the dangers of a perverse use of genuine knowledge. Within the sure framework of ecclesiastical history, Joan declared that learning was a disguise just as effective as borrowed clothing; she was a warning against the temptations of the pneuma that breathed inspiration into spiritually inclined women of the central Middle Ages. She showed that the seduction of illuminated woman, whether or not it was satanic, might be of the flesh. Flanked by the twin images of the Holy Virgin and the Foolish Virgin, Joan guarded the enclosed precincts of inspired women.

Ardors of the pneuma and the flesh incessantly undermined that construction, however. The type of the inspired woman, although subject to reversal, could not be dissolved by an ecclesiological discourse still reliant on the finely graduated level of belief that seeks veracity; within the firmly traced outlines of Joan's silhouette, female and inspirationalist heresy used colors of its own choosing to paint a miniature of the popess of the Holy Ghost, and after the twelfth century prophetesses continued to multiply.

The religious discourse of the central Middle Ages was thus obliged to create a place somewhere between the "sorceress" and the Chosen Woman for an inspired woman as domesticated as Joan but oriented toward the good. In short, a sexual polarization of the sacred offered four possible configurations: male domination (illustrated by orthodox pontifical history); female domination (illustrated, briefly, by the episode of the Milan popess); female subversion of the male model or the discovery of ways to get around that model (as conjured up by Joan's adventure); and male subversion of or discovery of ways to get around the female model (as in the Church version of the prophetess). Given that assigning gender roles continued to be a male and clerical prerogative (female domination emerged only briefly in one heretical parenthesis in Milan), counterfigures were oriented toward male domination. Female subversion (Joan) survived in memory only as a defeat and a danger (fear of which was projected onto the image of the witch). The only configuration that succeeded, as we shall see, was male subversion of female sacred prestige, which curbed the strong image of the prophetess, guiding it toward the male institution of the Church.

This means that it is the fourth configuration that we must explore, not for the simple (though real) pleasure of exhausting all combinations, but rather because it constitutes a response to Manfreda and to Joan. We must try to find a pendant to the female counterpope in the figure of a counterprophetess; a prophetess contradictorily integrated into the male model.

The Church had its work cut out for it, given the vigor of female mysticism in the West starting with the twelfth century. Women had little room in which to maneuver, however: as Peter Dronke remarks, Angela of Foligno and Marguerite Porete, two thirteenth-century lovers of Christ, were comparable as mystics, but Angela was revered and became the object of a cult, particularly among the Franciscans, whereas Marguerite was "atrociously put to death" at the stake in 1310.[55]

MARIE ROBINE: A PROPHETESS ON THE THRESHOLD OF THE CHURCH

Marie Robine provides another example of a female prophetic positioned at the limits of what the Church could accept.[56] If we view Marie Robine within the group of the many female prophets who flourished during the Great Schism (Bridget of Sweden and Catherine of Siena are two examples), she seems a double for Joan of Arc a quarter-century earlier. Marie arrived in Avignon some time in the 1380s (hence in the early years of the Schism). An illiterate peasant woman in poor health, she came there from her native Gascony in pilgrimage to the tomb of Pierre de Luxembourg, a cardinal who had died young in odor of sanctity. She regularly had apocalyptical visions. The Avignon pope, Clement VII, received her favorably, and in 1387–89 the pope participated in a prayer session at the tomb of Pierre de Luxembourg that cured Marie of her illness. Papal favor continued under Clement's successor, Benedict XIII, who granted Marie a pension, thus giving her a quasi-official status as prophetess, in a bull promulgated in 1395.

The revelations made to Marie, which were noted down and gathered together, became increasingly political and eschatological, and in 1398 she dictated a letter to Charles VI to oppose, in the name of heaven, the royal government's projected withholding of obedience from the pope and to preach the religious and moral reform of the kingdom. Following a pattern that reached from the visionary who contributed to Charles VI's first crisis of insanity in 1382 to Joan of Arc and continued all the way to "Martin l'Archange," a visionary who sought out Louis XVIII to lecture him on his conduct,[57] Marie went to Paris to see the king in June 1398. She was received with hostility by the masters of the University of Paris (thus throwing light on the trial of Joan of Arc in 1431), and she failed to see the king. After her return to Avignon, further revelations led Marie to express virulent criticism of the pontifical court in which she exalted the true Church and the congregation of the just while flaying the prelates. Leaving aside possible direct influences, Wycliffe's and Hus's theme of the true Church enjoyed immense and widespread popularity in a time when the Schism had rekindled questions regarding the truth of the Church first raised at the end of the thirteenth century.

Marie Robine embodied the ambivalence of the visionary: Clement VII and Benedict XIII had used her as a mystical guarantee of the authenticity of the Avignon papacy when ecclesiological arguments proved a weak defense. At the same time, however, opening the door to eschatology risked letting in the violent winds of antipapal reform. Marie Robine was probably spared the fate of Marguerite Porete and Joan of Arc only because she died in 1399.

The Great Schism demonstrated the defeat of a hierarchic male Church, which meant that the Holy Spirit had to inspire the simple faithful, especially the simplest among them, women. In his study of the spirituality of the many prophetesses who arose in that troubled period, André Vauchez notes that an expanded female religious role reactivated male and clerical fears, as in the first great treatise on demonology of the Middle Ages, the *Formicarius* of Johannes Nider, a work written between 1430 and 1435. Vauchez says of Nider: "He made particular mention of the cases of women 'appearing to be men who said they had been sent by God'—a formulation which in itself demonstrated that these women constituted a well-defined category and were not just isolated cases."[58]

If we want to find a "purer" (that is, less political, better accepted) instance of a Church prophetess, we will need to go back to an earlier period. The high point of tension between male and female sacrality is embodied in St. Hildegard of Bingen, a figure who also exemplifies the broadest extension of prophetic rights to a woman within the Church. In a sense, Hildegard was a quasi-popess. In discussing her, I shall rely on the translations of her works in the fine anthology of women's writings edited, with commentary, by Peter Dronke.[59]

HILDEGARD OF BINGEN: A MAJOR CHURCH PROPHETESS

Hildegard of Bingen (1098–1178) lived in times of theological and ecclesiastical renewal (in short, the century of St. Bernard), which may have spared her a confrontation with the Church. Hildegard's extraordinary status as a prophetess came only in 1136, when, at the age of forty and after her election as abbess of Disibodenberg, she let her revelations be known. She soon won the esteem and admiration of the powerful archbishop of Mainz, and the Synod of Trier (November 1147–February 1148), presided over by Pope Eugenius III, approved the redaction and distribution of her revelations. St. Bernard himself, who was present at Trier, praised her work. In 1150 Odo of Paris wrote to Hildegard to express his admiration and ask her to draw upon her visions to pronounce on the "deity" of God, a question that had been bitterly disputed at the Council of Reims between St. Bernard and Gilbert of Poitiers (Gilbert de la Porée), a debate of capital importance because it hinged on whether one could elaborate a logical, "scientific" theology.[60] Hildegard had thus become a high authority within the Church, to some extent analogous to St. Bernard. Although Bernard bore no particular title other than abbot of Clairvaux, he was always consulted, throughout the first half of the twelfth century, on questions of faith. He remarks in one of his letters that people said of him that he was the true pope.

The parallel between Bernard and Hildegard gives new vigor to a hypothesis suggested in chapter 4: when Martinus Polonus first stated that Joan came from Mainz, he may have been reflecting Hildegard's reputation as "popess" (a role attributed to her both as naive praise and as stinging criticism). There is another disturbing detail: around 1260 the priests, canons, and abbots of Cologne (still in the Rhine region) asked their archbishop to chase the Dominicans out of their city, taking as their authority a prophecy of Hildegard's that predicted the arrival of false preachers during the next century. The affair had important repercussions because Cologne was the central house of the Order of Preachers' immense German province, and it is conceivable that the Dominicans were furious at St. Hildegard. It is quite possible that Martinus Polonus, a decidedly inventive and mischievous person, might have lampooned Hildegard under the name of Joan. The importance of the private joke in medieval clerical culture has been sorely underestimated; the medieval Church laughed more often than is admitted. I might add that the Preachers had immense difficulties with Hildegard's heirs (legitimate and illegitimate), the tight-knit groups of mystics and béguines in the Rhineland who always operated at the edges of heterodoxy and insubmission.[61]

Hildegard counseled the greatest dignitaries of the Christian world, corresponding with popes Eugenius III, Anastasius IV, and Adrian IV and with such secular sovereigns as Conrad III, Frederick Barbarossa, Henry II of England, Eleanor of Aquitaine, and Irene, empress of Constantinople. She went so far as to give Emperor Frederick a good scolding. Moreover, she carried on pastoral activities (itinerant preaching, sermons delivered before monks, bishops, and the laity) usually reserved to male clerics.

Hildegard's aura as the "Rhenish Sibyl," as she was called, cannot be reduced to the prestige of her virtue or of her individual sanctity; the great consulted her not out of simple deference, but because she knew. God had revealed to her a message of universal salvation. This was what made her a prophetess and set her apart from the little lovers of Jesus who, from Angela of Foligno to Teresa of Avila, could only offer the world their private notes on their own loving relationship. Hildegard pursued the redaction of human contracts with God. She took great pains to publish everything, and even if her considerable oeuvre does not all concern revelation, her knowledge of God opened up the entire universe to her. One rarely encounters such an active encyclopedism in the Middle Ages: her fields of interest included cosmology, medicine, mystic poetry, physics, ethics, dramaturgy, and music.

Hildegard's high status is all the more surprising because it was never accompanied by any denial of her female condition. It is true that in her privileged relationship with the divine she attained a sort of sexual neutrality or "omnisexuality," to use Ferdinando Camon's felicitous neologism.[62] In one of her visions Wisdom (Sapientia) addresses her as "human creature"—in Latin *homo*, a generic term opposed to *vir* (man). When Hildegard sees herself in Moses or Daniel, she is referring to an inspired role, which implies neither her own transformation into a man nor (unlike Guglielma or Manfreda) any reversal of tasks from male to female.

THE FEMALE AND THE SACRED IN HILDEGARD

Hildegard's prophetic activities nonetheless had roots that were profoundly and specifically female: until she was forty, the age of sexual neutrality, her visions occurred within an all-female milieu. In the fragments of her autobiography that have been conserved, Hildegard states that God "fixed" a capacity for vision in her when she was still in her mother's womb, a quasi-Apollonian concept of the pythic gift to which we shall return. Hildegard's divine visions began when she was three years old. At the time her only companion was a nurse, who saw nothing and expressed a negative opinion about Hildegard's election. Hildegard was offered to the convent at the age of eight, and there for some time she said nothing about her visions, finally sharing them with the abbess, who had them noted down by a monk. The female nature of Hildegard's visionary activity was not limited to circumstances, but rather arose from a necessity in the history of salvation. When she speaks of her birth and her election, Hildegard indicates a context: "For, in the eleven hundredth year after Christ's incarnation, the teaching of the apostles and the burning justice which he had set in Christians and spiritual people began to glow sluggish and irresolute. In that period I was born, and my parents, amid sighs, vowed me to God." Hildegard's gift tended to compensate for the weakness of men *(homines* and *viri)* sunk into institutional torpor. In her autobiography she presents the Christian faithful in the grip of a habit that could only be broken by the shock of a new, female and divine speech. Those slumbering Christians wondered, "What are these things, and from where, which that woman utters as if they were from God? It's hard for us to live differently from our forefathers or the people of our time." Following the Christian scheme of inverted values, it was a woman without learning who received Knowledge. With neither humility nor vanity, Hildegard proclaimed the divine aspect of the female inheritance of the weak:

> In that same [experience of] vision I understood the writings of the prophets, the Gospels, the works of other holy men, and those of certain philosophers, without any human instruction *(ine ulla humana doctrina),* and I expounded certain things based on these, though I scarcely had literary understanding, inasmuch as a woman who was not learned *(indocta mulier)* had been my teacher.[63]

Hildegard seems clearly aware of what she is doing when she sets up an opposition between a dulled male learning and a living female knowledge, which exposed her to suspicions of imposture, and she describes a scandalized male reaction to her in terms that recall Origen's astonishment at the Pythia's inspired knowledge:

> Then the ancient deceiver put me to the ordeal of great mockery, in that many people said: "What's all this—so many hidden truths revealed to this foolish, unlearned woman, even though there are many brave and wise men around? Surely this will come to nothing!" For many people *(multi)* wondered whether my revelation stemmed from God, or from the parchedness *(inaquositas)* of aerial spirits, that often seduced human beings."[64]

A Mystical Female Sexuality

This physical note puts us on the track of the essentially female character of Hildegard's inspiration. As noted, God operated in Apollonian fashion to "fix" revelation in the foetus developing in Hildegard's mother's womb. That pythic relation to God is clear in her description of how her visions were revealed to her: "The fairest and most loving man" had appeared to her, "such that the look of him perfused all my womb with a balmlike perfume."[65]

Hildegard developed a genuine erotics of knowledge, which, before the fall, was penetration: "God gave Adam all creatures, that he might penetrate them with virile force *(virili vi eas penetraret)*. He knew them *(scivit et cognovit)*." Hildegard takes the biblical metaphor of "knowing" literally, for the act of knowing consists in a proper correlation of elements internal to man: "Man the human creature [*homo*, not *vir*] draws his sensuality *(sensualitatem)* and desire from fire; from air he draws thoughts and their power to roam; from water, knowledge and motion." Knowledge results from the proper circulation of fire in water through desire and sexuality: "When Adam gazed at Eve, he was entirely filled with wisdom."[66] The medieval physics of separation (man is hot and dry; woman cold and humid) is transformed here into a biology of harmonious mixture.

This mixture proved impossible after the fall, and the vital flux of knowledge (or "knowing") was dissipated: God created man so that all animated beings would be submitted to him:

> When man transgressed God's command, he was changed both
> in body and mind. For the purity of his blood was turned into an-
> other mode, so that, instead of purity, he now ejects the spume of
> semen. If man had remained in paradise, he would have stayed in
> an immutable and perfect state. But all these things, after his
> transgression, were turned into another and bitter mode. For
> man's blood, burning in the ardour and heat of lust, ejects a
> spume from itself that we call semen, as a pot placed on the fire
> brings up foam from the water because of the fire's heat.[67]

The dry heat of the man no longer produced anything but the froth of reproduction, but, for Hildegard, the nature of female pleasure and its orientation toward procreation permitted the woman to retain, in the act of love, the taste of paradise that makes possible communication with God and with the world. The woman holds the seed, the fruit, solidly in her womb, as did the Pythia in Giulia Sissa's analysis.

Thanks to the fire of her desire, woman is able to capture, in the sex act, the flux of enjoyment and knowledge. She seizes it; she conceives:

> When a woman is making love with a man [note that it is the
> woman who is the subject of this active verb], a sense of heat in

her brain, which brings with it sensual delight, communicates the
taste of that delight *(gustum ejusdem delectationis)* during the act
and summons forth the emission of the man's seed. And when
the seed has fallen into its place, that vehement heat descending
from her brain draws the seed to itself and holds it, and soon the
woman's sexual organs contract, and all the parts that are ready to
open up during the time of menstruation now close, in the same
way as a strong man can hold something enclosed in his fist.[68]

Hildegard sets up a contrast: to one side there is the continual, endless
heat of male desire and the foaming and dispersed flow of male sperm or
female menses (which she holds responsible for all sorts of ills when the
normal cycle is anticipated), to the other there is the good heat of female
desire, which is brief but is oriented toward creation and the creature to
come:

The man's love, compared with the woman's, is a heat of ardour
like a fire on blazing mountains, which can hardly be put out,
whilst hers is a wood-fire that is easily quenched; but the
woman's love, compared with the man's, is like a sweet warmth
proceeding from the sun, which brings forth fruits.

After the fall, man's desire sends him out to wander about in a world that
escapes him, whereas woman remains in the happy and paradisiac enclosure of the granary (yet another similarity with the Greek view of female
sexuality):

But the great love that was in Adam when Eve came forth from
him [in this case it is man who procreates in happiness], and the
sweetness of the sleep with which he then slept, were turned in
his transgression into a contrary mode of sweetness. And so, because a man still feels this great sweetness in himself, and is like a
stag thirsting for the fountain [the Danaides' image of endless de-
sire], he races swiftly to the woman and she to him—she is like a
threshing-floor pounded by his many strokes and brought to heat
when the grains are threshed inside her.[69]

Female sexuality, both real and metaphorical (virginity does not distinguish the nun from her lay sisters) is a welcoming and a grasping of the
world and God (both conception and a conceptualization), but male sexuality is dispersed in pursuit (endless desire, vain knowledge). This fine
exaltation of female sexuality, perhaps unequaled before our own days,
prompts our admiration. Its influence on mystics of the later Middle Ages,

though difficult to measure, is undeniable. St. Hildegard's exaltation of woman cannot be confined to mystico-biological speculation.

HILDEGARD'S TIARAS

Hildegard, who was by nature both haughty and vigorous, took command of her community of nuns and decided to leave the dual convent/ monastery of Disibodenberg and move to nearby Rupertsberg, a site on the Rhine, but one as desolate as Disibodenberg had been agreeable. Hildegard conducted herself like a "Desert Mother," a role that by no means inclined her to minimize the place of women in the Church. A vision noted in her first collection, the *Scivias*, led her to devise a habit for her nuns as striking as priestly vestments in the aim of showing honor to women in the history of salvation. This is how she describes the nuns' dress to the monk Guibert of Gembloux:

> As for tiaras: I saw that all the ranks of the Church have bright emblems in accord with the heavenly brightness, yet virginity has no bright emblem—nothing but a black veil and an image of the cross. So I saw that this would be the emblem of virginity: that a virgin's head would be covered with a white veil, because of the radiant-white robe that human beings *(homo)* had in paradise, and lost. On her head would be a circlet *(rota)* [the wheel was a figure of the natural and divine universe in Hildegard's cosomology] with three colours conjoined into one—an image of the Trinity—and four roundels attached: the one on the forehead showing the lamb of God, that on the right a cherub, that on the left an angel, and on the back a human being—all these inclining towards the [figure of the] Trinity.[70]

The habit that Hildegard designed for her nuns, with its headdress resembling a triple tiara and its symbolic ornaments, irresistibly recalls papal vestments: Hildegard gave a pontifical crown to her apologia of the sacred role of women.

Hildegard appears in this chapter as an illustration of male appropriation of the figure of the prophetess within the scheme of a gender-based division of sacred roles. But how did Hildegard make herself subject to the male order? Or, conversely, what distinguishes her from Manfreda or Guglielma? Perhaps not much, especially if we take into account that the records of the Inquisition trial, our only source, probably misrepresent the theology of Manfreda da Pirovano. There is an important difference, however: Hildegard chose to remain within the Roman Church. Her career as a churchwoman wholly conformed to canonical traditions: she only spoke in public or wrote after the age of forty, the age of the "sexual neutralization" of woman according to the Church. She became a public figure gradually, and she constantly and scrupulously requested the Church's approval, turning first to the archbishop of Mainz, then to the pope, during the Synod of Trier. She sought episcopal authorization for the transfer to Rupertsberg.

Moreover, Hildegard never challenged social order. She replied to Tengswindis, a canoness who had written to ask her why only women of high estate were admitted to her convent, that hierarchy on earth was desired by God, and that a wise farmer did not put oxen, asses, sheep, and goats in the same enclosure. Within a respect of these institutional limits, Hildegard could exalt woman in the Church; male control over female prophetic force was limited to her taking that respect of the Roman Church into account.[71]

Hildegard, an exceptional personality, takes the figure of the prophetess as far as it could go within the male framework of the Church. Her authentic participation should be seen, however, in the context of oblique, metaphorical forms of promotion that women controlled, such as the economy of salvation. This rhetorical aspect is clear in the twelfth-century Cistercian devotion to Jesus or to the abbot as mother, as analyzed by Caroline Bynum. The Cistercians used such maternal images to express "a need for affectivity in the exercise of authority and in the creation of community, and in a complex rhythm of renouncing ties with the world while deepening ties with community and between the soul and God."[72] Similarly, in his treatise *De religiosa habitatione in eremo*, St. Francis advised his friars to live "in the desert" in groups of four, two of them acting as "mother Marthas," taking care of all daily necessities while the other two "sons" gave themselves over to contemplation. The fact that these roles were reversed after a while shows that the maternal reference was not a concession to women but merely a figure of speech.[73]

A SHAM PROPHETESS: THE SYSTEM OF ROBERT D'ARBRISSEL

Even when feminization touched acts and not just language, it was kept to the realm of sham, of seeming reality. The founding of the Order of Fontevrault by Robert d'Arbrissel (ca.1045 – 1116) presents an ambiguous and interesting instance of this.

Michelet famously said about Robert that "he reopened the bosom of Christ to women." One of the original features of Fontevrault consisted in its inversion of gender roles. During his lifetime and again in his testament, Robert insisted that a woman be the head of the double (both male and female) Order of Fontevrault. Individual women reaped the benefits of Robert's interest in their sex, since he welcomed into the Order both prostitutes *(meretrices)* and high-ranking aristocrats. Pétronille de Chemillé was the first abbess of the Order; Hersende de Montsoreau, its first prioress. They were joined by Ermengarde, the wife of William VII of Poitou; Angès de Chateaumeillant; Philippa, the second wife of William, who had by then become William IX of Aquitaine; and Bertrade d'Anjou, the second of wife of King Philip I of France.

Jacques Dalarun has shown, however, that this promotion of women was a means for encouraging male asceticism. Robert, the son of a priest, grew up in the rough atmosphere of the Gregorian reform and was determined to combat "priestly incest"; for him, cohabitation with women was based in a desire for expiation; it was a trial, an ordeal of chastity of the highest sort. This is clear from Robert's writings: "This is why you must do your best, as long as I live, to remain willingly within your duty [and] to obey the commandment of the [female] servants of Christ, for the salvation of your souls." A similar statement in the *Life* of Robert written by André, one of his companions, accentuates that note of male obedience and courtly service to women (the theme was developed in lay terms in the age by the troubadour-duke, William of Aquitaine, Ermengarde's husband). Here Robert is quoted as saying: "I have ordered you to obey always in your life the servants *(ancelles)* of Jesus Christ, for the salvation of your souls, and to serve them, for love of their spouse, Jesus."[74]

One miracle that Dalarun mentions provides a good illustration of the female role in the Church in the early twelfth century. In it we can see a shift from an earlier horrified exclusion of women from the sacred (an attitude that persisted in canon law and hardened, by reaction, into a certain kind of male prophecy, as we saw in chapter 1) to a reasoned integration of women within the clerical universe. During his career as an itinerant preacher, Robert and his mixed troupe of disciples arrived, one day in or around 1114, at the church of Ménelay (now Menat, in the département of Puy-de-Dôme). Local tradition dictated that women could not enter the church, at the risk of death by immediate celestial fulmination. Robert and his group entered the church anyway, and no punishment ensued. The inhabitants of the place, piqued, implored St. Ménelay to take vengeance, but Robert preached a sermon to correct their error:

> Alas, simple people, do not make such silly, vain prayers! But
> know that the saints are not enemies of the spouses of Jesus
> Christ. For what you say is an absurd thing, and the purity of the

Catholic faith knows the contrary to be true, as it is said in the
Gospel of the blessed sinner who kissed the feet of the Redeemer,
washed them with her tears, and dried them with her hair, and
spread unguents on His most worthy head.

Robert's glittering, expiatory conception of woman was the very reverse of
the clear separation between male and female given in the anecdote on
which the prohibition was based, which presented an early prototype of a
cross-dressing Joan in an atmosphere close to the rough misogyny of the
Fathers of the Desert. In its discussion of a nearby church an ancient *Life* of
St. Calais, who had been a monk at Ménelay, states that he forbade entrance to his monastery to all women so that his face would always remain
hidden from the temptress. When a certain queen expressed a desire to
look at his face, he saw it as the devil attempting to snatch his soul. His *Life*
reports: "After his death a shameless woman, Gunda, a daughter of Eve, at
the urging of the serpent of lust and despite the prohibition, attempted to
enter into the sanctuary in which the body of St. Calais lay at rest. In order
to do so, she shaved off her hair and disguised herself as a man. Hardly
had she penetrated the holy place when she went blind and was betrayed
by a sudden loss of blood that flooded the floor."[75]

Once Robert d'Arbrissel had exorcised the satanic image of the
temptress disguised as a man who had been betrayed by her uterus (like
Joan), females, saints or sinners, could enter the church at Ménelay, but
this time to celebrate the Spouse, and under the spiritual direction of a
man. This supervised integration takes us away from the prophetess, but it
guides us toward a form of female prophecy that was more akin to that of
the visionaries (although both more specific and more general). After the
twelfth century, a stable and durable model associated an inspired, often
illiterate woman and a director of conscience who served as her guide,
promoter, and exegete, but concealed himself behind her.

THE TAMING OF THE PROPHETESS

The new model was fully developed in the thirteenth century, in particular
within the mendicant orders, which, thanks to their place in urban life
and their independence from parish and episcopal institutions, could lis-
ten to inspired voices among the people. The scheme of Christian inversion reintroduced by the Franciscans led the Spirituals, as we have seen, to
assert that Christ's truth could ultimately take refuge among the poor, the
infirm, children, and women. Beginning in the thirteenth century, the
conviction circulated (even outside the confines of the eschatological

drama of the Spiritual Franciscans) that "the privileged medium of divine revelation was young, poor, and female."[76]

We can see a remarkable and extreme example of that conviction, and of the male and clerical supervision it necessitated, in the little prophetess of Santa Maria a Cigoli in the late fourteenth century, whom Daniel Bornstein has studied.[77] The prophetess was a ten-year-old girl; veiled and separated from the faithful, she spoke through a priest. In Hildegard the prophetess was the organ of God; in this young visionary she was a humble part of a clerical and male mechanism. There are many examples of an apparent prophetess with a learned man at her side who speaks for her, but we will move outside the Church to the late sixteenth century, the end of the period considered in this chapter, and to a situation that produced a new Joan.

GUILLAUME POSTEL'S POPE JOAN

Guillaume Postel (1510–81) was one of the great luminaries of the Renaissance who mixed vast erudition with a highly syncretic hermeticism. His brilliant reputation and career keep us from reducing his genius to the ordinary madness of the many inventors of theosophical systems in the sixteenth century. In 1535, after solid studies (he won his *maître ès arts* in 1530), he accompanied the French ambassador, Jean de la Forest, to Constantinople, returning to France with a stack of manuscripts and a firm command of Eastern languages. He wrote the first grammar of the Arabic language in French, and was appointed a reader in mathematics and "pilgrim languages" at the Collège Royale. He received in benefice a diaconate in Anjou. He then went to Rome, where he joined the Society of Jesus, but the Jesuits soon expelled him because he was already working on his politico-theological system and loudly proclaiming its two principal tenets, the primacy of the Councils over the pope and the right of primogeniture of the king of France over the universal monarchy of the pope. In 1547 he was in Venice, busily working on a glossed translation of the Zohar, a principal literary production of the Jewish cabala. At the same time he took over the spiritual direction, at the hospital of SS. Giovanni e Paolo, of an illiterate *beata* (roughly the Mediterranean equivalent of a béguine) whom he calls Mère Joanne. The woman, whom we know only through Postel, declared herself pope and the spouse of Jesus, as Postel recounts:

> She told me, and I much marveled at it, that she, being a woman, was the angelic Pope and Reformer of the world. The which, since

> I considered her as a woman and not as being filled with the Holy
> Spirit and substance of Jesus, the sovereign duke of the Church,
> scandalized me. But when she said to me, "You will be my son,
> generated of my substance and of that of my spouse Jesus," I then
> well understood what she had meant, because it regarded me."[78]

Persuaded by this message of his election, Postel left once more for the Holy Land, returning to France in 1551. He proclaimed himself pope in 1552, taking the name Peter II. Despite his extravagances, the Church took little interest in Postel: the Inquisition declared him insane *(amens)*, and only when he penned an attack on Paul IV (when he was in Rome in 1559) was he imprisoned for a short time. Catherine de Médicis invited him to be preceptor to Hercule-François de Valois (who later reigned briefly as Francis II). Postel died a peaceful death in 1581.

Around 1550 Mère Joanne (whom Postel also called Jechochannah, "the grace of the Lord" in Hebrew) died, delegating her immortality to Postel. He promptly proclaimed himself, as his popess had taught him, the firstborn of Mère Joanne and her spouse, Jesus. Postel took the name of Cain, since he was the son of a new Adam and a new Eve. He then published a number of works in which he seemed to reiterate the message of Manfreda da Pirovano, in particular his best-known work, printed in Paris in 1553: *Très merveilleuses Victoires des Femmes du Nouveau Monde et comment elles doivent à tout le monde commander et mesme à ceulx qui auront la monarchie du monde vieil* (Most Marvelous Victories of the Women of the New World, and how they must command everyone, even those who will have sovereignty over the old world).

This apparent Manfredan feminism in fact conceals the model of male manipulation of illumination. Mère Joanne was useful to Postel as a source of personal humiliation ("The Spirit of God being hidden under the most abject creature in the world, as my Mother in this world has shown")[79] and as a metaphor that prepared his own revelation. In his *Rétractions de Guillaume Postel touchant les propos de Mère Jeanne* (a work in which Postel retracts none of his system, despite the title), he spells out the underlying meaning of his praise of women: "For I do not want the said women to understand by that (according to the way St. Augustine calls 'womanly' Inferior Reason in either sex) anything but natural reason."[80] He explains what had occurred in 1547: Jesus, both a male and a female figure, came twice, once in the male mode (which designates form, intelligence, authority, and the superior soul or *animus*) to redeem humankind by his Passion; he came again in 1547 to manifest, by female delegation, the "restoration" of the human being and its inferior, "feminine" part (the female principle, linked to matter, natural and inferior reason, execution, and the *anima*). What Mère Joanne had really done in 1547 was to give birth to Postel:

> The Mother of the World put her Spirit in me to the end that, just as the New Adam, her Spouse had, in Judea, given rise to the Papacy according to the order of Melchizedek, called Shem, son of Noah, so she in me (because a woman must not teach in the Church, whose authority has lasted up to now) was to instigate the Empire or Monarchy of the right of Japhet, the brother of the said Shem, as it was instituted in the golden age. And whosoever does not believe me will repent of it later.[81]

In the text of the *Victoires des femmes*, Postel speaks (perhaps cynically, perhaps ingenuously) of the principle that governs this male direction of women, whose inspiration he sees as a vain attempt to approach male reason:

> And as for [those women] who, because of their imperfection, have a desire to unite themselves with a superior, formal, and more perfect nature, they are not so much to be blamed as men are, because men, in obeying women against the nature of perfection, tend toward what is imperfect, but they [that is, women] tend to what is perfect, which is man.[82]

Mère Joanne and Hildegard stand at opposite extremes in the integration of the prophetess into male discourse, but we can see that those extremities touch in many ways, because the figures of the prophetess, the witch, the usurper, and the visionary are mixed or superimposed. All of them express, from different points of view and in different situations, one of the great aporia of medieval Christianity: how to give male (hence legal, legitimate) form to speech pronounced and conceived by a woman and transmitted by metasexual discourse? The only way for this to be possible was if this continual female assault on male institutions were an essential form of Christian sacrality.

In our search for a Joan as knowing, dominating female we have encountered a throng of women (Manfreda, Joan of Arc, Hildegard, Pétronille, Gunda, Mère Joanne, and all their cousins) who are variants of the same model—whether they were praised or scorned, feared or respected, free or in chains, according to fluctuating projections and rejections, compromises and condemnations. Up to this point, the image on the tarot card has been a convenient illustration of that sometimes threatening, sometimes desired cyclical presence: in the tarot the popess, both virtually and necessarily distributed or dealt out, takes or allows herself to be taken at a propitious or dreaded moment. History can do no more than comment on and categorize her decisive appearances; it cannot give them the necessity of laws. When Joan strays out of chronological discourse, she is guided, but only loosely, by a few institutional rules.

The image of the tarot brought into play a simulation of the real; if we detach the popess a bit more from life (either real or phantasmagoric), we construct the simulacrum that we call literature, to which we can now turn, thanks to the second iconographic representation of the popess in the Middle Ages.

Joan among Illustrious Women

Around 1400 two prestigious, richly illuminated manuscripts produced for the ducal court of Burgundy included a miniature depicting Joan giving birth during the procession in Rome. These are two copies of the French translation of Boccaccio's *De mulieribus claris*. In these representations Joan has none of the ambivalence, grave or joyous, of her portrait on tarot cards; here, rather than the working out of an enigma, the image shows its resolution. The brilliant costumes of the other characters (cardinals, bishops, monks) signal the public nature of the scene. Joan's child, shown coming through her papal robe to emerge at her feet, clearly denounces and announces her fall, which is also suggested by Joan's unsteadiness and her still-thick silhouette. The miniaturists chose to depict the event in all its spectacularity.[83]

They did not betray Boccaccio by doing so. In 1361 Boccaccio had retired to Certaldo, where he wrote, in Latin, a gallery of female portraits, following the ancient model of Illustrious Men, a genre that his friend Petrarch had just revived, as Boccaccio notes in his introduction to his own work.

Boccaccio writes on women who are more illustrious *(claris)* than they are simply famous, which is why I will use that term. His pantheon of 106 women draws its unity from female energy more than from moral or social greatness. Boccaccio's choice of Latin (as opposed to Italian, which he used in the *Decameron*) and the subjects he selects corroborate this impression. In 1361 Boccaccio put aside the use of Italian in order to exalt the ancient and Mediterranean heritage of strength of soul. Christian women occupy a very small place in the *Illustrious Women:* after the life of Eve with which the work begins, thirty-nine chapters (numbers II–XL) are dedicated to heroines of ancient mythology and poetry; the next sixty chapters (XLI–C) discuss remarkable women of ancient history, to whom he adds three women from the Bible, Athaliah, Nicaula, and Mariamne. Only the six final chapters present women of the Christian Middle Ages, and two of these were added during the summer of 1362 as a courtly gesture. Invited to Naples by Niccolò Acciaiuoli, the seneschal of that city, Boccaccio decided to dedicate the *Illustrious Women* to Andrea (or Andreola), his host's sister and the wife of the count of Capua, Bartolomeo II. He was at the time writing the chapter on Camiola, a Sienese widow well known in Messina, which in itself was a delicate homage to Andreola, also a Tuscan woman who lived in the South of Italy. He also wrote a new chapter on Queen Joan of Naples, the ruler of the kingdom where he was a guest. These details demonstrate that the popess's insertion within this series projected her into a new universe. In 1361 Joan left the Church to enter into literature and into feminist culture.

Here Joan measured her strength against other exceptional women, which also means that the ecclesiological question or concerns about the sacred were not what mattered. Boccaccio underplayed religious and moral themes in his evocation of female exploits that includes as many warrior women as courtesans.

Joan's new status seems difficult to define. Boccaccio makes no claims to being a historian; he is deliberately casual when using his sources, and at times he contradicts them, totally denying them. He gives himself the right to invent when he wants to. Should we thus speak of a literary existence for Joan? I will not attempt to justify the literary quality of the *Illustrious Women*, a risky task at best. For our purposes, it is enough to note that in this work Boccaccio was aiming more at signifying than at appealing to the reader's belief. This means that we will have to imagine a third type of belief in Joan, distinct from the veracity-based and the phantasmagoric. This new sort depends on an agreement tied to reading: the reader for whom Boccaccio writes (and only that reader, since all literary texts can be read according to unpredictable modes of belief) lends his adhesion by granting the text a signifying and metaphoric exemplarity. One does not believe in the historical existence of Marguerite Duras's Vice-Consul, for example; one adheres to his existence for the length of time it takes to read about him, and one judges his worth as a truth about a love-stricken man on that basis. These somewhat flat and ahistorical considerations have to be stated if we are to situate Joan's new status in Boccaccio or measure the complexity of her situation after 1360. In medieval minds, Joan was a nonauthentic pope (the first sort of belief), a true sorceress or prophetess (the second sort of belief), and a believable and exemplary heroine (the third sort of belief).

But the time has come to read Boccaccio's text. His reputation, the im-

portance of the occasion, and the charm of the narrative justify presenting
this short chapter of the *Illustrious Women* in its entirety.

BOCCACCIO'S "POPE JOAN"

Although John would seem from the name to be a man, in reality
she was a woman whose unheard-of audacity made her known to
the whole world and to posterity. Some say she was from Magon-
tiacum, but her real name is hardly known. There are, however,
some who say it was Giliberta. On the assertion of some this
much is known: she was loved by a young student when she was a
maiden. They say that she loved him so much that she cast aside
maidenly fear and shame and fled to him in secret from her father's house. Changing her name and dressing as a young man,
she followed her lover. While she studied with him in England,
she was taken for a cleric by everyone and pursued the study of
letters and of love.

When her lover died, Joan, knowing that she had a good
mind and attracted by the charms of learning, retained a man's
dress and refused to attach herself to anyone else or acknowledge
that she was a woman. She persisted diligently in her studies and
made such progress in liberal and sacred letters that she was
deemed to excel all others. Thus, endowed with admirable
knowledge, she left England and went to Rome when she was already mature in years. There for a number of years she lectured on
the trivium and had excellent students. Since in addition to her
scholarly knowledge she was very virtuous and saintly, everyone
believed her to be a man. She was so widely known that when
Pope Leo V died, she was elected to succeed him as Pope by the
unanimous vote of the cardinals. She was called John, and if she
had been a man she would have been the eighth of that name.
This woman was not afraid to mount the Fisherman's throne, to
deal with all the sacred mysteries and proffer them to others,
something which the Christian religion does not allow to any
woman, and she held the highest ecclesiastic office for a number
of years.

A woman, then, was the Vicar of Christ on earth. God from
on high was merciful to His people and did not allow a woman
to hold so lofty a place, govern so many people, and deceive them
with such a wicked fraud, and He abandoned that unduly audacious woman to herself. Spurred by the devil, who had led her

into this wickedness and made her persist in it, Joan, who in private life had been remarkably virtuous, now that she had risen to the lofty pontificate fell prey to the ardor of lust. And she, who for a long time had been able to hide her sex, did not lack the wiles necessary to quench her desire. And so, finding someone who would secretly mount on Saint Peter's successor and assuage her lecherous itching, the Pope happened to become pregnant. Oh, what a shameful crime! How great is God's patience! But what followed? This woman, who had been able to bewitch men's eyes for a long time, lacked the astuteness to hide the shameful fact that she was about to give birth to a child. For, being closer to the time of birth than she thought, as she went from the Janiculum to the Lateran in sacred procession around the city, between the Colosseum and the church of Pope Clement she publicly gave birth without the presence of any midwife. This made clear how she had deceived all men except her lover. And so she was thrown into a horrid dungeon by the cardinals, where this wretched woman died in the midst of her laments.

Down to our time, to condemn her dishonesty and perpetuate her infamy, when the Pope goes on a procession with the clergy and the people, at the halfway point, when they reach the place where Joan gave birth, the Pope turns away and takes different streets because of his hatred for that place. Having thus bypassed that shameful site, they return to their road and finish their procession.[84]

BOCCACCIO'S CONTRIBUTION

Boccaccio followed Martinus Polonus's narrative scheme fairly closely, developing it by a technique of amplification that might lead us to define his literary effort as primarily ornamentation. There is, for example, the mention of the detour taken by the papal processions, where the rhetorical device of painting a picture (*ekphrasis*) adds nothing to the story but virtuosity. Or there is the rhetoric of moral commentary glossing on the action: *O Scelus indignum!* (Oh, what a shameful crime!).

The atmosphere of this narration seems totally different, however. I have no intention of pausing over minor divergences that can be explained just as easily by positing that Boccaccio permitted himself a margin of freedom as by crediting them to approximations introduced into the manuscript transmission of Martinus's text as it was ceaselessly recopied and amended. Changing Leo IV into Leo V or the Vatican into the

Janiculum might have been the result of a faulty reading by a copyist or even by Boccaccio himself; these are details that do not entail anything of significance. Boccaccio's prehumanist learning might also have led him to replace Joan's studies in Athens with a brief sojourn in England (thus also solving the mystery of the English Johannes), and he knew Greek and Roman culture (as they survived in the Middle Ages) too well not to have been aware that Athens in the ninth century would have had little to teach Joan (a detail that, incidentally, would be used to refute the story of Joan in modern times). Another detail remains a mystery, the name "Gilbert" (Gilbertus; as a female, Gilberta) that was attached to Joan in her male but prepontifical career. This may attest to the existence of versions of the story that have disappeared, unless some copyist-glossator mixed up the histories of the bad popes, who were typically identified by the suffix "-bertus," which bore satanic overtones in the Middle Ages (as seen in Robertus, or Robert le Diable). We have seen, for example, that Jean de Mailly confused the names and the acts of Gerbertus (Gerbert, later Sylvester II, the necromancer) and Guibertus (Guibert of Ravenna, the antipope opposed to Paschal II), which are close both graphically and connotatively. Boccaccio is undoubtedly responsible for the transformation of John (Johannes) into Joan (Johanna) in the title of his chapter. It was a change essential to the development of the story, given that in the *Illustrious Women* the popess had to have a female name if she was to represent a woman within a collection of the portraits of women.

JOAN'S PASSIONS

These transformations and additions changed Martinus Polonus's narrative little more than the adaptations of the clerical chroniclers (discussed in the preceding chapter) had done. What was new in Boccaccio's narrative was its division of Joan's story into two parts, thus creating something like "The Grandeur and the Fall of Joan." Until Joan accepts the papacy, Boccaccio presents her with the same sympathy that he feels for all women who, thanks to a noble energy, rise above their female condition, even to the point of abandoning virginal modesty and female fears. Requited love (and mutual pleasure) justifies boldness: *a scolastico juvene dilectam quem adeo dilexisse ferunt*. Love and a passion for learning were what gave Joan her strength, and the fatal blow that dragged her to perdition could come only as a result of the death of her lover (a detail that Boccaccio invents). When Joan pursues her studies and keeps her male disguise, she expresses a sort of fidelity to her dead lover: a celibate ambition (and Boccaccio stresses the chastity of an inconsolable Joan) rechannels her lost love into a passion for knowledge, which had always accompanied it. Boccaccio, who was writing a work in praise of female culture, granted Joan a broader field of knowledge than had Martinus Polonus, who limited the popess's learning to the liberal arts of the trivium (grammar, logic, and dialectic). Boccaccio adds to this theology, the queen science. Jacques Verger has shown that the prestige of the arts faculties (which corresponded, roughly speaking, to the second cycle in a modern French lycée) was in continual decline during the Middle Ages, in comparison to upper-level studies in theology, law, and medicine.[85] Martinus Polonus had worked his usual mischief in this domain: the Dominicans did not usually follow the arts cycle, which had lost ground as first-year preparation, substituting a general formation of their own, imparted in the *studia* of the Order. Martinus may well have been aiming a perfidious barb at faculties directed by clerics who offered a superficial instruction amounting to seduction and deceit rather than the solid foundations of learning.

In Boccaccio, however, when Joan's high level of learning was turned outward, this ran counter to accepted values, dragging her toward usurpation and debauchery. Boccaccio opposes the mutual "delight" that Joan and her student lover found in ardent pleasure *(in ardorem libidinis)* to the burning desire (literally, an itch: *exurientem pruriginem*) that sends Joan into the arms of a lover whom Boccaccio describes as a mere sex object *(adinvento qui . . . exurientem pruriginem defricaret)*. One word that Boccaccio uses—*privata*—signals the emergence of a new value in the mid-fourteenth century. When he says of Joan that in her private life she remained "virtuous and saintly," *privata* refers to her status before she was elected to the papacy. The word has as much of a moral connotation as a social one, however: Joan's love and her appetite for learning could and must flourish only within the private sphere.

It is difficult to evaluate the meaning that Boccaccio gave to the second part of Joan's life. How are we to judge between Boccaccio's need to follow the clerical version of the Joan story (Joan uses trickery, thus inviting condemnation and profaning the throne of St. Peter) and limits that Boccaccio himself may have set to the acts of a woman (surpassing the female condition should not lead to a change of gender roles). This notion is suggested in chapter 3 of the *Illustrious Women* on Semiramis, queen of Assyria. Semiramis loses her husband, King Ninus, when her son Ninia is still too young to rule. She resorts to trickery and disguise (and Boccaccio's text uses many of the same expressions that describe Joan's acts: *astu quondam mulierbri; mentita sexum*). Taking advantage of the strong family resemblance between her beardless son and herself, she passes herself off as Ninia. Boccaccio praises both her motivation and the result: Semiramis took on male dress in order to save the dynasty and the kingdom, and when she judged that the danger had passed, she reestablished the truth. Her success as a female monarch is a shining example that sings of the glory of the female sex: "It was almost as if she wanted to show that in order to govern it is not necessary to be a man, but to have courage." In this spirit she carries Assyria's conquests into Ethiopia and India, thus outdoing her husband's achievements. Like Joan, however, she brings about her own downfall—*così fan tutte*—by sinking into debauchery: "Constantly burning with carnal desire [*assidua lubidinis prurigine*, the same term that he used for Joan], she added her own son to her many lovers.[86]

Women's weakness where lust is concerned does not refer back to the figure of the witch in Boccaccio, however: in fact, the religious versions of the Joan story and Boccaccio's version of it are poles apart. Learning and cross-dressing are a part of the lay, loving, and good life of Joan, which she lived with no hint of satanism. The witch, on the other hand, combines art (knowledge acquired through a pact with the devil) and seduction (Shakespeare has Joan of Arc take on instantaneous beauty by action of the devil) in order to dominate and overturn the good. Joan's fault derives from her passivity (she allows herself to be crowned with the papal tiara; she abandons herself to debauchery), as if the death of her beloved had broken the springs of her energy. If we really cared to hand out prizes for "feminism" (a somewhat vain exercise), we might hesitate, where Boccaccio is concerned, between two judgments. The first would praise him for his admiration of a female energy that rises above natural and social condition and avoids the pitfalls of a fascination with the male model; the second would note that he carefully doses his praise of women, reserving his highest accolades for female excellence attained within women's female nature and their relations with men.

Joan's transformation into a heroine of literature is at least as important as her "feminist" (better, pseudofeminist) rehabilitation. This change, as noted, is effected by neutralizing the ideological implications of the personage. Boccaccio is not interested in investigating the degree to which Joan was truly pope, nor in measuring her satanism. Nor does his gallery of outstanding women, in spite of determined exegesis, make a problem out of the question of the woman: as he himself says, he mixes truth and fiction from one chapter to another. The composition as a whole treats the various narratives as elements of a paradigm or variations on a theme (how does a woman becomes illustrious?). Boccaccio draws characters; the construction of each chapter, as we have seen with Joan and Semiramis, is based on the Aristotelian principle of tragedy as a gradual rise toward catastrophe. In the story of Joan, the note of the papacy creates the greatest possible gap between failure and success and between appearance and reality. In short, the popess represents an ideal tragic or romanesque literary figure.

BOCCACCIO'S PROGENY

Boccaccio's profoundly lay version of the Joan story met with considerable success, as we can see from the many manuscripts of his *Illustrious Women* that have been conserved and in its translation into many languages (including the French manuscripts mentioned above). Boccaccio's text was quoted abundantly by humanists throughout Europe, among them Chaucer, Laurent de Premierfait, Hans Sachs, Alvaro de Luna, and Alonso de Cartagena. Others adapted or continued the work: one of these was Jacopo Filippo Foresti of Bergamo, a Carmelite, who published a *De plurimis claris selectisque mulieribus* in Ferrara in 1497, a work that contains a chapter on the popess very much in the spirit of Boccaccio. I must note, however, that Christine de Pizan's feminism *avant la lettre* led her to exclude Joan from her *Cité des dames*, a work written in the early fifteenth century, even though she borrowed profusely from Boccaccio.[87] Jean Texier de Ravisy (Ravisius Textor), writing in 1501, brought the lay versions of the Joan theme to a point of anthropological neutrality by enumerating, in his *Officinae prima pars*, women who dressed as men whatever the reason: Semiramis; Christian saints such as Theodora, Marina, Euphrosyne, and Pelagia; and, to end the list, Joan of Arc (*Johanna gallica*) and Pope Joan (*Johanna anglica*).

When Boccaccio reshuffled the cards, Joan was no longer combined with popes, witches, or prophetesses. Henceforth she faced both men and the world as a strong but unfortunate heroine. Much later, when the various Reformations had stripped her of an ambiguity that led her, in Boccaccio, to the uncertain boundaries between fiction and history, she entered into a literary existence to which we shall return. The best we can do for the moment is to sketch out the various paths available to a female at the end of the Middle Ages, when only a few rare texts marked the path.

A writer interested in Joan's life might use Boccaccio's narrative as the basis for a romance of female revenge. In the early sixteenth century Mario Equicola d'Alveto stated in his treatise *On Women* (*De mulieribus*) that Providence had decreed that Joan sit on the throne of St. Peter's in order to prove that women are not inferior to men. A romance of the late thirteenth century, the *Roman de Silence* of Heldris de Cornuälle, provided a model for the genre.[88] The king of England had just forbidden transmission by the female line. Baron Cador, the heir to Cornwall, who had only a daughter, dressed her and educated her as a man, naming her Silence. Nature and Noreture (that is, culture) quarrel over her upbringing, but Reason rules in favor of Noreture: a woman can achieve the same levels of competence and the same rights as a man, thanks to her upbringing *(noreture)*. Silence's subsequent adventures prove them right. She leaves her paternal house and goes to the Continent, where she becomes a famous jongleur. Later she returns to England and goes to the king's court, where she accomplishes a difficult task (the capture of Merlin) and unmasks the queen's lover (who is disguised as a nun). Even though Boccaccio's narrative ended tragically, it suggested an orientation that we shall encounter again in later centuries.

A second reading of Joan's story, one emphasizing its romanesque and tragic aspects, prepared the fictional theme of ambition and love defeated by destiny or the world's laws. As noted in the context of the legendary (and the real) life of Pope Adrian IV, the Church offered the only possible way to rise in society by one's merits; there was nothing impossible about Joan's career in the Church, and it set people to dreaming.

In an anonymous manuscript of the fourteenth century conserved in the Abbey of Tegernsee in Bavaria (a region fond of the popess) Joan was not of humble origin, but her decision to break with her family to live with her lover reduced her to the lowest level of the social scale, from where she rose, with triumphant energy, by her own efforts. This curious text accentuates tendencies we have seen in Boccaccio, although no relationship between the two texts can be proved. Joan is by no means condemned in the Tegernsee version: the fact that Pircius, her lover, accompanies her throughout her career and becomes a cardinal eliminates all hint of moral degradation. If this couple of good managers of the Church's affairs had only been more aware of the female fertility cycle, they might have lived out their ecclesiastical careers and their love in peace and prosperity. The verse moral that ends this text dwells on the theme of the power of knowledge and wisdom to help people climb the echelons of human society. Joan's only fault (she is called Jutta here, but in Bavaria that name was used an as alternative to Joanna in other contexts) is that she lacks social legitimacy. The verse moral ends with a variant of the six-P formula in which, significantly, *Pater Patrum* becomes *Pater Pauperum* (the Father of the Poor). It is the author's way of recalling ironically that the usurpation of Jutta, a voluntary pauper, is not the gravest usurpation, and even though it was hidden, it was only apparent. Let us turn to this social and romanesque rehabilitation of Joan.

The Tegernsee Popess

This is the story of Pope Jutta, who was not German, as the chronicle of Martin mendaciously claims. Young Glancia was the daughter of a very wealthy citizen of Thessaly; she devoted her entire attention to wisdom. She was gifted with a sharp mind and a docile nature. Assiduous reading developed these qualities, and she soon earned a great reputation. And reality surpassed the praise. There was in the schools a young man of her age named Pircius; he was aware of the young girl's great studiousness, of the wealth of her father, and of her simplicity and her wisdom. Love brought closer those whom age had already brought together; they spoke of marriage, but their parents refused. Ardor and mutual desire grew in them, and as days went by and they grew older, they came to kisses and impatient embraces. Finally, one day, they found a refuge and joined together ardently. After having occupied themselves at Venus's game, they spoke of fleeing. She, among women, and he, among men, wanted to excel in virtue and studies, so they decided to go to Athens. Both one and the other, they provided themselves with as much money as they could; she took on the clothing and the manners of a man, and not only their clothes but also their minds made them extraordinarily like one another. Without delay they went to Athens, where they studied during many long years. She became more and more learned in both theology and the arts; similarly, he shone in all wisdom. They came to Rome; they taught there in all the faculties, [where] not only the students but the doctors in all sciences came to hear them, and the more their auditors entered into the profundity of their knowledge, the more they found abundant riches. Everyone, the doctors of all the faculties included, adored them; all the citizens venerated them. All Rome praised their merits, their modesty, their virtue, and their wisdom, word of which spread throughout the world. Finally, at the death of the pope, the woman was designated by unanimous choice, with no exceptions; at the supplication of the Romans, she was raised to the summit of the apostolate. Her lover Pircius was named cardinal; they led a quiet life, and under their governance the entire Church rejoiced. But because the seeds of adultery rarely take hold, or if they germinate they do not develop, or when they develop they do not last, it happened that the woman, who had never before conceived, found that she was pregnant once she had become pope. Since she was unaware of the usual rhythms of childbirth, she went to the church of St. John Lateran with all the clergy to celebrate a solemn Mass. But between the Coliseum and the church of St. Clement, stricken with labor pains, she fell, gave birth to a child, and died immediately. The popes still avoid that route, and before his coronation the virile organs of the pope are still verified manually.

See to what degree virtue and wisdom raise up
The small, they become high, protected by wisdom, but
All our learning and industry is naught against God.
　　See the poem that follows:

To learn all the laws, the young pilgrim
Glancia the brilliant transgressed men's laws by going to Athens
With a young man; she made herself man and Cupid,
　　But this Cupid
Moved crowds and taught the doctors of the City.
Pope she became, and engendering a child, she perished
　　Near the clergy.

Moral: Nothing rises to greatness more than the sage who enjoys the law;
Nothing sinks more than the man who enjoys no law.
Pope, Father of the Poor, the Popess
　　Produced a Popelet (*Papa, pater pauperum, perit papossa papellum*).[89]

　　The story of this Church couple, which is prefigured in the story of Abelard and Heloise, in turn prefigures the adventure of a monk and a nun further north in Germany who governed a church and defied the established powers. In another of history's ironies, it was precisely the success of that ex-monk Martin Luther that forcefully returned the popess to within the Catholic Church. The existential game that oscillated between seriousness and amusement turned to dispute, and Joan, denounced or rejected, was sentenced to burn at the stake of history, from where she escaped only thanks to the fumes of the imaginary.

PART III

DEATH AND
TRANSFIGURATION
OF THE POPESS

6. Illustration for the Apocalypse (Revelation) in Martin Luther's translation of the Bible, Wittenberg, 1522. Bibliothèque Nationale, Paris.

6

JOAN AT THE STAKE

FIFTEENTH — SEVENTEENTH CENTURIES

he Apocalypse according to Joan began in Prague in 1411. A procession organized by Voksa of Valdštejn, a favorite of Wenceslas IV, the king of Bohemia, wound through the streets of the city following a young man dressed as a prostitute with a mock papal bull around his neck. The ceremonial expressed the fury of the people and the king at the Roman Church and at Dietrich of Nieheim, the papal secretary, for the recent condemnation of Jan Hus.[1]

This scene is part of the history of Joan because it prefigures the polemical use that the Lutherans made of the episode of the popess a century later, when they connected the papacy with the Whore of Babylon (Revelation 17). Four years after the mock procession, Hus taunted Rome with the story of Joan at the Council of Constance. This was the first time the popess figured in a heretical arsenal of arguments (William of Ockham was only a schismatic; John Wycliffe mentioned Joan only in a brief polemical treatise with a limited circulation).

ENEA SILVIO PICCOLOMINI HAS HIS DOUBTS (1451)

It was also in Hussite Bohemia that for the first time the Church doubted that Joan had ever existed. In 1451 Enea Silvio Piccolomini, the bishop of Siena, who took the name Pius II when he became pope seven years later, was charged with an embassy to Bohemia for Emperor Frederick III of Germany. Piccolomini wrote a long and impassioned letter to Juan de Carvajal, cardinal of Sant'Angelo and formerly pontifical legate to Bohemia, about his mission to the heretical republic of Tabor (in southern Bohemia), in which he reported (and perhaps rewrote) a debate that had taken place among the three leaders of the republic: "Nicholas, whom they call their bishop, [whose] evil days were many, Joannes Galechus, who had just fled Poland in fear of the flames, and Wenceslas Coranda, an old servant of the devil, who states that the sacrament of the altar is merely a figure and a metaphor." After a long lecture in which he comments on the Taborites' anxieties, Piccolomini proposes to them the only road to salvation and peace:

> Eneas: Here is what I conjure you to do, Taborites. Present yourselves, with your doctrine, to the Roman pope; do what he orders you to do, without deviating either to the right or to the left. Those commands will assure you consolation for the spirit, peace and salvation for the soul.
>
> Nicholas: We would obey the apostolic majesty, and submit in full devotion, if it did not command things contrary to divine law.
>
> Eneas: Where faith is concerned, it has never been found that the apostolic see strayed, or approved perverse dogma.
>
> Galechus: But there was a manifest error in Agnes.
>
> Eneas: What Agnes are you talking about?
>
> Galechus: That woman, whom the Roman see honored as a man and placed at the summit of the apostolate.
>
> Eneas: But in that case, there was no error, either of faith or of law, but ignorance of a fact. And the story is not certain.
>
> Nicholas: But there were several criminal Roman popes, who now are serving out their sentences in hell.
>
> Eneas: I am unaware of that. However, if one of them may have sinned, it is because, like all humans, he fell, led astray by our fragility. But I insist: an uncontested Roman pope has never been heard to state publicly a false doctrine.[2]

This highly interesting debate continued, touching first on papal infallibility, then on the sacramental differences between Catholics and Taborites.

In this dialogue Piccolomini distinguishes fact from law, thus applying to Joan-Agnes the standard Church treatment that had been established by William of Ockham and reiterated (at about the same time as the Taborite controversy) by Tomás de Torquemada. The Catholic position had shifted slightly on its fixed axis, however: when Antoninus or Torquemada spoke of Joan, they were manipulating the factual argument and shaping belief ("according to what is said . . ."), but in general they accepted the existence of the popess. Piccolomini seems inclined to doubt her reality (neque certa historia est . . . quam Agnetem . . . nescio . . .). Nothing has changed: the popess still lay at the heart of a debate about papal infallibility, yet a fundamental shift had taken place between Dietrich of Nieheim (who was both Joan's historiographer, as we have seen, and Jan Hus's persecutor) and Enea Silvio Piccolomini, the first, still-hesitant Johannoclast and the Taborites' adversary. It was the opponents of the Roman Church who brought the name of Agnes into this ecclesiological debate. In other words, the history of the popess had passed from the status of a case or an example to that of a proof. Joan, always at the forefront in the ecclesiological battle, is a sign of a gaping breach, a "spiritual territorialism," to borrow the phrase that Lucien Febvre applied to Lutheranism,[3] opened by the Hussite revolution. In 1411 Jan Hus was still an ordinary heretic; in 1451 he had become the posthumous head of an other church, operating in another territory.

Henceforth ecclesiastical discourse lost its power to coopt or neutralize. Catholic totality was disintegrating: arguments and cases that had been common to all were divided between two camps. The change was felt slowly and gradually, after the emergence of Lutheranism, and it was not until 1562 that the first systematic refutation of the Joan story appeared on the Catholic side (although this trend did not prevent Jean Rioche, a Franciscan from Brittany, from reiterating the episode in the late sixteenth century). Doubts had been cast on Joan, and they chased her out of the Church and abandoned her to the Lutherans.

ROME AND GERMANY: FROM INVECTIVE TO PARODY

But to return for a moment to the 1411 procession in Prague: it was not simply a Czech survival of the Roman carnival. Carnival, and especially its more social and political form, the Cornomannia, involved rites of inclusion that inverted values and social position for a limited time, within the calendar cycle, and that encouraged integration; the Prague procession was a manifestation of exclusion that used inversion as an exacerbated figure for rejection and condemnation. Fifteenth-century Germany offers examples of intermediate forms, which used violent and profanatory carnivalesque rites and were prohibited by the authorities. In Cologne in 1441, for instance, carnival mannequins, one with an aspergillum, paraded a sham relic through the street, accompanied by flying banners; seventeen citizens of Frankfurt were punished for a similar parody in 1467. In Augsburg in 1503 some youths escorted a female goat seated on a cushion and adorned with ribbons, which a reveler dressed as a priest baptized. Genuine rites of contestation required only an accentuated and more aggressive context, which was precisely the case in Prague and Saxony. Robert W. Scribner has found traces of some twenty antipapal carnivals in Germany from 1320 to 1540.[4]

Representations of the Church as a prostitute *(meretrix)* have a long genealogy, quite apart from the Roman communal satire we have seen in part I. The tradition goes back at least to the genre of the "Invective against Rome," studied by Josef Benzinger.[5] Unlike Roman anticlericalism, here invective used a vocabulary more religious than sociopolitical, and it increased sharply in the late eleventh century with the controversy over investiture that set off the great struggle between the papacy and the Empire and continued, almost uninterrupted, to Charles V and the terrible Sack of Rome in 1527.[6] As this conflict persisted, it produced an almost ethnic hatred between Rome and the German nation, many traces of which can be found in Lutheranism. That mutual hatred is explicit in Frutolf of Michelsberg's continuation of the imperial chronicle of Ekkehardus of Aura: "This fact [the failure of the crusades] confirms that we were treated as enemies by the Romans just as much as we hated them."[7] In the three thick volumes of the *Monumenta Germaniae Historica, De Lite,* devoted to polemics between Rome and the Empire, a flood of insults, pamphlets, and treatises pours out Europe's fury (backed on one side by the imperial power). Within the binary structure of a simple, violent opposition ("we" are the German nation and its Ghibelline allies; "they" are Rome and the Guelfs) a process of mutual religious and political legitimation served as a channel for many sorts of rejection of the Roman power and primacy, which were denounced as a tyranny that betrayed the spirit of the Gospels. A striking example of heretical anarchism within anti-Roman invective (but one that comes, untypically, from an English source) is a famous treatise by an anonymous writer from York (or Normandy) around 1100. The author raises the question of whom Christians should obey in Rome, and by a succession of linked alternatives, he rejects an entire series of unacceptable obediences, all of which refer to some aspect of the Roman Church. In Rome, one should obey the Lateran, not the other churches; there, at the Lateran, one should obey men, not stones; among men, one should obey the members of Christ, not followers of the devil; among the members of Christ, one should obey a person, not the whole; in that person, one should obey the apostolic (the one who is sent), not the man; the one sent is to be obeyed if he has been sent by Christ, not by any other. Even when obedience to the pope was thus stripped of all Roman aspects, it made little sense:

> But, if he has been sent by Christ, to what end has he been sent?
> Either he has been sent to us to tell us the message of Christ and

> teach us, or for something else that we are unaware of and that
> has nothing to do with God's message; if that is the case, we
> should not even listen to him. But if he was sent to us to transmit
> the message of Christ and teach us, he becomes superfluous, be-
> cause we have available the prophetic, evangelistic, and apostolic
> Writings [the Old Testament, the Gospels, and the Epistles],
> which contain all of God's message; and knowledge of these writ-
> ings is more complete among us than in him.[8]

The only justifiable task of "the apostolic" (a nominalized adjective that insists on the etymological sense of "one who has been sent" and was fre-quently used in the Middle Ages to designate the pope) thus consisted in evangelizing the pagans. The Roman Church had no sacred legitimacy; quote to the contrary, "It includes few elect or sons of God, but many reprobates and sons of the devil; we could call it the Church of Satan rather than the Church of God." More than four hundred years before Luther, an ethnopolitical duality that used a violent rejection of the pa-pacy to put northern Europe and the Empire on one side and Rome on the other was the basis for an equally binary religious construct that pitted the Church of God against the Church of Satan.

Rhetorical and carnivalesque inversion flowed easily into that mold. Bonizo of Sutri (†1091), a virulent imperialist, took the evangelical image of the Shepherd and subjected it to the sort of reversal typical of the "world upside-down" (the hunter hunted, etc.): "The guardian himself having turned into a wolf, who will be there to protect the sheep?"[9] This reversal made good into bad, Rome into Babylon. As Sigebert von Gem-bloux said in the twelfth century: "Was there long ago any more confusion in Babylon than today in the Church?"[10] The figure of the Great Harlot of Babylon made a timid appearance in allegory in a passage of the *Planctus Ecclesiae in Germaniam* of Konrad von Megenberg (1337), who drew a par-allel between condemnation of Roman perversion and Germanic recrimi-nations: "The prostitute who is the pride and vainglory of the prelates of Christianity oppresses the eagle [that is, the German Empire]."[11]

BOHEMIA, OR, HERESY AS TERRITORY

What was new in the fifteenth century? Why did the 1411 masquerade in Prague mark a threshold? The answer is simple: that was when rhetoric be-came reality. The Prostitute made flesh was a signal and an announcement that the authentic Church—the congregation of the faithful that turned the Roman Church upside-down, inverting it so as to recover the right image of Christianity—was no longer constructed in Franciscan meditations or German invective, but in the reality of a country. Joan became incarnate (still implicitly, however) as a way to distinguish her from the *Corpus Christi* that was coming alive in Prague. Heresy too became a country: recent studies by František Šmahel and John Martin Klassen have shown that the Hussite revolution permitted (or caused) the emergence of a Czech national nobility that opposed both the monarchy and the Church.[12] In 1412 Jan Hus sent a letter to the dignitaries of the kingdom that was an ideological preparation for the antimonarchical Hussite League of 1415. Hus's intentions were completely different from Wycliffe's, since Wycliffe called on the king of England as protection against the pope and asked his help in putting into place his authentic Church. Dynasts can go far in the direction of speaking ill of the popes, but they think twice before moving on to religious secession, a risky venture in which they have little to gain and much to fear.

Tragedies aside (the bloody defeat of urban extremists and Taborites), the Peace of Kutná Hora in 1485 established a kingdom that was solidly controlled by the nobility and maintained the principal acquisitions of Jan Hus's doctrines. The invisible church had become visible, and in the sacramental domain it manifested itself clearly and rapidly. In 1414, before the trial and execution of Jan Hus, Jacobellus of Stříbro and Nicholas of Dresden had preached communion in two kinds, which gave rise to Utraquism and was a tenet that eliminated the priest as a barrier between the believer and God. The Hussites very soon developed a liturgy in Czech, and in 1420 the Taborites elected their bishop themselves.

ENEA AND JOAN AMONG THE SAVAGES

The Roman Church was shocked by that secession, as is clear from a letter written by Enea Silvio Piccolomini in 1451 in which he describes his horror at his discovery of Tabor, a church-city in southern Bohemia in which the extremists of the Hussite movement and the followers of Jan Žižka had gathered.

Piccolomini arrived in Tabor as a theologian; while he was there he discovered his vocation as an ethnologist of monstrosity: "I thought that this people was separated from us only by the rite of communion [in one or two kinds], but now I discover a heretic, infidel people, rebel to God, with neither thought nor religion."[13] He was describing an alien and monstrous population; a state peopled by heretics that was both organized and anarchical, ethnic and federated. This was prodigiously new. A sort of Islam (in the sense of a constituted religion, a scandal incomprehensible in a Christian era) had emerged at the heart of Christian Europe. There had of course been a crusade against the Cathars in the thirteenth century, but the Albigensians, although thickly settled in southern France, had never aspired to a prominent position in the world and had occupied a limited area. Piccolomini's letters on his discovery of the absolute otherness of heresy will help us to understand how Joan could become a monster among monsters and how she armed herself for religious war. Piccolomini saw

> a throng, rustic and without order although urban. . . . Some
> were nude, others had only a chemise, still others wore a leather
> tunic . . . their forehead bare, ears cut and nostrils slashed by a
> shameful wound. . . . No marching order, no moderation of
> words. They welcome us according to a barbarous and savage rite
> by offering us fish, wine, and beer. When we arrive inside the
> square, we see a place that I know not how to describe, if not as a
> fortress or an asylum for heretics; indeed everything that Chris-
> tianity knows in the way of monsters of impiety and profanation
> gathers here and finds refuge in this place, where there are as
> many heresies as there are individuals, and where everyone is free
> to believe whatever he wants.[14]

In the religious domain this savage appearance was a rejection of all order and all ritual:

> This pestiferous and abominable sect deserves the greatest pun-
> ishment. They reject the primacy of the Roman Church and the
> existence of any clergy. . . . They destroy the images of Christ and
> the saints, reject the fires of Purgatory [and] offer the Eucharist in
> bread and wine to children and madmen. . . . They bless no water
> and have no consecrated cemeteries; the cadavers of their dead
> are buried in the fields with the animals, as they deserve. . . . They
> make fun of consecrating churches, and perform the sacrament
> anywhere. . . . They condemn tithing.[15]

At that point it became clear to Piccolomini that Tabor, a radical inversion of the Church, was truly a creation of the devil. He remarks to his corre-spondent: "You have understood what this city is, what are the customs of this people, what is the site of this fortress, what this senate of heretics is, this synagogue of evil, this dwelling of Satan, this temple of Belial, this kingdom of Lucifer."[16]

We should take Enea Silvio Piccolomini's very emotional reaction quite seriously. He was a prelate, but in no way an inquisitor or a prophet.

Rather, he was a great humanist, the author of a delicate novel, *De duobus amantibus historia*, and a man familiar with the learned and skeptical milieu discussed in chapter 1 in connection with Platina. Although Piccolomini took holy orders rather late in life (in 1446, at the age of forty-one), he consistently held posts in the upper echelons of the Church. He participated in the rebel Council of Basel as secretary to Amadeus VIII of Savoy, who was proclaimed pope by that council, taking the name of Felix V. Reconciled with orthodoxy and Pope Eugenius IV, Piccolomini was soon named bishop of Trieste (in 1447), then of Siena (in 1450), and he was elected pope (as Pius II) in 1458. The barbarity of Tabor was a shock to the Mediterranean, juridical, and civilized order that had formed his personality and shaped his career, both literary and ecclesiastical. As a man of the humanist pre-Renaissance, Piccolomini believed in the progress of humanity. His very conception of pontifical infallibility demonstrates this: faith itself was untouchable, but aside from that principle variations in dogma were possible as societies progressed in a steady, beneficent fashion. For him, the Taborite republic had tipped over from a literal imitation of primitive Christianity to a military tribalism that lived by pillage alone and rejected working with one's hands. Thus it inverted the course of civilization. Piccolomini stated, addressing the king of Bohemia, George Poděbrad: "This kingdom was once quite flourishing, the richest of the eastern kingdoms; now it is a region that is miserable, downtrodden, torn apart. Why? Because our truth cannot lie when it says, by the Gospel, 'If a house be divided against itself, that house cannot stand.' You Bohemians are not only divided against yourselves, you are separated from the greater part of Christianity."[17] It is somewhat paradoxical that Piccolomini uses prophetic tones to express his horror of obscurantism; Tabor's thirty years of republican existence came to an end in 1452, only a few months after Piccolomini's visit, and its fall must have confirmed his progressive but apocalyptical conception of human history.

Enea Silvio Piccolomini demonstrates how the supple, all-englobing discourse of the Catholic Church at the summit of its doctrinal refinement could slide toward expressions of retrenchment and exclusion and toward what I have called "phantasmagoric belief." The diabolization of the heretic or the witch is perhaps better explained by the fifteenth-century fear of an immense backlash from the untamed strength of an ethnic Europe capable of producing a discourse and a Church of its own rather than by any mysterious and archaic fanatical return to ancient times. This was certainly an important reason for Rome's surprising intransigence toward Luther in 1517–20. In any event, Pius II did not forget the horror that Enea Silvio Piccolomini had experienced: in 1464, against all logic, he abrogated the *Compacta* that provided a reasonable compromise between the Hussites and the Catholic Church.

When Catholic discourse clashed with history, it shattered. The debate between Enea Silvio and the Taborites, which was literally analogous to many other disputes with the Church in the Middle Ages (with Berengar of Tours on the Eucharist in the twelfth century; with the Spiritual Franciscans on ecclesiology and primitive Christianity in the thirteenth and fourteenth centuries), differed sharply from those other disputes by taking place within the walls of a heretical city. A powerful and well-organized laity threw back at the Church the literal meaning of the Gospels and details of ecclesiastical history. The Church had lost the mastery of argumentation that had permitted it all things; henceforth, it had to look into the treasury of its doctrine and choose between telling arguments and dead weight. Joan was in the second category, among the domestic and familiar monsters that Catholic ecclesiology had toyed with. All detachment, all distance disappeared; figures and doctrines were inventoried and set out in twin columns headed "God" and "Satan." Once a metaphor, Joan became a metonymy, *pars pro toto;* she was part of Satan and part of heretical discourse.

JOAN AS GREAT HARLOT

The popess was one of the things that the Lutherans inherited from the Hussites. Before we reconstruct filiations and derivations, we would do well to look briefly at a work that established Joan's new status. During the 1540s Martin Schrott, a Lutheran, published a violently antipapal pamphlet titled *Von der Erschröcklichen Zurstörung und Niderlag dess gantzen Bapstum* (On the Terrible Destruction and Fall of the Papacy) that contained an illustration of a woman dressed as pope, a triple-crowned tiara on her head, perched on the back of a monstrous beast with seven horned heads. She is offering a chalice to several monarchs (one is the emperor of Germany) who kneel before her. A rectangular cartouche within the image bears the caption, *Angnes ain Weib au. Engelant Johanes der sieben[t] genant. Ā 851* (Agnes, a woman from England, called John VII in the year 851).[18]

The image is an illustration of the passage in Revelation 17 showing the Great Harlot (or the Whore of Babylon):

> I saw a woman seated on a scarlet beast which was covered with
> blasphemous names. This beast had seven heads and ten horns.
> The woman was dressed in purple and scarlet and adorned with
> gold and pearls and other jewels. In her hand she held a gold cup

that was filled with the abominable and sordid deeds of her lewd-
ness. On her forehead was written a symbolic name, "Babylon the
great, mother of harlots and all the world's abominations." I saw
that the woman was drunk with the blood of God's holy ones
and the blood of those martyred for their faith in Jesus. . . . The
angel said to me: "Why are you so taken aback? I will explain to
you the symbolism of the woman and of the seven-headed and
ten-horned beast carrying her. The beast you saw existed once but
now exists no longer. It will come up from the abyss once more
before going to final ruin. . . . Here is the clue for one who possesses wisdom! The seven heads are seven hills on which the
woman was enthroned. They are also seven kings: five have already fallen, another lives now, and the last has not yet come.[19]

The colors here and the gold, the cup or chalice, and especially the
seven hills that made up the kingdom of the harlot made it easy to identify
the woman as the Roman Church, a comparison that had already been
suggested in anti-Roman invective and in the Prague procession of 1411.
The name "Agnes" may have been a feminized and inverted version of the
Agnus who combats the Beast; it denotes Hussite influence and encour-
ages a historical application of the apocalyptical prophecy to the papacy.
Schrott based his engraving on an illustrious model, but that model simply compared the papacy to the Harlot with no explicit connection with
Joan. In September 1522 the German translation of the New Testament
produced by Martin Luther in his refuge of the Wartburg was published in
the Lutheran bastion of Wittenberg. Luther's friend Lucas Cranach illustrated the text of Revelation (and only Revelation, which gave his images
even greater thrust) with engravings in which he set up a detailed parallel
between Rome and Babylon and between the pope and the Antichrist or
the Great Harlot. The engravings showing the destruction of Babylon
(Rev. 18) includes a depiction of the Castel Sant'Angelo in Rome; the
beast (11.1–8) that devours God's witnesses is portrayed as a dragon with
clawed feet wearing the papal tiara; the apparition of the Harlot riding the
Beast (17) is a woman in contemporary dress with the papal tiara perched
on the side of her head. It is impossible to know whether or not Cranach
had the popess in mind; the illustrations function so strongly as a reflection of the text that any connection with the episode of Joan is difficult. It is interesting to note, however, that in the edition of the New
Testament that was published shortly after, in December 1522, the Harlot's tiara was pared down to a simple crown, whereas the other engravings were reprinted unchanged. Was the allusion perhaps too precise, too

"metonymical," at a time when Lutheranism was still fragile and dependent on the Empire? The Harlot is represented as pope, however, in the Basel New Testament (1523) illustrated by Hans Holbein the Younger, and again in Luther's complete Bible, published in Wittenberg in 1534.

These images, which circulated just as widely as Luther's Bible, account for only a part of the immense amount of pictorial propaganda that the Lutherans distributed throughout Europe in the first thirty years of the existence of Lutheranism (1520–50). They are admirably analyzed by Robert W. Scribner in *For the Sake of Simple Folk*.[20] Broadsides, at times printed in one thousand or fifteen hundred copies, publicized the basic polemical, antipapal themes of Lutheranism, using the popular and traditional forms of the world turned upside-down and pilgrim and carnival images, and reducing the Gospel texts to simple oppositions of good and evil, pope and pastor, Rome and Babylon. The simplicity and brutality of such images often had a broader impact and went farther than written polemical production or the apologetics of preaching. Luther himself was well aware of the power of the image. In 1545 he wrote: "I published these pictures and these images, each of which represents an entire volume that still remains to be written against the pope and his kingdom."[21] Images permitted an immediate grasp of powerful themes, inherited from the Middle Ages, that lent themselves to phantasmagoric belief and were difficult to discern in written discourse. A broadside titled *Vom Ursprung und Herkunft des Antichristi* (On the Origin and the Birth of the Antichrist) shows two devils using a large pestle to crush monks and nuns in a huge bloody tub; next to them, two other demons have used the resulting mash, or Host, to form a body, into which they are breathing life. When fully animated, this body, potbellied and naked except for the papal tiara on his head, will be the Antichrist.[22] This image communicates a message that could never be expressed in doctrinal terms; it emerges from the great tradition (mentioned in chapter 5) of the heretics' diabolic Host. The image satanizes the pope in much the same way that Guibert de Nogent had diabolized his depiction of the heretics of Soissons in the twelfth century. The power of the image resided in its essential indetermination: the image simultaneously represents and creates a metaphor, with no indication of the dividing line between invective and myth or between joke and belief.

SIGNS OF THE ANTICHRIST

Binary simplification of the image and Luther's violent attacks on the papacy soon gave wide circulation to the comparison of the pope to the Antichrist, the eternal enemy, past and present, of the evangelical movement.

Joan, the quintessence of the papacy, the proof that Satanic inversion reigned in Rome, and the incarnation of the Whore of Babylon, became part of a network of figures that gave the medieval Antichrist a dizzying number of new forms.

The legend of the Antichrist, founded on vague and fleeting allusions in the Bible (Daniel, 2 Thessalonians, Revelation), developed during the Middle Ages as an inverted mirror image of Christ. In this legend, the Antichrist, born in Babylon of the Devil and a prostitute and raised by sorcerers and magicians, arrives in Jerusalem at the age of thirty, where he has himself circumcised, denounces the usurpation of Christ, reconstructs the Temple, proclaims himself God and reigns three and a half years (the length of Joan's papacy in the early Franciscan versions of her story). God sends Enoch and Elijah against him, but he massacres them. He feigns death and stages a resurrection, but the archangel Michael strikes him down as he attempts to perform an Ascension from the Mount of Olives.[23] Uncertainty about how the Antichrist's dates related to the Last Times and about his precise nature (was he an individual? a number of individuals, returning cyclically? a population? In his second letter St. John speaks of several Antichrists) made him an even more menacing, infinitely malleable figure: many adversaries of the popes, Frederick II for one, were denounced as incarnations of the Antichrist. With each period of tension, speculation arose that the arrival of the Antichrist was imminent, as we have seen in connection with the events of 1360. That exact moment was predicted on the basis of calculation and the occurrence of "prodigies" because a current version of the legend stated that the Antichrist's coming would be accompanied by fifteen signs. There was a sharp rise of interest in themes related to the Antichrist, the fall of Babylon, and the coming of the Last Times in the late fifteenth century and the early sixteenth century, one sign of which was the publication of Joachim of Fiore's commentary on the Apocalypse (Revelation) in Venice by the Augustinians, under the general of their Order, Egidio da Viterbo (whom we have already encountered in connection with his Catholic denunciation of Rome and his views on Joan). A wave of combined vituperation and hope spread throughout Europe between 1490 and 1520, striking Florence with Girolamo Savonarola and Marsilio Ficino; Orvieto with Luca Signorelli; Alsace with Sebastian Brant, the *Book of a Hundred Chapters*, and Thomas Murner. What Lutheranism added was to locate the kingdom of the Antichrist in Rome.[24]

Luther had launched the identification of the Antichrist with Rome immediately after his excommunication in 1520 in the "Bull of the Antichrist" and in *De captivitate babylonica Ecclesiae* (On the Babylonian Captivity of the Church). Images helped to popularize this interpretation: in May 1521, Lucas Cranach published his *Passional Christi und Antichristi*, a series of engravings in pamphlet form in which thirteen double pages of engravings compared scenes of the life of Christ and the lives of the popes as Antichrist. Each of the twenty-six images was accompanied by a written commentary by Philipp Melanchthon, Luther's closest disciple. An edition in Latin was also published, and the German version was reprinted several times at Erfurt and Strasbourg. In 1536 Cranach decorated the great hall of the castle of Torgau with the final pair of scenes from the *Passional Christi und Antichristi*, the Ascension of Christ and the fall into Hell of the Pope-Antichrist.[25]

The Renaissance, which the hypertrophy of medieval symbolism and the extraordinary popularity of astrology had rendered even more sensitive to signs of the Antichrist, underwent what André Chastel calls "a sudden interest in teratology—the study of monstrosities—and a mania for omens." Chastel adds, "Fifty-six authors and one hundred thirty-three pamphlets devoted to forecasts and astrological calculations have been counted for the decade 1520–1530."[26] I shall concentrate here on the signs of the Antichrist that best show how the Lutherans denounced the pope, making use of such "prodigies" to bestialize and feminize him, satanizing Joan in the process. In 1496 a monstrous cadaver was fished out of the Tiber: a she-ass with a female human torso, the arms and legs of a variety of animals, and a dragon-like tail. It was immediately baptized "the Papal Ass" (*Die Bapstesel zu Rom*). The engraver Wenzel von Olmutz depicted the prodigy and published his image, with an antipapal exegesis, in Bohemia in the late fifteenth century. From there the image passed into Germany (providing another example of the connection between Hussites and Lutherans), and in 1523 Luther and Melanchthon published illustrations and commentary on the Papal Ass and another prodigy, the Monk Calf, as *Deuttung der czwo grewlichen Figuren* (Signification of the Two Frightful Figures). The images were a wild success: the paired figures together went through nine editions, with five editions for the Papal Ass alone and a number of translations into French, English, and Dutch.[27]

JOAN AMONG THE AMAZONS AND THE HERMAPHRODITES

A powerful concentration of "prodigies" around Rome completed the satanization of the popess. Sexual inversion exacerbated the religious inversion (the pope as Antichrist) that was one of the favorite themes of Lutheran imagery. Sexual inversion seems to have taken on a new, powerful, and disturbing significance in the sixteenth century,[28] one aspect of which was the many hermaphrodites reported by Polydore Vergil, Pierre Boaistuau, and Ambroise Paré. When men of the Renaissance treated transsexuality, they added to the usual medieval stigmatization of trickery, human or satanic, an even stronger terror before a natural or supernatural mystery or any threat to general stability. Montaigne gives instances of this in his *Journal de voyage,* where he juxtaposes two anecdotes (and of course very little is accidental in Montaigne). The first of these regards a voluntary and successful gender change; the second depicts the virility that lurks in all active women. In Vitry-le-François, Montaigne (or, rather, his anonymous secretary) tells us, he heard three remarkable stories. The first of these concerned the extraordinary sprightliness of the aged dowager duchess of Guise; the second and third were these:

> A few days before there had been a hanging at a place called Montier-en-Der, near here, upon this occasion: Seven or eight girls around Chaumont-en-Bassigni plotted together a few years ago to dress up as males and thus continue their life in the world. One of them came to this place under the name Mary, earning her living as a weaver, a well-disposed young man who made friends with everybody. At the said Vitry he became engaged to a woman who is still alive, but because of some disagreement that arose between them, their compact went no further. Later he went to the said Montier-en-Der, still earning his living at the said trade, and fell in love with a woman, whom he married and with whom he lived for four or five months, to her satisfaction, so they say. But she was recognized by someone from the said Chaumont, the matter was brought before justice, and she was condemned to be hanged, which she said she would rather undergo than return to a girl's status; and she was hanged for using illicit devices to supply her defect in sex.
>
> The other story is of a man still alive named Germain, of low condition, without any trade or position, who was a girl up to the age of twenty-two, seen and known by all the inhabitants of the town, and noticed because she had a little more hair about her chin than the other girls; and they called her Bearded Mary. One day when she made an effort in jumping, her virile instruments came out, and Cardinal de Lenoncourt, then bishop of Châlons, gave her the name Germain. Germain has not married, however; he has a big, very thick beard. We were not able to see him because he was in the village. In this town there is still a song commonly in the girls' mouths, in which they warn one another not

to stretch their legs too wide for fear of becoming males, like Marie Germain. They say that Ambroise Paré has put this story into his book on surgery. The story is very certain, and was attested to Monsieur de Montaigne by the most eminent officials of the town.[29]

Bringing up Montaigne's anecdotes in the context of the history of Joan will seem less gratuitous in the light of a remark by the French jurist, Etienne de Forcadel. He speaks of Joan in connection with a discussion of salic law in *De Gallorum imperio et philosophia,* a work published in Paris in 1580, where he suggests that perhaps she was a man when she was elected to the papacy and had changed gender after her election. He cites an instance of sex change in Livy in support of this hypothesis. The popess remained a monster, however, because in both Livy and Montaigne the change occurred in the "natural," "upward" direction from the imperfect female to the perfect male.

Lutheranism combated this sexual indecision by offering a secure division of gender roles founded in the family, a notion that was proclaimed publicly when Luther married, rejecting the prestige and the dangers of priestly omnisexuality. Luther constantly and proudly boasted of his own masculinity, as in the famous comment in his *Table Talk* on those who have themselves castrated for reasons of asceticism: "Ich wolde eher mir zewy par lassen ansetzen den ein par lassen ausscheiden" (I would rather have a second pair of testicles grafted onto me than have one cut off).[30]

This means that Joan, a figure of the Antichrist and a prototype for the religious and sexual inversion of Rome, occupied a choice position in Lutheran images. But just how did she come to be part of Wittenberg's arsenal of arguments?

SOURCES OF THE LUTHERAN JOAN

Around 1520 Joan seems to have been well remembered in Saxony. She arrived there through several channels:

1. Via Rome: in his *Tischreden* (Table Talk) Luther states that he saw a commemorative statue of Joan when he went to Rome late in 1510 on business for his Order, the Augustinians. He states: "In Rome, in a public square, there is a stone monument to commemorate the pope who was really a woman and who gave birth to a child on that very spot. I have seen the stone myself, and I find it astonishing that the popes permit it to exist."[31]

2. By means of print: two late-fifteenth-century printed texts gave the

story of the popess particularly broad circulation (as did many chronicles printed in the early sixteenth century, as we have seen). A popular edition of Boccaccio's *De mulieribus claris* was printed in Ulm in 1473 with a series of highly evocative woodcuts; the illustrations in Hartmann Schedel's *Weltchronik* (often called the "Nuremberg Chronicle"), published in Nuremberg in 1493, were reproduced frequently, in particular in Protestant circles. André Chastel has demonstrated that Cranach used the view of Rome in Schedel's chronicle to represent the destruction of Babylon in his own engravings for Luther's New Testament, September 1522.[32] The anonymous Latin translation of a work by Alexander Cooke, a Protestant, that was published in Oppenheim in 1616 as *Johanna papissa toti orbi manifestata* used another of Schedel's woodcuts, a charming Joan with child.

3. By the Bohemian connection: The mention of the name "Agnes" on Martin Schrott's broadsheet points to a link with Joan, which Luther confirms by using the name "Agnes" in his *Table Talk*. Lutherans knew Jan Hus's treatise *De Ecclesia* (On the Church), which alluded to the popess (see chapter 4). The dialogue that Enea Silvio Piccolomini reported as having taken place in Tabor in 1451 shows that the story was being transmitted, although it probably lost much of its currency after the destruction of Tabor, when a compromise was sought with the Taborites. Josef Macek, a specialist in Hussite texts, has been kind enough to search for traces of Agnes in those texts and has found none. One cannot exclude the possibility of oral circulation, however: in 1906, Hans Preuss discovered a late trace of the episode of Joan in a Hussite work that contrasted the election of a female pope with the choice of the Apostle Matthew to fill the place vacated by Judas (Acts 1.23).[33]

4. Through Bavaria and Thuringia: the Tegernsee version of the Joan story (presented in chapter 5) probably drew from a rich and lively autonomous tradition, one reflection of which can be seen in a play by Dietrich Schernberg that was performed at Mulhausen, in Thuringia, around 1480 and was printed by a Lutheran press in Eisleben in 1565. In chapter 7 we shall return to this *Fraw Jutta* (the Bavarian name for Joan). The summary of the legend given in Luther's *Table Talk* clearly refers to the Bavarian tradition (although the success of Schernberg's work must have spawned local variations throughout German lands).

5. Through Alsace and the Rhineland: the story of Joan found a resounding echo in the work of an astonishing personage, the Alsatian Franciscan Thomas Murner (1476–ca. 1537). An itinerant friar who had joined the Franciscans at a very young age (at fourteen, in 1490) Murner was in turn a universal student (he studied law in Friburg, arts and theology in

Paris, philosophy and mathematics in Krakow), court poet of Emperor Maximilian I (1506), the inventor (in Krakow) of the *Chartiludium*, a card game designed to teach logic (1507), and the popularizer and possibly the creator of the famous legend of Till Eulenspiegel. This career seemed to destine him to be a humanist, but, as a good Franciscan, he remained loyal to a popular, medieval vein, and his attachment to Alsatian dialect kept him apart from the humanists. Utopian and fideistic currents of thought were lively in Alsace in the late fifteenth century, as can be seen in texts close in inspiration to Sebastian Brant's *Ship of Fools* (*Das Narrenschiff*, 1494) such as *Die Narrenbeschworung* (The Conjuration of Fools), *Schelmenzunft* (The Corporation of Knaves, 1512), *Die Mulle von Schwyndelszheim* (The Mill at Schwyndelszheim, 1515), and others. Murner's interest in such themes should have led him to Luther, but he was instead a resolute adversary of Luther's and perhaps the only Catholic to respond to Luther's illustrated propaganda in the years from 1520 to 1535. An excellent draftsman, Murner illustrated his own *Great Lutheran Fool* (*Von dem grossen Lutherischen Narren*), where he appears with a cat's head (a play on his name attributed to him by Lutheran pamphleteers) and portrays himself as a hunter of Lutheran rats.[34]

Murner told the story of Joan on two occasions, in 1514 and in 1519. In 1514 he published in Strasbourg a *Badenfahrt* (Voyage to the Baths), an allegory of Christian salvation as a cure at a spa. In chapter 11, where he orders the patient to scratch his skin ("Die Hut kratzen") as a figure for doing penance, he uses Joan's choice of shame on earth over eternal damnation to illustrate his point. Murner gives a fuller version of the Joan story in *Die Gäuchmatt*, printed in Basel in 1519, a work that returns to the gallery of women, though in a more satirical and popular key, given that Murner's women are more scandalous than they are illustrious. Chapter 20 is dedicated to Joan ("Johannes ein babst"), and her neighbors are Potiphar's wife, Jezebel, Thaïs, and Venus (in the *Tannhaüser* version).[35]

Another German Franciscan, Johannes Pauli, mentions the popess in a late collection of exempla, *Schimpf und Ernst* (1522), where he recalls a scene from *Fraw Jutta* in which the devil's refusal to let a woman exorcise him exposes the pope as a woman.

The Franciscans—Murner, Pauli, and Rioche—were the last Catholics to cling to an attachment to Joan that had been so characteristic of their fellow friars in the fourteenth century. The logic of exclusion (which we have seen in connection with Enea Silvio Piccolomini) was ineffective in the populist, truculent universe of Thomas Murner. He seems unaware of the gap in Franciscan discourse in the fifteenth century; through a use of the theme of penitence (which came from the Bavarian tradition), that discourse, at once archaic and in tune with its times, could still include the history of the popess. Martin Luther was on his way, however.

Thanks to Lucas Cranach's and Martin Schrott's illustrations, the story of the popess became a lasting part of the Lutheran patrimony. Robert W. Scribner has found three broadsheets printed in the 1540s that narrate the story of Joan; the great Hans Sachs wrote a song about her in 1532.[36] It is curious, however, that the text history of the Lutheran Joan began only later, and outside the Saxon fortress.

THE FIRST LUTHERAN NARRATIVE: JOHN BALE (1548)

John Bale, an Englishman, mentioned the popess in a chapter on the popes and the Roman Antichrists in his *Illustrium majoris Britanniae scriptores Summarium* (Catalogue of the Illustrious Writers of Great Britain), published in Basel in 1548 and reprinted in that city in 1557. After a sojourn with the Carmelites in Norwich and studies at Cambridge, Bale was elected bishop of Ossory, in Ireland, but later he joined the Lutheran cause, was driven into exile in Germany, and married. Here is his version of the Joan story:

> John VIII received the surname of "Anglicus" from an English-
> man whom she loved, a monk in a monastery in Fulda; although
> she was a woman, she occupied the papal throne as pope for two
> years and six months. Of German origin, born in Mainz, her
> name was Gilberta; feigning to be a man, she went to Athens with
> her lover the monk. There she made great progress in all the disci-
> plines, and therefore when her friend died, she left for Rome, still
> dissimulating her female sex. Because of her great talent and her
> facility in speaking she was able to carry on difficult debates and
> give public lessons, prompting general admiration. She attracted
> so much sympathy that at the death of Leo IV she was elected
> pope. In that office, according to papal custom, she granted holy
> orders, created priests and deacons, named bishops, commanded
> the selection of abbots, celebrated Masses, consecrated altars and
> churches, administered sacraments, offered her feet to be kissed,
> and performed all the other pontifical functions. And everything
> that she accomplished in the Church was fully validated.[37]

Bale had obviously borrowed his version of the Joan story from several traditions. The name Gilberta and Joan's amorous and studious adventure come from Boccaccio, but Athens as a stop on the way to Rome comes from Martinus Polonus. Bale adds a new detail: the lover is a monk of Fulda, the large, prestigious abbey near Mainz. This addition is so typically Lutheran that it must be Bale's invention: antimonastic satire reached unheard-of levels of violence in early Lutheran propaganda; the lover here is one among many examples of the lustful, ambitious, and wandering monk. In the Lutheran context, the popess's enthusiasm for studies, which Boccaccio praises unconditionally, is no compliment: Lutheran apologetics pilloried medieval scholarship (Thomas Aquinas, Aristotle, William of Ockham, and Duns Scotus are often depicted in the company of demons and corrupt monks).

Bale is insistent in his commentary: sacraments performed by a canonically unqualified person were nonetheless valid, but most of the sacraments or rites that he specifies (ordination, the consecration of churches, veneration of the person of the pope) were ones that Lutheranism violently rejected and portrayed in its illustrated propaganda as blasphemous or purely terrestrial. Cranach, for example, pairs Christ washing the feet of the poor with the custom of kissing the pope's feet in his engravings for the *Passional Christi und Antichristi*.

Bale padded his narrative with political considerations on relations between the papacy and the lay powers, following the synoptic layout of the universal chronicles. The classic model of this genre, from the remote times of Eusebius and Jerome to Martinus Polonus, presented the chronicles of the popes and the emperors in two parallel columns, to which local chronicles at times added a third column for events concerning regional lay power, the diocese, or the abbey. The columns rarely corresponded chronologically, item by item, however. Bale chose to do so for polemical reasons, thus anticipating the method of the "Magdeburg Centuries" of Flacius Illyricus and others, the founding model of Reformed historiography. As Bale searched the legendary histories of lay sovereigns for events that coincided with the reign of the woman pope, he found interesting connections that made the female Antichrist the basis for the secular powers' ancient allegiance to the Holy See and for the shameful institution of tithing. Bale states:

> Under her papacy, the old emperor, Lothair, took the monastic habit, and when Louis II came to Rome, he received from her hands the imperial scepter and crown along with the blessing of Peter. By an act of the sort, the Harlot of Babylon showed that she was powerful enough to subject kings. Similarly, it was under her that Ætelwulf, king of the Angles, as Howedehus relates, of his own volition and like a weak woman conceded the tenth part of

his kingdom to clerics and monks. . . . In all of this you can see, pious reader, if truly the Roman Church did not err after the Mass of the Holy Spirit [the Mass preparatory to the election—divinely inspired—of the pope]. In reality, this specific fact shows very clearly that this Church is the seat of the Great Harlot and the Mother of all fornications, which no Apelles could paint in its real colors.[38]

Here Joan is personified as the mythical founder of the Babylonian perversion of Rome. At the end of this passage Bale describes the rite to verify the pope's manhood, repeating the witticism that the rite was unnecessary, given that all cardinals make sure they have progeny before being elected pope.

THE POPESS IN PIER PAOLO VERGERIO

The second Lutheran historian of Joan is a curious and interesting figure. Pier Paolo Vergerio was born in 1498 into a family made famous by the humanist of the same name. The younger Pier Paolo was ordained as the bishop of his native city of Capodistria by Paul III; he performed distinguished diplomatic service for Clement VII, Paul III, and Julius III and participated actively in the preparations for the Council of Trent. He met Luther in Wittenberg in 1535. That the two men met shows that Vergerio was open to Lutheranism, but the interview soon dissipated any attraction, and Vergerio pronounced Luther "a monster." Lutheranism made its effect slowly, however, and in 1549 Vergerio barely escaped being arrested by the Inquisition by fleeing, first to Switzerland, then to Germany, specifically to Tübingen.[39]

In his Tübingen hideaway, the new Lutheran soon produced a number of antipapal works, among them a pamphlet, *Historia di papa Giovanni VIII che fu femmina* (1556), a title that became more sharply critical when the work was reprinted the following year as *Historia di papa Giovanni VIII che fu meretrice e strega* (History of Pope John VIII, who was a prostitute and a witch). The work was reprinted again in 1562; it was translated into French in 1557, into German in 1559, into Latin in 1560, and into English in 1584.

Vergerio, who had certainly read Bale, was even more incisive and more abusive than his predecessor, and his vast culture provided him with even more violent historical examples and polemic thrusts:

Among all the tricks that the devil played on those miserable [papists], the worst was this one: about seven hundred years ago, in

the times of Emperor Lothair, that buffoon who later turned
monk (I say monk, and not friar, because in those days that
plague on the world, the friars, had not yet spread), the devil gave
them for most worthy leader a fat prostitute who ruled the synagogue, said solemn Masses, gave benedictions and absolutions,
created the bishops and other prelates (I do not say, created cardinals, because in those times those Sardanapalases, those beasts
and bloody monsters, had not yet been discovered). What should
happen but her Holiness became pregnant and gave birth in the
presence of all the clergy and the Roman people. Shame. Where,
oh papists, was the head of your Church then? Where was the
apostolic succession you boast of so much? In that necromancer,
or sorceress and prostitute (*In quella femmina nigromante o strega e
meretrice*)? Do you believe that she "consecrated" (as you say)
when she said Mass? Do you believe that she remitted sins when
she gave absolution? Who imprinted your famous indelible sign
on those whom she ordained and anointed? Who gave the Holy
Spirit? What a fine race, those bishops and those other priests
who issued from that necromancer's hands! And it is a fact that
all the popes who followed were the fabrications and the creatures of those gracious hands—that is to say, of the devils who
were in her and guided her. O miserable papists, ridiculous and
stupid![40]

After this amiable prologue of mixed invective and serious argument
about the interruption of the Petrine tradition, Vergerio relates the story of
Joan. He follows Boccaccio's version closely: the popess is named Gilberta; she goes to England with her lover; she succeeds Pope Leo V; lust is
her perdition. The story line so closely follows Boccaccio's that it seems
unnecessary to reproduce Vergerio's version here, but several incidental remarks dropped into the text by the perfidious but precise Vergerio are
worth noting. In making the point that it was the people and the clergy
who elected Pope Gilberta, he adds parenthetically, playing on the words
carnali, carnevali, and *cardinali*: "At that time they elected the pope, and
not only the carnal and the carnival ones, who stole that election just as
they stole the primacy."[41]

In a decidedly cavalier manner, Vergerio delivers a passing remark that
imputes to her a number of probable abortions and infanticides: "But unfortunately Her Beatitude became pregnant (it must not have been the
first time, but the other times she must have killed the babies, not yet born
or newborn)."[42] Vergerio makes the popess's baby a male (*un figliol mas-*

chio), but does not give further detail. One might expect Lutheran imagery to have made this child into the Antichrist (or an antichrist) begotten by the devil of a prostitute (and Vergerio does explicitly call Joan a prostitute *(meretrice).* The Catholic polemicist Florimond de Raemond was surprised at this lacuna in the usual Lutheran arguments. Vergerio may have thought that developing a mythic narrative about the Antichrist moved the question too far forward in time and weakened the contemporary thrust of his invective.

After Vergerio delivers his amended version of Boccaccio, he lists vestiges of the popess. He is unaware of the statue that Luther claimed to have seen in 1510, but of course he mentions the detour taken by papal processions. He also refers to a "very fine relief" on "the square in Bologna." There is no trace of any memorialization of Joan in that city; Vergerio may have been thinking of a bust of Joan in the gallery of the popes in the cathedral of Siena. He seizes on the tradition of the rite of the verification of papal manhood, which he describes with his customary crudity: "But so that they would never again be subjected to the shame of having a whore for a leader and a mother for a father, they took the precaution of having a stone seat made in St. John Lateran called *Stercoraria* because it is in the shape of a *cacatoio* [literally, shitting chair]." The confusion between the stercory chair and the porphyry thrones quite surely comes from Platina, who is one of the three sources that Vergerio mentions (along with Martinus Polonus's chronicle and Boccaccio's *De mulieribus claris,* in the Latin edition published in Bern in 1536). Vergerio goes out of his way to attack Platina, calling him "that great champion and adulator (for his own greater benefit; *per sua gratia)* of the papacy." This judgment is surprising, if we remember that Platina languished in the jails of Paul II, or if we think of the subtle perfidies of Platina's chapter on Joan. Indeed, if the two had changed places and, fifty years later, Platina were writing fictional history, he might have said as much of Vergerio. Vergerio blamed Platina for two things: first, Platina rejected the reason usually given for the verification of papal virility, turning the stercory chair into a metaphor for the human and natural fragility of the pope, subject, like all humankind, to the necessities of nature and of *chi bisogni cacare.* Vergerio, a neo-Lutheran but an expert in Catholic ritual, shows that puerile metaphor to be redundant, since the rite of burning a bit of tow at the end of a reed to the chanting of *Pater sancte, sic transit gloria mundi* was quite sufficient to remind the tyrant of his fragile humanity.[43]

Platina's second error, according to Vergerio, was that he distorted the truth. Platina had written, "Joan seized the papacy by magical arts, according to what is said *(Malis artibus [ut aiunt] pontificatum adeptus est)."*

Vergerio claims (the texts do not support this claim, however) that other historians had recognized that Joan could only have taken possession of the papal throne by beseeching the devil, which permitted him to class Joan within a long list of "other necromancer popes, intimate companions and as if brothers of the devil, both among ancient men and modern ones," and to pass on to further insults directed at Paul III and the entire Farnese family.[44]

John Bale and Pier Paulo Vergerio thus gave the story of Joan an ideological commentary to match Cranach's and Schrott's images. But Vergerio's astonishing statements in 1556, like those of Enea Silvio Piccolomini in 1451, raise the question of how cultivated men and humanists, prelates with such subtle minds, could have given credence to such coarse notions.

OUTBURSTS OF BELIEF

Did Vergerio truly believe in a diabolic papacy, or was he using the idea to give violent and rhetorical cover to his religious and/or personal anger at Rome? The second interpretation seems more probable, especially in the light of a chronological correlation suggested by Cesare D'Onofrio.[45] In 1556, the year of his first pamphlet on the popess, Vergerio published (also in Tübingen and in a format similar to his *Historia*) Cencio Savelli's *ordo* of 1192, following the manuscript now in the Vatican Library as Vat. Lat. 2145, and making no changes in the tenor of that work. That text, as we saw in chapter 3, mentions the porphyry seats and the stercory chair, but it keeps the two quite separate and mentions no rite verifying papal masculinity. As Vergerio republished it, this benign *ordo*, which offered no weapons to Lutheran argumentation, was preceded by an engraving showing the popess in the throes of childbirth similar to the one in Vergerio's first *Historia di papa Giovanni VIII*, and by a violently antipapal dedicatory letter addressed to Prince Albert of Brandenburg. If Vergerio had believed in a diabolic papacy according to the style of belief I have called phantasmagoric, he would have interpreted Cencio's text in some wild manner, making his own frenzied interpolations. It is clear, though, that, like Platina, he reserved his roving imagination and painstaking erudition for attacking contemporaries, Paul III or men of the Curia close to the pope. This means that we will have to theorize a fourth mode of belief in Joan (better, a subdivision of phantasmagoric belief) and speak of "intermittent belief," as the psychiatrists speak of "intermittent delirium." Such whiffs of belief touch on important emotions, and they affect only certain domains in certain circumstances.

Lutheran propaganda oscillated among three approaches to the story of Joan: first, Joan was a historical reality (for Bale, the 855 popess founded pontifical tyranny by subjecting sovereigns); second, Joan functioned as a sign (for Vergerio, a harbinger who revealed the Roman Antichrist); third, Joan was a metaphor, an emblem for the true nature of the papacy that operated as a condensation of Roman turpitude. Cyriacus Spangenberg wrote in 1562, "The Roman popes were often, although outwardly men, nothing but prostitutes,"[46] and Lucas Osiander used a metaphorical Joan in his *Bedencken ob der newe päpstliche Kalender ein Nottdurfft bey der Christenheit seie* (Considerations on the Need for a New Calendar; 1583), a polemical work written in 1583 to attack Gregory XIII's plan for a reform of the calendar. Osiander states: "The peddler Gregory has flattered himself that he can sell his calendars as profitably as indulgences were once sold. He has given birth to the calendar so as to avoid remaining sterile; before him, for the same reason Pope John VIII brought a pretty little boy child into the world."[47] It is difficult to differentiate clearly among these three interpretations; the polysemy (or the indetermination) of the image could easily appeal to all three traditions.

After first receiving such violent treatment from the Lutherans, Joan returned to a calmer (but still disapproving) historical existence in the enormous volumes of the Lutheran *Ecclesiastica historia,* a work compiled by scholars known as the Magdeburg Centuriators because they divided their history into centuries. In volume 5 (ninth century) of this work, published in 1565, the centuriators compiled a vast dossier of texts and other evidence proving the existence of Pope Joan.[48] Polemicists referred to this dossier constantly into the nineteenth century; Johann Wolf, whom we met in chapter 1, took it as his inspiration and gave its materials even broader distribution.

JOAN DENIED BY HER OWN: ONOFRIO PANVINIO (1562)

During the bitter years of the expansion of Lutheranism, what did the Catholic Church have to say about Joan? At first, nothing. In general Catholicism (with the notable exception of Thomas Murner) did not deign, or was not able, to respond to Lutheran polemics. André Chastel has analyzed this inability to adjust to new times in his presentation of the paintings done for the *Stanze* of the Vatican in 1520–25, some of which (the Donation of Constantine in particular) were a response to the Protestant threat. In 1518–19 Ulrich von Hutten, Luther's violent lay acolyte, alerted the world to the refutation of the spurious Donation written by the humanist Lorenzo Valla around 1440 and first published, with little resonance, in 1506. Chastel draws this conclusion:

The antagonism ran so deep that it declared itself in two totally opposing modes of graphic discourse: on the one side, the tradition of monumental Mediterranean painting at the height of its powers; and on the other, the direct, popular, and quickly produced art of Northern printmaking, which for the first time in history became a major force in cultural and religious life. Rome did not make use of the right weapons, the modern media; there could be no hope of victory.[49]

What was to be done with Joan? Up to that point the Church had put up with her, but now it felt the same embarrassment that Enea Silvio Piccolomini had experienced in 1451. St. Antoninus of Florence, writing in the mid-fifteenth century, had foreseen the most redoubtable questions posed by John Bale or Pier Paolo Vergerio and refuted them in advance. Antoninus claimed that the sacramental acts performed by the popess, although invalid, had received after-the-fact validation by divine grace (much like French public law today, in which a decree can be validated by passing catch-up legislation). In 1520, however, Antoninus's subtlety must have seemed dangerous because it implied precisely what Luther was thundering against: that the clergy was useless to the reception of grace. It was also dangerous to challenge the strict linearity of the Petrine inheritance, already threatened by the removal of the Donation of Constantine.

This means that the Church no longer cared to compromise itself over a more amiable Joan who was, however, dangerously familiar to the Lutherans. Still, a total turnabout seemed difficult: there were too many texts, from Martinus Polonus to Platina, that had certified Joan's existence, and too many usages that commemorated her. Only in 1562 did the Church deny Joan, thanks to the painstaking labors of an Augustinian friar (Luther's former Order!) from Verona, Onofrio Panvinio. Panvinio responded to the Lutherans publicly, not in another pamphlet, but by publishing a new edition of Platina's *Lives of the Popes* in Venice in 1562 (Italian translation, 1563).[50] The Curia had commissioned Panvinio to continue Platina's biographies of the popes to cover the pontiffs from Sixtus IV to Pius IV, Panvinio's own contemporary. He also added learned annotations to Platina's text. This was a carefully premeditated choice of means for refuting Lutheranism. Platina's work, with its quasi-official status and its pointed style, had been enormously successful, and the Lutherans had fallen upon it gleefully, as we have seen with Vergerio. Thus from the Catholic point of view, Platina had to be maintained, but also corrected. Panvinio reproduced Platina's earlier chapter on Joan in its entirety, but he added three pages of commentary to demonstrate that Joan's papacy had absolutely no reality.

Panvinio begins with general considerations on psychological and theological verisimilitude: the Romans, he claims, would never have been so stupid as to have elected to the papacy an unknown person of uncertain origin. Moreover, God would not have permitted such an imposture. Next he moves on to more convincing philological and historical refutations. Returning to the chronological listings of the popes, he remarks that between Leo IV and Benedict III (the position traditionally occupied by Joan's papacy) the vacancy lasted no more than a fortnight. Furthermore, he notes that Anastasius Bibliothecarius, whom he holds to be the author of the *Liber pontificalis*, does not mention Joan's papacy, and that the addition regarding Joan is by a different and later hand. He then broadens his inquiry to chronicles in general, remarking that no chronicler alludes to the popess until 1250 (the date he assigns to the redaction of Martinus Polonus's chronicle). Panvinio clearly had an excellent grasp of texts, and latter-day erudition has had little to add.

There is another possible argument: Panvinio notes that in 1054 Leo IX sent a letter to the Patriarch of Constantinople, Michael Cerularius, reproaching him for promoting eunuchs and a woman to high priestly functions (or so it was rumored in the West). How could Leo IX have been so imprudent as to launch such an accusation if Joan had indeed reigned as pope two centuries earlier?

Next, Panvinio returns to the institutional improbability of the story: the Church elected to the papacy only individuals who had been trained within its bosom. Finally, he stresses minor absurdities: the dual designation of Mainz and England *(Maguntinus Anglicus)* as Joan's places of origin; her studies in Athens, a city that, for all practical purposes, did not exist in the ninth century; her public lessons in Rome, at a time when that practice was unknown. As he comments on Platina's text, Panvinio stresses all the ways in which his predecessor hedged his bets ("according to what is said," etc.). He then goes on to list a long string of other unacceptable circumstances: it would have been impossible to conceal a pregnancy in a milieu always crowded with people; taking part in a procession at an advanced stage of pregnancy was highly imprudent; Joan successfully disguised her gender for an unbelievably long time. Panvinio follows this close criticism of the text from within and without with an attempt to reconstruct how the legend came into being. He explains the famous detour that processions took by appealing to Roman topography; Cesare D'Onofrio, a scholar well acquainted with Roman historical space, concurs with his overall description. Panvinio suggests that the fable was a transcription of the scandalous life of John XII (†962), one of whose many mistresses was named Joan. The similarity between their names and the rumor that Joan (the mistress) had so much influence over the pope as to be the real "popess" might have given rise to the story. This explanation, which has been ceaselessly repeated, with variants, up to our own day, was probably based on the account of an early-sixteenth-century Bavarian chronicler, Johannes Turmair, known as Aventinus after his native city of Abensberg. In his *Annalium Boiorum* (Annals of Bavaria), written around 1510, Turmair relates the papacy of John IX:

> Albert, a very wealthy prince of Etruria, held in his power
> Ravenna, Bologna, and Rome. His mother-in-law, Theodora, a
> noble and imperious courtesan, dominated in Rome; she im-
> posed John, her lover, on the Bolognese, then on the people of
> Ravenna, and finally on the Romans; she had him named to the
> supreme priesthood. This is, I believe, the origin of the fable that
> was so lightly repeated, according to which in those times a
> woman occupied the supreme priesthood and was supposedly
> named Joan.[51]

Thurmair's refutation stands high among the many mysteries surrounding the story of Joan. He was not an obscure, negligible writer, but the creator of modern Bavarian historiography, and he seems not to have been involved in the ecclesiological debates in which Joan flourished. Back in 1451, the eminent Enea Silvio Piccolomini had been unable to move from disquietude to refutation, and for over a century no Catholic voice had been raised to deny Joan's existence. Behind Panvinio's rather late refutation we sense pressure from the Curia and the weight of his own enormous erudition. Turmair forged right ahead to state with certitude that Joan had never existed, and he provided a plausible theory of how the legend had gotten started. His Erasmian spirit may have made him critical of all fables, partisan interests aside. The Church never expressed its gratitude for his "Johannoclasty," and in fact in 1564 his book was not only listed on the first Index of Prohibited Books, but was listed in the first category, works whose authors are heretics or suspected of heresy.

Thanks to its extraordinary erudition and its remarkable concision, Panvinio's Catholic refutation of the Joan legend provided the model for all further "Johannoclasties." Between 1562 and 1565—that is, between Panvinio and the "Magdeburg Centuries"—Joan's fate in polemics was sealed. To one side, she was rejected with solid arguments; to the other, an impressive quantity of medieval texts were published that proved, if not the existence of Joan, at least her long familiarity with the Catholic

Church. What followed in the wake of this dense controversy, as we shall see, was a never-ending reiteration of that same exchange of textual arguments.

The Catholic Church had at last determined its position and its tactic (erudite response), just when the Lutherans were moving from invective and visual propaganda to polemical discourse. There were three reasons for that shift, which corresponded to a decline (around 1550 or 1560) in the production of images. First, in general (and outside the religious domain), the image regressed in European printing of the late sixteenth century; second, Lutheranism, by that time well established and entrenched, gave more thought to giving a solid foundation to its institution than to vituperating Rome; third, new developments (the Council of Trent, the Calvinist and Zwinglian Reformations) required a more doctrinal, less polemical, style of argumentation.

JESUIT AND OTHER CATHOLIC ATTACKS

The Catholics were fairly quick to make use of Panvinio's erudition, and the first work entirely devoted to refuting the existence of Joan appeared in 1584. Its author was Georg Scherer, preacher to Archduke Ernst of Austria; its title, *Grundlicher Bericht ob es wahr sey, dass auf ein Zeit ein Pabst zu Rom schwanger gewesen und ein Kind gebohren habe* (Ingolstadt and Vienna, 1584; Italian translation, Venice and Milan, 1586). Scherer had nothing to add to Panvinio's arguments, but his work was new in two ways: it was written in German, thus carrying the debate into the Lutherans' own linguistic domain; it signaled the arrival of the Society of Jesus on the ideological terrain of the popess. The Jesuits were better qualified to adapt to the new struggles than the older congregations, and they had no need to take on the medieval inheritance of the Dominicans and the Franciscans, notably absent in controversy about Joan since the early sixteenth century. Jean Rioche, the Franciscan from Saint-Brieuc who rewrote a universal chronicle in 1576 in which he presents an ingenuous popess, was an exact contemporary of Scherer's. It would certainly be inaccurate to speak of a decline of the Dominicans or the Franciscans, but their efforts to combat Lutheranism kept to the ancient forms of the Inquisition, the Dominicans' heavy burden, and, for the Franciscans, popular preaching.

The Jesuits provided a resounding echo to Panvinio, and their entry into the fray culminated, in 1586, in a refinement of Panvinio's demonstration of the *De romano pontifice,* by Robert Bellarmine, the most eminent member of the Society of Jesus.[52]

Another Catholic refutation of the Joan legend appeared in Bordeaux in 1587: *L'erreur populaire de la papesse Jane* by Florimond de Raemond, a judge in the Parlement of Bordeaux and a friend of Montaigne and Blaise de Monluc (whose works he had edited). Raemond had shown Calvinist sympathies before he became an active Catholic propagandist close to the Jesuits (some claimed that Louis Richeome, a Jesuit, had inspired Raemond's book). The *Erreur populaire,* a work important for the extraordinary breadth of its erudition, was reprinted and added to many times, with twelve editions in French and Latin printed from 1587 to 1624 in Paris, Bordeaux, Lyon, Cambrai, Cologne, and Antwerp.[53] I will spare the reader an account of Raemond's version of the Joan story; he repeats and develops Panvinio's arguments, scrutinizing all aspects of Joan's history (texts, the context of 855, the various commemorations of the popess). His demonstration is less convincing that Panvinio's; at times it is better to leave well enough alone, or, as the French proverb goes, "Le mieux est l'ennemi du bien." Raemond attributes all texts before Boccaccio that mention the popess to the malignity of Lutheran (or quasi-Lutheran) forgers; for every manuscript that mentions the popess, he produces another that does not. This was not pure delirium; as we have seen, the earliest manuscripts of Martinus Polonus's chronicle bear no trace of a popess. Florimond de Raemond goes no further on that route, however, because he realized that he himself was using the corrosive Lutheran tactic of seeing forgeries everywhere. He was doubtless aware of the trauma caused by Lorenzo Valla's refutation of the Donation of Constantine, as relayed by Ulrich von Hutten.

Raemond's all-out search for reasons behind the invention of the Joan legend led him on some odd paths: in discussing Johannes Turmair's and Panvinio's thesis of a misunderstanding when a metaphor in which the pope's mistress was called "popess" was taken literally, he suggests that this version was a deliberate German invention dating back to the age of the Investiture Controversy. Raemond's passion for polemics compensated for his relatively unenlightened mind and led him to some unexpected illuminations: he writes some fine passages on the cultural mechanisms that induce authors to copy one another (out of fear of appearing ignorant) and on romantic fascination, thus sketching out a description of the autonomy of symbolic systems. If we add that he displays a certain structural agility in his speculations on the various successions of popes named Leo and Benedict, and that he made an extraordinary effort to evaluate texts philologically, we can see the benefit of polemic energy in historical research. It is also interesting that Raemond attempts a counterattack on two fronts. He states that the only real female usurper of papal rank is Queen Elizabeth of England ("Jezebel" for the League), who declared herself head of the Anglican Church after Henry VIII's break with Rome: "How, then, can one baptize a woman who calls herself the head of the Church, if not with the name 'popess'?"[54] On the Lutheran front, Raemond states that his adversaries are simply using the fable to mask the unheard-of novelty of the marriage of priests.

Raemond notes one troublesome trace of the popess, but rather than demolishing it he perpetuated it, proving an excellent illustration of just how intricately tangled mentions of Joan could be, and how easy it is to lose track of their origin. He states that in his day a sculpted bust of Joan still figured in the fifteenth-century gallery of papal portrait busts in the cathedral of Siena. Cardinal Cesare Baronio, who had read Raemond, alerted Clement VIII (1592–1605), who had the bust of Joan replaced by one of Pope Zacharias. This success was reported by Raemond himself in the later editions of his *Erreur populaire,* again by Antonio Pagi, the editor and commentator of Baronio's *Annales,* and yet again by Girolamo Gigli in his *Diario sanese* (Lucca, 1723), after which the anecdote became part of the greater Johannic tradition.

The fact that Raemond, Baronio, and Clement VIII were all genuinely disturbed by the idea of a bust of Pope Joan in no way implies that the statue in question was initially meant to figure Joan. The papal portraits are placed on a cornice high above the nave, where they are nearly inaccessible to sight. The busts themselves are quite undifferentiated, and the labels ascribing them to the various popes were placed on them at a much later date. They cannot even be matched to an accurate count of the pontiffs, given that the gallery does not have room for all the popes, which means that attributions can differ. I might add that it is unlikely that Pope Zacharias, a great pope well-known for his political dialogue with Pepin le Bref, would have been omitted from the original series. As with the rite of verification of the pope's manhood, it is difficult to separate good-faith error (occurring when the busts were made? when the names were read at some later date?) from malicious misinterpretation or horrified obsession.

In spite of its limitations, Raemond's work was echoed in such prestigious works as Gilbert Genebrard's *Chronographia* and, above all, in the *Annales ecclesiastici* of Cardinal Baronio, a highly important text that was compiled as a Catholic response to the "Magdeburg Centuries." In 1630, at the request of the Curia, the great Italian-Greek scholar Leone Allacci (Allatius) summarized the anti-Johannic arguments in his *Confutatio fabulae de Joannae papissae,* published in Rome.

THE END OF JOAN: SCORN FROM THE
CALVINISTS AND RATIONALISTS

The Catholic counterattack quite naturally prompted a flood of Protestant publications, and the process continued with an astonishing regularity: responses to the refutations elicited refutations of the responses, ad infinitum. I have noted forty pamphlet titles (thirty-two Protestant and eight Catholic) exclusively devoted to the popess that appeared between 1548 and 1700, not counting reprints and avowed and disguised translations, anonymous works often borrowed wholesale from a previous text. If we add to these figures reprints, new editions, translations, and lost or untraceable works mentioned in the extant literature, our total will have to be multiplied by at least four, which would give an average of one work per year for a century and a half, not even taking into account chapters on Joan in general works. This literature is not always cumulative, and it is often repetitive; such publications are usually more keyed to response than to advances. The two Reforms—the Protestant Reformation and the Catholic Counter-Reform—settled in to a sort of trench warfare in which vast amounts of human effort and paper were expended without making any notable progress.

This means that a rapid cartography of the Johannite war is more useful for our purposes than a full survey of this literature. There were two periods of intense activity, approximately 1585–1600, and approximately 1649–90. The first period corresponds to the Catholic counterattack (Scherer, Bellarmine, Raemond, Baronio); on the Protestant side interest in Joan was centered in the Lutheran bastions (Wittenberg, Dillingen, Eisleben) and in London, where the Anglican Church adopted Lutheran polemical tactics. In the second period this activity was centered in the Low Countries and in France. It originated in a precise event, the publication in Amsterdam in 1647 of a work that produced an important change in the history of Joan. David Blondel, a Calvinist pastor, published a refutation of the history of Joan that many Protestants considered a betrayal of their cause: *Familier esclaircissement de la Question si une Femme a este assise au Siège Papal de Rome entre Léon IV et Benoît III* (Familiar Clarification of the Question of Whether a Woman Sat on the Papal Throne of Rome between Leo IV and Benedict III). This work was reprinted in 1649 and was translated into Dutch in 1650 and into Latin in 1657. Fellow Calvinists responded vigorously, Nicolas Congnard with a *Traité contre l'éclaircissement donné par M. Blondel* (Saumur, 1655); Samuel Des Marets (Maresius), who had accused Blondel of receiving a pension for his refutation from Michel Particelli d'Emery, with a *Johanna restituta* (Groningen, 1658,

1661). Philippe Labbé, a Jesuit, joined this Calvinist debate with a *Ceno-taphium Joannae papissae* (Paris, 1660), a shining example of Catholic erudition (Labbé cites 150 texts) to which Friedrich Spanheim, a man from an illustrious Calvinist family, responded with his monumental *Disquisitio historica de papa foemina* (Leiden, 1691), a work popularized in France in its adaptation by Jacques Lenfant, *Histoire de la papesse Jeanne* (Cologne, 1694, much reprinted).

The change of direction that took place in 1647 is fairly easy to account for. Calvinism had always frowned on the use of legends and themes from popular culture (in iconography, of course, but also in texts). The list of Johannist publications after 1548 shows a remarkable lack of entries from Calvinist and Zwinglian Switzerland, even though Geneva was a major publishing center. Calvin tended to lump together Catholics and Lutherans, criticizing them both for superstition: "In papacy," he stated, "nothing is more widespread and worn out than the arrival of the future Antichrist."[55] In 1647 David Blondel's *Familier esclaircissement* was by no means an attempt to reach out to Catholicism. His scornful point was that Rome of his own day had enough demonstrable crimes and heresies without being reproached for a heavy dossier of dubious fables as well. Another fiercely anti-Catholic Calvinist, Pierre Jurieu, shared that attitude. Jurieu states in his *Histoire du papisme* (1683):

> I find that given the way in which this history is related, it grants
> more honor to the Roman see that it merits. It is said that this
> popess had studied well, that she was learned, clever, eloquent,
> and that her talents made her admired in Rome. . . . I say that it is
> granting much honor to the Roman see, at that time in which this
> popess is placed, some Roman lady's quality of lover being the
> only merit that led to the papacy.[56]

The time had passed for the joyous, bloody hand-to-hand combats of Luther's day, an age of aggressive conviviality in which the twin brothers of Rome and Wittenberg shared a taste for drama, for ornamental decor, for the flesh, and for eschatalogical scatology. Those were the days of the Catholic rumor that Luther had invented doctrinal innovations in the privies of the Wartburg, to which the Lutheran response was an image in the *Abbildung des Bapstum* (Description of the Papacy; Wittenberg, 1565) that shows a Lutheran peasant defecating into an upside-down papal tiara.[57] A more severe, more moralizing Calvinism refused to amuse itself with such games.

On a deeper level, however, French Calvinism participated in the emergence of critical rationalism, thanks to the Academy of Saumur and the example of the pastor Moïse Amyraut. Jesuit thought had already undermined the apocalyptical underpinnings of the controversy with the famous commentaries on Revelation of Francisco de Ribera (1591) and Luis de Alcázar (1614). Hugo Grotius, the illustrious Arminian, concurred in rejecting a millenaristic reading of Revelation.

Some years before Blondel's pamphlet appeared, Gabriel Naudé referred to Grotius, sagaciously noting the rise of a new orientation in the Reformation. In a letter from Rome that Naudé sent to Jacques Dupuy in 1641 he wrote: "I predict that Mr. Grotius, with his little pamphlets, will gradually make himself the leader of a third party which will perhaps be not inconsequential for the good of Christianity." Naudé was alluding in particular to a commentary that Grotius had published in 1640 to demonstrate that the pope could not be the Antichrist. Joan, once again, linked her existence to that of the papacy. A few lines later in his letter Naudé says of the *De primatu Petri* of Claude de Saumaise (a work that was published a bit later, in 1645): "Concerning the popess, he never should have embarked on wanting to support her, given that the galant men of his party laugh at her, and also that she will serve to discredit the other proposition as coming from a man too passion-ridden."[58]

Blondel's work stands somewhere between Descartes's *Meditationes de prima philosophia* (1641) and Hobbes's *Leviathan* (1651). For Descartes, the practice of clear and distinct ideas and of methodical doubt confined belief within the domain of the divine (the existence of God), and even there it was subsidiary, subject to a priori proof (the ontological argument of the existence of God). Everything else was open to judgment before the tribunal of reason, where Joan's chances, after the requisition so diligently promoted by Panvinio and the Jesuits, were slim. What is more, Descartes's epistemology and his anthropology of error, focused on the knowing individual, radically reversed the medieval perspective, where tradition constituted the first and primordial mental landscape in which the subject could move fairly freely to the four corners of knowledge. The Cartesian cavalier, standing alone before God and the Evil Genius, had drastically lightened his baggage, which leads us to the fourth mode of belief (and the dominant one from Descartes on), the rationalist mode that subsumed the strict alternation between the true and the false only to a nonobligatory (but desirable) adherence to God or to a Value.

Nothing represents this shift better (despite fundamental differences between Hobbes's thought and Descartes's) than the structure that Hobbes gave to his *Leviathan*. The work is divided into four parts: of man; of the commonwealth; of a Christian commonwealth; and of the Kingdom of Darkness. In the final section, which is quite short, Hobbes lists the errors of humankind; he demolishes broad swaths of time-honored beliefs, which he divides into four types: literal interpretations of Scripture, demonology, philosophical spiritualism, and "Fabulous Traditions."[59]

In spite of some rearguard skirmishes that continued until the late nineteenth century, Blondel's work signaled the death of Joan. No one wanted her anymore. Even the great Leibniz, in an elegant volume titled *Flores spersi in tumulum papissae* (Flowers Thrown on the Tomb of the Popess), published only shortly after Labbé's *Cenotaphium Joannae papissae*, suggests a new career for Joan:

> I am astonished that the popess, a worthy subject for a novelist in a time when people have such a taste for fables, has not yet, like Argenis or Clelia, found her writer. Such a writer would have a heroine and a lover just made for misfortunes: subject matter for a most elegant work. And truly, that illustrious woman concerns poets, not historians.[60]

Leibniz's appeal was heard, but only later, at the end of the eighteenth century, when Joan found a welcome among a new sort of jongleur—not the Franciscan *joculatores Dei*, who, from William of Ockham to Thomas Murner, had been so fond of her, but among literary folk who enjoyed buffoonery, tragedy, and Gothic horrors.

7

THE POPESS IN LITERATURE

oan's literary transfiguration could be viewed as having taken root in Thuringia in the mid-sixteenth century, even before Labbé and Leibniz had laid her in her tomb. This notion is supported by the title of a work that appeared in 1565 in Eisleben, Luther's birthplace: *The Apotheosis of John VIII, Roman Pope: Fine play on Dame Jutta, who became pope in Rome and who, on the throne of Rome, drew from her scrinium pectoris a newborn child. Made eighty years ago, but newly found and given to be printed for the reasons stated in the preface. Apocalypse XVIII: Pay her back as she has paid others; pay her double for her deeds! For she said to herself "I sit enthroned as a queen."*[1]

Why choose this *Fraw Jutta* as the beginning of the literary existence of the popess? Is the notion of "apotheosis" sufficient justification? Certainly not. We would risk sinking into endless subtleties by attempting to define the confines of the literary field of the popess; as late as the end of the nineteenth century, the appearance of a frothy novel based on Joan prompted a lively debate in which the fictional text was used to score polemical points. As early as the fourteenth century, Boccaccio's treatment of Joan was ambiguous in its status; as we have seen in chapter 5, Joan's inclusion in his gallery of "Illustrious Women" made the popess into a literary "character." But to use Boccaccio's text (in the sixteenth century, the main source for the historiography of Joan) brings that text back to the "veracity" status of chronicle or biography. The play published in Eisleben signals much more clearly the emergence of an autonomous literary sphere for the popess. There are several reasons for this:

1. *Fraw Jutta* was a theatrical piece and, by definition, drama suspends referential belief. It schematizes and represents, which removes it from the literal authenticity postulated by biography or chronicle.

2. Dietrich Schernberg's explicit use of the story of Joan in 1480 neu-

tralized the historical investments of the narrative. As we shall see from closer analysis of the text, Joan's adventure serves no polemical purpose here; the only thing at stake is the salvation of her soul. It is true that the 1565 edition of the work prepared by the Lutherans was part of the propaganda efforts described in the previous chapter: the title bears a malicious allusion to the famous adage of canon law, "The pope bears his archives in the jewel-case of his heart" (in scrinio pectoris)." Still, Hieronymus Tilesius, the editor of the work, treats the drama as an untouchable text, a "monument," limiting his own contribution to acting as an escort for the text by providing the title, the reference to Revelation 18.6 and 7, and a preface. The text itself was in no way antipapal.

3. Literary celebration of Joan, which is perceptible in the painstaking care taken by the editor of the 1565 edition, was continued in later publications. Despite the very limited diffusion of this text before the eighteenth century (the manuscript that Tilesius used in 1565 was lost, and only two copies of the Eisleben edition had been conserved, one in Berlin and one in Dresden), Johann Christoph Gottsched, the great eighteenth-century discoverer of German literature, hailed Fraw Jutta as "the oldest original tragic text printed in German" in his commentary on the text in his own meticulous edition in his Nöthiger Vorrath zur Geschichte der deutschen dramatischen Dichtkunst (1765).[2] Achim von Arnim, who did his own transposition of this text, learned of it thanks to Gottsched. Later scholarship picked up from there, with an edition of the work by Adalbert von Keller in 1853, another by Edward Schröder in 1911, and Richard Haage's inaugural dissertation in 1891.[3] I have insisted on the reception of Fraw Jutta because in the long run there is no better criterion of a work's "literary" quality than how it is received: a text is literary when it is treated as such.

FRAW JUTTA (CA. 1480)

For the circumstances surrounding the writing of Fraw Jutta we have to rely on the editor's preface in the 1565 edition. According to Tilesius, who headed the Lutheran Reformation in Mulhausen, in Thuringia, the play was written and performed in 1480. He supposed it to be the work of a priest (Tilesius says Mespfaffe), Dietrich Schernberg, who was born in the imperial city of Mulhausen. Schernberg supposedly left an autograph manuscript of the work, from which Tilesius worked. The language in Fraw Jutta confirms the date. The play resembles the sort of Christian drama offered during Carnival. Following the medieval model of the mystery or morality with several characters, the fairly long text (1,724 verse lines) was composed of a series of static dialogues marked off by brief indications of actions, events, and scene changes.

The first scene presents the devil's council: Luciper (Lucifer) has called together his acolytes: Vnversün (Universum, the universe), Lillis (Lilith, here Lucifer's grandmother), Sathanas (Satan), and Spiegelglanz (literally, mirror's glare). Lesser devils appear later in the play: Fedderwisch, Nottir, Astrot, Krentzelein. Luciper receives the homage of Jutta (and at this point we do not know about her previous history or her ambitions). The scene then changes to the earth, where we see Jutta leading her lover Clericus into adventure. Disguised as a man, she calls herself Johann von Engelland; the two of them go off to study in Paris. Jutta's rapid rise is sketched in a scene in which Jutta, Clericus, and a professor (Magister) have a brief verbal exchange, an honorarium is paid, and her program of studies is set (liberal arts, in particular logic, which allows her to manipulate and transform the law to her advantage). Magister's servant clothes the two lovers in doctoral gowns so they can leave with honors and money *(mit solden und ehren)*. Johann and Clericus then offer their services to the Curia, represented by four cardinals who take them to Pope Basilius, who receives their homage and makes them cardinals. A stage direction signaling the death of the pope is followed by a dialogued conclave that designates Jutta as pope. The next scene shows a Roman senator *(Rathsherr)* who brings his son, possessed by the devil, to the new pope to be exorcised. Jutta, horrified, attempts to pass on the task to her cardinals, but Vnversün, who inhabits the boy's body, reveals Jutta's secret to the assembled prelates: she is a woman, and she is bearing a child *(Nu höret zu alle gleich / Die hier in diesem saal gesamelet sind / Der Bapst da tragt fürwar ein Kind / Er ist ein Weib ind nich ein Mann)*. This scene is a transposition of the Franciscan and Thuringian version of the diabolic phrase with the six Ps that we saw in chapter 4; it borrows the devil's speech and the setting of an assembly of prelates from the same source. The extrapolation of this scene is important to our purposes, because it signals the persistence, in Thuringia, thus at the margins of the European development of the legend, of a tradition dating back to the mid-thirteenth-century chronicle of the anonymous Franciscan of Erfurt, traces of which seem to have been lost, after Siegfried of Balhusen and the *Flores temporum*, in the early fourteenth century. In reality, Joan lived on in Germanic lands from Bavaria, where the name "Jutta" probably came from, to Thuringia, which lay between Hussite Bohemia and a Saxony that was about to become Lutheran. The episode also demonstrates "literary" and/or "popular" creation moving from a theme to a dramatic performance that gives meaning to that theme, according to the same mechanisms as those governing the epic.

But to return to the adventures of Joan: leaving Rome to its emotions, Schernberg next transports his audience to Heaven, where Christ (Salvator) tells his mother that he has decided to have done with this popess. Mary persuades her son to grant Jutta a chance to redeem herself. The angel Gabriel then appears before Jutta to offer her a choice between immediate expiation and eternal damnation. This notion reflects the second episode of the German (and popular) tradition (found in Bavaria but also in the fourteenth-century Catalonian translation of Arnoldus of Liège that we saw in chapter 4) that explains the public scandal, but also the childbirth as a form of confession. The underground currents of the religious aspects of this scene might give us pause: this staging of a public scandal hints at the concept of the validity of confession without priestly intervention that was to become one of the essential tenets of Lutheranism.

After Jutta has made her choice, Death arrives to carry out the sentence. The most interesting aspect of this scene is its disrespect of the usual division of gender roles: Jutta invokes illustrious precedents: Adam, Peter, Thomas, Paul, Matthew, Theophilus, Mary Magdalene, Zacchaeus, and Longinus all betrayed, denied, or resisted Christ before being saved by his mercy. Jutta then appeals to the Virgin Mary, gives birth to her child, and dies. The devil Vnversün immediately bears her off to hell, where, with Nottir, he leads her before the master of the place, Luciper. Jutta's soul debates with the devils, while in Rome the bewildered cardinals decide to have a special chair made in order to be sure that from then on the candidate for the papacy is indeed a rooster and not a hen (*Ob er sen ein han oder ein henne*). The next scene is in hell. Jutta prays to the Virgin and to St. Nicholas to permit her to leave Purgatory (*Fegfewr*), and they in turn implore the Savior for mercy. The double supplication works, and Jesus sends the archangel Michael to deliver Jutta, whom he then receives as his daughter in Heaven ("Bis wilkomen du liebste Tochter mein").

In spite of its late date, Schernberg's text closely resembles the medieval miracle plays; its very theme is borrowed from Rutebeuf's thirteenth-century *Miracle of Theophilus*, a personage whom Jutta herself mentions, as we have seen.[4] The constant reappearance of demons, a scenic effect that delighted the medieval public, points to the same continuity. The play contains mild satire aimed at the university doctors and the Curia, but it is nothing like the satire of the *sotie*, for example in the antipapal attacks in the *Concile de Bâle*, a drama presented in 1434. Leaving aside the Lutheran reading of *Fraw Jutta* that Tilesius suggests in his preface, the play's novelty lay in its mix of genres: the highly popular theatrical form of the miracle or morality opened its arms to a theme more appropriate to farce or the *sotie*. This confusion of genres, which introduces the theme of the imposture in

Rome into the most religious form of theater, was a harbinger of graver troubles in store in nearby Saxony.

JOAN'S LITERARY PURGATORY (1480 – 1777)

Joan's literary career might have continued after Tilesius's edition of Schernberg's play, and she might have taken her place in the rise of German baroque drama (*Trauerspiel*), which prospered in a Lutheran milieu.[5] Another conduit existed at almost the same time, however, that condemned her to a different fate. The great polygraph Hans Sachs (1494 – 1576), who introduced "tragedy" into German literature, treated the subject of the popess in 1532 and again in 1558.[6] Sachs's version of the Joan story was not a dramatic elaboration (tragedy, comedy, or *Trauerspiel*), but first a song, then a simple "story" (*Historia*), genres closer to pamphlet literature than to literature proper, in which Sachs linked Joan to popes and prelates such as John XII, Sylvester II, and Udo of Magdeburg, whom Sachs lampooned in other "stories" of the sort. Between 1480 and 1777 Joan lived only within the world of controversy. It is understandable that Joan's Roman reputation made it impossible for her to occupy a place in the Catholic literary Pantheon, but the silence of the Protestants is harder to explain. Perhaps the liveliness of the debates over the existence of the popess made it impossible to establish any distance from the topic or to achieve the neutralization necessary to create a genuine character. The literal sense of Joan's life was too imposing to leave room for metaphorical meanings. If we consider how discontinuous the periods of Joan's literary life were—1360 with Boccaccio; 1480 with Schernberg; 1777 with Charles Bordes—we might even posit that those times corresponded to an upswelling of polemical investment in the topic (after the Franciscan use of Joan; after the conciliar debates that arose from the Great Schism; after the Protestant abandonment of the popess, completed several decades after Blondel had struck his Calvinist blow). The "apotheosis" promised by Tilesius was reduced to a polemic and ironic use of the term that excluded access to literary glorification, even if the long title that he gave *Fraw Jutta* seems to evoke the universe of the *Trauerspiel*. The date 1565 may be attractive as a pivotal point, but it was unimportant. Joan had no Renaissance.

This means that if we want to follow Joan in literature we must skip over three centuries. The neutralization of the question of whether or not she had existed endowed her with literary graces only very late, probably because in the course of an anticlerical eighteenth century the anecdote took on a serious cast on a secondary level. In France the philosophes considered the episode of Joan laughable, a grotesque object of dispute between two fanaticisms, Catholic and Protestant, both bent on falsification. The philosophic attitude was thus to disdain the facile effects of the fable and send both camps packing; any serious or literary use of the narrative would have abolished the superiority acquired by their scornful skepticism. This was why the philosophes treated the anecdote with a mocking, rationalist condescension and classified it as a superstitious tale. The *Encyclopédie* turns it into an old wives' tale:

> It was after Leo IV, who died in 855, that the false popess Joan is placed. In *Le songe du Vieil Pèlerin*, written by Philippe de Mézières in 1385, Queen Truth [Vérité] relates in chapter 51 of book 1 that an old woman told her one day, "In the court of Rome I saw a woman reigning who was from England." What is more, the old woman spoke badly in telling her tale, and Queen Truth did not believe it, nor did she believe another story from the same old woman about a bishop of Besançon, who, according to her, was carried away by the devil in Rome.[7]

Pierre Bayle had already given evidence, in his *Dictionnaire* (1694–96), of the distance that the thinkers of the Enlightenment chose to put between the narrative on Joan and its use. After analyzing the weakness of the arguments for the existence of the popess, Bayle shows that Reason had less interest in the content of the tale than in its use, and, from its lofty position, Reason might even find the ruses of the story and the controversy amusing. Bayle remarks that after "the story of the She-Pope" had been refuted "with the strongest arguments," the Protestants "ought to have abandoned it, and not to have used all their industry to keep up the dispute; for this was to point out to their adversaries the method of contesting all facts."[8]

Voltaire closes his *Essai sur les moeurs* (1756) with a "Catalogue des Empereurs et des Papes, etc.," a final version of the model set by Eusebeus and Jerome. In his listing he permits himself not only a skeptical smile but the pleasure of an explanation (which he borrowed from Baronio) of an error regarding Joan. He notes in connection with the assassination of John VIII (882): "It is not any truer than the story of the popess Joan. The role of that popess was attributed to him because the Romans said that he had shown no more courage than a woman against Photius."[9] It was probably the more benign view Voltaire borrowed from the philosophes that spared the popess the fate that he reserved for her more virtuous cousin, Joan of Arc, whom he treated quite roughly (but amusingly) in *La Pucelle* (1762). The fable of the popess did not belong to the realm of history, which one could and should parody, but rather to the history of history, where Voltaire found other fish (both Catholic and Protestant) to fry than our Joan.

The Joan story did not really fit in anywhere in the eighteenth-century categories of genres before the invention of the historical novel, which broke down barriers between the serious and the fantastic and between authenticity and fiction. The *conte* (short story) required more elbow-room; the burlesque poem demanded a more authentic subject to parody. Drama, a genre of infinite varieties, knew how to manipulate invention and history, but it required public consumption, and the censors were fierce. Until the French Revolution, ecclesiastical robes could not be shown on the stage. In 1764, however, Voltaire announced that Joan would soon triumph on the boards: "Some day we shall introduce Popes on the stage, as the Greeks represented their Atreus and Thyestes, to render them odious."[10] We get the feeling that his condescending and rationalist reserve would not long resist the coming floods of anticlericalism, mixed with the old current of Gallicanism, and further increased by the ritual exercise of flaying the Jesuits.

CHARLES BORDES: THE CLANDESTINE POPESS (1777)

Even before the French Revolution erupted, a temptation to indulge in the burlesque, which rationalist tactics (or a rationalist pose) had restrained, burst forth in the first modern "Pope Joan" of literature in a narrative poem by Charles Bordes, published anonymously with no place of publication under the title *La Papesse Jeanne* (1777; Leiden, 1778). With this long, roguish poem, which circulated clandestinely in France, we visit the marginal literature of the Enlightenment. We know these cultural zones better thanks to the works of Robert Darnton, who has shown how Enlightenment thought engendered a class of writers, more obscure than the established, recognized authors, whose inferior, scorned situation led them to express their rejection of the ancien régime in violent and often pornographic works.[11]

The works that these writers produced joined with the major works of the philosophes in a distribution system that moved into France from Switzerland and the Netherlands. As Darnton notes, a *Papesse Jeanne* figures prominently among the books that Bruzard de Mauvelain, a bookseller in Troyes, ordered from the Société Typographique de Neuchâtel in the 1780s.[12] This *Papesse* must have been Bordes's, as no other contemporary work by that title is known. The transfer from Leiden to Neuchâtel would have presented no difficulty. The *Papesse* figures among the 48 titles most ordered by Mauvelain; on six occasions he ordered 44 copies of the work. This places it fourth in popularity, after *Les fastes de Louis XV* (84 copies), *Les Muses du foyer de l'Opéra* (46 copies), and the *Chronique scandaleuse* (45 copies), three works that combined politics and pornography, and well ahead of the few serious works that Mauvelain ordered: Reynal's *Histoire philosophique* (18 copies), the *Oeuvres* of La Mettrie (16 copies) and of Helvétius (3 copies).

Charles Bordes's obscurity confirms his membership in the group of violent, opportunistic writers who lived in the shadowy zones of the Enlightenment. Bordes (1711–81), a minor and provincial philosophe (he was born in Lyon), won the approval of Jean-Jacques Rousseau for his *Blanche de Bourbon* (1736), but he later attacked Rousseau's *Discours sur les arts et sciences* (1750) and his *Discours sur l'origine et les fondements de l'inégalité parmi les hommes* (1755) and cultivated an acquaintance with Voltaire, who paid him a visit in Lyon in return for one that Bordes had paid to him at Les Délices. Bordes was a latecomer to anticlericalism; it was as if his failure to establish close relations with Rousseau and Voltaire had radicalized him, like many authors left at the threshold of the temple of Enlightenment. In 1766 Bordes inserted a *Catéchisme* into Dulaurier's *Evangile de la Raison;* his *Vers sur le bref du pape Clément XIV qui défend la castration dans ses états* was published posthumously. Clearly, prohibitions or censorship were not about to prevent Bordes from writing about the popess.

Moreover, Bordes invented an ingenious way to get around Voltaire's deontological or tactical reticence: although Bordes treated the episode of the popess with liberty, even license, he negligently placed a few scholarly notes at the foot of his pages to communicate the idea that if his unbridled fantasy was fictional, it was nonetheless based in fact. His narrative was just as rowdy as that of the most unyielding Protestants, but he avoided their apologetics. He hinted that there is no smoke without fire, which is roughly how the episode was perceived until our own day. The story of Joan was neither true nor false; it was significative. It might have had its origin in a true event; the Great Harlot of Babylon became a charming, lusty young woman. This technique of presenting a fantasy with a thin lining of truth set the scene for Joan's entrance into fiction. Giambattista Casti, Emmanuel Rhoides, and Lawrence Durrell were all to follow this route.

Bordes's poem (in ten *chants*) uses the techniques of the burlesque to paganize Roman customs, much as the Chevalier de Parny was to do, brilliantly, at the end of the eighteenth century in *La guerre des dieux*. In Bordes, an assembly of saints and celestial beings holds a council in heaven to remedy the sorry situation of the Holy See at the moment of Leo IV's death of syphilis, "The too bitter fruit of an agreeable error." The archangel Michael calls on St. Peter to do something about the sorry situation:

> How long, our loyal friend Peter,
> Will you suffer, seated on your throne
> A disloyal throng of scoundrels?

The archangel Raphael is dispatched to Rome to open a conclave, while in heaven holy women deliberate whether to demand access to the Holy See, because, as St. Monica says:

> There is [neither] honor nor dignity
> Where we have no full right to hope.

The council then considers Joan, whose career Bordes outlines. The daughter of a priest, she falls in love with René Fulda, a young monk whose life she decides to share by taking on the habit of St. Benedict. During her peregrinations she is separated from René, whom she believes dead, and she arrives in Tivoli, where she leads a retired life near a sepulchral monument that she has built to her lover's memory. In the meantime the holy women in heaven have sent an embassy to St. Peter, who grants their request and persuades the conclave to nominate the saintly monk, "John." The conclave sends to Tivoli Cardinal Marcel, who is none other than René Fulda. The lovers recognize one another, they consult oracles, and they return to Rome. The conclave elects "John," but it also revives "the law of the chair"—the use of the pierced chair used to verify the manhood of the pope. Cardinal Marcel/René Fulda, following the advice of the holy women, uses an expedient familiar to libertine literature:

> In the convents that are the most renowned
> For their cloistering and their chaste locks
> There is an art of imitating the jewels,
> Fresh and rosy, that always among you
> In the eyes of the [fair] sex have deserved the apple.

Thanks to a dildo, Joan was proclaimed pope.

As is obvious, Bordes makes radical changes in the Joan anecdote when he frees it from the constraints of history and uses it as a pretext for a ribald fantasy. His narrative fitted perfectly into its age. For one thing, recourse to a bawdy sort of fantasy provided the "Rousseau du ruisseau" (gutter Rousseaus), as Darnton calls them, with a substitute literary field. For another, the eighteenth-century genre of erotic fiction was filled with ecclesiastical persons and places (see *Le portier des Chartreux* and a number of similar *capucinades*). As in Oriental licentious tales, the remote time suggested by Bordes's footnotes permitted the pleasures of deliberate transposition, anachronism, and vague topography. Like the heroic genre, history seductively gauzes over (at once revealing and concealing) the crudity of situations. Ideological choice and licentiousness, the two historical anchors of the Joan story in a spicy key, inaugurated a tradition.

Later we will examine the combination of anticlerical and libertine inspirations in versions of Joan under the French Revolution. Before we do, however, we should turn to the European expansion of the popess in the harsher light of the north and the warmer sunlight of the south.

WINKOPP (1783): JOAN IN A GERMANIC LIGHT

In 1783, not long after Bordes, Peter Adolph Winkopp published in Leipzig a fictionalized version of the story of Joan inspired by Egbert Grim's *Pauselicke Heiligheit*, a polemical work published in Dutch in 1635.

Winkopp (1759–1813), an author now forgotten, had an interesting career that reflects the impact of the philosophic movement outside France, where Enlightenment ambitions were less fettered. A native of Lutheran Saxony but Catholic by upbringing, Winkopp left his Benedictine monastery of Petersberg, near Erfurt in Thuringia, at a young age, and between 1780 and 1785 he published a series of novels *(Serafine, Faustin, Prior Hartung, Die Päpstin Johanne)* whose settings were odious and oppressive convents. These works created such a stir that an official inquiry into conditions in cloistered institutions was launched. Winkopp then took up journalism, founding *Der deutsche Zuschauer* (The German Observer) in Zürich (1785–89). In 1786 his virulence led to his arrest and he was moved from Basel to the prisons of the archbishop of Mainz. On his release he first attempted (unsuccessfully) to enter the book trade, but he eventually prospered and won an official position at the court of Mainz. In 1790 he founded a periodical in Zürich that provided statistics on Rhenish Germany, and after the republican invasion of the Rhineland he became an observer and a propagandist for the Confederation of the Rhine until his death in 1813.

GIAMBATTISTA CASTI: AN ITALIAN JOAN

Joan also attracted the literary attentions of a quite remarkable Italian abbé, Giambattista Casti (1724–1803). A much-traveled, provocative man and a lively embodiment of the Enlightenment, Casti went everywhere in Europe from Malta to Russia, Istanbul to Paris, where he met the likes of Casanova, Goethe, and Napoleon Bonaparte and wrote opera libretti for

Paisiello and Salieri. He occupied posts as poet for the granddukes of Tuscany, a member of the Austrian diplomatic corps on mission to Catherine of Russia, and court poet to Francis II of Austria. In spite of his violent anti-Bonapartist sentiments, he was a guest of the Bonaparte brothers in Paris.[13]

Casti's *Papessa Giovanna* was published in Italian in Paris in 1804, a year after his death. It appeared in a collection of novellas in verse that was a republication, with additional material, of an edition of pieces that had been written as early as 1766 but were first published in Rome in 1790. This collection, which was dedicated to women who "can accompany virtue with reason," connects, on the one hand, with the time-honored tradition of Boccaccio (of the *Decameron*, not the *Illustrious Women*) and Masuccio (tales spun among women, furtive pleasures, women who invent clever ruses, friars who frequent bordellos, etc.) and, on the other hand, with the erotic "philosophical" narratives of the eighteenth century. In his *Novelle* Casti displays a lively hostility toward the temporal power of the popes (in particular in a tale titled "La bolla d'Alessandro VI"), toward Jesuit policies, and toward religious imposture; he praises divorce, sexual freedom, and the pursuit of pleasure. Like Bordes, Casti enjoyed transposing his subject matter to a new setting, a taste he had already displayed in *Poema Tartaro* (1783), where setting his tale in Mongol Russia of the Middle Ages conceals its denunciation of Catherine II.

Casti's version of the Joan story uses the same burlesque techniques that Bordes had used, but Casti remains more faithful to the canonical medieval model, including Joan's sorry end. He lightens the outcome, however, with a comic treatment of Joan's fate in hell, where Dante fails to notice her, and with a passing thought for the poor little soul of the tiny papal bastard:

> Alla povera animetta
> Del picciol pontificio bastardello.[14]

Casti enriched his classic story line, making malicious use of his vast erudition with remarks within the text and in notes on both the historical context and the historiography of the popess. This scholarly base permitted him a savory and satirical amplification modeled on what Spanheim and Lenfant had done in a serious, polemical vein in their versions of the Joan story. Joan's father becomes an English priest who had come to evangelize among the Saxons, thus offering Casti an opportunity to lampoon Charlemagne's bloody conversion methods. Later novelists (Rhoides, Jarry, and Durrell) copied this passage. Casti uses Joan's genealogy to embroider on his joyous anticlerical theme, given that before Joan's mother, Hildegarde, meets the English priest she is abducted from her native Ireland by a monk. Athens, which previous historians of Joan had found bothersome, is not only a place for studies but, in a subtle, preromantic shift, the setting for an amorous and artistic initiation and for a pilgrimage set among ruins.

The most striking aspect of Casti's narrative, however, is his total secularization of Joan. With an energy that she inherits from Boccaccio and a lively, joyous taste for pleasure, she lives a simple life with Fulda, her lover, in which studious days alternate with nights of pleasure. They part, still friends, to search out new desires and new discoveries: Fulda goes to the East, to Baghdad; Joan goes to the West, to Rome. In short, they reflect Casti's own life of pleasure and travel. Joan's arrival in Rome gives Casti an opportunity to deplore the decadence of Italy and to display an impatience with the archaism that gripped that land, both during the French Revolution and at the arrival of the French republican army. When Joan first sees the throne of St. Peter she judges it a worthy goal for her talents, but success bores her, so she takes as a lover a cardinal who delights her with his vigorous lovemaking:

> The room was then shaken.
> From high above a Christ fell and broke into pieces.
> A painted Virgin's cheeks turned red.
> The portrait of St. Peter turned black
> But still they carried on, full-tilt.

The birth of Joan's child puts an end to this Roman holiday, but not before Fulda, who had come to Rome, has a chance to play the jealous lover and state, in solemn Lutheran tones: "Surely it is of you that Revelation spoke."[15]

I have lingered at some length over Casti's novella; aside from its great charm, it is a prototype for an attitude of scholarly pleasantry that became the norm in treating the popess and that persists to our own day. The reader will be spared a full account of similarly romanesque works: the brilliant Casti was much copied but never equaled, let alone improved upon. In our move from Bordes to Casti, however, we have skipped over a capital moment in the literary genealogy of Joan, that of the French Revolution, to which we must return.

JOAN IN ANTICLERICAL THEATER (JANUARY 1793)

Within the space of less than a month (23 January–22 February 1793), Joan lent her name and her story to three theatrical works. The Revolution had totally liberated dramatic production in 1791, when it abolished censorship and did away with monopolies on repertory,[16] with the astonishing result that some 1,500 plays were created. For the year 1792–93 alone, the year in which our three popesses appeared, between two hundred and three hundred new plays were performed in some forty Parisian theaters.

Anticlericalism, ever present among the bourgeoisie and the people, rebounded with the new freedom: the famous *Charles IX* by Joseph Chénier, for example, could at last present on the stage the odious figure of the Cardinal of Lorraine. After the suppression of the monastic orders and the promulgation of the civil Constitution of the clergy in 1790, the theatrical repertory was flooded with antireligious plays. The old erotic fascination with the cloister exploded when the cloister was abolished. Sylvain Maréchal gleefully sang:

> Come out, dance, amuse yourselves
> Amuse yourselves, young little nuns!
> Let us perform together, with little noise
> The office, day and night.[17]

Within the span of only a few months in 1790 playgoers could see *Le couvent* (Laujon); *Les rigueurs du cloître* (Fiévée and Berton); *Les religieuses; Les religieuse délivrées; Les soeurs du pot; Le couvent, ou, Les voeux forcés* (Olympe de Gouges); and *La communauté de Copenhague* (Bertin d'Andilly). These were joined in 1791 by *Le mari directeur, ou, Le déménagement du couvent* (Flins des Oliviers); *Les Capucins; Amélia, ou, Le couvent;* and *Les victimes cloîtrées* (Monvel). Fleury, an actor and a playwright, stated:

> The performers at every one of the theatres, great and small, soon
> found it necessary to include among the articles of their wardrobe
> the chasuble, the surplice, the coif, and the girdle of St.
> Francis. . . . For our part, we had a cardinal in *Charles IX*, a cardi-
> nal in *Louis XII*, some Chartreux monks in *Le Comte de Com-
> minges*, and a group of pretty nuns in *Le Couvent ou Les fruits de
> l'éducation*.[18]

In this context, representing Joan's story on the stage became perfectly possible, but the specific reasons for her public appearance need to be seen in the context of the political history and social biography of her authors. Once again, we gain entry into a particular historical universe thanks to Joan.

JOAN'S MOMENT

In 1793 the story of the popess was a weapon against the papacy borrowed from the Protestants. After 1791–92 the pope had become an enemy of the Republic: Pius VI had condemned the civil Constitution of the French clergy; he sheltered refractory priests in his States; although the Papal States were not a member of the Coalition, he supported its cause in his briefs. The annexation of Avignon sanctioned placing the pope among the Tyrants. Sylvain Maréchal explicitly compared the pope to absolute sovereigns in a famous play, *Le Jugement dernier des rois,* performed 18 October 1793, three months after our three works on the popess. In Maréchal's play the pope dies, suffocated under the ashes of a volcano on the island to which the Sans-Culottes have deported him, together with the Emperor and the kings of England, Prussia, Russia, Naples, etc. Our three popesses mark an intermediary degree between the *capucinades*—jolly comedies about monks—of the years 1790–91 and the violence of the autumn of 1793.[19]

One specific circumstance may have set off this volley of popesses: on 13 January 1793, Jean de Bassvill, secretary of the French legation at Naples, went to Rome to demand that the pope permit the revolutionary emblems to be displayed at the door of the French consulate; during the ensuing riot (which French opinion attributed to the efforts of Cardinal Zelada, the Vatican Secretary of State) Bassvill was killed. The news spread rapidly to Paris. The Convention expressed its indignation, the populace took to the streets. An Italian revolutionary, Vincenzo Monti, hastened to compose a long poem in four cantos, the *Bassvilliana,* in memory of the martyr.[20]

The first play about the popess, written by Pierre Léger, was performed on 26 January in the theater of the rue Feydeau. It was common practice for a short comedy to be put together in only a few days. The foreword to August Defauconpret's play about the popess, printed in January 1793, confirms that haste. Defauconpret claims that his *Papesse,* written some time before, had been rejected by three theaters (the Feydeau, the Théâtre Français Comique et Lyrique, and the Vaudeville), and that he was publishing it because he had received word that two other plays on the same subject were about to be put on. Defauconpret continued to claim priority, even though he managed to have his play performed only on 23 February 1793, at the Théâtre Molière. He titled the second edition of his text *L'aînée des papesses* (The Elder of the Popesses).[21]

JOAN IN THE CAREER OF PIERRE LÉGER, AUTHOR-ACTOR

A consideration of the contents of these dramatic fictions (or at least the two that have come down to us) and of the social position of their authors shows that the benign antipapal attitude of January 1793 was a cultural and political compromise.

Pierre Léger avoids any troubling evocation of transsexuality in his *Papesse Jeanne*, which follows the light comedy model of lovers separated and disguised who find one another again by chance. Jeanne is engaged to Florello, but she is forced to flee, disguised as a man, to escape a rejected suitor. Florello finds her again at the moment of her election to the papacy. At the proclamation of her accession to the Holy See, she reveals her secret and declares her intention to remain as pope, but also to marry Florello. Coherent and revolutionary, she abolishes priestly celibacy and does away with tithing. Léger lampoons Cardinals Gireplante, Rolando, Jejunio, and Boivin (all obvious plays on words) with burlesque levity, but above all he stresses feminism and delights in bodily union in the spirit of the 1790–91 *capucinades*. Jeanne announces:

> And today, in my new state, I want
> To give a new brilliance to my ennobled sex.
>
> . . . .
>
> Celibacy is an infinite source of vice.[22]

Pierre Léger (1760–1823) came from a petit-bourgeois background (his father was a barber-surgeon in Bernay); he lived the precarious ancien-régime life of a second-rank intellectual, first as an abbé *au petit collet* (not ordained), then as a tutor. The Revolution promoted him to the rank of author and successful actor. He was sensitive to all the tendencies of the moment, as we shall see, and he was one of the first to put a cleric on the stage, in *L'orphelin et le curé* (1790). That short play, which was dedicated to a priest, had nothing of the anticlerical firebrand; to the contrary, it presents a worthy village parish priest who wholeheartedly accepts the civil Constitution of the clergy and the abolition of tithing and clerical privileges. The villain of the play, a *fermier* (tax collector) named Antoine, attempts to take advantage of the naive generosity of Auguste, a young orphan who is being raised by the curé and who stands to inherit a fortune. Auguste modestly does not admit to having lent money to the *curé* when the priest found himself unexpectedly short of cash, and through a series of misunderstandings the boy's wealthy benefactor, M. Dorval, thinks Auguste a thief and puts the boy's inheritance into the hands of Antoine. The dénouement finds Antoine confounded and M. Dorval and Auguste reconciled under the kindly gaze of the parish priest.

Léger and other author-actors created the Théâtre du Vaudeville in 1792.[23] The promoters of the enterprise, the Chevalier de Piis and Pierre-

Yves Barré, a composer, had made an earlier attempt (in the 1780s) to re-vive the French theatrical genre of the *vaudeville* (theatrical entertainments that mixed dialogue, song, and ballet), which Charles Favart had popular-ized but which had subsequently been abandoned in favor of Italian opera. After the institution of the new, more liberal regime in the theater, Piis and Barré attempted to revive *vaudeville,* using both the old repertory and new satirical sketches on current events. The municipal government of Paris gave its approval to the project, a former dance hall near the Lou-vre became the Vaudeville, and the theater remained at that site for some forty-six years. It soon became one of the most popular theaters in Paris, but equally soon the troupe became suspect in the eyes of the revolution-ary government, both for its ongoing satire of political events and for the fact that Barré's brother served in the Gardes de la Reine.

In 1792 Léger gave the revolutionaries more concrete reasons for charges against the Vaudeville troupe by writing a play, *L'auteur d'un mo-ment,* that fiercely lampooned Charles Palissot, but also Joseph Chénier, an author dear to the hearts of the patriots for his *Caïus Gracchus.* Léger im-mediately repeated his offense with a manifest, and Barré announced an-other incendiary play, *La revanche.* The fourth performance of *L'auteur d'un moment* was performed before a royalist public who maltreated the few Ja-cobins who had attended the play in order to protest it. The patriots re-sponded in kind, to the point that the presence of Danton and Pétion was required to reestablish order. The final outcome of the performance was three deaths (a soldier who had been taken for a Jacobin and two pages of the queen). The occasion also prompted the reinstatement of censorship after more than a year of total freedom for the theaters. In the days that fol-lowed, Barré was obliged to present his apologies to the public and to burn the manuscript of Léger's play.[24]

Léger was by no means an ideologue, however. Soon after the affair of *L'auteur d'un moment,* he pursued his career in parody with an attack on a play called *Lovelace* that was being performed at the Théâtre de la Nation by writing a purely literary satire, *Gilles Lovelace.* The rest of Léger's life as an actor-author shows both his opportunism and his loyalty to the trade he had pursued thanks to the Revolution's liberation of the theater. On 20 September 1793 he was imprisoned, along with Barré and Piis, for having continued to perform *L'auteur d'un moment.* He immediately wrote *Apoth-éose du jeune Bara,* a work celebrating Joseph Bara, the young martyr of the Revolution. In the same vein, he collaborated with Barré in the highly revolutionary *L'heureuse décade,* which was followed by a light comedy cel-ebrating the republican use of the familiar *tu,* written with Barré and Lecouppey de la Rosière, *Le sourd guéri, ou, Les tu et les vous*. In 1799 Léger and Piis took over the Théâtre Molière, without great success. As was his custom, Léger saluted the master of the moment by exalting Napoleon's coup d'état of 18 Brumaire in *La journée de Saint-Cloud*, written with René de Chazet and Armand Gouffé and performed at the Théâtre des Troubadours. In spite of his obstinate opportunism (in 1814 he wrote a play titled *Le berceau de Henri IV*), Léger's career faltered as the theater declined under the Empire and the Restoration, and he was forced to return to the less prestigious occupations of teacher, secretary at a city hall, and court recorder, eventually returning in the theater at Nantes before his death in 1823. In spite of the ups and downs of his career, the cultural revolution of 1789–90 had given this proletarian of ancien-régime culture a status as a man of the theater that he could never have dreamed of at the start. In January 1793, the time of the Bassvill affair, a lighthearted but moralizing anticlericalism offered a way for a suspect but supple and ambitious author to become part of a political movement much greater than himself.

Léger's *Papesse Jeanne* was not performed at the Vaudeville, but at the theater of the rue Feydeau. Was this a prudent move to play down the scandal of *L'auteur d'un moment*, which was still being performed? At the time, January 1793, the troupe at the Vaudeville was playing *La chaste Suzanne* by Jean-Baptiste Radet and Georges-François Desfontaines. The Vaudeville found that it had unexpectedly worsened its case: the quite anodyne play simply related the biblical episode of Susanna and the Elders, but after the incidents of 1792 the Vaudeville had a reputation for being reactionary. The supporters of the Convention, a somewhat paranoid public, complained of a line they thought political: "You were her accusers; you cannot be her judges as well." The authors moved quickly to change the offending phrase, but in vain: on 28 January Jacques-René Hébert applied to the Convention for a prohibition of the play, which he obtained, and Radet, Desfontaines, and Barré were thrown into prison.[25]

This was when Flins des Oliviers's *Papesse* was performed at the Vaudeville. Did the troupe, deprived of its leadership, appeal to Flins, whose plays had been very successfully received in the most illustrious theaters (the Comédie Française and the Richelieu) as a way to reestablish themselves financially and ideologically? And did Flins's *Papesse* replace Léger's play? Was this a move of revenge directed at Léger for deserting the Vaudeville after the incidents of 1792 and 1793? We will never know.

In any event, Léger's *Papesse Jeanne* was performed on 26 January at the Théâtre Feydeau, and a year later, when he emerged from jail, he offered the same theater his play about Joseph Bara. The Feydeau, in former times the Théâtre de Monsieur, renamed in 1791, was by no means a revolutionary theater: in late 1793 it was even the only place where the moderates could gather. Its repertory, however, made it one of the most popular theaters in Paris, along with the Vaudeville and the Favard. Above and beyond all his mistakes and the fluctuations of his career, Léger was a theater professional, and his gay, opportunistic Joan floated on the current of the times.

To believe *Les Spectacles de Paris*, Léger's *Papesse* even met with a certain success: "Feydeau: *La papesse Jeanne*, comedy in one act in verse, mixed with *vaudeville*, par Citizen Léger, on 26 January 1793. Success." In a later issue the same publication stated: "The applause that Citizen Verneul obtained in her debut in the role of Popesse Jeanne in the play by that name has demonstrated to that actress that the Public would like to see her given more important roles."[26] Two editions of the play were printed (by André Charles Cailleau), a further indication of its success.

THE OBSTINATE DEFAUCONPRET AND JOAN

Defauconpret's *La Papesse* is harder to classify. The action of this play also takes place at the moment of the conclave, but at the price of an astonishing compression of time: it follows the canonical scheme of the Joan story but presents the birth of her child in its final scene. What makes the work stand out is its political tone. Two clans, the young cardinals and the older ones, who are called *porteurs de perruques* (wig wearers) have reached a stalemate over the election of a new pope; a messenger from the Roman people announces that the cardinals will be locked in with no food or drink until they have made a definitive choice. Cardinal Morini insists on having his mistress, Jeanne, at his side and has her disguise herself as a monk. In return she demands support for her own candidacy for the Holy See. Maffeo, the leader of the younger cardinals and a suitor of Jeanne's, promises his vote in exchange for her favors. She is elected. Is it forcing the argument too much to see in this plot a satire of factional struggles that were tearing apart the Convention at just that time? If so, who was it who was resorting to a disguise in order to obtain a unanimous vote?

The songs in this *vaudeville*, which were so numerous that Defauconpret called his play an *opéra-bouffon*, were even more virulent than in Léger's play: popular airs were fitted with words on such themes as "Elle aime à rire, elle aime à boire" (She likes to laugh; she likes to drink), "Quand je vois ma maîtress" (When I see my mistress), and more. There was also a hymn to St. Roch, and the work concluded with a finale sung to the tune of the republican "Ça ira":

When on Jeannette's forehead
The tiara shines,
All Rome will applaud
Our choice, my little chick.
Ho ho ho ho, Ha ha ha ha,
What a pretty pope she is!
Before the beauty that adorns you
The vain brilliance of the tiara
Will soon be eclipsed.
Ah, ça ira, ça ira, ça ira.

We know little about the personality of Defauconpret (1767–1843). His plays were unpublished. He became a notary (1795–1815), and in 1799 he published a work titled *Nouveau Barême, ou, Tableau de réduction des monnaies et mesures nouvelles analogues* (New Barême, or, Table for calculating the new equivalent money and measures). Oddly enough, he shared this combined taste for figures and for the story of Joan with Winkopp. After he was ruined as a notary Defauconpret moved to London, where he became a prolific translator, responsible for French translations of dozens of English-language works, including such authors as Sir Walter Scott and James Fenimore Cooper.

Defauconpret and Léger fitted the same social paradigm. Both were of humble birth and were in their early twenties in 1789. The Revolution permitted them (or permitted them to hope) to enter into the Republic of Letters, but the weight of social tradition sent one of them into primary school teaching and the other to a notary's office (probably at the lower end of the scale, given that Defauconpret's failure forced him into exile). Neither man had more than a limited success in new careers linked to a new cultural industry that arose out of the shock of the Revolution: Léger benefited from the extraordinary expansion of the theatrical scene after 1790 and managed to eke out a living in the theater until his death; Defauconpret made his living from the legal development of the popular book trade and from the romantic era's fondness for all things English.

We have already seen their rivalry in January 1793. Léger had connections with two of the three theaters that had rejected Defauconpret's *Papesse*. In the preface to *L'aînée des papesses*, the second edition of his play (and that it had a second edition attests to a degree of success) Defauconpret explains why it had been rejected: "I thought that an air of novelty might create a welcome for me: things turned out quite differently. It was regretted that I was not of a sort to be shown in a theater like the Feydeau." The fact that Léger's play was performed there shows that this was not the reason. Although Léger's work neither preceded Defauconpret's nor copied it, the episode nonetheless demonstrates that an author had to be known among the tight circle of the actors to have his play performed. The Vaudeville (which presented Flins des Oliviers's *Papesse*) rejected Defauconpret's play for "the same reasons that had led to the decision of the [theater] of rue Feydeau." The third theater that rejected the play, the Théâtre Français Comique et Lyrique, seems a replica of the Feydeau and the Vaudeville. Founded in June 1790, it operated in a small hall across from the Opéra on rue de Bondy, where it offered *vaudevilles* (before Piis and Barré attempted to revive the genre) and occasional works. It became successful only in November 1790. In October an anticlerical play by Olympe de Gouges, *Le couvent, ou, Les voeux forcés*, had been a total failure, but a production of *Nicodème dans la lune* by Cousin Jacques played for 363 performances, until late 1793, and turned the tide in their favor. *Nicodème* seems to have been a success thanks to a mix of fantasy and moderate politics (indeed, Cousin Jacques was arrested in 1793). Thus our popess found her *habitus*, real or desired, on a level without high ambitions at the crossroads between entertainment and current events. In Defauconpret's view, however, it was Léger (at the Vaudeville and the Feydeau) and Cousin Jacques who had barred Joan's access to topical *vaudeville*, even though Defauconpret declared that the reason for the Théâtre Français's rejection was the bad management that caused the theater to close its doors in 1793 in spite of the resounding success of *Nicodème*. He states, "I needed a costume that never was deemed possible with the funds of that spectacle, already on the decline."[27] Even after more open policies had been instituted in 1790, the literary career was too narrow for many aspiring writers. The author who went by the name of Cousin Jacques was an exception within the social paradigm of dramatic authors. His name was Beffroy de Reigny, and under the ancien régime he, like Léger, had taught school. He had also written burlesque poems in a Voltairean vein, and he founded a satirical review, *Les Lunes*. He threw himself into writing plays, but he never managed to have one performed at the Comédie. His first success came in 1790 with a light topical work, and after a brief period with a patriotic review, his hit his stride with *Nicodème*.

When Defauconpret finally managed to get his *Papesse* performed at the Théâtre Molière on 23 February 1793, he faced a totally different public. The Théâtre National Molière had been founded in June 1791 by Jean-François Boursault Malherbe, a deputy to the National Assembly and a businessman, for the presentation of vehemently patriotic and revolutionary works with such titles as *La Ligue des Fanatiques et des Tyrans* (Roncin), *Louis XIV, ou Le masque de fer* (Legrand), or *Le Comte Oxtiern* (the marquis de Sade); under the Terror the theater changed its name to Théâtre du Sans-Culotte. Despite Boursault's zeal, he aroused the suspicions of Robespierre, but he eluded his long grasp thanks to the friendship of Collot d'Herbois and his own timely disappearance from the scene.[28] Oddly enough, Léger and Piis took over the theater in 1799, renaming it the Théâtre des Troubadours.

Defauconpret thus attempted to move from competition in the theater (in the *vaudeville* genre) to competition in the political arena. The maneuver might have succeeded, given that Léger seemed compromised, but Defauconpret did not follow up on his advantage and we lose trace of him. He had missed his cue for entering the Republic of Letters, even though he became one of its citizens twenty years later through the back door or translation.

This episode proves that it would be a mistake to lend too much importance to the ideological content of the various plays on the popess: obscure allusions may have played a role in this battle, but success depended more on the authors' supple and varied tactics. Once again, Joan served a purpose.

THE LOST POPESS OF FLINS DES OLIVIERS

We still have not spoken of the third of the rival popesses in the play written by Carbon Flins des Oliviers. Unfortunately, the text either was never printed or has been lost; the only mention of it is a brief notice in a periodical that reviewed current offerings: "La Papesse Jeanne in one act by Citizen Fleins [*sic*]. Wit, pretty couplets, but a subject poorly handled. Little success." The play's lack of success was probably the reason it was not printed. Still, Flins des Oliviers was not an unknown. He offers another variant, on a higher level than Léger or Defauconpret, of the model of the literary Bohemia of the age of the Revolution. Chateaubriand has left us a portrait of Flins in his *Mémoires d'outre-tombe* that confirms Robert Darnton's picture of the species. The year is 1787; Chateaubriand is paying a visit to Delisle de Sales, a popularizer of Enlightenment thought.

> I met at his rooms Carbon Flins des Oliviers, who fell in love with Madame de Farcy [Chateaubriand's sister]. She laughed at him; he put a good face upon it, for he prided himself upon being a man of breeding. Flins introduced me to his friend Fontanes, who became mine.
>
> Flins was the son of an administrator of woods and forests at Rheims, and had received a neglected education; he was for all

that a man of sense, and sometimes of talent. It was impossible to imagine anything uglier than he: short and bloated, with large, prominent eyes, bristling hair, dirty teeth, and yet a not over-vulgar air. His manner of life, which was that of nearly all the men of letters in Paris at that time, deserves to be told. Flins occupied a lodging in the Rue Mazarine, pretty near La Harpe, who lived in the Rue Guénégaud. He was waited upon by two Savoyards, disguised as flunkeys by means of livery cloaks; they followed him at night, and opened the door to his visitors in the daytime. Flins went regularly to the Théâtre Français, which at that time was situate in the Odéon and excelled particularly in comedy. Brizard had only just retired; Talma was commencing; Larive, Saint-Phal, Fleury, Molé, Dazincourt, Dugazon, Grandmesnil, Mesdames Contat, Saint-Val, Desgarcins, Olivier were in the full vigour of their talent, pending the arrival of Mademoiselle Mars, daughter of Monvel, who was preparing to make her first appearance at the Théâtre Montansier. The actresses protected the authors, and sometimes became the occasion of their fortune.

Flins, who had only a small allowance from his family, lived on credit. When Parliament was not sitting, he pawned his Savoyards' liveries, with his two watches, his rings and underclothing, paid his debts with the amount thus raised, went to Rheims, spent three months there, returned to Paris, redeemed, with the money his father had given him, the articles which he had pledged at the pawnshops, and resumed his round of life, ever gay and popular.[29]

If we are to understand Flins's place within the cultural and social context of Paris in 1793 we need to add a few remarks to this admirable portrait. Flins (1757–1806) was of a social level much higher than that of Léger or Defauconpret; born into a family of bourgeois officeholders, he pursued a dual career under the ancien régime (he was some ten years older than his rivals in the Joan competition) as a *conseiller* (magistrate) at the Cour des Monnaies and an opportunistic author. While still a very young man he published an *Ode sur le Sacre de Louis XVI* after attending the coronation in his native Reims, and in 1779 he followed that work with an *Ode en l'honneur de Voltaire*, composed on the occasion of Voltaire's death in 1778. At the time he was a member of the Masonic Lodge of the Nine Sisters. He seems to have been more financially secure than it would appear from Chateaubriand's account of him, although it is true that Chateaubriand met him in 1787, when Flins was drifting toward a literary Bohemia and frequenting the circles of the Comédie. On 25 August 1781 Flins read a poem titled "Sur la servitude abolie dans les domaines du roi" at a public session of the Académie Française. His social position and the friendships that it offered him, even during the Revolution, gave him a base and a security that contrast with the fragility of Léger's and Defauconpret's positions. Chateaubriand mentions Flins's friendship with the marquis de Fontanes (Flins's exact contemporary), the future Grand Maître of the University under Napoleon and a man who knew La Harpe. That friendship quite probably had something to do with the post of *procureur impérial* (imperial prosecutor) of the civil court of Vervins that Flins occupied under the Empire until his death in 1806.

Flins, a man of the Enlightenment, welcomed the Revolution, even though he lost his post as *conseiller* because of it (as Chateaubriand states, it brought him little income). In 1789–90 he published six issues of *Les Voyages de l'Opinion dans les Quatres Parties du Monde*, one of many little reviews that flourished for a time. The news was given in the periodical by the allegorical figure of Opinion, who frequented the National Assembly and royalist circles of the first wave of emigration in Brussels. The review reflects an anticlerical bias that seems to have been characteristic of Flins from that time on. For instance, when the first émigrés arrive in Brussels disguised as priests, they are urged to say Mass. Their host asks accusingly: "Why do you not say it like any other [priest]? Are you more atheist than a bishop, more ignorant than a Capuchin, more greedy than a canon, more libertine that an beneficed abbé? Yet they say Mass every day." In the fourth issue of his journal Flins analyzed the success of Cagliostro, and in the process he offered a curious version of a religious sociology worthy of Max Weber:

> Religion was close to its fall; Baile [Bayle] and Fréret had uprooted faith by proofs and reasons. . . . Voltaire had done more by rendering it ridiculous. Still, food is needed to feed men's curiosity and their unquiet minds. And I thought that it was time for new superstitions to replace the old ones [Cagliostro is speaking]; men who are blasé, old women and stupid people unmoved by the gentle passions need to be agitated by violent passions; fanaticism is as necessary to them as strong spirits to a jaded palate. . . . In England . . . love of business replaced love of women. In France . . . the disquietude that survives the passions of youth was usually directed toward the objects of religion: this is what produced the Jesuits, the Calvinists, the Jansenists, Molinism . . . [30]

It did not take Flins long to win a place for himself as a dramatic author of a certain importance: in 1790 (and thanks to Chateaubriand we know that Flins had prepared the terrain before 1789) the Comédie Française produced *Le réveil d'Epiménide à Paris,* a work that presented that immortal classical philosopher waking up in Paris in 1789. Epimenides is astonished at the changes that have taken place during his slumber, and Flins takes the occasion to catalog the early achievements of the Revolution, along the way lampooning an abbé who laments the loss of his benefice. The play's success prompted imitations (*Le souper magique* by Pierre-Nicolas Murville, *L'Epiménide français* by Riouf, *Le convalescent de qualité* by Fabre d'Eglantine).[31] Flins's play was revived at the Théâtre de Monsieur (later the Feydeau). Performances were halted in July 1790 only because of a quarrel between Talma and friends of Joseph Chénier, who wanted the Comédie Française to produce the latter's *Charles IX.*

In February 1791 the Comédie Française produced Flins's *Le mari directeur, ou, Le déménagement du couvent.* In this play a convent is "liberated" by the Revolution; a government commissioner disguises himself as a superior of the Order so as to hear the confessions of his wife and his daughter, who admits that she loves a monk. The commissioner defrocks the monk and marries him to his daughter, and everything ends in merry song. In Flins we finally find an author sincerely dedicated to Joan and fond of disguises and religious settings. Flins contributed to establishing the thematic material of the theater under the Revolution, because he was the first to give a joyously licentious tone to an antireligious play, at a time when Léger was offering his worthy, constitutional parish priest to an admiring audience. Flins continued in his career with a play at the Théâtre Richelieu titled *La jeune hôtesse,* an adaptation of Carlo Goldoni's *La locandiera,* a work that proved its worth because it was still being performed in 1821 at the Richelieu's successor, the Théâtre Français. After his *Papesse* Flins entered a period of silence and retirement that coincided with a general decline in the theater in 1793: the company of the Comédie Française broke up when the actors were subjected to repression in 1793; the Richelieu turned radical. The Vaudeville, which was facing difficult times in January 1793 with the imprisonment of its directors, offered Flins a substitute theater before he retreated into a prudent silence. Given these circumstances, Joan's function seems clear: in the moment of extreme tension before the antireligious explosion of the summer of 1793 and the return to religion in 1794, the subject of Joan's papacy was cloaked in a merry anticlericalism that lent itself to *vaudeville* and song and that could interest an opportunistic practitioner of the theater, an author in search of a stage, and an experienced, prudent playwright.

JOAN AND THE REVOLUTIONARY NOSTALGIA
OF THÉODORE DESORGUES (1801)

Before we leave the French Revolution, a final, later popess deserves mention. It will be rapid, because Michel Vovelle has provided an excellent, exhaustive study of the career and works of the play's author, Théodore Desorgues (1763–1808).[32]

Le Pape et le Mufti, ou, La réconciliation des cultes was never performed, but it was published in 1801. The publication date is a good indication that the play, unlike the 1793 plays on the popess, had little to do with the preoccupations of an era when Chateaubriand's famous Génie du christianisme, published in 1802, was all the rage. In Desorgues's play the Joan anecdote retains little of its traditional story line, and the action takes place in a timeless fictional present. As in Léger's play, there are separated lovers: the Turks under Mufti Ali are besieging Rome, where the pope happens to be Azémis, a young Turkish woman disguised as a man so she can live with her lover, Azolan, who has become a cardinal. This runs counter to the wishes of her father, who is of course the selfsame Mufti Ali. The Roman people are beginning to chafe under the Christian religion, and Penetranti, the barigel (commander of the guard) of Rome, suggests to the pope that he renounce celibacy:

> You must marry, infallible vicar,
> And finally merit the title of Holy Father.[33]

Prominent Romans suggest negotiating a peace with the Mufti and Islam, which is reputed to be fond of the pleasures of Venus. When Mufti Ali comes to discuss his conditions, he engages in a long debate with the pope over the merits of Islam and Christianity, but eventually he recognizes his daughter. Azémis and Azolan marry, but the Romans refuse to remain under their domination, and Azémis agrees to teach young girls while Azolan teaches young boys in the tolerant atmosphere they have found in Rome.

Desorgues's work is fully as sprightly and droll as the 1793 Papesses, but its anti-Christian charge is much stronger. During the long debate between Ali and Azémis, the Mufti details all of Christianity's failings. One speech should be enough to indicate the tone:

> That compiling God, in order to preach wisdom,
> Translates the sages of Greece into bad Greek,
> Claims that it is new; and without their fine sermons
> He may perhaps not have wearied his lungs.
> Out of a thief on the gibbet he makes a convert;

He expires in public, resuscitates in secret;
From the son of a carpenter, He becomes the son of God:
The world would have suffered less if he had stuck to his trade.[34]

Desorgues's latter-day anti-Christian attitude was out of tune with the times, and it sets him apart from his fellow authors. Michel Vovelle sees him as representing some sort of last-ditch, desperate fidelity to the Revolution, by then a lost cause. Desorgues's fate confirms that interpretation: he was imprisoned in Charenton, along with the marquis de Sade, and he remained there from 1803 to his death in 1808. Tradition tells us that his crime was refusing a lemon ice at the Café de la Rotonde by saying "Je n'aime pas l'écorce," a pun on "le Corse," or Napoleon, who was born in Corsica. His pun was taken all the more seriously because a song that was currently popular began, "Oui! Le grand Napoléon est un caméléon" (a chameleon; a turncoat).[35] Desorgues's popess was a brilliant, final, hopeless fireworks display more than a continuation of the poetic activities of the Revolution.

How did Desorgues reach that point? The grandson of a notary in the region of Manosque and the son of a prosperous and influential lawyer in Aix-en-Provence, Desorgues was on his way up in society when the Revolution approached, even though his situation as a younger son and his physical handicap (he was hunchbacked) channeled most of the family fortune to his elder brother. We know nothing of his life before 1789, but we find him in 1792 in the company of Abbé Delille, busy penning gallant verse. Then, in 1794 (Year II) the Desorgues brothers, who were suspect because their father had achieved noble (or quasi-noble) status, suddenly offered their services to the Comité d'Instruction Publique, and not long after Robespierre chose Théodore Desorgues to write a Hymn to the Supreme Being for the celebration of 20 Prairial, Year II (an honor in which he supplanted Joseph Chénier). Desorgues became a major poet of the Revolution, writing many hymns and odes. The anti-Christian theme appears in these early writings, in particular in a poem, "Les transtévérins, ou, Les Sans-Culottes du Tibre," which appeared in the Mercure Français of 11 September 1794, but anti-Christian sentiment counted for much less in these works than a predominantly republican and Rousseauistic inspiration. Desorgues reached a turning point only in the last days of the Revolution, in the Year VII, with a strange, pre-Johannic poem, "Mon Conclave." Joan was no longer providing a service; she was doing a disservice. She no longer linked; she excluded. Thus ended Joan's revolutionary adventure.

From 1777 to 1804, from Bordes to Casti, Joan had taken all sorts of liberties with history and permitted herself broad license; she, who had lived within storms of discord and in fear of the flesh, now offered the world opportunities for a facile accord and for bodily pleasures. That joyous vein never ran out, and we will survey its contemporary appearances rapidly. In spite of the brilliant reputations of some of the authors, they brought nothing new: Joan had reached her height with Casti. Before turning to these offshoots at the close of the chapter, there is one other version of Joan that deserves attention. It appeared soon after Desorgues and Casti but in a totally different universe, in the Prussian romanticism of Achim von Arnim.

THE GENEALOGY OF ACHIM VON ARNIM'S POPESS (CA. 1815)

Achim von Arnim's *Päpstin Johanna*, the last major halt on our literary pilgrimage, deserves attention, in part because Arnim develops the theme so fully (there are 465 pages in the posthumous edition by the brothers Grimm) and his version is so rich and so handsome, and in part because his treatment so clearly shows the status of the popess in literature. Arnim takes Joan to the outer limits of her story and fully achieves what we might call literary distance. In chapter 5 we saw Joan's birth in literature in Boccaccio (1360), and we noted that a certain displacement had occurred: the popess left the papal context to become a literary character when she joined a gallery of illustrious women. At the same time, Joan left her empirical but enigmatic existence (Had she ever existed? How did she change the course of Church history?) to take on a metaphorical life (What does the popess reveal about woman? about sexuality? about ambition?). Joan's second literary epiphany took place with Dietrich Schernberg, where, more radically, she moved from displacement to condensation (these terms are not used in their precise psychoanalytic senses). Schernberg brought into the papal anecdote an entire universe of anxiety and hope (sin and atonement, purgatory, intercession of the saints and the Virgin). He transposed the miracle of Theophilus and prefigured the *Trauerspiel* but, unlike Boccaccio, he seems unconcerned about literal fidelity to the traditional Joan story. Schernberg's invention was different in nature from the rectifications and manipulations of historians of the popess from Martinus Polonus to Friedrich Spanheim. Although at times the Enlightenment popesses continued to benefit from reference to history, they pursued condensation by other means: a denunciation of imposture and celibacy; a joyous exaltation of the flesh. Arnim's version is even further detached from historical reference, because he neutralizes the polemical themes that had previously prompted invention, substituting for them new configurations that form a universe apart. Arnim was not fascinated by either the Vatican or the cloister. The question of Roman clericalism did not come up in a writer like Achim von Arnim (1781–1831), born into the old Lutheran landed aristocracy in a country strongly secularized by Frederick II, far from the Rhineland where Winkopp had flourished. Like most German romantics, Arnim felt a certain attraction for the aesthetic and mystical sides of Catholicism, but it was hardly strong enough to threaten the Lutheranism that he considered an essential part of the north-German character and that was of prime importance to him. Nor was he attracted by themes of a fear of women or women's revenge. Romantic Germany had benefited, without convulsions, from the combined effects of Lutheranism and the Enlightenment. Arnim lived surrounded by great and highly respected women writers: Bettina von Arnim, his wife and the sister of Clemens von Brentano; Cunegunde von Savigny, another of Brentano's sisters and the wife of the great jurist Friedrich Karl von Savigny; Carole von Günderode; Hermine von Klencke; Rahel Varnhagen; Henriette Vogel; and many other women who rightfully and fully participated in the German cultural expansion of the years from 1800 to 1820.

The popess came to Arnim as an already constituted cultural object and a part of German tradition. First and foremost, Joan was the heroine of the oldest German drama, *Fraw Jutta*. After the harshness of the Prussian Enlightenment, the disaster of the Napoleonic invasion, and the fragmentation of the Germanic nation, the most important task at hand was to discover the cultural roots of a national unity. Arnim's first major text, *Des Knabenwunderhorn* (the child's magic horn), a collection of popular songs that he rewrote in collaboration with Brentano, claimed to reforge a connection among the various classes and dispersed tribes of Germany. Arnim became acquainted with Schernberg's text quite soon in his career: in a letter to Brentano of 2 April 1805 he warmly advises him to read the issue of Gottsched's *Nöthiger Vorrath zur Geschichte der deutschen dramatischen Dichtkunst* that included an edition of *Fraw Jutta*.[36]

The popess first appears in Arnim's works as a fragment that summarizes her story, inserted into part 4 of his great novel, *Armut, Reichtum, Schuld und Busse der Gräfin Dolores* (Poverty, Wealth, Fault and Expiation of the Countess Dolores; 1810), an immense and complex masterwork that remains too little known, like most of Arnim's works, and that still awaits translation into French or English.[37] As it appears in this novel, the Joan story shows all the characteristics of traditional popular culture that appealed to Arnim. After a number of vicissitudes, the count and the countess, the German protagonists of the novel, are living in Sicily with their twelve children. On Carnival Day they go to the monastery of St. Lawrence to attend a theatrical performance; the chevalier Brülar, a French émigré who is their children's tutor (the action is set immediately after the French Revolution) is critical of the excursion, saying "One cannot take children to see such senseless buffooneries, subject to no rule." The prior, too, seems critical of the low cultural level of this traditional amusement, but he cannot oppose the popular will: "The prior apologized: his proposition of playing a new and good Italian play by Metastasio had not been adopted, because the people (das Volk) wanted to stay with the old tradition of Pope Joan."[38]

The performance awakens the mind of Johannes (the masculine form of Joan, I might note), the couple's eldest child, born, as a first step in her repentance, one year after the countess had had an adulterous affair. Johannes himself draws the parallel between his own subjection to the learned and cynical domination of his tutor, Brülar, and Johanna's (that is, Joan's) subjection to Speigelglanz, a philologist delegated by Satan to train a popess destined to shake the throne of Rome as Antichrist. This launches the family on a great ascetic pursuit of salvation, and after the sinful countess dies a saintly death, the others return to Germany, where they rediscover their roots by their participation in the simple and authentic community of the German nation. Pope Joan is thus a metaphor for a renunciation of the temptations of "civilization" and a metonymy of the new but also traditional convivial "culture"—to borrow an opposition in terms that was highly important to German national ideology in the early nineteenth century, as Norbert Elias has demonstrated.[39] The old constellation of the people, the woman, the child, and holy ignorance that had shone through in the Joan story since the fourteenth century appears here in a new context.

It took some time for Armin to complete Joan's transformation into a character fully his own. The fine scene that he had worked out in Countess Dolores was repeated word for word in his play, but in the shorter novel form the end of the adventure conformed to the story line in Schernberg and that Schernberg had in turn inherited from the long Johannic tradition (the fatal childbirth following Joan's choice of earthly punishment in exchange for eternal salvation). In his final version of the story, Arnim modified that schema.

Arnim continued to elaborate the Joan story for several years, doubtless encouraged by the very favorable reception that readers had given to Countess Dolores. Clemens von Brentano speaks in a letter to the painter Philipp Otto Runge (June 1810) of the "masterly" dramatic episodes of Arnim's novel (the popess; Hylos and the Ring). In an article written for the *Heidelberger Jahrbücher* in 1810 Wilhelm Grimm declared his admiration for the "sublime" scene of Joan in the garden. Jakob Grimm wrote to Arnim on 24 September 1810 to tell him that it was the finest thing he had ever written: "It is a piece as important as Goethe's *Faust*."[40] Arnim set to work. In a letter to the brothers Grimm of November 1812 he declares that he has almost finished his drama, and that he rejoices in the encouragements of his brother-in-law, Savigny. But in a letter to Brentano in 1813 Arnim states that he had in part given up the earlier form of the work: a tragedy in rhymed iambs, probably on the model of the baroque *Trauerspiel* of Gryphius (Andreas Grief), whom Arnim much admired, and that he had inserted lengthy prose passages into the work.[41] The publication of the first volume of Arnim's theatrical works *(Schaubühne)* in 1813 includes another fragment on the popess ("Des Frülingsfest," The Feast of Spring), a cantata for choir with dialogue. After that we lose sight of the play, aside from a fleeting allusion to it in a letter from Arnim to the Grimm brothers. It was unpublished at Arnim's death in 1831, but we know that he had completed it, if not given it the final polishing. Bettina von Arnim had it published it in 1846 in volume 19 of Arnim's complete works, edited by the Grimms. Since that date, if we except the fragments in anthologies (Montague Jacobs, 1908; Reinhold Stein, 1911) and two short studies (H. Specken, 1903; Paul Merker, 1933),[42] this great popess lies abandoned in total and undeserved oblivion. The least we can do to compensate for this dreary fate is to offer a summary of the play. It is also indispensable to an understanding of this Prussian, romantic Joan, the last truly creative work on the popess.

Arnim's Popess

Arnim's *Die Päpstin Johanna* begins in Iceland, a land that once was a paradise and cradle of the German nation before freezing over and becoming the refuge of Lucifer. In the depths of his cavern, the devil is working to make an Antichrist who will destroy the work of the Son of God. At the same time, Melancholy has just given birth to a child who, because its father is an earthling, cannot claim a place in the superterrestrial world. Melancholy places the child, a girl, under a glass bell, where Lucifer finds her and takes her to be the happy result of his antichristic alchemy. Lucifer gives over the child to Spiegelglanz, "the most terrible of the philologists," to be educated, in exchange for a promise that Spiegelglanz will serve as a prophet in the coming kingdom of the Antichrist. A she-wolf nurses the child before Spiegelglanz, who is a professor at the University of Paris, whisks her away to that city. When they get there, however, he keeps her away from people, hiding her in a gypsum cave so that he can protect her from outside influence and linguistic contamination and can determine experimentally humanity's original language. When Joan speaks it is in German, but rather than croaking in the Satanic mode, she launches into a song in praise of God. At that point Spiegelglanz decides to leave for Germany with the little Johanna, but his chief adversary, a student named Raphaël, has had enough time to imprint the three-year-old child with his shining spirituality.

The end of part 1 and all of part 2 of Arnim's work take place in the Rhineland. With the help of the giant Oferus (who is Johanna's father), Spiegelglanz establishes himself in the castle of the count Palatine, where an aged knight watches over the child count to protect him from parents who hate him. The philologist (Spiegelglanz) tutors the two children, who love one another tenderly, though each is unaware that the other is of a different sex than it seems: Lucifer's plan includes disguising Johanna as a boy (Johannes), and in a move to foil his parents' plots, the young count Palatine is dressed as a girl and named Stephania. Spiegelglanz quarrels with the aged knight and moves (with Johanna/Johannes) to the cathedral school of the archbishop of Mainz. There Spiegelglanz, who is unaware that he is being watched by Lucifer, under the disguise of Crysoloras, a professor of Greek, works to repress Johannes/Johanna's childish fantasy and love of nature. He initiates Johannes into fraud by composing a poem on the feast of spring that the youth, who has supposedly written it, presents at the ceremony that replaces final examinations in the episcopal school. Johannes wins the prize and receives a scholarship to study in Rome, for which city he/she and Spiegelglanz then depart.

The third part of Arnim's drama depicts the irresistible rise of Johannes, who becomes a priest, thanks to the aid of Chrysoloras/Lucifer and Spiegelglanz. The study of ancient texts moves him/her even further away from the Christian world. He/she falls under the influence of two Roman women, the imperious Marozia and Reinera, a lady whose pagan tendencies lead her to worship Venus in secret. When Johannes again encounters the young count Palatine (still disguised as Stephania), he/she is invincibly attracted to him/her. Spiegelglanz, who senses a threat to the execution of his master plan, reveals to Johannes her female nature; Johannes sinks into despair and, in her desire to become a man, turns to the universe of the ancient gods and participates in a ceremony in honor of Venus. At the same time, however, Stephania (that is, the count Palatine) is also informed of his true gender, and as a result he promptly throws off his disguise, thus reviving Johanna's amorous hopes. Lucifer succeeds in distracting Johanna, however: with the help of Spiegelglanz, he persuades her that her (half) superterrestrial birth gives her the powers of a goddess, but she begins to have her doubts about Lucifer when she notes his terror at the sight of a crucifix. At that point Pope Anacletus dies and Johanna allows herself to be pushed into taking the papal throne, where she increasingly comes under the influence of Spiegelglanz, who has become the papal physician.

Part 4 presents Johanna's papacy. She tries to forget her love for the count Palatine by dilapidating the wealth of the Church in extravagant festivities and tourneys. During a visit to the palace of Princess Venus (Marozia's daughter) Johanna falls into delirium. That very morning the count Palatine arrives at the same palace, but he disappears, enslaved by a magic potion that he has drunk. On her way back from the palace of Princess Venus Johanna meets a hermit who harangues her about his anxieties and warns her to repent. In the meantime, Marozia and Venus have taken over the pontifical court.

In part 5 Arnim resolves all these tensions. The German emperor arrives in Rome and reestablishes order in the city. He has Johanna's father, the giant Oferus, declared pope (he has converted to Christianity in the meantime, taking the name of Christophorus, the Christ-Bearer). Johanna is reunited with the count Palatine, and they escape, first to a hermit's mountain retreat, then back to Germany. Spiegelglanz drowns in the Tiber, and Lucifer retreats to his subterranean kingdom.

The considerable liberties that Arnim takes with the Johannist tradition can be attributed to a German romantic taste (see Johan Ludwig Tieck, Brentano, and the Grimms) for popular legends charged with strong, primordial signification. That same taste is responsible for several themes that Arnim added to the main plot: the tale of St. Christopher, the giant who serves Satan but passes over to the service of God; the legend of the enchanted realm of Venus (as in the Tannhaüser legend); the anecdote of children deprived of human contact in order to discover humanity's primeval language (an episode credited to Frederick II Hohenstaufen in the Middle Ages), and more.

Although the Roman episodes (the domination of Marozia, the arrival of the German emperor) that evoke Pope John XII, supposedly the model for Joan, show that Arnim was to some extent aware of the scholarly controversies regarding the popess, Schernberg's play occupies a central place in his rewriting of the legend. Arnim borrows from Schernberg the notion of the satanic plot and the happy ending that transcribes redemption through Christ into secular terms. Joan's Germanic characteristics, which had been prepared by a long tradition of medieval versions of the story from Thuringia and Bavaria and was continued by Schernberg, Murner, Pauli, and Sachs, are given a truly national stamp. The narrative takes on the dimensions of a founding myth of the German nation, first fragmented, then rediscovered. It includes the idea of election (the language of origins is German; the German emperor arrives in Rome to save the day); a lost paradise (Iceland); a time of wandering (Johanna's vagabondage to Paris, Mainz, and Rome); and a return (the popess returns to Germany to marry the count Palatine). This presents a new paradox: Joan, a figure who emerged out of the communal movement in Rome and out of Catholic universality, becomes a figurehead for the German nation.

Beyond this cultural determination, however, the legend of Joan offered Arnim an opportunity to crystalize the essential theme of his entire oeuvre, which is that of the double. Joan, a creature at first manipulated but who achieves humanity, evokes the related figures of the mandragora or the golem in Arnim's novellas "Isabella von Ägypten" and "Melück Maria Blainville, die Hausprophetin aus Arabien" (1812). Thanks to her transfer from the service of Lucifer to the service of God, to her internal hesitation between her male and female nature (which is intensified by the symmetrical disguise of the count Palatine), and to her oscillations between awareness and forgetfulness, sin and repentance, Arnim's Joan takes her place among others of his characters who, like Countess Dolores, live not as subjects but as battlefields. The difficult conquest of humanity, fighting against knowledge and power, is achieved through suffering and by abandoning oneself to fate and chance. This is what makes Joan—as Jakob Grimm rightly saw—a new Faust. In Arnim, through Schernberg, Joan found her strength in the weakness of her soul.

A BRIEF THEORETICAL INTERLUDE

The literary history of the popess might be made to end on these Arnimian heights. The year 1831, the date of Arnim's death and Hegel's, would thus mark the end of philosophy, history, and Joan. In academic terms, we could say that what came after is rightly called "contemporary" history.

At that point, however, the historian is master of nothing and the sociologist takes over: with romanticism, literature becomes an autonomous cultural field with a logic of its own. Our 1793 popesses in revolutionary Paris were still history, because (albeit in burlesque fashion) they reflected a possible event (Joan's papacy), specific ways of thinking (those of the

French political and literary Bohemia), and the social situation of her interpreters (men on their way to becoming professionals, as we have seen). With Arnim the episode of the popess becomes self-referential: literature is made out of literature. Arnim's Joan emerges, not out of reality (empirical or imaginary) but out of Gottsched's *Nöthiger Vorrath,* where Schernberg's text was already marked with the seal of literature ("the first German tragedy"). Werner Kraft, whose 1925 inaugural dissertation was the first literary analysis of the motifs of the Joan legend,[43] wrote as a technician of literature when he noted that the two rival theoreticians of German drama of the eighteenth century, Gottsched and Lessing, offered their disciples two very different versions of the theme of seduction (in Jutta and in Faust). Arnim followed one of these versions; Goethe, the other.

That situation puts an end to our task, because literary production regarding Joan, which is still considerable, becomes fragmented, following no genuine order discernible to the historian. Thus far the various interpretations of the popess have been organized according to how they fitted into various systems of belief, successive and/or simultaneous. From here on, however, Joan's literary autonomy as a character and her solidarity with specifically cultural entities (the vogue for the Gothic novel, German nationalism, the historical novel, decadent farce, etc.) remove Joan from all spheres of belief, which were contracting. A sociology that takes inspiration from Pierre Bourdieu might draw up a map of cultural fields in which Joan figured, distinguishing among popesses naively emblematic of some sort of access to historical knowledge, metaphorical popesses with a strong cultural stamp (symbolism is a criterion of distinction here), and popesses of a third level, such as those of Alfred Jarry and Bertolt Brecht, who affect a vulgarity that signals a liberation from the norms of documentation and from symbolist art. Such an analysis requires special competence. Rather than risk it, we will have to be content with an inventory of contemporary versions of the popess, arranged by type.

Texts on the popess have proliferated from 1831 to our own day, but they display little genuine novelty. They can be divided into three ways of treating the topic; three readings of the episode.

Burlesque Readings

Bordes and Casti had laid the foundations for a burlesque reading of the Joan episode, and the theater of the French Revolution had freed their invention from the malicious counterweight of their anticlerical erudition. The nineteenth century fairly exactly reproduced that division of literary tasks. In 1831, the year we have taken as symbolic, one final *vaudeville* on Joan appeared, *La Papesse Jeanne*, "*vaudeville*-anecdote in one act by Messieurs Simonnin and Théodore N., performed for the first time in Paris at the Théâtre de l'Ambigu-Comique, on Saturday 15 January 1831." Two prolific authors are concealed under these pseudonyms, Benjamin Antier (1787–1870), the author of famous melodramas such as *L'Auberge des Adrets* (1823) and *Robert Macaire* (1834), and Théodore Nezel. I will not inflict yet another plot summary on the reader; suffice it to note that these authors burdened an antipapal romp with embellishments borrowed from the current fashion for the Gothic Middle Ages (Joan is the flighty wife of a crusader) but also reflected nineteenth-century familial themes (clever ways to commit adultery was a staple in the long tradition of the "théâtre de boulevard"). Comparison between the 1831 Joan and her sisters of 1793 displays the width of the gap separating the Revolution of 1789 from the Revolution of 1830.

Nineteenth-century anticlericalism took quite different forms from those of the Revolution. In the later age it rallied opinion ranging from the Reaction to the Movement, which structured politics in Europe. After 1815 reaction in Europe was strongly papist and ultramontane. We need think only of Joseph de Maistre and his *Du Pape* (1817), or of all the well-brought-up young men who rushed to the defense of the papacy of Pius IX (1846–78) as he struggled to retain the Patrimony of St. Peter (that is, the Papal States), under threat since 1859; instituted the dogmas of the Immaculate Conception of the Virgin (1854) and of papal infallibility (1870); and condemned liberalism and socialism (with the bulls *Quanta cura* and *Syllabus*, 1864). On the other side, anticlericalism played a role in forming a republican compromise after the great crises of 1830, 1848, and 1870.

One fictionalized version of the popess gave full expression to both these tensions and these points of agreement, thus occupying a place in the Johannist tradition disproportionate to its literary worth. In 1866 Emmanuel Rhoides (1840–1904), a Greek, published a burlesque *Papissa Joanna* in Athens that was a close imitation of Casti's novel, complete with long anticlerical digressions. There is nothing astonishing about the fact itself: Greece, which had won its independence in 1830, was still dominated by the traditionalist attitudes of the diaspora under Ottoman rule that inspired dreams of a Hellenic empire centered on Constantinople. The appearance of this *Papissa* soon after the fall of Otto I, the Bavarian king of Greece, and the redaction of the Constitution of 1864 displayed a sort of anticlerical ecumenism. Rhoides had probably encountered the subject matter of his tale in Genoa, where his father served as consul, or in Berlin, where he studied. His own career as director of the National Library of Athens and as the translator of Chateaubriand and Macaulay shows that he was sensitive to European culture.

Rhoides's novel met with considerable success in Europe; it was translated into German (by Georg Buvar in 1875 and by Paul Friedrich in 1904, both published in Leipzig); in Italian (published in Athens in 1876); and in French (Paris, 1878). The French translation caused a scandal. Barbey d'Aurevilly wrote an indignant review of it in the *Constitutionnel*, which was followed by another by Charles Buet. The work was believed a forgery, with authorship attributed to Edmond About or Francisque Sarcey. The publisher responded by adding to the seventh edition of the work (1882) a portrait of Rhoides, a facsimile of the frontispiece of the Greek edition, and Rhoides's response to Barbey's critique, published in full.

Curiously enough, this novel, which was itself imitated from Casti and/or Spanheim, gave rise to two adaptations that tended to efface Rhoides: Joan had a tendency to thrust her successive mediators into the shadows. In 1905 the illustrious Alfred Jarry, seemingly unaware of the 1878 translation, undertook the translation of Rhoides's book into French. Two years earlier, on the occasion of the death of Leo XIII in 1903, Jarry had told Claude Terrasse, a musician, that he wanted to write an operetta on the subject of the popess in collaboration with the composer Eugène Demolder. Jarry added: "As precedents, there were two nonfarcical 'Pope Joan' plays, one under the Revolution, the other in the middle of the century." The project had to wait, and in 1905 Jarry wrote to the publisher Edward Sansot to announce his discovery of Rhoides: "I have received from Greece the reviled work, which made its little *Quo vadis* in that country and has never been translated, Ἡ Πάπισσα Ἰωάννα [La Papesse Jeanne]."[44] Jarry translated the work with the aid of a friend, Jean Saltas, but he died before he could review the translation. It was published by Fasquelle et Charpentier in 1908. The translation is quite faithful, and it is no improvement on the 1878 French translation. Jarry's genius found better scope in *Le Moutardier du Pape*, a reworking of the 1903 project for an operetta, which was published in 1907. The play is a wild, Ubuesque farce involving "Jane of Eggs, popess under the name of John VIII"; Macaro, the Grand Moutardier du Pape (mustard-maker to the pope; a reference to a French saying, typically prefaced by "Who does he think he is?"); Man Forte de Costo, colonel of the pontifical Guards; and a throng of "ambassadors, cardinals, tourists, salvationists, muledrivers, bull-bearers, staff-bearers, gondoliers, Guards, *petits moutardiers* of the Sixtine Chapel, the faithful, ballets of wise and foolish virgins, indignant apothecaries."

Another famous translator, the English novelist Lawrence Durrell, crushed the unfortunate Rhoides under his own prestige.

An Episode in German and English Cultural History (1890-1930)

The poor and approximate logic of our classification of contemporary readings of the Joan legend incites us to include in the series of burlesque versions of the popess a dramatic sketch written in 1922 by Bertolt Brecht for the actress Tilla Durieux.[45] Brecht relates the story of Joan in the expressionist mode typical of that early period of his production; it is close in style to the parody and the grating affirmation of brute individuality that Brecht developed in his first play, *Baal* (1918–22). In his sketch about Joan, Brecht contrasts the ambitious calculation of Cardinal Matteo, the promotor of the popess, with the earthly, carnal, and simple calculation of Joan, who, after her public childbirth, "rests in a low house of the Vatican, numb, at peace, and calm, near a wooden cradle." Brecht's presentation of the cardinals as meat merchants and thieves prefigures *Die heilige Johanna der Schlachthöfe* (Saint Joan of the Stockyards; 1930–32) and *Der aufhaltsame Aufstieg der Arturo Ui* (The Resistible Rise of Arturo Ui; 1941).

Without forcing this youthful sketch into the mold of *Verfremdungeffekt*, a term drawn from the theoretical operations of the Russian formalists, usually translated as "device of strangeness,"[46] I might note that Brecht's choice of this episode enables him to transpose the world of power, his prime target, out of its familiar framework and move it elsewhere (here the medieval Curia; in other works, the world of gangsters, of ancient China, etc.) in order to expose the mechanisms of power in the contemporary world. The simple, effective logic of alienation may perhaps explain many contemporary popesses.

Something else was at work, however: German writers of the years between 1890 and 1920 were preoccupied by Joan, as evidenced by Richard Haage's inaugural dissertation on Schernberg's *Fraw Jutta* in 1891 and by the republication of *Fraw Jutta* itself in Edward Schröder's edition in 1911.[47]

The *Kulturkampf* launched by Bismarck between 1871 and 1878 against the powerful Catholic party of the Zentrum had revived an interest in Lutheran and pre-Lutheran culture. Neo-Lutheran and misogynist versions of the Joan legend included a play by the little-known Max Weitemeyer (Erfurt, 1900) and a work (Munich, 1905) by Adolf Bartels (1862–1945), later a preeminent figure in Nazi literary criticism, who earned a certain sinister fame for his anti-Semitic attacks on the memory of Heinrich Heine.[48] A rapid enumeration of the other popesses of the time shows that Joan had acquired the light weight and the versatility of a disputed literary motif. In 1920 there was a metaphysical and symbolist *Päpstin Jutta* by Rudolf Borchardt (1877–1945), a poet and a friend of von Hofmannsthal's;[49] in 1920 Richard Alexander Edon published a fanciful version of the Joan story; in 1924, Georg Reicke was responsible for a new *Jutte* set in ancient times. These texts were implicit responses to and contestations of one another.

Confirmation of the arbitrary nature of the literary sign might be found, *a contrario*, in the surprising lack of English popesses during that same period, even though circumstances seemed favorable.

Roman Catholicism exerted a great attraction in the milieu of English aesthetes close to Oscar Wilde. One would think that as a female and an imposter, Joan might have offered such circles an image of refined and decorative suprasexuality. I am thinking of such figures as Frederick Rolfe, known as Baron Corvo (1886–1913), an Anglican who converted to Catholicism and determined to become a priest. He went to Rome in 1890, where he lived in the vain hope of receiving ordination. He expressed both his fascination with the Roman court and his distaste for it in such works as *Chronicles of the House of Borgia* and *Don Tarquinio*, but especially his major work, *Hadrian the Seventh*, which presents an English, homosexual pope. There was also Ronald Firbank (1886–1926), a friend of Oscar Wilde's and one of his admirers. His last novel, *Concerning the Eccentricities of Cardinal Pirelli* (1926), presents a series of decadent scenes set within the Roman Church (a dog receives Catholic baptism, a cardinal cross-dresses as a woman, etc.).[50]

ROMANESQUE READINGS

Joan seems to have met with little success in the early nineteenth century, an age in which the production of historical novels was nonetheless intense. Was this because the anecdote is resolutely non-Gothic? Or perhaps because of the influence of burlesque interpretations or ceaseless but warmed-over controversy? The only genuine historical novel on the Joan theme was that of Friedrich Wilhelm Bruckbräu, *Der Papst im Unterrocke* (The Pope in Petticoats; Stuttgart, 1832). Bruckbräu was a prolific author of spicy historical narratives that occupied a place halfway between the licentious tale of the eighteenth century and the historical novel of the romantic period. The parents of his unfeminine Joan saw her as a male: "The child seems destined for great things. It is doubtful that she can achieve them as a girl." Bruckbräu's plot includes innumerable adventures, kidnappings, pursuits, and disguises. All turns out well in the end when Joan, pregnant, escapes the fury of the Roman Church thanks to two accomplices, Basile, a monk, and Odon, a Turkish pirate converted to Christianity.

There are other facile, free, and romanesque treatments of Joan's fate, but they are hardly worth pausing over. One is Léo Taxil's *Un pape femelle* (1882). Taxil was an astonishing personage who made a veritable industry of anticlerical publications. He converted to Roman Catholicism in 1885 (receiving absolution from Leo XIII), but later, in 1897, denounced his own conversion as a masquerade.[51] Ernesto Mezzabotta's *La Papessa Giovanna* (Rome, 1885), and Claude Pasteur's *La Papesse* (Paris, 1983, which was followed by *Le manuscrit d'Anastase*, 1986) are works in which the simple pleasures of disguises and revealing the secrets of the Vatican lack both mystery and depth.

METAPHORICAL READINGS

If Arnim's oeuvre had not been so completely neglected, his name might figure at the head of a lineage of writers who examine Joan's extraordinary destiny more in the light of the mystery of cross-dressing or the penetration of superficial appearances than in terms of the popess's ambitions and adventures within the Church.

Michelet might have written Joan's praises. He did not do so, but instead glorified (and rather flatly) another woman in man's garb, Joan of Arc. There is a version of the popess's story worthy of Michelet in a curious work published in Marseille in 1878 (the year in which Rhoides was causing such a stir in France). It was written by Jean Pierre Cansson, an author otherwise totally unknown, and titled *Histoire de la papesse Jeanne, mademoiselle Agnès Alla Etelbert née en Angleterre, montée sur le trône pontifical le 17 juillet 855 à 858 sous le nom de Jean VIII*. This work is divided into sections headed "The Woman" and "The Fairies"; it praises Joan as a glorious figurehead of the necessary triumph of women: Cansson goes so far as to state that "Christianity is the pontificate of the woman." Joan's adventure, which he strips of all its dubious and immoral taint, illustrates the radiant trajectory of The Woman toward the humanization of the species.

Rather than pursuing descriptions of the metaphorical life of Joan (in Bartels, for example, or Borchardt), I prefer to end this literary survey by narrowing the paradigm of the popess and considering two contemporary works in which the spirit of Joan is strong even though the literal anecdote is absent.

Yentl, or, Ambivalence

In the short story "Yentl" (1962), Isaac Bashevis Singer relates the Joan story within the setting of Polish Judaism.[52] Yentl is inhabited by a passion for Talmudic knowledge; she rejects her female condition, disguises herself as a young man (taking the name Anshel), and sets off to seek instruction in Judaic teachings far from her native village. She lodges in the house of a man whose daughter, Hadass, has just broken her engagement with Avagdor, a fellow student and friend of Anshel/Yentl. Acting out of some obscure desire, Anshel/Yentl marries Hadass, but abandons her and pushes Avagdor into marrying her after a divorce arranged from a distance. Singer's text, so close to the Christian legend, is an asymptote of the Joan story in their shared nostalgia for androgyny, figured as a desire for knowledge.

A Crime, or, The Female Christ

Un Crime, a detective story written by Georges Bernanos in 1935, takes us far from the pontifical question, but plunges us into the heart of Joan's fascination. It describes the mysterious presence of a female Christ, the central figure and the essence of a text in which Bernanos sacrifices to plot only the final few pages, needed to tie up loose ends. The key to the mystery, which Bernanos gives only in those final pages, is this: a young woman (never named) who is the daughter of a nun forced to flee her convent at her approaching childbirth, comes to the Alpine village where her mother lives as nurse-companion to an elderly and wealthy lady. The daughter has come to assassinate the rich old lady so that her grand-niece, Evangeline, whose companion and lover she has become (in full knowledge of the old woman's fortune), will inherit her wealth. In the dark of night, as our assassin is fleeing the scene of the crime, she unexpectedly encounters the new parish priest, who has just arrived at the village. She and the priest had already met during her voyage, so she is obliged to eliminate him. She does so, then takes his place and presents herself, dressed in his cassock, as the new curé.

When this new curé arrives unexpectedly in the middle of the night, after the village had given up hope that he would come that day, the priest's housekeeper, Céleste, takes him for an apparition: "The face appeared very distinctly, right in the center of the luminous halo. . . . 'You have come,' she repeated mechanically, 'You have come. . . .' " This sudden appearance had been preceded (or announced) by a sort of noisy silence: "What she [Céleste] had just heard was scarcely a noise for she could not have situated it in space and yet it seemed as if this noise had never ceased but continued to float closely around her. 'Bless me,' she said aloud, 'the wind has dropped.'"[53]

The blade of the angel (or rather, its pistol) arrives to cut through the heavy slumber of this godforsaken village and separate out the elect (of God? Of Satan?). The opening scene prepares this coming of the angel by a sort of heavily drawn parody, a false feminization (in this village that Bernanos names "Mégère," shrew) of the angelism of the woman curé. As Céleste nervously awaits the arrival of the new parish priest, Phémie *la sonneuse* (the bell-ringer; the one who spreads the news) arrives instead, "without making any more noise than a weasel." A mannish sort of woman who spits and drinks gin, Phémie offers to keep Céleste company, on the condition that she be permitted to smoke "the dead man's pipe"— that is, the pipe of the old priest whose replacement they are awaiting.[54]

The young curé charms Mégère and soon the villagers are won over. Céleste is the first to be smitten by a smile that conquered her heart and won her loyalty. For Céleste, the spiritual attraction of the priest is expressed as a direct inspiration that conjures up imagery of the Holy Spirit: "Even before he'd opened his mouth, you'd imagine that his thought was already in you, in your breast, that it had jumped into your heart. And the words to answer him came out in the same way, as if he'd only to make a sign and call them; he looks as if he charmed doves, like the old Italian who came here last year." The next to succumb is an adolescent choirboy and aspirant seminary student, who follows in the curé's footsteps even unto his death, despite the priest's warning: "When God places us in the presence of a master, the future may depend upon a first clear, frank look."[55]

Outside the orbit of the presbytery, the *juge d'instruction* charged with investigating the old lady's murder succumbs to the same charm; fascination reduces him to a state of innocence and, to the great surprise of the police officers under him, he lets the curé, a major witness, slip away. His superior, the *inspecteur de police,* cannot believe how soft he has become, and Céleste complains, when she tries to overhear the judge interviewing the priest as a witness, "Well, just as well try to hear the grass growing. A magistrate who has nothing to be ashamed of doesn't whisper like a girl in a confessional." The judge does not recognize the priest as an angel; trying to remember him, he has only a vague reminiscence: "The likeness of the curé of Mégère also rose from the depths of his memory. The whole likeness or some peculiarity of expression, voice, gesture?"[56] Moreover, when the priest disappears, the judge becomes impatient with what he sees as veils, complaining that nobody in the village resigns himself to seeing things in the ordinary way, with his own eyes. Rumor abounds, and he feels he is going crazy. All he has to go on is a photograph of a young girl that he has found in the priest's wallet and that he contemplates cease-lessly, to no end, for no reason.

What can we make of this breath, this wind, this spirit that blows over Mégère? A somewhat flat reading would see this intrusion as a metaphor for the violence of grace, which shakes and turns things upside-down, as in the evangelistic model. In reality, the constellation Céleste-the adoles-cent acolyte-the village idiot (who is the only person to have seen the "an-gel" as a woman, between her two crimes, and in all her savagery: "A real woman in a hairy jacket. I could as easily have taken her for an animal, she moved with so little noise") evokes the saving trilogy of the woman, the child, and the fool that fourteenth-century Franciscans thought should re-place the bad pope. Phémie reports the new priest's arrival: "A curé who arrives in their midst after midnight, in the idiot's cart. . . . And supposing the law had something to do with it, my beauty?"[57]

On a deeper level, however, the priest's seduction comes from the gap that he creates and from the fear that devours him and that he propagates like an affection: "There is no love without fear," he/she writes to Evange-line. That same terror (of the exterminator or of the Messiah) is what at-taches both Céleste and the adolescent to the priest: the narrator says of Céleste, "Her terror no longer had a purpose. She simply attached her fears to this unknown priest's footsteps." The same terror is what disarms the judge, a new St. Paul. To these "elect" the priest appears like a being come from exile or from some distant capital. The woman curé, by murder and imposture (an inversion of the Passion or a true restoration of it) forces her destiny to become grace. He/she assumes and disperses female inheritance (both the fortune of her victim and maternal atavism) so as to extract from it the weapon of a predominantly female suprasexuality, an angelic femi-ninity (revenge, or God's truth), against its village parody (Mégère), its af-fective parody (her misdirected love for Evangeline), and its clerical parody. The authorial narrator comments at the end: "She had really lived a sinister nightmare in her waking hours. There a lucid examination would have recognized, one by one, the abnormal pictures born of maternal re-morse, the priestly obsession, his manners, his language, which for so many years had poisoned the conscience of the unfrocked nun."[58]

Bernanos's fine novel may not closely follow the anecdote or the his-tory of Joan, but it returns to the stupor that Jean de Mailly felt in the pres-ence of the original tale, and it persuades us to close this book with one final examination of the methodological fascination that underlies this long search for the popess. We must conclude.

EPILOGUES

8

FIRST EPILOGUE

HISTORIOGRAPHY OF THE POPESS

am proposing two separate epilogues to the history of Joan, our bird of passage of ambivalent plumage, numbering them chapters 8 and 9 to emphasize that they are not intended to be conclusive. Refusing to conclude is not just a worn-out rhetorical device: to whom could we grant the right to have the last word on the popess? Thus far our enquiry has placed Joan within realms of discourse, universes of belief, or cultural fields that gave her a function and totally absorbed her. What is left that might permit us to think of the popess outside of those successive, mutually exclusive fractures and crystallizations? At best, to continue the discussion would risk adding new versions to offer the next commentator.

The two epilogues will nonetheless attempt a phenomenological reduction of the anecdote by setting aside the historical emergence of the legend and considering the act of relating the history of Joan as it has been surveyed in this book. As the last of the faithful followers of the popess, I shall situate my own version. In the first epilogue I will interrogate the protocol underlying the position I take as it relates to the historiographic tradition regarding Joan; in the second epilogue I will situate my participation in the continuing curiosity that the popess evokes, above and beyond differences in interpretation.

Can one legitimately trace a historiography of the popess? Certainly not, if we consider that Joan has been a historical object ever since Jean de Mailly. This means that the historiography of Joan is one with discourse on her, including fictional versions (Casti's or Rhoides's scholarly apparatus bring their works close to historical description).

Otherwise we would have to proclaim the truth about Joan, recognize the authors who followed the right road, and distribute certificates of historical merit to them. A teleology of the sort seems to have been at work in our own times, given that (with the exception of Cesare D'Onofrio) historians have been as good as immobile since 1836, when Döllinger fixed the truth of Joan (she never existed), drew up a historiographical table of honor of the skeptics, and pilloried the credulous. Joan never existed: that was the historical fact. That means that her true history began in the sixteenth century with Panvinio, then reached completion thanks to Blondel (for his disinterested criticism), Leibniz (for his comprehensive criticism), and Döllinger (who brought to the service of criticism the new tools of German philology).

It is in fact true that the popess probably never existed. Leibniz said as much, soberly and with elegance, in two lines that are worth volumes of controversy: "Cui in justo temporum ordine nullum relinquit series rerum personnarumque" (In the proper order of time, the series of events and persons leaves no room for her).[1] Modern and contemporary scholarship leaves no gap in ninth-century papal chronology. Still, there is nothing to stop someone from feminizing one or another of the popes; it has been done to Homer and Shakespeare.[2] We know that any imaginary construction can be justified somehow.

But that would give us only one truth about Joan, and the meagerest one to boot. The fact of believing in the existence of the popess or of rejecting that belief constitutes a historical object. Moreover, that probable truth has attracted historians' efforts, rather than the other way around. It would thus be vain to seek a method where simple means were used. I shall attempt to discern some constants in modern and contemporary interpretations of the Joan legend by analyzing the intellectual mechanisms that accompany the decision to treat the subject. I shall examine the case of an *honnête homme* who wrote on the question of the popess in the early nineteenth century, well after the great religious controversies. This last witness, whom we shall hear at some length, is Stendhal, chosen not for his fame but for the unexpected but exemplary nature of his encounter with Joan:

> Who would believe that there are people in Rome today who attach much importance to the story of Popess Joan? A personage of considerable stature, who aspires to the cardinal's hat, attacked me this evening on the subject of Voltaire who, according to him, had indulged in many impieties concerning the Popess Joan. It is my impression that Voltaire says not a word about her. In order not to be *disloyal to my cloth* (the worst of faults in the eyes of an Italian), I maintained that the popess had in fact existed, using as best I could the reasons that my opponent let slip.

Several contemporary authors relate that after Leo IV, in 853, a woman, German by nationality, occupied the See of St. Peter, and had as successor Benedict III.

I have said that one must not expect of history a kind of certainty that it cannot offer. The existence of Timbuctu, for example, is more probable than that of the emperor Vespasian. I should be more inclined to believe in the reality of the most singular ruins that some travelers claim to have seen, in the heart of Arabia, than in the existence of King Pharamond or King Romulus. It would not be a strong argument against the existence of Popess Joan to say that the thing is improbable. The exploits of the Maid of Orleans are far more shocking to all the rules of common sense, and yet we have a thousand proofs of them.

The existence of Popess Joan is proved by an extract from the chronicles of the ancient monastery of Canterbury (founded by the famous Augustine, who had been sent to England by Gregory the Great). Immediately after the year 853, in the catalogue of the bishops of Rome, the chronicle (which I have not seen) bears these words:

"*Hic obiit Leo quartus, cujus tamen anni usque ad Benedictum tertium computantur, eo quod mulier in papam promota fuit.*"

And after the year 853: "*Johannes. Iste non computatur quia femina fuit. Benedictus tertius,*" etc.

This monastery of Canterbury had frequent and intimate relations with Rome; it has been adequately proved, moreover, that the lines I have just quoted were set down in the register at the very time that is marked by the dates.

The ecclesiastical writers who look to the court of Rome for their advancement still believe it useful to establish that the *power to remit our sins*, which the pope enjoys, has been transmitted to him from pope to pope, by the successors of St. Peter, who had himself received it from Jesus Christ. As it is essential, I do not know why, that the pope be a man, if from the year 853 to the year 855 a woman occupied the pontifical throne, the transmission of the power to remit sins was interrupted.

At least sixty authors, Greek, Latin, and even *holy*, tell the story of Popess Joan. The famous Etienne Pasquier says that the immense majority of these authors had no ill-will toward the Holy See. The interest of their religion, of their advancement and the very fear of some chastisement required that they keep this strange adventure concealed. During the ninth and tenth centuries, Rome was rent by factions, and disorder was at its height. But the popes were hardly more wicked than the princes who were their contemporaries. Agapet II was elected pope before the age of eighteen (946), Benedict IX mounted the throne at ten and John XII at seventeen. Cardinal Baronius himself, the *official* writer of the court of Rome, admits this. Is there much difference between the face of a young man of eighteen and that of certain women of bold and determined character such as is needed in order to aspire to the papacy? In our own day, despite the intimacy that military life enforces, have not several women disguised as soldiers won the cross of the Legion of Honor, and this in the time of Napoleon?

I see that this appeal to the facts greatly embarrasses my antagonist, who based his chief arguments on *improbability*, for the historic texts are inexorable.

Marianus Scott, a Scottish monk, who died in 1086, relates the story of the popess. Bellarmin, a papist writer, says of him, *"Diligenter scripsit."*

Anastasius, surnamed the *Librarian*, a Roman abbot, a learned man and of high merit, who was a contemporary of the popess, relates her story. It is true that in many of Anastasius's manuscripts, this scandalous page was omitted by the copying monks. But it has been proved a thousand times that it was their custom to suppress everything that they considered contrary to the interests of Rome.

Le Sueur, in his *Ecclesiastical History,* and Colomesius, in his *Historical Miscellany,* quote an Anastasius in the library of the king of France that contains the whole history of Popess Joan. There were two similar Anastasiuses in Augsburg and in Milan. Saumaise and Freher had seen them.

Anastasius was sufficiently informed, he lived in Rome, he spoke as an eye-witness. He wrote the lives of the popes up to Nicholas I, who came after Benedict III.

Martin Polonus, the archbishop of Cosenza and penitentiary of Innocent IV, has written the history of Popess Joan.

This singular woman is sometimes called *Anglicus,* at other times *Moguntinus.* Roolwinck, the author of the *Fasciculus Temporum,* says, *"Joannes Anglicus cognomine, sed natione Moguntinus."* Mézeray, in the *Life of Charles the Bald,* says that the existence of Popess Joan was accepted as a *constant truth for five hundred years.*

The reader is well aware, from the serious turn of the pages he has just read, that this discussion, which had begun in the salons of his excellency, the ambassador of . . . , ended up in the Barberini Library, where my learned antagonist had made an appointment to meet me. Here we verified most of the texts. A M. Blondel, a Protestant, but who lived in Paris under Louis XIV, and who *sought advancement,* composed a quite unconvincing dissertation to disprove the existence of Popess Joan, who probably reigned from 853 to 855.

But what does the truth of this anecdote matter? It will never reach the kind of men who have their sins remitted. "Give a French *Civil Code* to your subjects," I told my adversary, "and no one will seriously revive the memory of the young German woman who so awkwardly placed herself between St. Peter and Leo XII. She was young, for her sex was revealed by a childbirth occurring in the midst of a procession. In the Louvre museum a porphyry bath chair is shown that is mixed up with the history of Popess Joan." But I do not wish to become scandalous.[3]

The Roman scene that Stendhal sets quite clearly exemplifies the nature of the historiography of Joan: imposture reigns in it, as if Joan's ruse had gushed forth, splattering those who came too close to her. In reality, Stendhal's text is copied, almost textually and without crediting his source, from two letters in François Maximilien Misson's *Voyage d'Italie,* a work published in 1694 and often used by travelers (the marquis de Sade among them). Even the appointment in the Biblioteca Barberini comes from Misson, who breaks the monotony of his dissertation on Joan with a description of the library.[4] The falsity of the setting contains, *en abyme,* a falsification of the arguments: the would-be cardinal wrongly incriminates Voltaire, who was a convinced Johannoclast, as we have seen. Anastasius is taken (wrongly) as the author of the *Liber pontificalis.* What is more, it was known from the sixteenth century on that the mentions of the popess had been added to that work in the fourteenth century. The allusion to Anastasius is in fact a reference to a shady affair in the early seventeenth century between Jesuits and Protestants in Cologne in which a manuscript on loan was claimed to have been relieved of the page on Joan. In this war of falsifications waged since the sixteenth century, historians of Joan incessantly copied from one another, stole from one another, and distorted and rearranged materials. This overwhelming presence of falsity is not based on the psychology of historians of Joan (although certain deserters to the other side—Bale, Vergerio, Raemond—were particularly severe cases). Rather, it was the question itself that elicited vituperative debate.

Stendhal provides a good illustration of this when he presents two adversaries whose polemical decisiveness derives from a tactical situation: the Johannoclast, a "person of considerable stature" who "aspired to the cardinal's hat" "attacks" a representative of anticlericalism and a countryman of Voltaire's. The Johannist narrator stands up for Voltaire out of national and cultural solidarity ("in order not to be disloyal to my cloth"). Although the stakes are anodyne here and the dispute is treated with humor, the outcome of the game has been decided in advance. The acid conversation that takes place between the narrator and the prelate is a mirror image of the life of Joan in historical controversy, which is an incessant dialogue that tirelessly reiterates borrowed arguments, swallowed whole and blown out of all proportion, rather than springing from mature thought. One example of this repetitive dialectic ought to suffice. In 1844 a Dutch scholar, Nicolaas Christiaan Kist, wrote a new treatise favorable to the existence of the popess, *De pausin Joanna;* the following year, Justus Henricus Wensing responded with a work, *De verhandeling van N. C. Kist,* in which the author's aggressive attack on Kist was clearly more important to him than the matter at hand; the exchange continued with *Een woord an Wensing,* a "word" of several dozen pages addressed to Wensing by Ludwig Tross.[5] The leading historical revues in Europe noted the Kist-Wensing-Tross dispute, which was followed by yet another cycle of responses.

This late flurry of activity, even after all the previous controversy, poses the difficult question of the survival of certain seemingly timeless, indestructible representations that live on even when the issues themselves have changed or disappeared. The revival of the debate that takes the place of historiography springs from a strange automatism that had little to do with reason; it is as if people needed a set of disputed questions to give themselves the illusion of playing the judge or the prosecutor and instituting a poorly argued case.

And indeed, all that rage for dialectic, that copious argumentation, and that untiring verve define the judiciary tone of the historiography of Joan since the sixteenth century. Joan has had lawyers for the defense and for the prosecution, occasionally judges, but rarely historians. Since Panvinio—that is, since Joan became a counter in a vaster game—the procedure may have been refined, but it remained the same.

The prosecution (who are Johannist in that they believe in Joan's existence) employ two types of means: testimony given by witnesses and a narrative reconstruction of the crime. The defense responds by calling other witnesses and by forging an alibi.

1. *Testimony.* As we have seen, the prosecution accumulates written evidence beginning with Anastasius Bibliothecarius and Marianus Scotus; the principle of accumulation rules here, as it does in the courts. Spanheim and Lenfant managed to assemble 160 texts. Another trait that signals judiciary influence (at least, in the sixteenth century) is the prosecution's preference—against all historical logic—for recent evidence given by contemporary historians, as if the witness's reputation, guaranteed by temporal proximity, counted more than how old the testimony was.

The defense responds with contrary testimony, drawing up long lists of authors who fail to mention the popess. It challenges the prosecution's witnesses, noting falsifications, interpolations, and ignorant copying errors. Florimond de Raemond went quite far in this direction: according to him, no author (poets aside) ever spoke of Joan!

Authors with more subtle minds take this criticism of testimony to a higher level; in Panvinio and Leone Allacci it becomes a genuine philological evaluation of the texts that pays careful attention to paleography and to the relation of one manuscript to another. Their demonstrative ardor engenders scholarly agility, and Bayle was quite right when he noted that the Protestants had turned against themselves arms that they had forged to destroy Catholic error. Philology could not triumph, however, because its victories opened a continual series of new battlefields that penetrated ever deeper into traditions. Textual criticism was a corrosive acid that ate away the parchment too.

2. *Narration.* The basic means used in the Roman model of the formal plea, which Cicero perfected in his Orations and is still followed today, is the "narration," a purposeful and likely reconstruction of the facts *(ex facto oritur jus)*. Here too, Spanheim and Lenfant provide a prime example because they begin their brief in favor of the existence of the popess with an extremely long relation that absorbs all the chroniclers' excrescences. Moreover, the story that they tell is inserted into known, hence incontestable, contexts. In this manner, the English origin of Joan one or two generations after the conversion of Saxony elicits a description of monastic missions in Britain. As with juridical narrative, the technique is to create belief through a careful amalgam of the certain, the false, and the hypothetical. The use of Joan in an elaboration of this sort is a sign that cracks exist in certain areas of a general historiography established on the soft foundations of narrative categories (drawing causality from chronology, relying on psychology for explanation, confusing the true and the possible).

3. *Alibi.* The defense responds to a line of argumentation based on verisimilitude with a linear chronology of the popes that leaves no place for an extraneous papacy. Because of the temporal uncertainty of the early Middle Ages, however, this argument is insufficient to ward off the possibility that a female pope may have reigned under a male name. Hence the defense has to propose a positive explanation of the legend, which is that the popess is not to be found in the reality of the papacy as an institution, but rather elsewhere, in the imaginary world of the metaphor.

From Panvinio to our own day the defense has offered that alibi, reconstructing the error supposed to have produced a wrong belief. The argument runs thus: collective memory (whatever that may be!) took literally an insulting or mocking metaphor directed at women, and in particular at the mistresses of weak or lustful popes. There were plenty of candidates for the role of a pope mistakenly credited with being a woman. For Wouters (1870) it was John VII; for Baronio, Mai, Hergenroether (1868), and Hefele (1879), it was John VIII; for Weiland and Lapôtre (1895), it was John XI; for Panvinio, Raemond, and Moroni (1845), it was John XII; for Vernet (1911), it was all the popes named John in the ninth century, from John X to John XIII; for Arnaldi (1986), it was the antipope Anastasius Bibliothecarius.[6] For other writers the legend was an ironic denunciation of a presumptuous woman rather than an insult addressed to a pope. For Leone Allacci (1630) and Alfonso Chacón (1677), that woman was the pseudoprophetess Thiota, condemned by the Council of Mainz in 847; for Bishop Suares (quoted by Théophile Reynaud in 1603), this "popess" (against all chronological evidence) was Giovanna, the wife of the antipope Nicolas V (1328); Félix Vernet thought that the famous Marozia, the mother of John XI, fit the bill, for hadn't the chronicler Benedictus of Mont-Soracte said that at the time Rome was ruled by the hand of a woman?[7]

Joan's alibi is offered more casually by Robert Bellarmine and Leibniz, who simply remove the affair from the papal sphere with no explanation. Bellarmine sees the legend as a distortion of a fable from Constantinople regarding a woman patriarch that Leo IX alluded to in 1054 in a letter to the patriarch of Constantinople, Michael Cerularius. Leo states that he does not believe in the existence of the female pope, but he nonetheless uses her as a reason to condemn the Byzantine custom of permitting eunuchs to rise to the patriarchate.[8] Leibniz, always the peacemaker, suggests that the legend refers to some bishop and was subsequently attributed to a pope.

Finally, some historians thought the legend could be explained as an erroneous decoding of theological symbolism (see Cesare D'Onofrio's hypothesis of the misunderstood metaphor for *Mater Ecclesia*). Others thought it satirical allegory (for Carlo Blasco in 1778 and August Friedrich Gförer in 1848, the legend was a mocking personification of the False Decretals); still others, a simple mysterious inscription translated maliciously or naively (Döllinger's thesis).[9]

Some attempted to blame these transpositions on a person or group. For many, the malicious, mischievous spirit of the Roman people played a determinant role; for others it was the Dominicans of a later century who were responsible.

We will not linger over these adventurous and aleatory hypotheses. They do little to explain a silence of two or three centuries before the story suddenly appeared in thirteenth-century narratives. Even if we accept the proposition, suggested earlier, of the legend's existence in a verbal and ritual state in the century before it was written down, what oral memory, however tenacious, could have preserved the story for such a long time?

The judiciary procedures of the controversy elude control by historical discourse because they multiply the subjects involved, whereas history can only determine agents and systems. Putting Joan at the center of a process already in existence sets her up as a subject who must respond for her acts. Taking advantage of the presence of Leibniz in this historiography, we might speak of a veritable "Johannodicy" just as constraining as the "Theodicy" that claims to tie God down to a judiciary evaluation of good and evil in the world. The postulate that the popess did not exist simply replaces the subject under accusation with other subjects who are deceivers, abused, ignorant, mockers, or a wandering ghost bearing an infamous metaphor. These subjects, detached from their time, seek an aleatory anchorage (any John will do) or a mythical connection (to the People, the Greeks, the Germans, the Dominicans, etc.).

In contrast to the judiciary ontology of the popess that has used ideological implications to retain such a firm hold on the episode until recent times, I have tried to offer a historical anthropology of Joan. I hope I will be forgiven an instant of theoretical ambition whose goal is defining a project more than celebrating a task accomplished.

I have attempted to discern the strong, overall significance of the story of Joan in the societies through which it traveled, but also to avoid limiting that significance to ecclesiastical history, folklore, or simple anecdotal curiosity. Legend—this legend (and some others) in particular—has a power to crystalize and precipitate. It has a capacity for guiding how people think that make a "total historical fact" as important (no more, no less) as the price of wheat or a political reform. My reference to anthropology is intended to demand for the historian the virtue of "alienation" that leads anthropologists to realize that the complexity of the societies they study means that they must take just as much care to gain access to the symbolic system as to the social and economic system.

Beyond the true affection that I bear her, the popess seemed to me to offer a convenient entry into worlds of belief very remote from our own, but that convenience cannot be reduced to a simple interest in a case study that permits exhaustive mastery of the materials. Joan varies little as she moves through times and contexts; her history, linked as it is to the perpetuity of the institution of the papacy, is extremely stable. This means that when the popess is used as a reference point, she has the status of a historical object in a first, methodological, sense. She also operates somewhat like a fixed pole around which the moving fields of belief can, at least in part, be organized.[10] Thus she is a historical object in a second, empirical sense as well.

The procedure that I have followed here has been to historicize the legend by a deconstruction (a rejection of the ontological point of view), a multiple contextualization, and a functional reconstruction within signifying nuclei.

The task begun here thus consists in using other poles to examine other partial configurations: the fluid but real entities that I have called systems of belief. In common parlance the term "belief" evokes a content (one believes one dogma or another, one narrative or another) but also an act (adherence or comprehension). It is perhaps more accurate not to speak of an "act" or "activity," but rather, with Jürgen Habermas, of an *acting*, a disposition toward action that conditions it and prescribes its possibilities, constraints, and limits. Belief, seen as a mechanism, is distinct from both its apparatus (which can be as concrete as the parish or as abstract as the sacrament) and ideology, its product. In short, it would be the instrument, concretely and historically determined (the narrative tradition of the popess is one example), that connects the deep and inert levels of *mentalités*, that is, ways people think with the manifest surface of the action (the conduct to be followed during the Great Schism, the condemnation of Rome, etc). That "acting" must not be taken in isolation: it forms a system with other spheres at the boundaries between transitive activity (the transformation of the world) and the activity of representation, where it operates, as we have seen, along with ritual, speculative, aesthetic, and communicative practices. The system of belief is thus shaped differently in each age.

The study of systems of belief must thus aim at three things: the universe of belief, which is made of specific knowledge and historically available representations and is marked by a few poles around which these representations are organized; the various modes of belief, at once succes-sive and concomitant; and the agents of belief, who are its constantly in-teracting producers and consumers.

The interpretation I offer has all the facility and all the danger of any system: abstraction and the arbitrary lie in wait. This is why I have taken on this monographic project, while dreaming of a future cartography of the universes of belief.

It would be sad to abandon Joan with these cold considerations of method. The slight, fugitive form of the popess continues to move through time and appropriations: let us follow her a bit longer.

9

SECOND EPILOGUE

JOAN'S BODY

e have reached the end of this inquiry, but the question with which we started remains unanswered: What is this story of Pope Joan? We have treated it as a being of language, following Wittgenstein's famous adage, "Do not seek significations, seek usage." Joan has, in fact, served us well as a mannequin, a target for thirteenth-century derision or fear; as a case of the obliteration of law or grace by fact (with William of Ockham and the fourteenth-century Franciscans); as a precedent for a pope too many at the time of the Great Schism; as a proof of the Roman Antichrist for the Lutheran sixteenth century; as a joking, merry charge against the Roman Catholic Church in anticlerical witticisms of the French Revolution and the nineteenth century; as a metaphor for female virtualities (praised or dreaded) or for a bewildering human malleability in certain literary versions of her story from Boccaccio to Achim von Arnim.

These uses of Joan's story do not exhaust her being, however. What envelope could be big enough or supple enough to contain her scattered existences? A lazy response to that question would simply place the story within the immense reservoir of "legends." But that would render it banal, treat it as a pretext. The historiographic enterprise that I have attempted here in surveying the uses of Joan fits the famous definition of the novel that Stendhal borrowed from Saint Réal: "A novel is a mirror that one shines along a road." Joan seems to be a truly singular mirror: because it is concave, it focuses the rays projected toward it; rather than reflecting, it concentrates heat and brightness, producing fusion or effusion. Moreover, this terminological neutralization eludes one of the crucial elements of this history, the question of belief. As we have seen, Joan moves through very different registers and modes of belief (belief that seeks veracity, phantasmagoric belief, rational belief, and belief by contract). To subject

310

the episode to norms suspends the dynamic of the narrative essential to its force. Finally, and I do not intend to justify the statement, Joan has a different stature from the paper creatures who people "legends."

Joan's life either falls short of what people say of her or goes beyond it. But what life does she live? The question is not rhetorical. It addresses a glimmer that flickers within our own contemporaries, who usually do not know the previous states of Joan's service. When I happened to mention this project to a friend or colleague, I was never asked why I was taking up the topic (as might have been the case if I had mentioned Prester John or Gog and Magog). An immediate complicity, mocking or warmly approving, seemed to signal a shared experience, a rediscovered familiarity with a being that had been to some extent forgotten, but who was still present. It was as if I had pulled out of my wallet the yellowed photograph of a common cousin who was attractive but scandalous, vaguely extravagant and slightly compromising.

That vague but sure familiarity, that recognition that does not require real knowledge, would perhaps enable us to treat the history of Joan as a myth. Brutally but as if experimentally, we might dare to seize a Christian echo of Tiresias in Joan by stressing the theme of the transgression of gender separation in the story of the popess. That facile choice would have done nothing but annoy: one can just imagine the banal harmonies filling the air at the popess's final procession as she leaves her church and moves toward the great square, the common ground where everything converges. No: thus far, the history of Joan and of the configurations over which she reigned has left no room for universalizing vibratos. But let us play with the idea for a moment, with the proviso that the dissonances of criticism will be heard later.

Tiresias, then. To recall the most common version of the Greek myth: Tiresias, a Theban, was walking on Mount Cyllene when he saw two snakes mating; he separated them, and he was instantaneously turned into a woman. Seven years later he/she returned to the spot and again watched snakes mating; separated them, and immediately became a male once more. These metamorphoses made him famous. Zeus and Hera appealed to him to decide a question that had come up between them: Who, the man or the woman, felt the most pleasure while making love? Tiresias alone could speak from experience. He answered the gods, declaring unhesitatingly that if sexual pleasure were divided into ten parts, the woman would have nine of them. Hera, furious at Tiresias for revealing women's secret, struck him blind, but Zeus, in compensation, gave him the gift of prophecy and promised him long life.

Joan's story contains the same elements but distributes them differently: she moves from female to male and back to female (in her public childbirth); she enjoys the unique privilege of breaking the rule that divides the sexes in the priesthood and the papacy. Both stories show a connection with superior knowledge (Joan's prodigious learning) and blindness (Joan is blindly unaware of her own body, which leads to the scandal of public childbirth). The high stakes involved in the myth of Tiresias would explain the high level of interest in Joan, beyond the personal investments that she attracted. The complicity I have spoken of perhaps comes down to something that radiates from the word "popess," which puts in the feminine a term that was one of the last bastions of the separation of the sexes in the West.

One might object that Joan's story is a truly minor episode that belongs among the "curiosities" of Western history. That "curiosity" should be taken at its full value, however: Tiresias and Joan are indeed curious beings: on the one hand, they are strange, unique beings of whom the divinity is jealous; on the other hand, they are practitioners of the will to know. They express both the need to travel in the black continent of the other sex and the impossibility of doing so; they present the fulfillment of curiosity and the punishment for it.

There is another reason for rejecting the theme of Joan as a female Tiresias: Joan changed her appearance, not her gender. Only eighteenth-century licentious literature found sexual confusion amusing.

Still, if we want to account for the unity that subsumes the very different uses of this episode, we will have to accept the idea that a metastasis of meaning (the various uses) develops from a nucleus that is not directly signifying (do I dare say, that is unconscious?), always present in the name of the popess but never expressed. That structure (an unknown nucleus and metastases of meaning) takes us away from myth, which is a perfectly explicit statement; a permanent, founding narrative that is reactivated metaphorically along the same lines as its original meaning. When Marcel Jouhandeau, somewhat late in life, described his astonished discovery of sodomy, he related his experience in a book that he titled *Tirésias*. According to my hypothesis, Joan's story has no meaning; no intentional, original signification. The Roman archaeology of Joan that was presented in the first three chapters in no way reconstitutes a first, founding intention: carnivalesque inversion had already become custom. The first text, Jean de Mailly's, expressed simple bewilderment; twenty years later, Martinus Polonus gave Joan a jurisprudential meaning by his narration and his commentary. Other narratives (Boccaccio's, for example) substituted other meanings, on the basis of no better traces than the event, as crystalized by the name of popess. I may be taxed with naive realism in suggesting the permanent existence of an unknown nucleus (a Christian Tiresias), but I am not claiming to have discovered a hidden, covered meaning, but only a place where effects of meaning converge geometrically.

To draw a further distinction: The Greek myth and its metaphorical occurrence, the fable, have a universal scope tied to their explicit signification. Joan's story is applicable only within a specific symbolic field—Christianity and its annexes—where the suprasexual but dominantly male status of the priestly and papal figure is located. Moreover, like other Christian narratives, this episode takes place among men and within human history. Joan lived around 854, which much bothered the Lutherans, who did their best to place her at the mythic origins of Rome as Antichrist. Putting Joan in the middle of things was essential. When God became flesh, incarnated as a man at a time remote from the Origin (Genesis), He forced Christians to struggle with all-too-human narratives in which one cannot tell where spirit begins and the letter ends. A lack of canonical authentification (thus a lack of signification) is a shadow that hangs over postevangelical narratives (which are, nonetheless, virtually sacred, for the Parousia arrives without warning). Under such conditions, Joan takes her place among literal beings in search of a spirit (we receive their existence, not their signification), at the side of the saints, prodigies, Judas, the wood of the cross, etc. In Joan the scarlet letter (the color of the cardinalate and of the Whore of Babylon) on Christian flesh is as important for the mark it leaves as it is for the endless deciphering it requires.

Thus we can label the story of Joan a "symbolic object," meaning by the term that its field of belief is not homogeneous, but strongly polarized around points of attraction. The symbolic object is characterized by a certitude of the existence of an uncertain meaning. The force that Joan continues to display (as do many other objects) leads us to suppose that the laicization of the Christian symbolic field produced little change in its contours or in the poles around which it turns.

How are we to approach that unknown nucleus that is constantly replaced by a proliferation of narrated meanings? Georges Bernanos's analogical, nonliteral contemporary version of the Joan story in *A Crime* provides us with one image, one metaphor for that nucleus. Bernanos inverts the proportions of the Joan story: meaning (usage) and the final outcome (strongly loaded with meaning) disappear under the convenient mechanisms of the mystery (in the common sense) that has to be safeguarded in the "mystery story" genre. Romanesque development (which is, once again, favored by the literary constraint of an inquiry that must be long and an outcome that must be unpredictable) is limited to describing the effect of the imposture. We see a woman-priest before her deception is revealed; to the very end, all the characters in the book are unaware of the real sexual identity of the curé. The reader, too, learns only in the brief final chapter of the novel that she is a woman. Within the novel, the woman-priest appears exclusively in the almost physical mark she/he leaves on the other characters. Bernanos constructs a phenomenology of the popess.

The last chapter of A Crime, the only place in the book where the curé is shown to be a woman, gives the reader three successive versions of her last will and testament in three letters that she writes to Evangeline before committing suicide. These three texts, none of which gives the final word on this story, ring changes on the theme of a Christ-like Coming and the betrayal of Judas/Evangeline, who has turned away from the Advent toward an earthly, male love. After her betrayal, her rejection of the Messiah, the void reigns: "'For me alone your long watch, for henceforth you will await no one'" (letter 1). The Parousia remains a threat, however: "'Your life stands open to me: I shall force it when it I choose.'" Evangeline is still her prey (letter 2). The third letter prepares the arrival of the adolescent, the angel's parthenogenetic offspring: "'It pleases me more to leave you, to leave in your life a being so like myself, of a race so akin to mine, so familiar that I recognized him for mine at the first glance.'"[1] All this is in vain: in fact, none of the letters are sent, and the adolescent *clergeon* whom the curé had intended to send to Evangeline commits suicide.

When she is crushed under the wheels of a train, the end of the woman-curé does not bring anything to a conclusion, any more than Christ's Passion does; rather, it leaves the same terror at a missed Opportunity and the same expectation of a Return. Bernanos integrates into the story of Joan the medieval intuition of a divine femaleness (God, Jesus, or the Holy Spirit as a woman). This recalls Guglielma, the Incarnation of the Holy Ghost around 1300, the erotic physiology of the knowledge of God in Hildegard of Bingen, and the veneration of Jesus as a mother among twelfth-century Cistercians. Bernanos's black-cassock version presents, more dramatically than in the white-robed or purple versions centered on the papacy, a Tiresias/Joan who, placing herself for an instant at the point of human contact with the Spirit (the designation of the pope, the ordination of a priest), leaves a vague, floating suspicion, at times muffled, at times shockingly clear, inscribed by the Incarnation (the becoming flesh) at the center of human history. What if neglect of the female or its exile (and the female is a quality as closed to women as it is to men, even though it was highly carnal, *hic et nunc*, the day God was born—of woman or as woman?) had robbed us of nine-tenths of enjoyment and of salvation?

CHRONOLOGICAL BIBLIOGRAPHY OF WORKS

OR FRAGMENTS OF WORKS ABOUT POPE JOAN

~~~~~

ca. 1260   Jean de Mailly. *Chronica universalis Mettensis. MGH, Scriptores,* 24: 514.

ca. 1261   Etienne de Bourbon (Stephanus de Borbone). *Tractatus de diversis materiis praedicabilibus.* MS, B.N. Paris, Latin 15970, fol. 574r.

ca. 1261   Erfurt, Anonymous Franciscan of. *Chronica minor.* Edited by Oswald Holder-Egger. *MGH, Scriptores,* 24: 184, 212.

ca. 1280   Martinus Polonus (Martin of Troppau). *Chronica de Romanis Pontificibus et imperatoribus. MGH, Scriptorum,* 22: 428.

ca. 1280   Maerlant, Jacob van. *Spiegel Historiael.* Leiden, 1857, 3: 220.

ca. 1280   Enikel, Jansen. *Weltchronik.* Edited by Philipp Strauch. *MGH, Scriptores qui vernacula lingua usi sunt, Deutsche Chroniken,* 3: 434.

ca. 1290   *Flores temporum.* Franciscan chronicle. *MGH, Scriptores,* 24: 248.

1293   Robert d'Uzès. *Le livre de visions.* In Jeanne Bignami Odier, "Les Visions de Robert d'Uzès." *Archivum Fratrum Praedicatorum* 25 (1955): 258–320, esp. 274.

ca. 1295   Geoffroy de Courlon. *Chronique de l'Abbaye de Saint-Pierre-le-Vif de Sens.* Edited by Gustave Julliot. Sens, 1876, 296–99.

ca. 1297   Jacopo da Voragine. *Chronica Januensis.* See *Iacopo de Varagine e la sua Cronaca di Genova dalle origini al MCCXCVII.* Edited by Giovanni Monleone. Rome, 1941, 2: 4.

ca. 1300   Martinus Polonus. *Cronica.* Variant. *MGH, Scriptorum,* 22: 428.

ca. 1304   Siegfried of Balhusen (or of Meissen). *Compendium historiarum, MGH, Scriptorum,* 25: 684.

ca. 1307   Arnoldus of Liège. *Alphabetum narrationum.* In Colette Ribeaucourt, "L'Alphabetum Narrationum: Un recueil d'exempla compilé au début du XIVe siècle." *Thèse,* Université de Paris X-Nanterre, 1985.

ca. 1312   Tolomeo da Lucca. *Historia ecclesiastica. Rerum Italicarum Scriptores.* Edited by Ludovico Antonio Muratori. Milan, 1717, XI, 2: 1013–14.

ca. 1315–25   Gui, Bernard. *Catalogus Pontificum Romanorum cum inserta temporum historia.* Fragment. *Spicilegium Romanum.* Edited by Angelo Mai. Rome, 1823–38, 6: 202.

ca. 1315   Heinrich von München. *Weltchronik.* Fragments. *Die Weltchronik*

Heinrichs von München in der Runkelsteiner Handschrift des Heinz Sentlinger. Edited by Paul Gichtel. Munich, 1937, 391–92.

ca. 1315   Leone da Orvieto. *Chronica.* In *Deliciae eruditorum seu Veterum ANEKΔΟΤΩΝ opusculorum collectanea.* Edited by Giovanni Lami. Florence, 1737, 3: 337.

ca. 1316   Colonna, Landolfo. *Breviarium historiarum.* MS B.N. Paris, Latin 4912. The same fragment appears in the anonymous compilation, *Breviarium historiale.* Poitiers, 1479.

ca. 1318   Sozomenus of Pistoia. *Historiae.* Fragment quoted in Jean Mabillon, *Iter Italicum.* Paris, 1687, 173.

ca. 1330   Higden, Ranulf. *Polychronicon.* Edited by Churchill Babington and Joseph Rawson Lumby. London, 1876, 6: 330.

1332   William of Ockham. *Opus nonaginta dierum.* Edited by J. G. Sykes et al. *Guillelmi de Ockam Opera politica.* Edited by R. F. Bennet and H. S. Offler. London, 1940, volume 1.

ca. 1340   William of Ockham. *Octo quaestiones de potestate Papae. Opera politica.* Manchester, 1963, 2: 854.

ca. 1340   Johannes of Winterthur. *Chronica. MGH, Scriptores rerum germanicarum, Nova series,* 3: 33.

ca. 1340   Barlaam of Seminara (Baralaam Calabro). *On the Power of the Pope* (Περὶ τῆς τοῦ Πάπα ἀρχῆς). *Pat. Graeca.* Volume 151, column 1274.

1362   Boccaccio, Giovanni. *De mulieribus claris.* Edited by Vittorio Zaccaria. *Tutte le opere di Giovanni Boccaccio.* Edited by Vittore Branca. Second edition, Milan, 1970, chapter 101, pages 414–19.

1362   Amalric d'Augier. *Actus Pontificum Romanorum. Corpus Historicum Medii Aevi.* Edited by Johan Georg von Eckhart. Leipzig, 1723, 1627.

1366   *Eulogium historiarum sive temporum.* Edited by Frank Scott Haydon. London, 1858–63, 1: 243.

ca. 1368   Stefano da Nardo. *Chronica. Rerum Italicarum Scriptores.* Edited by Ludovico Antonio Muratori. Milan, 1738, 24: 885–87.

1369   Golein, Jean. French translation of a *De Romanis Pontificibus.* Vatican Library, MS Reg. Lat. 697, fol. 38v.

ca. 1370   Petrarca, Francesco. *Cronica delle vite de Pontifici et imperatori Romani.* Venice, 1507, 55; Strasbourg, 1555; Frankfurt, 1624.

ca. 1370   Jacopo d'Acqui. *Chronicon imaginis mundi. Historiae Patriae Monumenta. Scriptores,* volume 5, columns 1357–1626.

ca. 1379   Johannes, abbot of Viktring. *Liber certarum historiarum. MGH, Scriptores rerum germanicarum.* Hannover, 1909–10, 1: 106–7.

1382   Gerson, Jean. *De jurisdictione spirituali.* Gerson, *Opera.* Edited by Louis Ellies Du Pin. Paris, 1704, 2: 207.

1382   Wycliffe, John. *Cruciata. John Wiclif's Polemical Works in Latin.* Edited by Rudolf Buddensieg. London, 1883, 2: 618–19.

ca. 1386   Philippe de Mézières. *Le songe du Vieil Pèlerin.* Edited by George William Coopland. Cambridge, 1969, 1: 338, 370.

ca. 1386   Bonet, Honoré. *L'arbre des batailles.* Paris, 1493. Among the many subsequent editions, see that of Ernest Nys. Brussels and Leipzig, 1883, 21–22.

ca. 1386   Twinger, Jacob, of Köngshofen. *Chronicke.* Augsburg, 1476, 1480; Strasbourg, 1698, 179.

ca. 1386   *Österreische chronik von den 95 herrschaften.* Edited by Joseph Seemüller. *MGH, Scriptorum qui vernacula lingua usi sunt: Deutsche chroniken.* Volume 6, 82.

ca. 1399   Amaury du Peyrat. *Chronique.* Fragment. *Notes et extraits des manuscrits de la Bibliothèque Nationale.* Paris, 6: 82.

Fourteenth century: Interpolations to the *Liber pontificalis*

Interpolation. *Liber pontificalis.* Edited by Louis Duchesne. Paris, 1892, 2: xxvi. New editions, 3 volumes, Paris: Thorin, 1955–57; 3 volumes: Boccard, Paris, 1981.

Interpolation. Marianus Scotus. *Chronicon.* In *Scriptorum qui rerum a Germanis gestarum historias reliquerunt.* Edited by Johann Pistorius. Frankfurt, 1583, 442.

Interpolation, Sigebert von Gembloux. *Chronographia.* In Pistorius, ed., *Scriptorum qui rerum,* 565.

Interpolation. Otto of Freising. *Chronica.* In *Germaniae historicorum illustrium ab Henrico IV ad annum 1400.* Edited by Johann Pistorius. Frankfurt, 1585, 1: 163.

Interpolation. Richard of Poitiers. *Chronique.* In *Histoire littéraire de la France.* Paris, 1869, 12: 479; 13: 534.

Interpolation. Geoffroy of Viterbo. *Pantheon sive Memoriae saecolorum.* *Pat. Latina.* Volume 198, column 1017.

Interpolation. Gervase of Tilbury. *Otia Imperialia.* MS mentioned in Paul Colomiès, *Mélanges historiques.* Orange, 1675, 57.

Fourteenth century:

Chronica Campidonense (Chronicle of the Abbey of Kempten). *Lectiones memorabiles et reconditae.* Edited by Johannes Wolf. Second edition, Frankfurt, 1671, 177.

Abbey of Tegernsee. Cod. Lat. 781. In Johann Joseph Ignaz von Döllinger. *Die Papst-Fabeln des Mittelalters: Ein Betrag zur Kirchengeschichte.* Second edition, Stuttgart, 1890, 440–41 n. 6.

Early fifteenth century:

Arnoldus of Liège. *Alphabetum narrationum.* Catalan adaptation. *Recull de eximplis e miracles, gestes et faules e altres ligendes ordenades per ABC.* Edited by A. Verdaguer. Barcelona, 1881, 147. English translation. *An Alphabet of Tales.* Edited by Mary Macleod Banks. London, 1904–5.

1403   Gerson, Jean. Sermon. "Apparuit" ("De Pace"). Gerson, *Oeuvres complètes*. Edited by Palémon Glorieux. Paris, 1960–65, 5: 64–90, especially pages 86–87.

ca. 1405   Adam of Usk. *Chronicon*. Fragment. Ugo Balzani, "La storia di Roma nella Cronica di Adamo da Usk." *Archivio della Società Romana di Storia Patria* 3 (1880): 473–88.

ca. 1410   Jacopo d'Angelo of Scarperia. Letter to Emmanuel Chrysoloras. In appendix to *Leonardi Dathi . . . Epistolae XXXIII*. Edited by Lorenzo Mehus. Florence, 1743.

1412   Hus, Jan. *De Ecclesia*. Mainz, 1520, 46.

ca. 1412   Dietrich of Nieheim. *Historia de gestis Romanorum Principum*. Edited by Katharina Colberg and Joachim Leuschner. Stuttgart, 1980, 27–28.

ca. 1415   Roques, Jean (Jean de Rocha). *Contra evasiones Johannis de Gersono super suis assertionibus erroneis*. Jean Gerson. *Opera omnia*. Edited by Louis Ellies Du Pin. Antwerp, 1706, 5: 456.

1415   Hus, Jan. Declarations at his trial during the Council of Constance. See Matthew Spinka. *John Hus at the Council of Constance*. New York and London, 1965, 192, 209, 212.

ca. 1423   Engelhusen, Dietrich. *Chronicon Theodorici Engelhusii*. *Scriptores Brunsvicienses*. Edited by Gottfried Wilhelm von Leibniz. Hannover, 1707–11, 2: 1065.

ca. 1435   Korner, Hermann. *Chronica novella*. *Corpus historicorum Medii Aevi*. Edited by Johann Georg von Eckart. Leipzig, 1723, 2: 442.

ca. 1441   Stadtweg, Johan. Chronicle in Lower Saxon dialect. Leibniz, ed., *Scriptores Brunsvicienses*, 3: 263.

ca. 1447   Hemmerli, Felix (Malleolus). *De nobilitate et rusticitate dialogus*. N.p., n.d., fol. 99.

ca. 1450   Lefranc, Martin. *Le champion des dames*. Paris, 1530, fol. 335.

ca. 1450   Rucellai, Giovanni. *Della bellezza e anticaglia di Roma*. In *Codice topografico della città di Roma*. Edited by Roberto Valentini and Giuseppe Zucchetti. Rome, 1953, 4: 407.

ca. 1450   Antoninus, archbishop of Florence. *Chronica Antonini*. Lyon, 1543, fol. 148.

1451   Piccolomini, Enea Silvio. Letter to Juan de Carvajal. *Die Briefwechsel des Eneas Silvius Piccolomini*. Edited by Rudolf Wolkan. Vienna, 1918, III, 1: 36.

ca. 1455   Torquemada, Tomás de. *Summa de Ecclesia*. Venice, 1561, 394–95.

ca. 1455   Alonso de Cartagena. *Recapitulationes*. Chapter 56.

ca. 1455   Palmieri, Matteo. *Liber de temporibus*. Basel, 1570, 112. Edited by Gino Scaramella. *Rerum Italicarum Scriptores*. Città di Castello, 1903.

1462   *Chronicle of Ulm*. Ulm, 1482, fol. 22.

ca. 1464   Chalcocondylas, Laonicos. *Historiarum de origine ac rebus gestis Tur-carum*, IV. *Pat. Graeca*, volume 159, columns 299–302.

ca. 1464   Janus Pannonius. Epigram VIII. *Epigrammata*. Venice, 1544, 70.

ca. 1470   Brewyn, William. *De septum . . . Ecclesiis Romae.* In *Commentarius de scriptoribus ecclesiae antiquis illorumque scriptis.* Edited by Casimir Oudin. Leipzig, 1722, 3: 2678.

1472   Platina, Bartolomeo (Bartolomeo Sacchi). *Vitae Pontificum (Liber de vita Christi ac omnium Pontificum).* Venice, 1479. Many subsequent editions. See also the modern edition by Giacinto Gaida. *Rerum Italicarum Scriptores.* Bologna, 1932, 1: 151–52.

1473   Boccacce, Jean (Giovanni Boccaccio). *De la louange et vertu des nobles et claires dames.* Paris, 1473. This was the first print edition of *De mulieribus claris.*

1474   Rolevinck, Werner. *Fasciculus temporum.* Cologne, 1474. Many later editions and translations.

ca. 1474   *Chronica S. Ægidii in Brunswig.* Leibniz, ed., *Scriptores Brunsvicienses,* 3: 580.

ca. 1474   Kemnat, Mathias. *Chronicle.*

1474   Riccobaldo of Ferrara (ninth century). *Cronica summorum pontificum imperatorumque.* Edited by Joannes Philippus de Lignamine with an interpolation mentioning Pope Joan. Rome, 1474. This is the first printed trace of the Joan story.

ca. 1480   Marulić, Marko, of Split (Marcus Marullus Spalatensis). Epigram. Wolf, ed., *Lectiones memorabiles,* 1: 187.

ca. 1480   *Chronicon Episcoporum Verdensium* (Chronicle of the Bishops of Werden). Leibniz, ed., *Scriptores Brunsvicienses,* 2: 211.

ca. 1480   Schernberg, Dietrich. *Fraw Jutta.* Published in 1565 (see at that date).

1484   Maino, Jason. *In Digestum et Codicem commentarium.* Dig. Vet., book I, title 14, law 3, note 64. Venice, 1573–74.

1485   Fregoso, Battista. *De gestis et dictis memorabilibus.* Venice, 1485; Cologne, 1726, fol. 254v.

1486   Foresti, Jacopo Filippo, of Bergamo. *Supplementum chronicis libri II.* Venice, 1486, year 858, fol. 262b.

1486   Burchard, Johann. *Diarium.* Edited by Louis Thuasne. Paris, 1883, 1: 233.

1489   Bothone, Conrado. *Chronicon Brunsvicensium picturatum.* Leibniz, ed., *Scriptores Brunsvicienses,* 3: 299.

1490   Battista Mantovano. *Alfonsus. Baptisae Mantuani Opera omnia.* Bologna, 1502, fol. 279v.

1492   Corio, Bernardino. *Storia di Milano.* Milan, 1503, R IIIIv.

1493   Schedel, Hartmann. *"Nuremberg Chronicle" (Chronicarum liber).* Nuremberg, 1493, fol. 169.

1495   Trithemius, Johannes (Trithemius). *Chronica Monasterii Hirsaugiensis.* Fragment. Wolf, ed., *Lectiones memorabiles,* 1: 181.

ca. 1497   Le Jards, Jean (Lazardius). *Epitome historibus ecclesiasicis.* 2: 3.

1497   Foresti, Jacopo Filippo, of Bergamo. *De plurimis mulieribus claris.* Ferrara, 1497, fol. 133.

1499   *Chronicle of Cologne.* Cologne, 1499, fol. 199a.

Late fifteenth–early sixteenth century:

            Several works entitled *Mirabilia urbis Romae* or *Indulgentiae.* See Valenti and Zucchetti, eds., *Codice topografico della Città di Roma,* 1958.

ca. 1500   Naucler, Jean (Johannes Nauclerus). *Chronica.* Cologne, 1544, 649.

ca. 1501   Equicola d'Alveto, Mario (Olivetanus). *De mulieribus.*

1501   Bade, Josse. *Ascensius.* Paris, 1501, volume 3, fol. 26.

ca. 1503   Krantz, Albert (Cranzius). *Ecclesiastica historia sive Metropolis.* Cologne, 1575, II, 1: 40.

1504   Coccio, Marco Antonio (Sabellico). *Enneades.* Venice, 1504; Basel, 1560, volume 2, column 625.

1505   Stella, Johannes. *Vitae Pontificum.* Venice, 1505, 108.

ca. 1506   Maffei, Raffaele (Volterranus). *Anthropologia.* Basel, 1544, fol. 252.

1507   Pico della Mirandola, Giovanni. *Tractatus de Fide.* Strasbourg, 1507.

1511   Le Maire de Belges, Jean. *Traité de la différence des schismes et des conciles de l'Eglise.* Lyon, 1511, part III, 2.

1513   Tarcagnota, Giovanni. *Delle historie del mondo.* Venice, 1580; 1586–93, 2: 374–75.

1513   Tiraqueau, André. *De legibus connubialibus.* Paris, 1561, 298.

1514   Murner, Thomas. *Badenfahrt.* Strasbourg, 1514. Edited by Ernst Martin. Strasbourg, 1877.

1515   Floriszoon, Adrien (later Pope Adrian VI). *Quaestiones quotlibeticae.* Qu. XI. Louvain, 1515, 1518; Paris, 1527, 1531; Lyon, 1546. See the edition of Paris, 1531, fol. 246v.

1516   Ricchieri, Lodovico (Coelius Rhodiginus). *Lectionum antiquarium libri XVI.* Venice, 1516, fol. 370. This work was also published in Paris and in Basel.

ca. 1517   Giacobazzi, Domenico. *Tractatus de Concilio.* In *Sacrorum Consiliorum nova et amplissima collectio.* Edited by Giovanni Domenico Mansi. Paris and Rome, 1870, 400. This edition is based on the seventeenth-century edition by Philippe Labbé and Gabriel Cossart.

1517   Mariano da Firenze. *Itinerarium urbis Romae.* Edited by Enrico Buletti. Rome, 1931, 169.

1517   Vellius, Caspar Ursinus. *Monosticha.* Louvain, 1532, fol. DIr.

1518   Friedlieb, Franz (Irenicus). *Germaniae exegesos volumina XII.* Nuremberg, 1518; Basel, 1567; Frankfurt, 1570, 2: 3.

1519   Murner, Thomas. *Die Gäuchmatt.* Basel, 1519. Edited by Wilhelm Uhl. Leipzig, 1896, 89–90.

1519   Ebser, Johann, bishop of Chiemsee. *Onus Ecclesiae.* Chapter XIX. Landshut, 1524; Cologne, 1531, fol. 34v.

1522   Pauli, Johannes. *Schimpf und Ernst.*

1522   Turmair, Johannes (Aventinus). *Annalium Boiorum.* Nuremberg, 1522. Ingolstadt, 1554; 1580, 368.

1524   Texier, Jean, de Ravisy (Johannes Ravisius Textor). *Officina prima pars.* 1524; Venice, 1541, fols 147–48.

ca. 1525   Egidio da Viterbo. *Historia XX Saeculorum.* In François Secret, "Notes sur Egidio de Viterbe." *Augustiniana* 27 (1977): 299–30.

1528   Molther, Menrad. *Romanorum Pontificum omnium, a S. Petro, ad Clemente VII, usque, vita et mores.* Speyer, 1528.

1529   Chasseneux, Barthélemy de. *Catalogus gloriae mundi.* Lyon, 1529; 1546, part 2, cons. 9, no. 33, fol. 52v.

1530   Agrippa von Netteshein, Heinrich Cornelius. *Declamatio de nobilitate et praecellentia foeminei sexus.* Chapter 32.

1531   Valeriano Bolzani, Giovanni Pierio. *Pro sacerdotum barbis.* Rome, 1531; 1621, 9.

1534   *Biblia.* Translated by Martin Luther. Illustration for Revelation 17.

1534   Seidenstücker, Paulus "Constantinus" (Phrygius). *Chronicum.* Basel, 1534, 402.

1537   Johannes Lucidus. *Emendationes Temporum.* Venice, 1537, fol. 62r. Other Venice editions, 1545, 1575.

1539   Du Moulin, Charles. *Commentaire sur la coutume de Paris.* Paris, 1539; 1603, title I, no. 26, p. 8.

1540   Nevizzano, Giovanni. *Sylvae nuptialis.* Venice, 1540, 277. Other editions, Venice, 1570, 1572; Lyon, 1545; Frankfurt, 1647, 4: 19.

1540   Massacus, Chrétien (Christianus Massaeus). *Chronicorum.* Antwerp, 1540, 211.

1540   Ryd, Valerius Anselmus. *Catalogus annorum et principum.* Bern, 1540.

ca. 1540   Luther, Martin. *Tischreden.* In French translation as *Propos de table.* Translated by Louis Sauzin. Paris, 1932, 292.

ca. 1540   Schrott, Martin. *Von der Erschrocklichen Zurstorung des Bapstums.* See Robert W. Scribner, *For the Sake of Simple Folk.* Cambridge, 1981, 172.

1541   Bouchet, Jean. *Annales d'Aquitaine.* Poitiers, 1541, volume 2, fol. 61a.

1542	Mexia, Pedro. *Silva de varia Lección.* Seville, 1542. Many editions and translations into French, Latin, Italian, Flemish, etc.
1542	Scultetus, Alexander. *Chronographia.* Rome, 1546, fol. 7.
1546	Carranza, Bartolomé. *Summa omnium Conciliorum et Pontificum.* Venice, 1546; Lyon, 1587 (?), fol. 229v.
1545	Rabelais, François. *Le tiers livre.* Paris, 1546. Edited by Pierre Michel. Paris, 1996, 189.
1548	Rabelais, François. *Le quart livre.* Paris, 1548. Edited by Robert Marichal. Geneva, 1947, 199–200.
1548	Bale, John. *Illustrium majoris Britanniae scriptores Summarium.* Basel, 1548, fol. 62; Basel, 1557, 118.
1549	Wassebourg, Richard de. *Antiquitez de la Gaule Belgicque, Royaulme de France, Austrasie & Lorraine.* Paris, 1549, fol. 3.
1550	Muntzer, Valentin. *Chronographia.* Cologne, 1550, fol. 60.
1550	Vitalis, Janus. *Elogium Papum.* N.p., 1550.
1550	Alberti, Leandro. *Descrittione di tutta Italia.* Bologna, 1550; Venice, 1561. Latin edition, Cologne, 1564, 167.
1551	Gilles, Nicole. *Annales et chronique des Gaules.* Paris, 1551, fol. 66b.
1553	Guazzo, Marco. *Cronica.* Venice, 1553, fol. 176a.
1554	Egnazio, Giovanni Battista. *De Exemplis.* Venice, 1554, 97, 246, 265.
1556	Alfonso de Castro. *De justa haereticorum punitione.* Antwerp, 1556.
1556	[Vergerio, Pier Paolo]. *Historia di Papa Giovanni VIII che fu femina.* N.p. [Tübingen], 1556.
1557	[Vergerio, Pier Paolo]. *Historia di papa Giovanni VIII che fu meretrice e strega.* Tübingen, 1557. Republished in 1562, this work was translated into French in 1557, into German in 1559, into Latin in 1560, and into English in 1584.
1557	Curio, Jakob (Hosemius). *Chronologicarum rerum liber.* Basel, 1557.
1558	Sachs, Hans. *Historia von Johanna Anglica, der bäpstin.* In *Hans Sachs.* Edited by Adelbert von Keller, Stuttgart, 1874, 8: 652–55.
ca. 1560	Soto, Domingo de. *In quartum sententiarum librum.* Dist. XXV, quaest. 1, art. 2. Louvain, 1573; Venice, 1575, 1598; Douai, 1613.
1560	Pasquier, Etienne. *Recherches de la France.* 1560. Paris, 1596, fols 103, 262b.
1562	Panvinio, Onofrio. Revision of Platina, *Vitae Pontificum.* Venice, 1562. Italian translation, Venice, 1563. Many subsequent editions.
1564	Carion, Johannes. *Libri III chronicarum.* Basel, 1564, 372.
1564	Marconville, Jean de. *Traité de la bonté et de la mauvaiseté des femmes.* Paris, 1564, 51.
1565	*Ecclesiastica historia . . . congesta, per aliquot studiosos et pios viros in*

urbe Magdeburgica ("Magdeburg Centuries"). Magdeburg, 1565, 5: 333, 357.

1565   Tilesius, Hieronymus. *Apotheoses von Johann VIII*, an edition of Dietrich Schernberg, *Fraw Jutta*. Eisleben, 1565. See also *Dietrich Schernbergs Spiel von Frau Jutten (1480) nach der einzigen Uerberlieferung im Druck des Hieronimus Tilesius (Eisleben 1565)*. Edited by Edward Schröder. Bonn, 1911.

1566   Cope, Alan. *Dialogi sex contra Pontificatus oppugnatores.* Antwerp, 1566, 46–48.

1570   Genebrard, Gilbert. *Chronographia.* Louvain, 1570; Lyon, 1609, 538–40.

1572   Frantz, Laurent Albert (Franzius). *Bericht vom Pabst Johanne VIII, welcher soll ein Weib gewesen seyn.* Dillengen, 1572.

1576   Rioche, Jean. *Compendium temporum et historiarum ecclesiasticarum.* Paris, 1576, fol. 230v.

1577   Girard, Bernard de, seigneur du Haillan. *Histoire de France.* Paris, 1577, 1: 451–52.

1578   Cornelis de Dordrecht. *Sermones.* Bruges, 1578, 2: 452.

1580   Rosières, François de. *Stemmatum Lotharingiae ac Barri ducum tomi VII.* Paris, 1580, fol. 178a.

1580   Forcadel, Etienne de. *De Gallorum Imperio et philosophia, libri septem.* Paris, 1580, book VII, 477–78.

1583   Osiander, Lucas. *Bedencken ob der newe päpstliche Kalender ein Nottdurfft bey der Christenheit seie.* Tübingen, 1583, 19.

1584   Scherer, Georg. *Grundlicher Bericht ob es wahr sey, dass auf ein Zeit ein Pabst zu Rom schwanger gewesen und ein Kind gebohren habe.* Vienna and Ingolstadt, 1584. Italian translation, Venice and Milan, 1586.

1586   Belley, Pierre. *Moyen d'abus contre la bulle de Sixte V.* Paris, 1586.

1586   Bellarmine, Robert. *Disputationes de controversiis christianae fidei.* Ingolstadt, 1586, I, III, chapter 24.

1587   Raemond, Florimond de. *L'erreur populaire de la papesse Jeanne.* Bordeaux, 1587. Twelve editions in French and Latin from 1587 to 1614 at Paris, Bordeaux, Lyon, Cambrai, Cologne, and Antwerp.

1588   *Simplex narratio . . . exponens meretriculam quamdam Anglam nunquam papam fuisse.* Strasbourg, 1588.

1588   [Witekind, Hermann]. *Jesuitas pontificis maximi Romani emissarios, falso et frustra negare papam Joannem VIII fuisse mulierem.* N.p., 1588; second edition, 1588; German translation, 1598.

1591   Mayo, John. *An Anatomie of Pope Joan.* London, 1591; 1594.

1596   Elfenhold, Elias. *Confutatio der Jesuiten, das sie mit verschwiegener Wahrheit dürfften fürgeben, Johannes IIX sey kein Wiebes-Bild gewesen.* N.p., 1596.

1597   Boissard, Jean-Jacques. *Romanae urbis topographiae et antiquitatum.* Frankfurt, 1597–1602, 1: 70.

1598   [Perkins, William]. *Assertio contra Jesuitas, papam Johannem VIII fuisse mulierem.* London, 1598.

1599   *The Romaine Jubilee of 855.* London, 1599.

1602   Baronio, Cesare (Baronius). *Annales ecclesiastici.* Rome, 1602, volume 10.

1606   Doglioni, Giovanni Nicolò. *Theatrum universale principum.* Venice, 1606, 1: 413.

1606   Binius, Severinus. *Concilia Generalia.* Cologne, 1606, 3: 657.

1609   Herrenschmidt, Jacob. *Papa mulier, sive vera et infaillibilis narratio de papa Johanne VIII femina.* Wittenberg, 1609, 1611, 1643.

1610   Cooke, Alexander. *Pope Joane, a dialogue between a Protestant and a Papist proving that a woman called Joane was Pope of Rome against the surmises and to the contrarie objections made by Robert Bellarmine and Caesar Baronius.* London, 1610, 1622. Latin translation, 1616. French translation, 1633.

1611   Laval, Sylvain de. *Les justes grandeurs de l'Eglise romaine.* Paris, 1611.

1611   Fauchet, Claude. *Les Antiquités et histoires gauloises et françaises.* Geneva, 1611, 701.

1612   Decker, Conrad. *Liber de papa Romano et papissa Romana.* Oppenheim, 1612.

1612   Sanders, Nicholas (Nicolas Sanderus). *De papa Romano et papissa Romana Demonstrationes.* Oppenheim, 1612.

1614   Serarius, Nicolaus. *Tractatus de Joanna papissa.* Cologne, 1614.

1614   Nicolaï, H. *Vom Pabst Johann VII, dass er eine Frau gewesen.* Goslar, 1614, 161.

1616   Aubigné, Théodore Agrippa d'. *Histoire universelle.* Edited by Alphonse de Ruble. Paris, 1886, 185.

1624   *The Anatomie of Pope Joan.* London, 1624. This work is possibly a reprint of John Mayo, 1591.

1624   *Partus Papae prodigiosus perpetuo P productus.* 1624.

1630   Allacci, Leone (Allatius). *Confutatio fabulae de papissa Joanna ex monumentis graecis.* Rome, 1630. Enlarged edition, edited by Bartold Nihus. Cologne, 1654; Rome, 1650. The text is reprinted in Allatius, *Opera,* Rome, 1653, volume 2.

1630   Chacón, Alfonso (Ciaconius). *Vitae et res gestae Pontificum Romanorus et S.R.E. cardinalium.* Rome, 1630; 1677, 1: 631–32.

1631   Stalen, Johann (Stalenus). *Een corte doch grondticke Resolutie op de vrage wat sekere historie van Paus Johanna ofte Jutta te houden.* Rees, 1631.

1633   La Salle, Jean de. *Confutatio Joannae papissae.* Louvain, 1633.

1633   La Montagne, Jean de. *La Papesse Jeanne, ou Dialogue entre un protestant et un papiste.* Seden, 1633. This work is an adaptation in French of Alexander Cooke, *Pope Joane*, 1610.

1635   Grim, Egbert. *Pauselicke Heiligheit, dat is Catholyck ende authentyck vertoogh dat Joannes, gemeenlick Paus Iutte genoemt, een vrouwe gesweest is.* Wesel, 1635.

1639   Stalen, Johann (Stalenus). *Papissa monstrosa et mera fabula, sive dissertatio historico-theologica.* Cologne, 1639.

1640   Hulsemann, Johann. *De Ecclesia papistica non habente successionem episcoporum continuam.* Wittenberg, 1640, 1689.

1641   Naudé, Gabriel. Letter to Jacques Dupuy. *Lettres de Gabriel Naudé à Jacques Dupuy: 1632–1653.* Edited by Phillip Wolfe. Edmonton, 1982, Letter 43, 132–34.

1641   Ehinger, Elias. *Dissertatio de papa mulieri sive de papa Joanna VIII.* Augsburg, 1641, 1724.

1645   Banck, Lars. *Roma Triumphans, seu actio inaugurationum et coronationum Pontificum Romanorum, et in specie Innocentii X P.M., brevis descriptio.* Frankfurt, 1645, 1656.

1647   Blondel, David. *Familier esclaircissement de la Question, si une Femme a esté assise au Siège Papal de Rome entre Léon IV et Benoît III.* Amsterdam, 1647. Enlarged edition, Amsterdam, 1649. Latin translation, with preface by Etienne de Courcelles, Amsterdam, 1657. Dutch translation, Amsterdam, 1650.

1648   Nihus, Bartold. *Hypodigma.* Cologne, 1648, 213.

1650   *Gespräch ob es wahr sey, dass ein Weib zu Rom sey Papst gewesen.* N.p., 1650.

1655   Capel, Rudolph. *Discursus historicus de Joanna VIII papissa.* Giesen, 1655.

1655   Congnard, Nicolas. *Traité contre l'esclaircissement donné par Blondel en la question, si une femme a esté assise au siège papal de Rome entre Léon IV et Benoît III.* Saumur, 1655.

1658   Des Marets, Samuel (Maresius). *Joanna papissa restituta, sive animadversiones et annotationes historicae ad Dav. Blondelli . . . librum posthumum.* Gröningen, 1658.

1660   Labbé, Philippe. *Cenotaphium Ioannae papissae, ab heterodoxis . . . et utopia in Europam nuper revocatae, eversum funditusque excisum demonstratione chronica.* In Labbé, *De Scriptores ecclesiasticis.* Paris, 1660, 1: 835–1006, and in his *Concilia.* Paris, 1672, 8: 150–222.

1661   Des Marets, Samuel (Maresius). *Animadversiones chronologicae in Joannam papissam.* Gröningen, 1661.

1662   Bernegger, Matthias. *Historiae Joannis VIII, Romani pontificis, virum primo simulantis, postea sexum suum partu in publica via editio prodentis.* Helmstadt, 1662, 1667; Leiden, 1677.

1663   Reynaud, Théophile. *Dissertatio de sobria alterius sexus frequentatione per sacros et religiosos homines.* Lyon, 1663, 465.

1666   Chifflet, Jean-Jacques (Chiffletius). *Judicium de fabula Joannae papissae.* Antwerp, 1666.

1669   Lehmann, Johann. *Infelix puerpera Johannes VIII pontifex dissertatione historica exhibita.* Wittenberg, 1669.

1669   Voet, Gisbert (Gisbertus Voetius). *Spicilegium ad disceptationem historicam de papissa Joanna.* Utrecht, 1669.

1673   Artopoeus, Johannes Daniel. *Dissertatio de Joanna VIII papissa.* Leipzig, 1673.

1675   *A Present for a Papist, or The Life and Death of Pope Joan.* London, 1675.

1678   Diecmann, Johann. *De primis et antiquissimis Johannae papissae praeconibus.* Stade, 1678.

1678   *Päpstlich Kindbett, oder Zeugniss dass Pabst Johann VIII eine Weibsperson gewesen.* Munich, 1678.

1678   *Zerstörung des also falschlich papstlichen offenbaren Kindbettes . . . oder Widerlegung der Fabel vom Papst Johannes dem achten.* Vahrstadt, 1678.

1680   Settle, Elkanah. *The Female Prelate, Being the History of the Life and Death of Pope Joan.* London, 1680, 1689.

1683   Jurieu, Pierre. *Histoire du calvinisme et celle du papisme.* Rotterdam, 1683, part III, *Histoire du papisme.*

1688–98   Cave, William. *Scriptorum ecclesiasticorum historia literaria.* London, 1688–98. Oxford, 1740–43, 2: 323.

1689   *Pope Joan, or, An Account out of Romish Authors before and since Luther . . . that there was a She Pope who sat in that See and Ruled the Same.* London, 1689.

1691   Spanheim, Friedrich. *Disquisitio historica de papa foemina inter Leonem IV et Benedictum III.* Leiden, 1691. Many subsequent editions. Adaptation in French by Jacques Lenfant, 1694.

1691   Misson, François Maximilien. *Voyage d'Italie.* Paris, 1691; 1694, 2: 180–212.

1694   Lenfant, Jacques. *Histoire de la papesse Jeanne, fidèlement tirée de la dissertation latine de Fred. Spanheim.* Cologne, 1694. Edited, with notes, by Alphonse de Vignoles. The Hague, 1720, 1736, 1758. German translation, Frankfurt and Leipzig, 1737.

1695   Bayle, Pierre. *Dictionnaire historique et critique.* 1695–97; s.v. "Papesse (Jeanne la)."

ca. 1695   Leibniz, Gottfried Wilhelm. *Flores spersi in tumulum papissae.* In *Bibliotheca Historica Goettingensis.* Edited by Christian Ludwig Scheidt. Göttingen, 1758, 297–392.

ca. 1695   Leibniz, Gottfried Wilhelm. Letter. In Jacques André Emery. *Pensées sur la religion et la morale.* Second edition of *Esprit de Leibniz.* Paris, 1803, 2: 417.

1699   Basnage, Jacques. *Histoire de l'Eglise depuis Jésus-Christ jusquà présent.* Rotterdam, 1699, 1: 408.

1699   Haendel, Christophe Christian. *Dissertatio de Joanne VIII, pontifice optimo maximo, qui foemina fuit sexum mentita.* Wittenberg, 1699.

1711   *Beweis das ehedessen eine Frau.* N.p., 1711.

1721   Fabricius, Johann Albert. *Bibliotheca Graeca,* 10: 432–35, 11: 470–73.

1722   Hearne, Thomas. *Scriptores historiae Anglicae,* 15: 1568–69.

1722   Joannis, Georg Christian. *Scriptores rerum Moguntinarum.* Frankfurt, 1: 131–50.

1722   *Leven van Johanna, paus van Rom, onder den naam van Johannes VIII.* Amsterdam, 1722.

1722   Oudin, Casimir. *Commentarius de scriptoribus Ecclesiae antiquis illorumque scriptis.* Frankfurt, 1722, 2: 285–307, 3: 534–45.

1723   Leyser, Polykarp. *Prodromus ad Joannae papissae existentiam probandam.* Helmstadt, 1723.

1723   Rydelius, Magnus. *Dissertatio de pontifice Johanne VIII.* Lund, 1723.

1723   Gigli, Girolamo. *Diario Sanese.* Lucca, 1723, 2: 434–35.

1724   Irenaei. In *Bibliotheca historico-philologico-theologica.* Bremen, 1718–27, 7: 901–6, 8: 469–92.

1724   Brueys, David Augustin de. *Histoire des Papes.* Paris, 1724, 2: 29.

1727   Goringius, A. M. In *Bibliotheca historico-philologico-theologica,* 8: 900–901.

1728   Palthenius, Johann Philip. In *Amoenitates literarum,* 9: 817–21.

1730   Altdorf Academy. *Argumenta potiora quae a viris eruditis contra historiam de Joanna papissa afferi solent.* In *Amoenitates literarum,* 1: 195–221.

1730   Wagenseil, Johann Christoph. *Dissertatio de Joanna papissa.* In *Amoenitates literarum,* 1: 142–94.

1730   Launoy, Jean de. *Opera omnia.* Edited by Franciscus Granet. Cologne, 1731, V, 2: 562–69.

1735   Oeder, Georg Ludwig (Sincerus Pistophilius). *Epistola . . . qua mulierem inter Leonem IV et Benedictum III papatu Romano functam, idoneis rationibus asseritur.* 1735.

1735   Fabricius, Johann Albert. *Bibliotheca latina mediae et infimae aetatis.* Hamburg, 1734–46, 4: 116–17.

1739   Schumann, Johann Daniel. *Dissertatio de origine vera traditionis falsae de Johanna papissa.* Göttingen, 1739; Jena, 1741.

1741   *Hinlänglicher Beweis, dass ehedessen eine Weibesperson, Namens Gilberta, insgemein Pabst Agnese genannt, unter dem Nahman Pabst Jo-*

hann VIII den Stuhl Petri wirklich besessen und verunehret habe. N.p., 1742.

1744   Gleichmann, Johann Zacharias. *Wahrheit der Geschichte von der Päbstin Johanna, wieder die Recension des Heumann.* Frankfurt and Leipzig, 1744. This work was a response to Schumann, 1739.

1744   *The Surprising History of Pope Joan.* London, 1744.

1749   Artigny, Antoine Gachet d'. *Nouveaux mémoires d'histoire, de critique et de littérature,* 1: 415–25, 2: 49–55.

1749   Garampi, Giuseppi. *De nummo argenteo Benedicti III . . . in qua plura ad pontificum historiam illustrandum et Joannae papissae fabulam repellandam proferuntur.* Rome, 1749.

1756   Voltaire. *Essai sur les moeurs.* In Voltaire, *Oeuvres complètes.* Paris, 1878, 13: 196.

1762   Walch, Johann Georg, ed. *Bibliotheca theologica.* 4 volumes, Jena, 1757–65. Volume 3 (1762), 548–54.

1765   *Encyclopédie, ou, Dictionnaire raisonné des sciences, des arts et des métiers.* Edited by Denis Diderot and Jacques d'Alembert. Neuchâtel, 1765, s.v. "Papesse Jeanne."

1765   Gottsched, Johann Christoph. *Nöthiger Vorrath zur Geschichte der deutschen dramatischen Dichtkunst.* Leipzig, 1765, 81–138. These pages contain Dietrich Schernberg, *Fraw Jutta,* 1480, 1565.

1771   *Dictionnaire de Trévoux,* 6: 502.

1778   Blasco, Carlo. *Diatriba de Joanna papissa, sive de ejus fabulae origine.* Naples, 1778.

1778   Natalis, Alexander. *Historia ecclesiastica.* Venice, 1778, 4: 319–26.

1778   Bordes, Charles. *La Papesse Jeanne: Poème en X chants.* N.p. (The Hague?), 1778.

1783   Winkopp, Peter Adolph. *Die Päpstin Johanne.* Leipzig, 1783.

1788   *Geschichte der Päpstin Johanna.* Leipzig, 1788.

1793   Léger, Pierre. *La Papesse Jeanne.* Play. Paris, 1793.

1793   Defauconpret, August Jean Baptiste. *La Papesse Jeanne.* Play. In the second edition titled *L'aînée des papesses.* Paris, 1793.

1793   Flins des Olivier, Claude Carbon. *La Papesse Jeanne.* Play, unpublished.

1801   Desorgues, Théodore. *Le Pape et le Mufti ou la réconciliation des cultes.* Play. Paris 1801. Reprinted in Michel Vovelle, *Théodore Desorgues ou la désorganisation: Aix-Paris, 1763–1808.* Paris, 1985, 235–73.

1802   Cancellieri, Francesco. *Storia de' solenni possessi de' Sommi Pontefici, detti anticamente processi, dopo la loro coronazione, dalla basilica Vaticana alla Lateranense.* Rome, 1802.

1804   Casti, Giambattista. *La Papessa Giovanna.* In Casti, *Novelle.* Paris, 1804. Bilingual edition, *La Papesse,* Paris, 1878.

1809   [Reich, H. P.] *Ueber die Wahrscheinlichkeit der Existenz der Päpstin Johanna, eine historische Untersuchung.* Regensburg, 1809.

1810   *Dictionnaire Universel.* Paris, 1810. S.v. "Benoît III."

1810   Arnim, Achim von. *Armut, Reichtum, Schuld und Busse der Gräfin Dolores.* Berlin, 1810. See Arnim, *Sämtliche Romane und Erzählungen.* Edited by Walter Migge. Munich, 1962–65, part 4, chapter 6, 348–63.

1811   *Bibliothèque Universelle.* Paris. S.v. "Papesse."

1813   Arnim, Achim von. "Das Frülingsfest." In Arnim, *Schaubühne.* Berlin, 1839–42, volume 1.

ca. 1820   Arnim, Achim von. *Die Päpstin Johanna.* Published in 1846 in Arnim, *Sämmtliche Werke.* Edited by Wilhelm Grimm. Berlin, 1839–42, volume 19.

1821   *Die Päpstin Johanna, keine wahre Geschichte.* Mainz, 1821.

1828   Ciampi, Sebastiano. *Disamina sull'opinione del Boccaccio intorno alla cosi detta papessa Giovanna.* Florence, 1828.

1829   Smets, Wilhelm. *Das Mährchen von der Päpstin Johanna, aufs neue erortet.* Cologne, 1829. Enlarged edition, Cologne, 1835.

1830   Stendhal. *Promenades dans Rome.* In Stendhal, *Oeuvres complètes.* Edited by Victor Del Litto. Geneva, 1974, volume 7.

1830   *Diccionario historico o Biografia universal.* Barcelona, 1830, 2: 241–46, 444.

1831   Simonnin, M., and Théodore N. (Benjamin Antier and Théodore Nézel). *La Papesse Jeanne. Vaudeville-anecdote.* Paris, 1831.

1832   Bruckbräu, Friedrich Wilhelm. *Der Papst im Unterrocke.* Stuttgart, 1832.

1841   *Encyclopédie des gens du monde.* Paris, 1841. S.v. "Jeanne la papesse."

1841   Moroni, Gaetano. *Dizionario di erudizione storico-ecclesiastica.* Venice, 1841, 8: 171–73.

1842   Peake, R. B. Article in *Bentley's Magazine* 12 (1842): 148.

1843   *Juana la papesa, novela historica.* San Sebastián, 1843.

1844   Kist, Nicolaas Christiaan. *De pausin Johanna, (Eine sanwijzing, dat het onderzoek harer geschiedenis nog gunszins afgedaan of gesloten is).* Leiden, 1844.

1845   Wensing, Justus Henricus. *De verhandeling van N. C. Kist, over De pausin Joanna, nagelezen en getoetst.* The Hague, 1845.

1845   Tross, Ludwig. *Een woord an Wensing over zijn geschrift wegens de pausin Joanna.* Leiden, 1845.

1845   Bianchi-Giovini, Aurelio Angelo. *Esame critico degli atti e documenti relativi alla favola della papessa Giovanna.* Milan, 1845.

1848   Gförer, August Friedrich. *Geschichte der ost-und westfränkischen Carolinger, vom Tode Ludwigs der Frommen bis zum Ende Conrads I (840–918).* Freiburg im Breisgau, 1848, 1: 288–93.

1850   "Facts and Documents Relating to Pope Joan." *North British Review* 12 (1850): 354.

1854   *Bibliographie biographique universelle.* Edited by Eduard Maris Oettinger. Paris, 1854. S.v. "Jeanne."

1855   Kleine, Georg. *Die Päpstin Joanna keine Fabel.* Einbeck, 1855.

1862   Brunet, Gustave (Philomneste junior). *La Papesse Jeanne, étude historique et littéraire.* Paris, 1862. Enlarged edition, Brussels, 1880.

1863   Döllinger, Johan Joseph Ignaz von. *Die Papst-Fabeln des Mittelalters: Ein Betrag zur Kirchengeschichte.* Munich, 1863. Enlarged edition, Stuttgart, 1890. French translation, Paris, 1865. Italian translation. In English translation by Alfred Plummer as *Fables Respecting the Popes of the Middle Ages.* London, 1871.

1863   *La Vérité historique.* Various articles: 12 (1863): 24–58, 94–116, 132–58.

1864–65   *L'Intermédiaire.* Various articles: 1 (1864): 339–40; 2 (1865): 176, 400.

1866   Andreae, Otto. *Ein Weib auf dem Stuhle Petri oder das wieder geöffnete Johanna, eine Vergleichung der für und wider dieselbe sprech: Zeugnisse, mit den Zeugnissen für und wider das Papsttum.* Gütersloh, 1866.

1866   Rhoides, Emmanuel. *La Papesse Jeanne.* Athens, 1866. Two German translations: Leipzig 1875; 1904. French translation, 1878, the seventh edition of which was published with a preface reprinting an article of Barbey d'Aurevilly. Italian translation, 1876. English translation by Lawrence Durrell, 1971.

1868   Hergenroether, Joseph. *Photius.* Regensburg, 1868, 2: 365.

1869   Meline, J. C. "The Fable of Pope Joan." *Catholic World* 9 (1869): 1–14.

1870   Gastineau, Benjamin. *Les courtisanes de l'Eglise.* Paris, 1870.

1870   Wouters, Henricus Guilielmus. *Dissertationes in selecta historiae ecclesiasticae capita.* Louvain, 1870, 3: 158.

1875   Barthélemy, Charles. *Erreurs historiques.* Paris, 1875, 1: 1–37.

1876   Backer, Aloys de. In *Bibliothèque de la Compagnie de Jésus,* 3 (1876): 607, 614–15, 2467.

1876   *Die Päpstin Johanna und ohre Namens Vettern: Eine kirchengeschichtliche Excursion des kath. Volke.* Würzburg, 1876.

1878   Buet, Charles. Article. *Revue du Monde Catholique* 35 (1878): 31–63.

1878   Buet, Charles. *Etudes historiques: La Papesse Jeanne, réponse à Em. Rhoidès.* Paris, 1878.

1878   Cansson, Jean-Pierre. *Histoire de la papesse Jeanne, mademoiselle Agnès Alla Etelbert, née en Angleterre, montée sur le trône pontifical le 17 juillet 855 à 858 sous le nom de Jean VIII.* Marseille, 1878.

1878   Herran y Valdivielso. "Faits historiques de la papesse." *Comercio de Santander,* 1878.

1878   Mateos Gago y Fernández, Francisco. *Juana la papissa: Contestacion a un articulista papisero de Santander.* Seville, 1878. French translation, Paris, 1880.

1879   Hefele, Karl Joseph von. *Conciliengeschichte.* Second edition, Freiburg im Breisgau, 1879, 4: 458.

1882   Taxil, Léo. *Un pape femelle.* Paris, 1882.

1885   Mezzabotta, Ernesto. *La papessa Giovanna: Romanzo storico Romano.* Rome, 1885.

1885   Stegagnini, Leopoldo. *Sulla sconcia favola della papessa Giovanna.* Verona, 1885.

1889   *Kirchenlexicon,* 1889. S.v. "Jeanne." By Franz Xavier von Funk.

1890   Bernheim, Ernest. "Zur Sage von der Päpstin Johanna." *Deutsche Zeitschrift* 3 (1890): 412.

1895   Zürner, Hugo. *Frau Jutta: Ein neues lustig Spiel von Frau Jutten.* Zurich, 1895.

1895   Lapôtre, Arthur. *L'Europe et le Saint-Siège à l'époque Carolingienne, Première partie, Le pape Jean VIII (872–882).* Paris, 1895, 359–67.

1897   Douais, Célestin. "La papesse Jeanne." *Bulletin de l'Institut Catholique de Toulouse,* 189, 2d ser., 9 (1897): 210–21.

1900   Weitemeyer, Max. *Die Päpstin Johanna.* Play. Erfurt, 1900.

1900–1901 Müntz, Eugène. "La légende de la Papesse Jeanne dans l'illustration des livres, du XVe au XIXe siècle." *La Bibliofilia* 2 (1900–1901): 325–39.

1903   Michael, Emil. *Geschichte des deutschen Volkes seit dem dreizehten Jahrhundert bis zum Ausgang des Mittelalters.* Freiburg im Breisgau, 1903, 3: 383–88.

1905   Bartels, Adolf. *Die Päpstin Johanna, Römische Tragödien.* Munich, 1905.

1907   Jarry, Alfred. *Le Moutardier du pape.* Paris, 1907.

1907   Chevalier, Ulysse. *Répertoire des sources historiques du Moyen Age . . . Bio-bibliographie.* Second edition, Paris, 1907, columns 2553–57.

1908   Jarry, Alfred. Translation (with Jean Saltas) of Emmanuel Rhoides, *La Papesse Jeanne* (1866). Paris, 1908.

1909   Mourret, Fernand. *Histoire générale de l'Eglise.* Paris, 1909, 3: 464–67. In English translation by Newton Thompson under the title *A History of the Catholic Church.* St. Louis, 1930.

1911   *Dictionnaire apologétique de la foi catholique.* Paris, 1911. S.v. "Jeanne (la papesse)." By Félix Vernet.

1914   Thurston, Herbert. "Pope Joan." *The Month* (May, 1914): 450–63.

1919   Gorm, Ludwig. *Päpstin Johanna.* Munich, 1919.

1920   Borchardt, Rudolf. *Die Päpstin Jutta: Ein dramatisches Gedicht.* Erster Teil, *Verkündigung.* Berlin, 1920.

1920   Edon, Richard Alexander. *Der Antichrist: Die Tragödie der Päpstin Johanna*. Berlin, 1920.

1922   Brecht, Bertolt. *Päpstin Johanna*. Draft for a play. In Klaus Völker, *Päpstin Johanna*, 1977.

1923   Vacandard, Elphège. *Etudes de critique et d'histoire religieuse*. Paris, 1923, 4: 15–39.

1924   Reicke, Georg. *Päpstin Jutte*. Leipzig, 1924.

1925   Kraft, Werner. *Die Päpstin Johanna: Eine Motivgeschichtliche Untersuchung*. Inaugural dissertation. Frankfurt, 1925.

1931   Ince, Richard Basil. *When Joan Was Pope*. New York, 1931.

1931   Wood, Clement. *The Woman Who Was Pope: A Biography of Pope Joan, 853–855 A.D*. New York, 1931.

1947   Borodin, George. *The Book of Joanna*. London, 1947.

1971   Rhoides, Emmanuel. *Pope Joan*. Translated by Lawrence Durrell. London, 1971. French translation of Durrell, Paris, 1974.

1972   Perrodo-Le Moyne, Henri, and Gérard Caillet. *Un pape nommé Jeanne*. Levallois-Perret, 1972.

1977   Völker, Klaus. *Päpstin Johanna: Ein Lesebuch*. Berlin, 1977.

1979   D'Onofrio, Cesare. *La Papessa Giovanna: Roma e papato tra storia e leggenda*. Rome, 1979.

1983   Pasteur, Claude. *La Papesse*. Paris, 1983.

1984   Boureau, Alain. "La Papesse Jeanne: Formes et fonctions d'une légende au Moyen Age." *Comptes Rendus de l'Académie des Inscriptions et Belles Lettres* (1984): 446–64.

1986   Pasteur, Claude. *Le manuscrit d'Anastase*. Paris, 1986.

1986   Boureau, Alain. "Un papa o piuttosto una papessa." *Storia e Dossier* 1, 1 (1986): 26–29.

1988   Boureau, Alain. *La papesse Jeanne*. Paris, 1988.

1988   Pardoe, Rosemary and Darroll. *The Female Pope: The Mystery of Pope Joan*. Wellingborough, 1988.

1998   Cross, Donna Woolfolk. *Pope Joan: A Novel*. New York: Ballentine Books, 1966. Translated into French by Hubert Tézenas under the title *La Papesse Jeanne*. Paris: Presses de la Cité, 1998.

1998   Stanford, Peter. *The She-Pope*. London, 1998; *The Legend of Pope Joan*. New York, 1999.

NOTES

ABBREVIATIONS

MGH   *Monumenta Germaniae Historica*

Pat. Graeca   *Patrologiae cursus completus . . . Series Graeca*, ed.
                      Jacques-Paul Migne

Pat. Latina   *Patrologiae cursus completus . . . Series Latina*, ed.
                      Jacques-Paul Migne

CHAPTER ONE

1. Maurice Clavel, "Quand l'Eternel éternue," *Le Nouvel Observateur* 728 (23–29 October 1978): 91–93.

2. Martinus Polonus, *Chronica de Romanis Pontificibus et imperatoribus*, in *MGH, Scriptorum*, ed. Georg Heinrich Pertz, 22: 428. On the success of Martinus's *Chronicle*, see Bernard Guenée, *Histoire et culture historique dans l'Occident médiéval* (Paris: Aubier Montaigne, 1980), 305–7.

3. Geoffroy de Courlon, *Chronique de l'Abbaye de Saint-Pierre-le-Vif de Sens*, ed. Gustave Julliot (Sens, 1876), 296–99.

4. This text is published in Jeanne Bignami Odier, "Les visions de Robert d'Uzès," *Archivum Fratrum Praedicatorum* 25 (1955): 258–320. The passage quoted appears on p. 274.

5. The text of "Anonymous Leoliensis," probably written at Vienna around 1379, repeats and continues Johannes of Viktring, *Liber certarum historiarum* (1340–43); it appears, edited by Fedor Schneider, following Johannes of Viktring's chronicle: 2 vols. (Hannover and Leipzig: Hahn, 1909–10), 1: 106–7. My thanks to Jean-Marie Moeglin for pointing out this text to me.

6. Adam of Usk, *Chronicon*, in Ugo Bolzani, "La storia di Roma nella Chronica di Adamo da Usk," *Archivio della Società Romana di Storia Patria* 3 (1880): 473–88, quoted from *The Chronicle of Adam Usk, 1377–1421*, ed. and trans. C. Given-Wilson (Oxford: Clarendon Press; New York: Oxford University Press, 1997), 187–89. Many of the instances that follow are given in Cesare D'Onofrio, *La Papessa Giovanna: Roma e papato tra storia e leggenda* (Rome: Romana Società Editrice, 1979); in Johann Joseph Ignaz von Döllinger, *Die Papst-Fabeln des Mittelalters: Ein Betrag zur Kirchengeschichte* (Munich, 1863), reprint of the 1st ed.

(Frankfurt: Minerva, 1962), 2d ed. (Stuttgart, 1890); and in Johann Wolf, *Lectiones memorabiles et reconditae* (1600), 2d ed. (Frankfurt, 1671), 1: 176–89. There is a French translation of the first edition of Döllinger's *Papst-Fabeln,* but it is less complete than the second edition. A translation of the first edition is available in English as *Fables Respecting the Popes of the Middle Ages,* trans. Alfred Plummer (London, Oxford, and Cambridge, 1871).

7. Jacopo d'Angelo of Scarperia, in *Leonardi Dathi . . . Epistolae XXXIII . . . recensente Laurentio Mehus . . . accessit Elegantissima Jacobi Angeli Epistola ad Emmanuelem Chrysolaram addita ejusdem vita* (Florence, 1743).

8. For the episode of the withered arm in the *Gospel of James,* see *Le Protévangile de Jacques et ses remaniements latins,* ed. with commentary by Emile Amann (Paris: Letouzey, 1910), 326–28. The anecdote was rediscovered in the middle of the thirteenth century: See Alain Boureau, "Les vignes de Bolzano: Edition de l'Epilogus de Barthélémy de Trente sur la Nativité du Seigneur," in *Contributi alla Storia della Regione Trentino-Alto Adige, Civis: Studi e Testi,* supplement 2 (Trent, 1986), 91–104.

9. Hermann Korner, *Chronica novella,* in *Corpus historicorum Medii Aevi,* ed. Johan Georg von Eckhart (Leipzig, 1723), 2: 442.

10. Giovanni Rucellai, *Della bellezza e anticaglia di Roma,* ed. Roberto Valentini and Giuseppe Zucchetti, in *Codice topografico della città di Roma,* Fonti per la storia d'Italia, 81 (Rome: Tipografia del Senato, 1940–), vol. 4 (1953), 407.

11. William Brewyn, *De septum . . . Ecclesiis Romae,* in Casimir Oudin, ed., *Commentarius de scriptoribus ecclesiae antiquis illorumque scriptis* (Frankfurt, 1722), vol. 3, col. 2678, quoted from *A XVth Century Guide-Book to the Principal Churches of Rome, Compiled in c. 1470 by William Brewyn,* trans. C. Eveleigh Woodruff (London: Marshall Press, 1933; reprint, New York: AMS Press, 1980), 33.

12. Laonicos Chalcocondylas, *Historiarum de origine ac rebus gestis Turcarum,* VI, in *Pat. Graeca,* vol. 159 (Paris, 1866), cols. 299–302.

13. Felix Hemmerli, *De nobilitate et rusticitate dialogus* (Strasbourg, ca. 1495–1500), fol. 99, quoted in D'Onofrio, *Papessa Giovanna,* 94–95.

14. On Platina, see D'Onofrio, *Papessa Giovanna,* 23–38.

15. For the passage on Joan in Platina's *Life of the Popes,* see Bartolomeo Platina, *Platynae historici Liber de Vita Christi ac omnium pontificum (aa. 1–1474),* ed. Giacinto Gaida (1913), new, enlarged ed. (Città di Castello: S. Lapi, 1932), 151–52.

16. Janus Pannonius, *Epigrammata* (Venice, 1544), Epigram 58, p. 70, quoted in D'Onofrio, *Papessa Giovanna,* 95.

17. Marcus Marullus Spalatensis, in Wolf, *Lectiones memorabiles,* 1: 187.

18. Jean-Jacques Boissard, *Romanae urbis topographiae et antiquitatum* (Frankfurt, 1597–1602), 1: 70.

19. Hartmann Schedel, *Chronicarum liber* (Nuremberg, 1493), fol. 169. At nearly the same date (on the occasion of the coronation of Pope Alexander VI in 1492), the chronicler Bernardino Corio also reports the rite of verification.

20. Jacopo Filippo Foresti, *De plurimis mulieribus claris* (Ferrara, 1497),

quoted in D'Onofrio, *Papessa Giovanna*, 100. I shall return to the topic of the "Mirrors of Women" in chap. 5.

21. *L'Opera de messer Giovanni Boccaccio de mulieribus claris* (Venice, 1506), available in English translation as *Concerning Famous Women*, ed. and trans. Guido A. Guarino (New Brunswick, N.J.: Rutgers University Press, 1963).

22. Joannes Stella, *Vitae Pontificum* (Venice, 1505), 108.

23. Giovanni Pierio Valeriano Bolzani, *Pro sacerdotum barbis* (Rome, 1531), 1621 edition, p. 9.

24. Wolf's *Lectiones memorabiles* clearly reflects the influence of the Reformation tradition of the "Magdeburg Centuries," a topic to which we shall return in chap. 6.

25. Wolf, *Lectiones memorabiles*, 2d ed., 1: 187.

26. To cite a few such works: see Giovanni Briccio, *Relatione della cavalcata solenne fatta in Roma alli 23 di novembre 1644* . . . (Rome, 1644); Lucio Flori, *Apparato fatto per la cavalcata nel pigliare il possesso a S. Gio. Laterano* . . . (Rome, 1644); Antonio Gerardi, *Trionfal possesso della sanctità di nostro signore Innocentio X*; Giorgio Maria Bonelli, *Copioso e compito della cavalcata e ceremonie* . . . (Rome, 1644). All of these brief works are in the Vatican Library.

27. Lars Banck, *Roma triumphans, seu Actus inaugurationum et coronationum Pontificum Romanorum, et in spetie Innocentii X Pont. Max. brevis descriptio* (Frankfurt, 1645).

28. Ibid., 1656 edition, 387 – 89.

29. Ibid.

30. This image is reproduced in D'Onofrio, *Papessa Giovanna*, 98, fig. 62.

31. Ibid., 109, fig. 69.

32. See Paul de Vooght, *Les pouvoirs du concile et l'autorité du pape au Concile de Constance* (Paris: Cerf, 1965); Heinz Angermeier, "Das Reich und der Konsiliarismus," *Historische Zeitschrift* (1961): 529 – 88.

33. D'Onofrio, *Papessa Giovanna*, 15 – 20.

34. See Eugenio Dupré Theseider, *Roma dal Commune di popolo alla signoria pontificia (1252–1377)* (Bologna: Capelli, 1952).

35. See Roger Chartier, "Espace social et imaginaire social: Les intellectuels frustrés au XVIIe siècle," *Annales E.S.C.* 37, 2 (1982): 389 – 400.

36. This pasquinade is given in Francesco Cancellieri, *Storia de' solenni possessi de' Sommi Pontefici* . . . (Rome, 1802), 246. On pasquinades, see Renato and Fernando Silenzi, *Pasquino: Quattro secoli di satira romana* (Florence: Vallecchi, 1968), and Vittorio Cian, *La satira*, 2d ed. rev., 2 vols. (Milan: Vallardi, 1945).

37. André Chastel, *Le sac de Rome, 1527* (Paris: Gallimard, 1984), 10; see also *The Sack of Rome, 1527*, trans. Beth Archer (Princeton: Princeton University Press, 1983).

38. François Rabelais, *Le quart livre des faicts et dicts héroiqes du bon Pantagruel*, critical edition by Robert Marichal (Geneva: Droz, 1947), 199 – 200, quoted from *The Complete Works of Rabelais: The Five Books of Gargantua and Pantagruel*, trans.

Jacques Le Clercq (New York: Modern Library/Random House, copyright 1936), 626-27.

39. François Rabelais, *Le tiers livre*, critical edition by Pierre Michel (Paris: Gallimard, 1966), 189, quoted from *Complete Works*, Le Clercq translation, 336.

40. Lucien Febvre, *Le problème de l'incroyance au XVI siècle: La religion de Rabelais*, 2d ed. (Paris: Albin Michel, 1968), 144-50, quoted from *The Problem of Unbelief in the Sixteenth Century: The Religion of Rabelais*, trans. Beatrice Gottlieb (Cambridge, Mass.: Harvard University Press, 1982), 153.

41. Robert d'Uzès, in Bignami Odier, "Les Visions de Robert d'Uzès." Henceforth, references to this source will give "Robert" and the page number in this edition.

42. Marjorie Reeves, *The Influence of Prophecy in the Later Middle Ages: A Study in Joachimism* (Oxford: Clarendon Press, 1969).

43. Robert, 272-73.

44. Ibid., 283.

45. Ibid., 285.

46. Ibid., 284.

47. Ibid., 303.

48. William of Saint-Thierry (Guillelmi Abbatis Sancti Theodorici), *De natura et dignitate amoris*, in *Pat. Latina*, vol. 184 (Paris, 1879), col. 401, available in English translation as *The Nature and Dignity of Love*, trans. Thomas X. Davis (Kalamazoo; Cistercian Publications, 1981).

49. Gerhoch of Reichersberg (Gerhohus Reicherspergensis), *In Psalmo II*, 29, in *Pat. Latina* (Paris, 1854), 193, col. 671.

50. Peter of Blois (Petrus Blesensis), Sermon 38, "In nativitate Beatae Mariae," in *Pat. Latina*, vol. 207 (Paris, 1855), cols. 672-77, esp. col. 672.

51. See Alain Boureau, "L'inceste de Judas: Essai sur la genèse de l'antisémitisme au XIIe siècle," *Nouvelle Revue de Psychanalyse* 33 (1986): 25-41.

52. Domenico Giacobazzi, *Tractatus de Concilio* in *Sacrorum Conciliorum nova et amplissima collectio* (Paris and Rome, 1870), 400, 171.

53. On the question of women in canon law in the twelfth and thirteenth centuries, there is one work that is well documented but more theological than historical: Ida Raming, *Der Ausschluss der Frau vom priesterlichen Amt: Gottgewollte Tradition oder Diskriminierung?* (Cologne, 1973). I have used the English translation, *The Exclusion of Women from the Priesthood: Divine Law or Sex Discrimination?*, trans. Norman R. Adams (London and Metuchen, N.J.: Scarecrow Press, 1976). The passages from Gratian's *Decretals* quoted can be found in *Corpus Juris Canonici*, ed. A. Friedberg, new edition (Graz: 1955), vol. 1, cols. 86, 1304. They are quoted here from Raming, *Exclusion of Women*, 8, 10.

54. *Die Summa decretorum des Magister Rufinus*, ed. Heinrich Singer (1902), reprint (Aalen: Scientia Verlag, 1963), 192 n158.

55. Paucapalea, *Die Summa des Paucapalea, über das Decretum Gratiani*, ed. Jo-

hann Friedrich von Schulte (1890), reprint (Aalen: Scientia Verlag, 1965), 11, quoted here from Raming, *Exclusion of Women*, 48.

56. Note on Decretal X.5.40.10 in the Lyon edition (1671) of the *Corpus Juris Canonici*, vol. 2, col. 1936, quoted here from Raming, *Exclusion of Women*, 82; see also ibid., 211 n85.

57. For Huguccio, *Summa*, see Raming, *Exclusion of Women*, 62, 192 n158.

58. Ibid., 62, 193 n161.

59. Gratian, *Decretals*, Cause III, Q VII, c. 1, in *Corpus Juris Canonici*, ed. Friedberg, 1, col. 524.

60. Egidio da Viterbo, *Historia XX saeculorum*, MS Naples, cod. IX B 14, fol. 221, fragment published in François Secret, "Notes sur Egidio de Viterbe," *Augustiniana* 27 (1977): 229–30.

61. See Jack Goody, *The Development of the Family and Marriage in Europe* (Cambridge and New York: Cambridge University Press, 1983).

62. Roberto Zapperi, *L'uomo incinto: La donna, l'uomo e il potere* (Cosenza: Lerici, 1979), available in English translation as *The Pregnant Man*, trans. Brian Williams, rev. ed. (Chur, Switzerland, and New York: Harwood Academic, 1991), 3–32, and in French translation as *L'homme enceint: L'homme, la femme et le pouvoir*, trans. M. A. Maire-Vigueur (Paris: Presses Universitaires de France, 1983), 19–46.

63. Henricus de Segusio, Cardinal Hostiensis, *Summa aurea*, for which see Raming, *Exclusion of Women*, 83, 212 nn89, 90.

64. See Raming, *Exclusion of Women*, 62, 192 n159.

65. Thomas Aquinas, *Summa theologica*, Suppl. Qu. 39 a 1; given from the translation of the Fathers of the English Dominican Province, 3 vols. (New York, Boston, etc.: Benziger Brothers, 1947–48), 3: 2698.

66. Robert, 199.

67. Burchardus, abbot of Bellevaux, *Apologia de barbis*, in *Apologiae duae*, ed. R. B. C. Huyghens, with an introduction on "Beards in History" by Giles Constable, in *Gozechini Epistola ad Walcherum; Burchardi ut videtur abbatis Bellevallis, Apologia de barbis* (Turnhout: Brepols, 1985), 151–224.

68. Martinus Polonus, *Margarita Decreti* (Speyer, ca. 1482–89), s.v. "femina." Concerning the prohibition against transdressing, I might note that one of the charges against Joan of Arc was to have presented herself to receive communion dressed in men's clothing: see Marie-Christine Pouchelle, "L'hybride," *Nouvelle Revue de Psychanalyse* 7 (1973), 60.

CHAPTER TWO

1. Christian Jouhaud, "Imprimer l'événement: La Rochelle à Paris," in Roger Chartier, ed., *Les usages de l'imprimé (XVe–XIXe siècle)* (Paris: Fayard, 1987), 381–438, in English translation as "Printing the Event: From La Rochelle to Paris," in

The Culture of Print, trans. Lydia G. Cochrane (Oxford: Polity Press/Blackwell, 1989), 290–333. The first part of this chapter on the rite of verification has profited from a friendly but critical reading in a workshop on politics and society led by Christian Jouhaud at the Ecole des Hautes Etudes en Sciences Sociales, with the participation of Jean-Pierre Berthe, Marie-Noëlle Bourguet, Simona Cerutti, Marie-Elisabeth Ducreux, Robert Descimon, Arlette Farge, Michèle Fogel, and Jacques Revel.

2. Ernst H. Kantorowicz, "Mysteries of the State: An Absolutist Concept and Its Late Medieval Origins" (1955), in Kantorowicz, *Selected Studies* (Locust Valley, N.Y.: J. J. Augustin, 1965), 381–98, in French translation as "Mystères de l'Etat: Un concept absolutiste et ses origines médiévales (bas Moyen Age)," in Kantorowicz, *Mourir pour la patrie et autres textes* (Paris: Presses Universitaires de France, 1984), 75–103.

3. Martinus Polonus, *Chronica de Romanis Pontificibus et imperatoribus*, in *MGH, Scriptorum*, ed. Georg Heinrich Pertz, vol. 22 (Hannover, 1872), 377–475, esp. p. 428.

4. Jean de Mailly, *Chronica universalis Mettensis*, in *MGH, Scriptores*, vol. 24 (Hannover, 1879), 502–26, esp. p. 514.

5. Anonymous text transcribed in Johann Wolf, *Lectiones memorabiles et reconditae* (1600), 2d ed. (Frankfurt, 1671), 1: 176. See also Jacopo Filippo Foresti of Bergamo, *Supplementum chronicis libri II*, Year 858 (Venice, 1486), and others.

6. Jacopo da Voragine, *Chronica Januensis*, in a modern edition as *Iacopo de Varagine e la sua Cronaca di Genova: Dalle origini al MCCXCVII*, ed. Giovanni Monleone, 3 vols. (Rome: Tipografia del Senato, 1941), 2: 268–69.

7. Jean de Mailly, *Chronica*, 514. Other versions of this inscription will be examined in chap. 4.

8. See Francesco Cancellieri, *Storia de' solenni possessi de' Sommi Pontefici . . .* (Rome, 1802), 60–112.

9. Raniero Gnoli, *Marmora Romana*, 2d ed. (Rome: Edizioni dell'Elefante, 1971), 187–91.

10. Frédéric de Clarac, *Musée de sculpture antique et moderne ou description du Louvre* (Paris, 1841), 2: 993.

11. *Realencyclopädie der Classischen Altertumswissenschaft*, ser. 2, vol. 7 (Stuttgart, 1931), 403.

12. See Josef Deér, "The 'Porphyry' Thrones of the Lateran Palace," in *The Dynastic Porphyry Tombs of the Norman Period in Sicily*, trans. G. A. Gillhof, Dumbarton Oaks Studies, 5 (Cambridge, Mass.: Harvard University Press, 1959), 142–46.

13. Walther Amelung, *Die Skulpturen des Vatikanischen Museums*, vol. 2 (Berlin: 1908), 109; Wolfgang Helbig, *Führer durch die offentlichen Sammlungen klassischer Altertümer in Rom*, vol. 1, *Die päpstlichen Sammlungen im Vatikan und Lateran* (Tübingen: E. Wasmuth, 1963), 156–57.

14. Cesare D'Onofrio, *La Papessa Giovanna: Roma e papato tra storia e leggenda* (Rome: Romana Società Editrice, 1979).

15. Ole Borch (Olaus Borricuius), *De antiquitate Urbis Romanae*, in Johannes Georgius Graevius, ed., *Thesaurus antiquitatum romanarum*, vol. 4 (Venice, 1732), col. 1596.

16. Quoted in D'Onofrio, *Papessa Giovanna*, 163.

17. Museum of Ostia Antica, reproduced in D'Onofrio, *Papessa Giovanna*, 168, fig. 111.

18. Avicenna, *De impregnatione et partu*, in D'Onofrio, *Papessa Giovanna*, 172.

19. Michele Savonarola, *Ad mulieres ferrarienses de regimine pregnantium et noviter natorum usque ad septennium*, ed. Luigi Belloni as *Il trattato ginecologico-pediatrico in volgare Ad mulieres* . . . (Milan, 1952), mentioned in D'Onofrio, *Papessa Giovanna*, 172 – 73.

20. Anna Comnena, *Alexiade*, VI, 8,1 and VII, 2,4; in D'Onofrio, *Papessa Giovanna*, 169 – 70.

21. See D'Onofrio, *Papessa Giovanna*, figs. 140 – 43, pp. 190 – 91.

22. *Ordo* "of Basel." For this text, discovered and edited by Bernhard Schimmelpfennig, see Schimmelpfennig, "Ein bisher unbekannter Text zur Wahl, Konsekration und Krönung des Papstes im 12. Jahrhundert," *Archivum Historiae Pontificae* 6 (1968): 43 – 70, esp. p. 68.

23. For this passage, see Marc Dykmans, *Le cérémonial papal de la fin du Moyen Age à la Renaissance*, vol. 1, *Le cérémonial papal du XIIIe siècle* (Brussels and Rome: Institut Historique Belge de Rome, 1977), 123.

24. See Caroline Walker Bynum, *Jesus as Mother: Studies in the Spirituality of the High Middle Ages* (Berkeley: University of California Press, 1982). We shall return to this metaphorical tendency in chap. 5.

25. See Pierre Champagne de Labriolle, "Une esquisse de l'histoire du mot 'papa,'" *Bulletin d'Ancienne Littérature et d'Archéologie Chrétienne* 1 (1911): 215 – 30, and Walter Ullmann, *The Growth of Papal Government in the Middle Ages: A Study in the Ideological Relation of Clerical to Lay Power* (London: Methuen, 1955), 21 n6; 3d ed. (1970), 22 – 23 n6.

26. *Le liber pontificalis*, ed., with commentary, by Louis Duchesne (Paris, 1886 – 92), new ed., 3 vols. (Paris: E. Thorin, 1955 – 57), 2: 269. See also 3 vols. (Paris: E. Bocard, 1981). On Paschal's reticence to accept election, see François Louis Ganshof, "Note sur l'élection des évêques," *Revue Internationale des Droits de l'Antiquité* 4 (1960): 487.

27. Arnold van Gennep, *Les rites de passage* (Paris: E. Nourry, 1909), available in English translation as *The Rites of Passage*, trans. Monika B. Vizedom and Gabrielle Caffee (Chicago: University of Chicago Press, 1960).

28. See Schimmelpfennig, "Ein bisher unbekannter Text."

29. Stephen Kuttner, "Universal Pope as Servant of God's Servants; The Canonists, Papal Titles and Innocent III," *Revue de Droit Canonique* 31, 2 (1981): 109 – 49.

30. See Ullmann, *Growth of Papal Government*. All of Ullmann's works are of capital importance, however.

31. See Deér, "The 'Porphyry' Thrones."

32. Kuttner, "Universal Pope," Appendix II, 137.

33. Ibid., 138–39.

34. Lucan, *Pharsalia*, III, 103–9. I have consulted *La guerre civile (La Pharsale)*, ed. Abel Bourgery, 2 vols. (Paris; Belles Lettres, 1962), 2: 68. Lucan is quoted here from *Lucan: The Civil War, Books I–X*, trans. J. D. Duff (Cambridge, Mass.: Harvard University Press; London: William Heinemann, 1951), 121–23.

35. Gerhoch of Reichersberg, *De investigatione Antichristi*, 1: 72, MGH, *De lite*, 3: 391.

36. Peter Cantor, *Verbum abbreviatum*, *Pat. Latina*, vol. 205, col. 117.

37. Innocent III, letter (Reg. 2, 202), *Apostolicae sedis, Pat. Latina*, vol. 214, col. 763.

38. "Stephanus II, papa Pippino, Carolo, Carolomanno," *Codex Carolinus*, in *MGH, Epistolae Merowingici et Karolini Aevi . . . 755,*" vol. 3 (Berlin, 1892), 488–90, esp. p. 489.

39. Ullmann, *Growth of Papal Government*, 61–62; 3d ed., 54–74.

40. See Paolo Brezzi, *Roma e l'impero medioevale (774–1252)* (Bologna: L. Cappelli, 1947), 4–5.

41. See Stephen Kuttner, "Cardinalis," *Traditio: Studies in Ancient and Medieval History* 3 (1945): 129–214, and Johannes Baptist Sägmüller, *Die Tätigkeit und Stellung der Cardinäle bis Papst Bonifaz VIII* (Freiburg im Breisgau: Herder, 1896).

42. *Das Constitutum Constantini*, ed. Horst Fuhrmann, in *MGH, Fontes Juris Germanici Antiqui*, vol. 10 (Hannover: Hahn, 1968), 88, quoted here from Christopher B. Coleman, *The Treatise of Lorenzo Valla on the Donation of Constantine* (New Haven: Yale University Press, 1922), reprint (Toronto, Buffalo, and London: University of Toronto Press, 1993), 15.

43. Gabriel Le Bras, *Institutions ecclésiastiques de la chrétienté médiévale*, tome 12, vol. 2 of *Histoire de l'Eglise depuis les origines jusqu'à nos jours*, gen. eds. Augustin Fliche and Victor Martin, pt. 1 (Paris: Bloud et Gay, 1964), 340–48.

44. Jean Gaudemet, with Jacques Dubois, André Duval, and Jacques Champagne, *Les élections dans l'Eglise latine des origines au XVIe siècle* (Paris: F. Lanore, 1979), 193–212.

45. Peter Damian (Petrus Damianus), *Contra Phylargyriam*, in *Pat. Latina*, vol. 145 (Paris, 1867), col. 540.

46. Deusdedit, *Collectio canonorum*, IV, edited by Victor Wolf von Glanvell as *Die Kanonessammlung des Kardinals Deusdedit* (Paderborn, 1905), 1: 17, reprint (Aalen: Scientia, 1967).

47. See Walter Ullmann, "The Legal Validity of the Papal Electoral Pacts," *Ephemerides Juris Canonici* 12 (1956): 246–78.

48. Gaudemet, *Les élections*, 201–202.

49. See Carlo Servatius, *Paschalis II (1099–1118): Studien zu seiner Person und*

seiner Politik (Stuttgart: Hiersemann, 1979), 42–72, and Jürgen Ziese, *Wibert von Ravenna: Der Gegenpapst Clemens III (1084–1100)* (Stuttgart: Hiersemann, 1982).

50. See Brezzi, *Roma e l'impero medioevale*, 14–15.

51. See Dykmans, *Le cérémonial papal*, 1: 178.

52. Sidonius Apollinaris, Letters, in *Sidoine Apollinaire*, ed. and trans. André Loyen, 3 vols. (Paris: Belles Lettres, 1970), 2: 46, available in English translation as *The Letters of Sidonius*, ed. and trans. O. M. Dalton, 2 vols. (Oxford: Clarendon Press, 1915).

53. See Walter Ullmann, "The Pontificate of Adrian IV," *Cambridge Historical Journal* 11 (1955): 233–52; Ullmann, "Cardinal Roland and Besançon," *Miscellanea Historiae Pontificiae* 18 (1954): 107–25.

54. Monsignor Maccarrone has written many works on the throne of Saint Peter, in particular in the context of a papal commission created by Paul VI in 1967. For all these texts and for the work of his collaborators, see the abundant bibliography given in the notes to the latest stage of his research in a long article, Michele Maccarrone, "La 'Catedra sancti Petri' nel Medioevo da simbolo a reliquia," *Rivista di Storia della Chiesa in Italia* 39, 2 (1985): 349–467. See also Nikolaus Gussone, *Thron und Inthronisation des Papstes von den Anfängen bis zum 12. Jahrhundert* (Bonn: Röhrscheld, 1978).

55. Cyprian, *Lettres*, 43, 5, 2, quoted in Maccarrone, "La 'Catedra sancti Petri,'" 375; quoted here from *The Letters of St. Cyprian of Carthage*, trans. and annotated by G. W. Clarke, Ancient Christian Writers, 43–47 (New York and Ramsey, N.J.: Paulist Press; Newman Press, 1984), 44: 64.

56. Quoted in Maccarrone, "La 'Catedra sancti Petri,'" 375.

57. *Liber pontificalis*, 1: 366.

58. "Concilium Romanum A.769," in *MGH, Concilia*, vol. 2, ed. Albert Werminghoff (Hannover: Hahn, 1907), pt. 1, pp. 74–92, esp. p. 86.

59. *Liber pontificalis*, 1: 470.

60. Ibid., 2: 72.

61. Ibid., 2: 142. See also Jésus Hortal Sanchez, *De initio potestatis primatialis Romani Pontificis*, Analecta Gregoriana, 167 (Rome: Università Gregoriana, 1968): 37–70.

62. Pierre Toubert, *Les structures du Latium médiéval: Le Latium méridional et la Sabine du Xe à la fin du XIIe siècle* (Rome: Ecole Française de Rome, 1973).

63. See Carlrichard Brühl, "Das 'Palatium' von Pavia und die 'Honorantiae civitatis papiae,'" in *Atti del 4° Congresso Internazionale di Studi sull'Alto Medioevo* (Spoleto: Centro di Studi sull'Alto Medioevo, 1969), 189–220, esp. pp. 218–20.

CHAPTER THREE

1. Arthur Lapôtre, "Le Souper de Jean Diacre," *Mélanges d'Archéologie et d'Histoire* 21 (1901): 305–85, reprinted in *Etudes sur la papauté au IXe siècle*, foreword

by André Vauchez, introduction by Paul Droulers and Girolamo Arnaldi, reprint, 2 vols. (Turin: Bottega d'Erasmo, 1978), 2: 439 – 519.

2. John Hymmonides, Latin text given in Lapôtre, "Le Souper de Jean Diacre."

3. Paul Fabre, *Le Polyptyque du chanoine Benoît (Etude sur un manuscrit de la Bibliothèque de Cambrai)* (Lille, 1889). The passage on the Cornomannia in Benedictus's text appears on pp. 18 – 23. This annotated edition is fundamental for an understanding of the Cornomannia, and it will be referred to henceforth as *"Polyptyque,"* followed by a page number in this edition. The question of the Cornomannia is also treated in Martine Boiteux, "Cornomannie et carnaval romain médiéval," in the collective volume, *Le Carnaval, la fête et la communication,* Actes, Rencontres internationales de Nice, March 1984 (Nice: Serre, 1985), 11 – 125. My thanks to Claude Gaignebet for calling this essay to my attention.

4. On the Feast of Fools in the Middle Ages, see Jacques Heers, *Fêtes des fous et carnavals* (Paris: Fayard, 1983).

5. From a letter by Egino, abbot of Farfa, published in Johann Baptist Matthias Watterich, ed. *Pontificum Romanorum . . . Vitae,* vol. 2 (Leipzig, 1862), 138.

6. *Polyptyque,* 28.

7. Ibid., 28 n2. See also Ernst H. Kantorowicz, "The 'King's Advent' and the Enigmatic Panels in the Doors of Santa Sabina," in Kantorowicz, *Selected Studies* (Locust Valley, N.Y.: J. J. Augustin, 1965), 37 – 75.

8. See Johann Schlemm, *De phillobolia Veterum* (Jena, 1666), and Johann Nicolai, *De Phyllobolia, seu Florum et ramorum sparsione in sacris et civilibus rebus usitatissima,* in Johan Dieterici, *Dissertatio de sparsione florum* (Frankfurt, 1698).

9. See Francesco Cancellieri, *Storia de' solenni possessi de' Sommi Pontefici . . .* (Rome, 1802), 8 – 9 n1.

10. Claudius of Turin, *Apologeticum atque rescriptum Claudii Episcopi adversus Theutmirum Abbatem,* in *Pat. Latina,* vol. 105 (Paris, 1864), cols. 459 – 66, esp. col. 462. See my commentary on this text in Boureau, "Les théologiens carolingiens devant les images religieuses: La conjoncture de 825," in *Nicée II, 787–1987: Douze siècles d'images religieuses,* Actes du colloque international Nicée II held at the Collège de France, Paris, 2, 3, 4, October 1986, ed. François Boespflug and Nicolas Lossky (Paris: Cerf, 1987), 247 – 62.

11. Bonizo, bishop of Sutri, quoted in Watterich, ed., *Pontificum Romanorum . . . Vitae,* 1: 314.

12. *Polyptyque,* 26.

13. Heers, *Fêtes des fous.*

14. Ottorino Bertolini, "Per la storia delle diacone romane nell'Alto Medioevo sino alla fine del secolo VIII," *Archivio della Società Romana di Storia Patria,* 60 (1947), ser. 3, vol. 1, fasc. I–IV, 1–145, reprinted in Bertolini, *Scritti scelti di storia medioevale,* ed. Ottavio Banti, 2 vols. (Livorno: Il Telegrafo, 1968), 1: 309 – 460.

15. *Descriptio sanctuarii sanctae Lateranensis ecclesiae,* quoted in Reinhard

Elze, "Das 'Sacrum Palatium Lateranence' im 10. und 11. Jahrhundert," *Studi Gregoriani* 4 (1952): 27-54, esp. p. 41.

16. On the Four Times, see the commentary on the Ordo XXXVI A in Michel Andrieu, *Les Ordines romani du Haut Moyen Age*, Spicelegium Sacrum Lovaniense, 28, 5 vols. (Louvain, 1931-), 4: 213-32; text of the Ordo, 235-38.

17. See Jean Mabillon, *Museum Italicum* (Paris, 1687), 2: 187.

18. *Polyptyque*, 27.

19. Ibid., 24-25.

20. Ibid., 25-26. On the symbolism of the cock (here linked with Carnival and with Christian imagery), see Lorrayne Y. Baird, "Priapus Gallinaceus: The Role of the Cock in Fertility and Eroticism in Classical Antiquity and the Middle Ages," *Studies in Iconography* 7-8 (1981-82): 81-111. My thanks to Aline Rousselle for providing me with this text.

21. On the earliest traces of Roman Carnival, see Filippo Clementi, *Il Carnevale romano nelle cronache contemporanee* (1899), 2d ed., 2 vols. (Città di Castello: Edizioni R.O.R.E., 1939), 1: 10-40.

22. Johann Wolf, *Lectiones memorabiles et reconditae* (1600), 2d ed. (Frankfurt, 1671), 1: 183-84.

23. Clementi, *Il Carnevale romano*, 1: 10-40.

24. For an analysis of this maxim, see Pierre Legendre, *L'amour du censeur: Essai sur l'ordre dogmatique* (Paris: Seuil, 1974).

25. See Michele Maccarrone, "La 'Catedra sancti Petri' nel Medioevo da simbolo a reliquia," *Rivista di Storia della Chiesa in Italia* 39, 2 (1985): 349-467, esp. pp. 410-19.

26. For the *Ordo* of Basel, see Bernhard Schimmelpfennig, "Ein bisher unbekannter Text zur Wahl, Konsekration und Krönung des Papstes im 12. Jahrhundert," *Archivium Historiae Pontificae* 6 (1968): 43-70. The *ordines* of Cencio and Albinus are published in Paul Fabre and Louis Duchesne, eds., *Le Liber Censuum de l'église romaine*, 3 vols. (Paris: A. Fontemoing, 1910-51). For the text of Cencio's *ordo*, with Albinus's text in appendix, see ibid., 2: 85-137.

27. See Eduard Eichmann, *Weihe und Krönung des Papstes im Mittelalter* (Munich: K. Zink, 1951), and Hans Walter Klewitz, "Die Krünung des Papstes," *Zeitschrift für Rechtsgeschichte*, 61, *Kanonisches Abteilung XXX* (1940): 96-130.

28. *Ordo* of Basel, in Schimmelpfennig, "Ein bisher unbekannter Text," 65-66. Henceforth this *Ordo* will be referred to as "Basel," followed by the page number in this article.

29. See the description of the coronation of John XXII at Lyon in Marc Dykmans, *Le cérémonial papal de la fin du Moyen Age à la Renaissance*, 4 vols. (Brussels and Rome: Institut Historique Belge de Rome, 1977-85), vol. 2, *De Rome en Avignon, ou, Le cérémonial de Jacques Stefaneschi* (1981), 290-305.

30. This fragment of Benedictus's *Polyptych* is published in the *Liber Censuum*, ed. Paul Fabre and Louis Duchesne, 2: 154.

31. See the topographical analysis and the many interesting illustrations in Cesare D'Onofrio, *La Papessa Giovanna: Roma e papato tra storia e leggenda* (Rome: Romana Società Editrice, 1979), 212–40.

32. Basel, 61.

33. See Dykmans, *Le cérémonial papal*, vol. 1, *Le cérémonial papal du XIIIe siècle*, 177.

34. See Ibid., 62.

35. D'Onofrio, *Papessa Giovanna*, 152–62.

36. Maccarrone, "La 'Catedra sancti Petri,'" 403 n198.

37. David L. D'Avray, *The Preaching of the Friars: Sermons diffused from Paris before 1300* (Oxford: Clarendon Press; New York: Oxford University Press, 1985), 225–59.

38. See Michele Maccarrone, "Innocenzo III teleologo dell'eucaristia," in Maccarrone, *Studi su Innocenzo III*, Italia Sacra, 7 (Rome: Herder, 1972), 341–431.

39. Cyrille Vogel, *La réforme culturelle sous Pépin le Bref et sous Charlemagne*, in Erna Patzelt, *Die karolingische Renaissance*; and Cyrille Vogel, *La réforme culturelle sous Pépin le Bref et sous Charlemagne* (Graz: Akademische Druck- und Verlagsanstalt, 1965), 173–242.

40. see Dykmans, *Cérémonial papal*, 1: 38–39.

41. Ibid., 15.

42. Quoted in Albert Poncelet, "Vie et miracles du pape Saint Léon IX," *Analectia Bollandiana* 25 (1906): 258–97, esp. p. 290.

43. Testament of Roger II, given in Reinhard Elze, "Zum Königtum Rogers II von Sizilien," in *Festschrift Percy Ernst Schramm zu seiner siebzigsten Geburtstag*, ed. Peter Classen and Peter Scheibert, 2 vols. (Wiesbaden: Franz Steiner, 1964), 1: 102–16, esp. p. 111.

44. Cardinal Lothar, *De miseria humane conditionis*, III, 4, 4, quoted in Reinhard Elze, "Sic transit gloria mundi: Zum Tode des Papstes im Mittelalter," *Deutsches Archiv für Erforschung des Mittelalters* 65 (1978): 1–18, esp. n.45. For a modern edition of Cardinal Lothar, see *De miseria humane conditionis*, ed. Michele Maccarone (Lugano: Thesauri Mundi, 1955); see also Lothario dei Segni (Pope Innocent III), *On the Misery of the Human Condition*, ed. Donald R. Howard, trans. Margaret Mary Dietz (Indianapolis and New York: Bobbs-Merrill, 1969).

45. Elze, "Sic transit gloria mundi." Carlo Ginzburg and a seminar under his leadership have published an important updating of information on ritual destruction: "Saccheggi rituali: Premesse a una ricerca in corso," *Quaderni Storici* 65 (1987): 615–36.

46. Jacques de Vitry, *Lettres*, ed. R. C. B. Huyghens (Leiden: Brill, 1960), 1: 73, quoted in Elze, "Sic transit gloria mundi," 1.

47. See *MGH, Epistolae*, 8 vols. (Berlin: Weidemann, 1887–1939), vol. 1 (1887), 364, quoted in Elze, "Sic transit gloria mundi," 4.

48. F. de Saint-Palais d'Aussac, *Le droit de dépouille (Jus spolii)*, Thesis, Université de Strasbourg, Faculté de Théologie, 1930 (Paris: A. Picard, 1930).

49. For a similar situation in the French sphere, see Andrew W. Lewis, *The Royal Succession in Capetian France: Studies on Familiar Order and the State* (Cambridge, Mass.: Harvard University Press, 1981), in French translation as *Le sang royal, La famille capétienne et l'Etat, Xe–XIVe siècle,* trans. Jeannie Carlier (Paris: Gallimard, 1986).

50. Ernst Kantorowicz, *The King's Two Bodies: A Study in Medieval Political Theology* (Princeton, N.J.: Princeton University Press, 1957), new ed. (1997), and Ralph E. Giesey, *The Royal Funeral Ceremony in Renaissance France* (Geneva: E. Droz, 1960).

51. Carlrichard Brühl, "Das 'Palatium' von Pavia une die 'Honorantae civitatis papiae,'" in *Atti del 4° Congresso di Studi sull'Alto Medioevo* (Spoleto: Centro di studi sull'Alto Medioevo, 1969), 189–220; Helmut Beumann, "Zur Entwicklung transpersonaler Staatsvorstellungen," in *Das Königtum: Seine geistigen und rechtlichen Grundlagen,* Vorträge und Forschungen, 3 (Lindau and Konstanz: Jan Thorbecke, 1956), 185–224.

52. Wipo, *Gesta Chuonradi II,* ed. Harry Bresslau, *MGH, Scriptores Rerum Germanicarum* (Hannover, 1915), quoted in Elze, "Sic transit gloria mundi," 13.

53. See Françoise Autrand, *Charles VI: La folie du roi* (Paris: Fayard, 1986). See also my commentary on the state question: Alain Boureau, "Toujours, déjà, soudain là: L'Etat devant l'historien," *Nouvelle Revue de Psychanalyse* 34 (1986): 185–95.

54. On Augustinus Triumphus, see Michael Wilks, *The Problem of Sovereignty in the Later Middle Ages* (Cambridge: Cambridge University Press, 1963).

55. See *Atti del convegno di studio: VII centenario del 1° Conclave (1268–1271)* (Viterbo, 1975).

56. Dykmans, *Le cérémonial papal,* 1: 158.

57. See Agostino Paravicini-Bagliani, *Il corpo del papa* (Turin: Einaudi, 1994); *The Pope's Body,* trans. David S. Peterson (Chicago: University of Chicago Press, 2000). Paravicini-Bagliani delivered a highly informative lecture at the Institut Historique Allemand, Paris (21 May 1987) on "La curie pontificale du XIIIe siècle au carrefour des sciences," and he presented a talk on funerary practices within the Curia before Jacques Le Goff's seminar at the Ecole des Hautes Etudes en Sciences Sociales in 1985.

58. My thanks to Simona Cerutti for her careful reading of the draft of this chapter, this passage in particular.

59. Gaetano Moroni, *Dizionario di erudizione storico-ecclesiastica da S. Pietro sino ai nostri giorni* (Venice, 1840–), vol. 11 (1841), 66–68.

60. Paride Grassi, *Diario,* published in Johann Joseph Ignaz von Döllinger, *Beiträge zur politischen, kirchlichen und culture-Geschichte der sechs letzen Jahrhunderte,* vol. 3 (1882), 428, quoted in Elze, "Sic transit gloria mundi," 17.

61. See Walter Ullmann, *The Growth of Papal Government in the Middle Ages: A Study in the Ideological Relation of Clerical to Lay Power* (London: Methuen, 1955), 3d ed. (1970), 328 and notes.

62. Armando Petrucci, *La scrittura: Ideologia e rappresentazione* (Turin: Einaudi,

1986), in English translation as *Public Lettering: Script, Power, and Culture*, trans. Linda Lappin (Chicago: University of Chicago Press, 1993). The importance of mastering monumental writing is clear in a detail that the same anonymous Roman gives of the tactics of Cola di Rienzo, the great Roman tribune of the fourteenth century who attempted to reestablish the ancient Republic. According to this source, Cola "reflected all day long on the marble reliefs that lay about Rome. He alone knew how to read the ancient epitaphs. He transposed the ancient writings into the vernacular tongue. He accurately interpreted these marble figures." Cola's scholarship had a political aim, because he discovered and deciphered a tablet of the law referring to the Empire under Vespasian that he accused Pope Boniface VIII of having hidden. Cola contended that this law, according to which the Senate granted the Empire to Vespasian, nullified the Donation of Constantine, on which the temporal power of the popes was founded. In the twelfth century, no one possessed either Cola's knowledge or his political will, and the mocking decipherment of the inscription with the six Ps attributed the commemoration of Pope Joan to him, providing yet another example of revenge on the alienation of meaning. The text of this anonymous source is quoted and commented on in Chiara Frugoni, "L'antichità: Dai 'mirabilia' alla propaganda politica," in *Memoria dell'antico nell'arte italiana*, ed. Salvatore Settis, vol. 1, *L'uso dei classici* (Turin: Einaudi, 1984), 5–72, esp. p. 33. See also Augusto Fraschetti, "Rome: Un sujet double au Moyen Age," *Mi-dit: Cahiers Méridionaux de Psychanalyse* 10–11 (1985): 68–74. I have used Fraschetti's translation of this anonymous author.

Chapter Four

1. Jean de Mailly, *Chronica universalis Mettensis*, in *MGH, Scriptores*, vol. 24 (Hannover, 1879), 502–26, esp. p. 514.

2. See Ludwig Weiland, "Die Chronik des Predigermönches Johannes von Mailly," *Archiv der Gesellschaft für alter deutschen Geschichtkunde* 11 (1874): 419–73, and Antoine Dondaine, "Le dominicain français Jean de Mailly et la Légende dorée," *Archives d'Histoire Dominicaine* 1 (1946): 53–102.

3. Etienne de Bourbon, quoted in Dondaine, "Le dominicain français Jean de Mailly."

4. Jean de Mailly, *L'Abrégé des gestes et miracles des saints*, trans. Antoine Dondaine (Paris: Cerf, 1947).

5. On Bartholomew of Trent and his *Liber epilogarum*, see Alain Boureau, "Les vignes de Bolzano: Edition de l'Epilogus de Barthélémy de Trente sur la Nativité du Seigneur," in *Contributi alla Storia della Regione Trentino-Alto Adige, Civis: Studi e Testi*, supplement 2 (Trent, 1986), 91–104. For a more general presentation, see Boureau, "Barthélémy de Trente et l'invention de la 'Legenda nova,'" in *Raccolte di Vite di Santi dal XIII al XVIII secolo: Strutture, messaggi, fruizioni*, the Acts of a colloquy, Rome, May 1985, ed. Sofia Boesch Gajano (Fasano di Brindisi: Schena, 1990), 23–39.

6. See Alain Boureau, *La Légende dorée: Le système narratif de Jacques de Vo-

ragine (†1298) (Paris: Cerf, 1984), and Barbara Fleith, *Studien zur Überlieferungs-geschichte des lateinischen Legenda aurea,* a dissertation on the manuscript tradition of the *Golden Legend,* University of Geneva, 1986 (Brussels: Société des Bollandistes, 1991).

7. For a concrete illustration of this mobility, see the biography of Bernard Gui in Bernard Guenée, "Bernard Gui (1261–1331)," in Guenée, *Entre l'Eglise et l'Etat; Quatre vies de prélats français à la fin du Moyen Age, XIIIe–XVe siècle* (Paris: Gallimard, 1987), 49–85, available in English translation as *Between Church and State: The Lives of Four French Prelates in the Late Middle Ages,* trans. Arthur Goldhammer (Chicago: University of Chicago Press, 1991), 37–70.

8. Jacopo da Voragine, *Legenda aurea,* ed. Theodor Graesse, 3d ed. (Dresden, 1890), 260, quoted from *The Golden Legend: Readings on the Saints,* trans. William Granger Ryan, 2 vols. (Princeton, N.J.: Princeton University Press, 1993), 1: 238.

9. Jacques Le Goff, "Culture ecclésiastique et culture folklorique au Moyen Age: Saint Marcel de Paris et le dragon," in Le Goff, *Pour un autre Moyen Age: Temps, travail et culture en Occident: 18 essais* (Paris: Gallimard, 1977), 236–79, available in English translation as "Ecclesiastical Culture and Folklore in the Middle Ages: Saint Marcellus of Paris and the Dragon," in *Time, Work and Culture in the Middle Ages,* trans. Arthur Goldhammer (Chicago: University of Chicago Press, 1980), 159–88.

10. Jacopo da Voragine, *Legenda aurea,* 164; *Golden Legend,* 1: 148.

11. Hermann Korner, *Chronica novella,* ed. Johann Georg von Eckhart, *Corpus historicum Medii Aevi* (Leipzig, 1723), 2: 442.

12. See Vittorio Coletti, *Parole dal pulpito: Chiesa e movimenti religiosi tra latino e volgare* (Genoa: Marietti, 1983), in French translation as *L'éloquence de la chaire: Victoires et défaites du latin entre Moyen Age et Renaissance,* trans. Silvano Serventi (Paris: Cerf, 1987).

13. Bartolomeo Platina, *Platynae historici Liber de vita Christi ac omnium Pontificum (aa. 1–1474),* ed. Giacinto Gaida (1913), new enlarged ed. (Città di Castello: S. Lapi, 1932), 152.

14. Dondaine, "Le dominicain français Jean de Mailly."

15. Ibid.

16. Jean de Mailly, *Abrégé des gestes et miracles des saints,* 93.

17. See Boureau, "Les vignes de Bolzano," 100.

18. Quoted from Georges and Andrée Duby, *Les procès de Jeanne d'Arc* (Paris: Gallimard, 1973), 15.

19. See *Dictionnaire apologétique de la foi catholique,* (1911), s.v. "Jeanne (la papesse)" (Félix Vernet).

20. Jansen Enikel, *Weltcronik,* ed. Philipp Strauch, in *MGH, Scriptores qui vernacula lingue usi sunt,* vol. 3, *Deutsche Chroniken,* vol. 3 (Hannover and Leipzig, 1900), p. 434 (verses 22, 295–22, 520). My thanks to Jean-Marie Moeglin for calling this text to my attention.

21. Jacob van Maerlant, *Spiegel historiael,* vol. 3 (Leiden, 1857), 220.

22. Jacques Berlioz and others are preparing a critical edition of Etienne de Bourbon, *Traité de divers matériaux de la prédication* (*Tractatus de diversis materiis praedicabilibus*).

23. I am paraphrasing here the definition given by Claude Bremond, Jacques Le Goff, and Jean-Claude Schmitt in *L'exemplum* (Turnhout: Brepols, 1982), 37–38, omitting one term of their definition, "donné comme véridique." Fables in the spirit of Aesop are never given as truthful, but rather as signifying. See below, on the development of belief in the Middle Ages.

24. Etienne de Bourbon, *Tractatus de diversis materiis*, MS Bibliothèque Nationale, Paris, Latin 15970, fol. 574r.

25. Jacopo da Voragine, *Chronica Januensis*, in a modern edition as *Iacopo de Varagine e la sua Cronaca di Genova: Dalle origini al MCCXVII*, ed. Giovanni Monleone, 3 vols. (Rome: Tipografia del Senato, 1941), 2: 4.

26. See Boureau, *Légende dorée*, 45 – 63.

27. Mariano da Firenze, *Itinerarium urbis Romae*, ed. Enrico Bulletti (Rome: Pontificio Istituto di Archeologia Cristiana, 1931), 169, quoted in Cesare D'Onofrio, *La Papessa Giovanna: Roma e papato tra storia e leggenda* (Rome: Romana Società Editrice, 1979), 213 – 14.

28. Jacopo de Voragine, *Iacopo de Varagine e la sua Cronaca di Genoa*, 2: 268 – 69.

29. There is a critical edition of the Latin text of Arnoldus of Liège: *L'Alphabetum narrationum: Un receuil d'exempla compilé au début du XIVe siècle*, ed. Colette Ribeaucourt, *thèse* defense, Ecole des Hautes Etudes en Sciences Sociales, Paris 1985.

30. Arnoldus of Liège, *Recull de eximplis e miracles, gestes et faules e altres ligendes ordenades per ABC*, ed. A. Verdaguer (Barcelona, 1881), 147.

31. *Chronica minor auctore minorita Erphordiensi*, ed. Oswald Holder-Egger, *MGH, Scriptores*, vol. 24 (Hannover, 1897), 172–204, esp. p. 184.

32. Ludwig Weiland, "Die Chronik des Predigermönches Johannes von Mailly," *Archiv der Gesellschaft für alter deutschen Geschichtkunde*, 12 (1875): 1–78.

33. Martinus Polonus, *Chronica de Romanis Pontificibus et imperatoribus*, in *MGH, Scriptorum*, vol. 22, ed. Georg Heinrich Pertz (Hannover, 1872), 428.

34. See Ernst H. Kantorowicz, "An 'Autobiography' of Guido Faba," reprinted in Kantorowicz, *Selected Studies* (Locust Valley, N.Y.: J. J. Augustin, 1965), 194–212.

35. *Cronica pontificum et imperatorum sancti Bartholomaei in insula romani*, ed. Oswald Holder-Egger, *MGH, Scriptorum*, vol. 31 (Hannover: Hahn, 1903), 218.

36. Jacopo de Voragine, *Legenda aurea*, 190; *Golden Legend*, 1: 172. The source of the pun is older, however (John Hymmonides).

37. Alberto Milioli, *Liber de temporibus*, ed. Oswald Holder-Egger, *MGH, Scriptores*, vol. 31 (Hannover: Hahn, 1903), 353 – 668, esp. p. 420.

38. Geoffroy de Courlon, *Chronique de l'abbaye de Saint-Pierre-le-Vif de Sens*, ed. Gustave Julliot (Sens, 1876), 296 – 99.

39. This exemplum is translated in Albert Lecoy de la Marche, *Anecdotes historiques, légendes et apologues tirés du receuil inédit d'Etienne de Bourbon, Dominicain du XIIIe siècle* (Paris, 1877), anecdote 376.

40. Leone da Orvieto, *Chronica de temporibus et gestis Romanorum Pontificum*, Biblioteca Riccardiana, Florence, 338, fols. 99 – 163. The manuscript was published by Giovanni Lami in *Deliciae eruditorum, seu Veterum* ΑΝΕΚΔΟΤΩΝ *opusculorum collectanea* (Florence, 1736 –), vol. 3 (1736), 337.

41. Pietro Calo da Barletta, quoted in Baudouin de Gaiffier, "La nativité de saint Etienne: A propos des fresques de Tivoli," *Atti e Memorie della Società Tiburtina di Storia e d'Arte* 41 (1968): 105 – 112.

42. Guibert de Nogent, *De vita sua*, consulted as *Autobiographie*, ed. and trans. Edmond-René Labande (Paris: Belles Lettres, 1981), 213 – 25, available in English as *Self and Society in Medieval France: The Memoirs of Abbot Guibert of Nogent*, ed. John F. Benton (Toronto and Buffalo: University of Toronto Press in association with the Medieval Academy of America, 1984).

43. John Lathbury, quoted in Beryl Smalley, *English Friars and Antiquity in the Early Fourteenth Century* (New York: Barnes and Noble, 1960), 225.

44. Innocent IV's letter is quoted in Solomon Grayzel, *The Church and the Jews in the XIIIth Century* (Philadelphia: Dropsie College for Hebrew and Cognate Learning, 1933), 268 – 71.

45. Martinus Polonus, *Chronica*, 428.

46. See "Les pouvoirs informels dans l'Eglise," special issue, ed. André Vauchez, *Mélanges de l'Ecole française de Rome* 98, 1 (1986).

47. Marie-Dominique Chenu, *La théologie comme science au XIIIe siècle*, 3d ed. rev. and enlarged (Paris: J. Vrin, 1969).

48. Guenée, *Entre l'Eglise et l'Etat*, 141, quoted from *Between Church and State*, 116.

49. Guenée, *Entre l'Eglise et l'Etat*, 141; *Between Church and State*, 117.

50. Daniel Milo, "Laboratoire temporel grandeur naturelle: Le calendrier révolutionnaire," in Milo, *Trahir le temps (histoire)* (Paris: Belles Lettres, 1991), 193 – 224.

51. Bartolomé Carranza, *Summa omnium Conciliorum et Pontificum* (1546) (Rome, 1665), 734.

52. Jean Rioche, *Compendium temporum et historiarum ecclesiasticarum . . .* (Paris, 1576), fol. 230v.

53. Ranulf Higden, *Polychronicon . . .* , ed. Churchill Babington and Joseph Rawson Lumby, 9 vols. (London, 1865 – 86), vol. 6 (1876), 330.

54. See *Histoire littéraire de la France*, vol. 12 (Paris, 1869), 479, and vol. 13 (1870), 330.

55. Bernard Gui (Bernardus Guidonis), *Catalogus Pontificum Romanorum cum inserta temporum historia*, in Angelo Mai, *Spicilegium Romanum*, vol. 6 (Rome, 1841), 202 – 3.

56. See the report of a discussion given after Alain Boureau, "La papesse

Jeanne: Formes et fonctions d'une légende au Moyen Age," *Comptes-Rendus de l'Académie des Inscriptions et des Belles-Lettres* (1984): 446 – 64; esp. p. 464.

57. Tolomeo da Lucca, *Historia ecclesiastica*, published in Ludovico Antonio Muratori, *Rerum Italicarum Scriptores* (Milan, 1723 – 51), XI, 2: 1013 – 14.

58. *Chronik Johanns von Winterthur* (*Cronica Iohannis Vidodurani*) in *MGH, Scriptores rerum germanicarum, Nova Series,* vol. 3 (Berlin: Weidmann, 1924), 33.

59. *Vita Urbani V,* ed. G[uillaume] Mollat, in *Vitae Paparum avenionnensium,* 4 vols. (Paris: Letouzey et Ané, 1914 – 27), 1: 366.

60. Johann Burchard, *Liber notarum,* ed. Enrico Celani (Città di Castello: Lapi, 1907 – 10), 1: 82 – 83.

61. Dietrich of Nieheim, *Historia de gestis Romanorum Principum,* ed. Katharina Colberg and Joachim Leuschner, in *MGH,* Staatsschriften des späteren Mittelalters (Stuttgart: Hiersemann, 1980), 27 – 28.

62. *Chronica minor autore minorita Erphordiensi,* 184.

63. Siegfried of Balhusen (or of Meissen), *Compendium historiarum,* in *MGH, Scriptorum,* ed. Oswald Holder-Egger, vol. 25 (Hannover, 1880), 679 – 718, esp. p. 684.

64. See Jean-Marie Moeglin, *Les ancêtres du Prince: Propagande politique et naissance d'une histoire nationale en Bavière au Moyen Age (1180 – 1500)* (Geneva: Droz, 1985), 59 – 61.

65. *Flores temporum,* in *MGH, Scriptores,* ed. Oswald Holder-Egger, vol. 24 (Hannover, 1847), 228 – 50, esp. p. 248.

66. See Jean-Jacques Nattiez, *Fondements d'une sémiologie de la musique* (Paris: UGE, 1975, 1978).

67. See Jean Rychner, *La chanson de geste: Essai sur l'art épique des jongleurs* (Geneva and Lucca: Droz, 1955), which refers to Lord's works. See also Marcel Jousse, *Etudes de psychologie linguistique: Le style oral rythmique et mnémotechnique chez les verbo-moteurs* (Paris: 1925), available in English translation as *The Oral Style,* trans. Edgard Sienaert and Richard Whitaker (New York: Garland, 1990).

68. Johann Joseph Ignaz von Döllinger, *Die Papst-Fabeln des Mittelalters: Ein Betrag zur Kirchengeschichte (1863),* 2d ed. (Stuttgart, 1890), in English translation of the first edition, *Fables Respecting the Popes of the Middle Ages,* trans. Alfred Plummer (London, Oxford, and Cambridge, 1871), 44 – 47.

69. Christian Jouhaud, "Lisibilité et persuasion: Les placards politiques," in *Les usages de l'imprimé (XVe–XIXe siècle),* ed. Roger Chartier (Paris: Fayard, 1984), 309 – 42, in English translation as "Readability and Persuasion: Political Handbills," in *The Culture of Print,* trans. Lydia G. Cochrane (Oxford; Polity Press/ Blackwell, 1989), 235 – 60.

70. *Chronica S. Ægidii in Brunswig* and *Chronicon Theodorici Engelhusii,* in *Scriptores Brunsvicienses,* ed. Gottfried Wilhelm von Leibniz (Hannover, 1707 – 11), 3: 580, 2: 1065, respectively.

71. The text of this chronicle is apparently lost, but the fragment pertaining to Joan is published in Johann Wolf, *Lectiones memorabiles et reconditae* (1600), 2d ed. (Frankfurt, 1671), 1: 177.

72. Heinrich von München, *Weltchronik,* is unpublished. Extracts (which include the passage concerning Joan) appear in Paul Gichtel, *Die Weltchronik Heinrichs von München in der Runkelsteiner Handschrift des Heinz Sentlinger* (Munich: C. H. Beck, 1937), 391 – 92, for the passage on Joan. My thanks to Jean-Marie Moeglin for calling this text to my attention.

73. This is one of the themes of the legend of St. Eustace and of the constellation of tales from which that legend was drawn. See *Les avatars d'un conte,* ed. Claude Bremond, special issue on narrations of *Communications* 39 (1984).

74. Joinville, *Histoire de Saint Louis,* ed. Francisque Michel (Paris, 1830), 23, quoted from *The Life of St. Louis,* trans. René Hague from the text edited by Natalis de Wailly (New York: Sheed and Ward, 1955), 30.

75. *De perfectione statuum ordinis fratrum minorum,* quoted in Brian Tierney, *The Origins of Papal Infallibility, 1150 – 1350; A Study on the Concepts of Infallibility, Sovereignty and Tradition in the Middle Ages* (Leiden: E. J. Brill, 1972), 166 – 68.

76. See Marjory Reeves, *The Influence of Prophecy in the Later Middle Ages: A Study in Joachimism* (Oxford: Clarendon Press, 1969).

77. See, in particular, Marie-Dominique Chenu, "Conscience de l'histoire et théologie," in Chenu, *La théologie au XIIe siècle* (1957) (Paris: J. Vrin, 1976), 62 – 89.

78. Tierney, *Origins of Papal Infallibility,* 76.

79. Peter of John Olivi, *Lectura super Apocalypsim,* quoted in Tierney, *Origins of Papal Infallibility,* 107.

80. Jacopone da Todi, in Brian Tierney, *The Foundations of the Conciliar Theory: The Contributions of the Medieval Canonists from Gratian to the Great Schism* (Cambridge: Cambridge University Press, 1955), 159.

81. Jacopo da Voragine, *Iacopo de Varagine e la sua Cronaca di Genova,* 2: 409 – 10.

82. On the pairing of Martha and Mary and its polemical currency, see Jean-Claude Schmitt, *Mort d'une hérésie: L'Eglise et les clercs face aux béguines et aux bégards du Rhin supérieur du XIVe au XVe siècle* (Paris, The Hague, and New York: Mouton, 1978), 101 – 4.

83. *Gesta Boemundi archiepiscopi Treverensis,* in *MGH, Scriptores,* vol. 24 (Hannover, 1879), 476. The term "dialogic" is used in the sense given to it by Mikhail Bakhtin.

84. Olivi, *De renuntiatione,* as mentioned in Tierney, *Origins of Papal Infallibility,* 102.

85. Jean de Paris (Jean Quidort), *De regia potestate et papali,* ed. Fritz Bleiestein (Stuttgart: Klett, 1969), available in English translation as *On Royal and Papal Power,* trans. Arthur P. Monahan (New York: Columbia University Press, 1974).

86. Robert d'Uzès, in Jeanne Bignami Odier, "Les Visions de Robert d'Uzès," *Archivum Fratrum Praedicatorum* 25 (1955): 258 – 320, esp. pp. 285 – 86.

87. Leone da Orvieto, *Chronica,* in Lami, *Deliciae eruditorum,* 3: 335. See also Arturo Graf, "Il rifiuto di Celestino V," in Graf, *Miti, leggende e superstizioni del*

Medio Evo, 2 vols. (Turin, 1892–93), reprint (Milan, 1894), 287–92. Graf's brief but penetrating analysis does not mention Leone da Orvieto's version of these events, however.

88. Tierney, *Origins of Papal Infallibility.*

89. See Wilhelm Kölmel, *Wilhelm Ockham und seine kirchenpolitischen Schriften* (Essen: Ludgerus, 1962).

90. William of Ockham, *Opus nonaginta dierum,* ed. J. G. Sykes and H. S. Offler, in *Guillelmi de Ockam Opera politica,* ed. R. F. Bennett and H. S. Offler, 4 vols. (Manchester: University of Manchester Press, 1940–97), vol. 2 (1963), 854. The first part of the *Opus nonaginta dierum* appears at the end of vol. 1, ed. J. G. Sykes (1940).

91. See ibid.

92. Ibid., vol. 1.

93. Claudio Sergio Ingerflom, "De l'inversion au despotisme et à l'imposture: Quelques réflexions sur les représentations du pouvoir dans la Russie des XIVe et XVIIe siècles."

94. Tomás de Torquemada, *Summa de Ecclesia* (Venice, 1561), 394.

95. Antoninus, *Chronica Antonini* (Lyon, 1543), fol. 148.

96. Leone da Orvieto, in Lami, *Deliciae eruditorum,* 337.

97. Martin Lefranc, *Le champion des dames* (ca. 1430) (Paris, 1530), fol. 335; in Casimir Oudin, ed., *Commentarius de scriptoribus ecclesiae antiquis,* 3 vols. (Leipzig, 1722), 3: 2466.

98. John Wycliffe, *Cruciata,* in *John Wiclif's Polemical Works in Latin,* ed. Rudolf Buddensieg, 2 vols. (London, 1883), 2: 619.

99. Here and below, quotations regarding Hus are taken from Matthew Spinka, *John Hus at the Council of Constance* (New York: Columbia University Press, 1965), 192, 209, 212.

100. See Walter Ullmann, "The University of Cambridge and the Great Schism," *Journal of Theological Studies,* n.s., 9 (1958): 53–77.

101. Guenée, *Entre l'Eglise et l'Etat,* 153.

102. Philippe de Mézières, *Le songe du Vieil Pèlerin,* ed. George William Coopland, 2 vols. (Cambridge: Cambridge University Press, 1969), 1: 338.

103. Ibid., 370.

104. Dietrich of Nieheim, *Historia de gestis Romanorum Principum.*

105. Dietrich of Nieheim, *De modis uniendi et reformandi ecclesiam in concilio universale,* ed. Hermann Heimpel (Leipzig: Tübner, 1933), 55–56.

106. *Eulogium historiarum sive temporum,* ed. Frank Scott Haydon, 3 vols. (London, 1858–63), 1: 243.

107. Ullmann, "The University of Cambridge and the Great Schism," 60.

108. Jean Gerson, Sermon, "Apparuit" ("De Pace"), in *Oeuvres complètes,* ed. Palémon Glorieux (Paris and New York: Desclée, 1960–), 5: 64–90.

109. John XII was deposed by Otto, the emperor, not by the Church. He re-

turned to power and was assassinated. The absence of a number after "John" in Gerson's text might seem to point to Joan, in Martinus's version. The text seems to infer that "John" was deposed. This was true of Joan in only two versions, which we have seen.

110. Jean Gerson, "Apparuit," 87.

111. See Howard Kaminsky, "Cession, Substraction, Deposition; Simon de Cramaud's Formulation of the French Solution to the Schism," in *Post Scripta: Essays on Medieval Law and the Emergence of the European State, in Honor of Gaines Post*, ed. Josephus Forchielli and Alphonsus M. Strickler, Studia Gratiana, 15 (Rome: Studia Gratiana, 1972), 295–318.

112. Jean Roques (de Rocha), *Contra evasiones Johannis de Gersono super suis assertionibus erroneis*, in Gerson, *Opera omnia*, ed. Louis Ellies Du Pin (Antwerp, 1706), 5: 456. It is probable that Joan appears in many other places in the immense polemical literature (still largely unpublished) that developed around the Great Schism. For example, Honoré Bonet speaks of Joan in a juridico-apocalytical context in *Arbre des batailles* (ca. 1386). For this passage, see *Arbre des batailles*, ed. Ernest Nys (Brussels and Leipzig, 1883), 21–22, available in English translation as *The Tree of Battles*, ed. and trans. George William Coopland (Liverpool: University Press, 1949).

113. See John Saward, *Perfect Fools: Folly for Christ's Sake in Catholic and Orthodox Spirituality* (Oxford and New York: Oxford University Press, 1980), 91, in French translation as *Dieu à la folie; Histoire des saints fous pour le Christ* (Paris: Seuil, 1983).

Chapter Five

1. Michael Dummett with Sylvia Mann, *The Game of Tarot from Ferrara to Salt Lake City* (London: Duckworth, 1980).

2. For the Ferrara text, see Robert Steele, "A Notice of the Ludus Triumphorum and Some Early Italian Card Games," *Archaeologia* 57 (1900): 189–200.

3. The reference is of course to Johan Huizinga's classic work, available in English translation as *The Autumn of the Middle Ages*, trans. Rodney J. Payton and Ulrich Mammitzsch (Chicago: University of Chicago Press, 1996).

4. On the expansion of this signifying image, see Alain Boureau, "Les livres d'emblèmes sur la scène publique: Côté jardin et côté cour," in *Les usages de l'imprimé*, ed. Roger Chartier, 343–97, in English translation as "Books of Emblems on the Public Stage; Côté jardin and côté cour," in *The Culture of Print*, trans. Lydia G. Cochrane (Oxford: Polity Press/Blackwell, 1989), 261–89.

5. Gisèle Lambert, "Les tarots humanistes," in *Tarot, jeu et magie*, catalog of an exhibition, Galerie Mazarine, Bibliothèque Nationale, Paris, 17 October 1984–6 January 1985 (Paris: Bibliothèque Nationale, 1984), 45–48.

6. See Dummett, *Game of Tarot*, 68.

7. Giuliana Algeri, *Gli Zavattari: Una famiglia di pittori e la cultura tardogotica in Lombardia* (Rome, 1981).

8. Ibid. See also the fine reproduction of the Visconti-Sforza Tarot and Calvino's commentary in Italo Calvino, *Tarots: Le jeu de cartes Visconti de Bergame et New York* (Milan and Paris: Ricci, 1974).

9. Gertrude Moakley, *The Tarot Cards painted by Bonifacio Bembo for the Visconti-Sforza Family: An Iconographic and Historical Study* (New York: New York Public Library, 1966).

10. For Guglielma, see the excellent summary in *Dictionnaire de théologie catholique* (1925), s.v. "Guillelmites." For a transcript of the trial of 1300, see Felice Tocco in *Rendiconti della R. Accademia dei Lincei*, Classe di scienze morali, series V, vol. 8 (Rome, 1899), 309 – 469. Carlo Ginzburg has kindly brought to my attention a recent summary of the Guglielmite afffair: Luisa Muraro, *Guglielma e Maifreda: Storia di un'eresia femminista* (Milan: La Tartaruga, 1985). This work contains a complete bibliography, and Muraro has completely revised the Tocco transcription. See also Marina Benedetti, *Io non sono Dio: Guglielma di Milano e i Figli dello Santo Spirito* (Milan: Edizioni Biblioteca Francescana 1998). I have preferred the classic form of the name Manfreda to Muraro's "Maifreda," but the two forms are found in the trial report.

11. *Dictionnaire de théologie catholique*, s.v. "Guillelmites."

12. Ibid.

13. Johannes of Wissenbourg, *Annales Colmarienses majores,* in *MGH, Scriptores,* vol. 17 (Hannover, 1861), 226.

14. I owe the notion of a "change of scale," important to the question of the difficult relationship between "macro-" and "micro-" history, to Jacques Revel.

15. Jack Goody, *The Development of the Family and Marriage in Europe* (Cambridge and New York: Cambridge University Press, 1983).

16. See Antonio Corvi, *Il processo di Bonifacio VIII: Studio critico* (Rome: Officina Grafica Bodoni, 1948).

17. Boniface VIII, bull *Nuper au audientiam,* quoted in *Dictionnaire de théologie catholique,* s.v. "Guillelmites."

18. Gabrio de Zamorei, *Sermo De Fide,* quoted in Muraro, *Guglielma e Maifreda,* 106. See ibid., 206 for the bibliographic reference.

19. Norman Rufus Colin Cohn, *Europe's Inner Demons: An Enquiry Inspired by the Great Witch-Hunt* (New York: Basic Books, 1975), in French translation as *Démonolâtrie et sorcellerie au Moyen Age: Fantasmes et réalités* (Paris: Payot, 1982).

20. Adhémar de Chabannes, *Historia Francorum,* 3: 59; see Cohn, *Europe's Inner Demons,* 20; *Démonolâtrie et sorcellerie,* 40.

21. Paul, Monk of Chartres, *Liber Aganonis,* cited in Cohn, *Europe's Inner Demons,* 20 – 21; *Démonolâtrie et sorcellerie,* 40.

22. Guibert de Nogent, *De vita sua;* in *Autobiographie,* ed. and trans. Edmond-René Labande (Paris: Belles Lettres, 1981), 429, in English translation as *Self and Society in Medieval France: The Memoirs of Abbot Guibert of Nogent,* ed. John F. Benton (Toronto, Buffalo, and London: University of Toronto Press, in association with the Medieval Academy of America, 1984).

23. Carlo Ginzburg, "Présomptions sur le sabbat," *Annales E.S.C.* 39, 2 (1984): 341–54.

24. Carlo Ginzburg, *I benandanti: Stregoneria e culti agrari tra Cinquecento e Seicento* (Turin: Einaudi, 1966, 1972), in English translation as *The Night Battles: Witchcraft and Agrarian Cults in the Sixteenth and Seventeenth Centuries,* trans. John and Anne Tedeschi (Baltimore: Johns Hopkins University Press, 1983).

25. Cohn, *Europe's Inner Demons,* 217; *Démonolâtrie et sorcellerie,* 271.

26. I have used the very convenient anthology of texts drawn up by Georges and Andrée Duby, *Les procès de Jeanne d'Arc* (Paris: Gallimard, 1973). For excellent complete critical editions of the two trials of Joan of Arc, see Pierre Tisset, *Procès de condamnation de Jeanne d'Arc,* 3 vols. (Paris: Klincksieck, 1960–71), and Pierre Duparc, *Procès en nullité de la condamnation de Jeanne d'Arc,* 5 vols. (Paris: Klincksieck, 1977–86). Some quotations from the trial proceedings have been taken from *The Trial of Jeanne d'Arc,* trans. W. P. Barret (New York: Gotham House, 1932).

27. Duby and Duby, *Procès de Jeanne d'Arc,* 156; Barrett, ed. *Trial of Jeanne d'Arc,* 316.

28. Duby and Duby, *Procès de Jeanne d'Arc,* 115; Barrett, ed., *Trial of Jeanne d'Arc,* 126.

29. See Alain Boureau, "L'inceste de Judas; Essai sur la genèse de l'antisémitisme au XIIe siècle," *Nouvelle Revue de Psychanalyse* 33 (1986): 25–41.

30. Duby and Duby, *Procès de Jeanne d'Arc,* 129; Barrett, ed., *Trial of Jeanne d'Arc,* 154.

31. François Neveux, *L'évêque Pierre Cauchon* (Paris: Denoël, 1987).

32. Duke of Bedford, quoted in ibid., 132.

33. *Journal d'un bourgeois de Paris,* quoted in ibid., 133; quoted here from *A Parisian Journal,* trans. Janet Shirley (Oxford: Clarendon Press, 1968), 240.

34. Duby and Duby, *Procès de Jeanne d'Arc,* 61; Barrett, ed., *Trial of Jeanne d'Arc,* 68.

35. Duby and Duby, *Procès de Jeanne d'Arc,* 62 (for Joan's letter); see also Barrett, ed., *Trial of Jeanne d'Arc,* 68 (for the trial record).

36. Duby and Duby, *Procès de Jeanne d'Arc,* 130; *Trial of Jeanne d'Arc,* 160.

37. My thanks to Michael Barry for calling these passages to my attention.

38. Duby and Duby, *Procès de Jeanne d'Arc,* 257.

39. Ibid., 262.

40. Bernard McGinn, "*Teste David cum Sibylla;* The Significance of the Sibylline Tradition in the Middle Ages," in *Women of the Medieval World: Essays in Honor of John H. Mundy,* ed. Julius Kirshner and Suzanne F. Wimple (Oxford and New York: Basil Blackwell, 1985), 7–35.

41. Giulia Sissa, *Le corps virginal: La virginité féminine en Grèce ancienne,* preface by Nicole Loraux (Paris: Vrin, 1987), available in English as *Greek Virginity,* trans. Arthur Goldhammer (Cambridge, Mass.: Harvard University Press, 1990).

42. Origen, quoted in Sissa, *Corps virginal,* 48, quoted here from *Greek Virginity,* 22.

43. John Chrysostom, quoted in Sissa, *Corps virginal,* 48 – 49; *Greek Virginity,* 23.

44. The best introduction to the work of Oskar Panizza (to whom we shall return) is still his "Autobiography," given in the French translation of his *Liebeskonzil,* his best-known text: *Le concile d'amour* (Paris, 1964), translated into English by Oreste F. Pucciani under the title *The Council of Love: A Celestial Tragedy in Five Acts* (New York: Viking, 1973).

45. See McGinn, *"Teste David cum Sibylla"*; Bernard McGinn, "Joachim and the Sybil: An Early Work of Joachim of Fiore from Ms 322 of the Biblioteca Antoniana in Padua," *Cîteaux* 24 (1973): 97 – 138; McGinn, *Visions of the End: Apocalyptic Traditions in the Middle Ages* (New York: Columbia University Press, 1979).

46. See *Virgile au Moyen Age* (Rome: Ecole Française de Rome, 1985), and Domenico Comparetti, *Virgilio nel Medio Evo* (Livorno, 1872), new edition, ed. Giorgio Pasquali, 2 vols. (Florence: La Nuova Italia, 1937 – 41), available in English as *Vergil in the Middle Ages,* trans. E. F. M. Benecke (London and New York, 1895).

47. See McGinn, *"Teste David cum Sibylla,"* 20.

48. Jacques Le Goff, *La naissance du Purgatoire* (Paris: Gallimard, 1981), available in English translation as *The Birth of Purgatory,* trans. Arthur Goldhammer (Chicago: University of Chicago Press, 1984).

49. Alfons Kurfess, "Dies irae," *Historisches Jahrbuch* 77 (1957): 328 – 38.

50. Alain Boureau, "Les vignes de Bolzano: Edition de l'Epilogus de Barthélémy de Trente sur la Nativité du Seigneur," in *Contributi alla Storia della Regione Trentino-Alto Adige, Civis: Studi e Testi,* supplement 2 (Trent, 1986), 91 – 104.

51. See Luigi Paolucci, *La Sibilla Appenninica* (Florence: Olschki, 1967), and Antoine de la Sale, *Le paradis de la Reine Sibylle* (Paris: Stock, 1984), an adaptation in modern French.

52. Sissa, *Corps virginal,* 61; *Greek Virginity,* 36.

53. Quoted in McGinn, *"Teste David cum Sibylla,"* 24 – 25.

54. Nicole Loraux, "Sur la race des femmes et quelques-unes de leurs tribus," in *Les enfants d'Athéna: Idées athéniennes sur la citoyenneté et la division des sexes* (Paris: Maspero, 1981), 75 – 118, available in English translation as "On the Race of Women and Some of Its Tribes: Hesiod and Semonides," in *Athenian Ideas about Citizenship and the Division between the Sexes,* trans. Caroline Levine (Princeton: Princeton University Press, 1993), 72 – 110.

55. Peter Dronke, *Women Writers of the Middle Ages: A Critical Study of Texts from Perpetua (†203) to Marguerite Porete (†1310)* (Cambridge and New York: Cambridge University Press, 1984), 217.

56. For a published version of the visions of Marie Robine, with commentary, see Matthew Tobin, "Le 'Livre des Révélations' de Marie Robine (†1399): Etude et édition," *Mélanges de l'Ecole Française de Rome, Moyen Age, Temps Modernes,* 98, 1 (1986): 229 – 64.

57. See Philippe Boutry and Jacques Nassif, *Martin l'Archange* (Paris: Gallimard, 1986).

58. André Vauchez, *Les Laïcs au Moyen Age: Pratiques et expériences religieuses* (Paris: Cerf, 1987), 284, quoted from *The Laity in the Middle Ages: Religious Beliefs and Devotional Practices*, ed., with an introduction, by Daniel E. Bornstein, trans. Margery J. Schneider (Notre Dame: University of Notre Dame Press, 1993), 262. See also (as Vauchez suggests) Evelyne Patlagean, "L'histoire de la femme déguisé en moine et l'évolution de la sainteté féminine à Byzance," *Studi medievali,* 3d ser., 17 (1976): 597–623.

59. Dronke, *Women Writers of the Middle Ages*, 231–64 (for the Latin texts); 144–201 (for commentary and English translation).

60. See Alain Boureau, "De la félonie à la haute trahison: La trahison des clercs, version du XIIe siècle," *Le Genre Humain* 16–17 (1987): 267–91.

61. See Jean-Claude Schmitt, *Mort d'une hérésie: L'Eglise et les clercs face aux béguines et aux bégards du Rhin supérieur du XIVe au XVe siècle* (Paris, The Hague, and New York: Mouton, 1978), chap. 4, n. 81.

62. Ferdinando Camon, *La malattia chiamata uomo* (Milan: Garzanti, 1987), available in English translation as *The Sickness Called Man*, trans. John Shepley (Marlboro, Vt.: Marlboro Press, 1992) and in French translation as *La maladie humaine*, trans., with an introduction, by Yves Hersant, 2d ed. (Paris: Gallimard, 1987), 18.

63. Hildegard of Bingen, *Autobiography*, fragment published in Dronke, *Women Writers of the Middle Ages*, 145, 150, 145 (for the English translation); 231, 236, 232 (for the Latin).

64. Ibid., 150 (English); 233 (Latin).

65. Ibid., 164 (English); 239 (Latin).

66. Hildegard of Bingen, *Causae et curae*, fragment published in Dronke, *Women Writers of the Middle Ages*, 175, 175 (English); 243, 244 (Latin).

67. Ibid., 176–77 (English), 244 (Latin).

68. Ibid., 175 (English); 244 (Latin).

69. Ibid., 176 (English); 244 (Latin).

70. Hildegard of Bingen, letter to Guibert of Gembloux, in Dronke, *Women Writers of the Middle Ages*, 169 (English), 253 (Latin).

71. Dronke, *Women Writers of the Middle Ages*, 165.

72. Caroline Walker Bynum, *Jesus as Mother: Studies in the Spirituality of the High Middle Ages* (Berkeley: University of California Press, 1982), 166.

73. See Schmitt, *Mort d'une hérésie*, 102.

74. Jacques Dalarun, "Robert d'Arbrissel et les femmes," *Annales E.S.C.* 39, 6 (1984): 1140–60, esp. pp. 1149, 1150.

75. Ibid., 1152–53.

76. Daniel Bornstein, "The Shrine of Santa Maria a Cigoli: Female Visionaries and Clerical Promoters," *Mélanges de l'Ecole Française de Rome, Moyen Age, Temps Modernes*, 98, 1 (1986): 219–28, quotation, 228.

77. Ibid.

78. Guillaume Postel, quoted by François Secret in the preface to his edition of Guillaume Postel, *Thresor des prophéties de l'univers* (The Hague: Martinus Nijhoff, 1969), 21.

79. Guillaume Postel, *Les Tres Merveilleuses Victoires . . .*, ed. Gustave Brunet (Turin, 1869), 42, quoted (in French) in M. A. Screech, "The Illusion of Postel's Feminism," *Journal of the Warburg and Courtauld Institute* 16 (1953): 162–70.

80. Guillaume Postel, *Rétractions*, quoted (in French) in Screech "The Illusion of Postel's Feminism," 163.

81. Postel, *Tres Merveilleuses Victoires*, 27, quoted (in French) in Screech, "The Illusion of Postel's Feminism," 168.

82. Postel, *Tres Merveilleuses Victoires*, 9; quoted (in French) in Screech, "The Illusion of Postel's Feminism," 169 n2.

83. Giovanni Boccaccio, *De mulieribus claris*, French translation, MS Bibliothèque Nationale, Paris, 12420, fol. 155v, and Bibliothèque Nationale, Paris, 226, fol. 252. See also Brigitte Buetnner, "Profane Illustrations, Secular Illusions: Manuscripts in Late Medieval Courtly Society," *Art Bulletin* 74, 1 (March 1992): 75–90.

84. Giovanni Boccaccio, *De mulieribus claris*, ed. Vittorio Zaccaria, vol. 10 of *Tutte le opere di Giovanni Boccaccio*, ed. Vittore Branca, 2d ed. (Milan: Mondadori, 1970), chap. 101, pp. 414–19, "Pope Joan" quoted here from *Concerning Famous Women*, trans. with introduction and notes by Guido A. Guarino (New Brunswick, N.J.: Rutgers University Press, 1963), 231–33.

85. Jacques Verger, "Pour une histoire de la Maîtrise ès-arts au Moyen Age: Quelques jalons," *Médiévales* 13 (1987): 117–30.

86. Boccaccio, *De mulieribus claris*, 32–38; *Concerning Famous Women*, 5, 6.

87. Christine de Pizan, *Le livre de la Cité des Dames*, translated, with an introduction, by Eric Hicks and Thérèse Moreau (Paris: Stock, 1986), available in English translation as *The Book of the City of Ladies*, trans. Earl Jeffrey Richards (New York: Persea, 1982).

88. Heldris de Cornüälle, *Le roman de Silence*, ed. Lewis Thorpe (Cambridge: W. Heffer & Sons, 1972). For the Old French text with English translation, see *Silence: A Thirteenth-Century Romance*, ed. and trans. Sarah Roche-Mahdi (East Lansing, Mich.: Colleagues Press, 1992).

89. Abbey of Tegernsee, Cod. Lat. 781, published in Johann Joseph Ignaz von Döllinger, *Die Papst-Fabeln des Mittelalters: Ein Betrag zur Kirchengeschichte* (1863), 2d ed. (Stuttgart, 1890), 40–41. The Latin text (with a summary in English) is available in the English translation of the first edition of this work, *Fables Respecting the Popes of the Middle Ages*, trans. Alfred Plummer (London, Oxford, and Cambridge, 1871), Appendix B, pp. 280–82.

CHAPTER SIX

1. See Matthew Spinka, *John Hus at the Council of Constance* (New York and London: Columbia University Press, 1961), 38.

2. Enea Silvio Piccolomini, letter of 21 August 1451, published in *Der Briefwechsel des Eneas Silvius Piccolomini*, ed. Rudolph Wolkan, Fontes Rerum Austriacarum, 2d ser., vol. 69, tome III, vol. 1 (Vienna: Hölder, 1918), 36, 40.

3. Lucien Febvre, *Un destin: Martin Luther* (1928), 4th ed. (Paris: Presses Universitaires de France, 1968), 142, in English translation as *Martin Luther: A Destiny*, trans. Roberts Tapley (New York: E. P. Dutton, 1929).

4. R. W. Scribner, "Reformation, Carnival and the World Turned Upside Down," *Social History* 3 (1978): 303 – 29.

5. Josef Benzinger, *Invectiva in Romam; Romkritik im Mittelalter vom 9. bis 12. Jahrhundert* (Lübeck and Hamburg: Matthiesen, 1968).

6. See André Chastel, *The Sack of Rome, 1527*, trans. Beth Archer, A. W. Mellon Lectures in the Fine Arts, 1977, vol. 26, The National Gallery of Art, Washington, D. C., Bollingen Series, 35 (Princeton, N.J.: Princeton University Press, 1983); *Le sac de Rome: Du premier maniérisme à l'art de la Contre-Réforme* (Paris: Gallimard, 1984).

7. Frutolf of Michelsberg, *Chronica Frutolfi*, continuation of *Ekkehardi Uraugiensis Chronica*, ed. Georg Waitz, in *MGH, Scriptores*, vol. 6 (Hannover, 1844), 214.

8. Anonymous of York (Anonymous Norman), quoted in Benzinger, *Invectiva in Romam*, 59 – 60. See also Harald Scherrinsky, *Untersuchungen zum sogenannten Anonymus von York (Tractatus Erboracenses)*, Inaugural Dissertation, Berlin, 1939 (Würtzburg: K. Triltsch, 1940; 1946).

9. Bonizo of Sutri (Bonithonis Sutriensis), *Liber . . . ad amicum*, in *MGH, De Lite*, 1: 571 – 620, esp. p. 580.

10. Sigebert von Gembloux, quoted in Benzinger, *Invectiva in Romam*.

11. Konrad von Megenberg, *Planctus Ecclesiae in Germaniam*, in *MGH, Staatsschriften des späteren Mittelalters*, vol. 2 (Leipzig: Hiersemann, 1946), chap. 10, p. 30.

12. František Šmahel, *Husitská revoluce* (Prague: Historický ústav, 1993), in French translation as *La Révolution hussite, une anomalie historique* (Paris: Presses Universitaires de France, 1985); John M. Klassen, *The Nobility and the Making of the Hussite Revolution* (Boulder, Colo.: Eastern European Quarterly; distribution: New York: Columbia University Press, 1978).

13. Piccolomini, *Briefwechsel*, III, 1: 27.

14. Ibid., 23, 26.

15. Ibid., 24.

16. Ibid., 26 – 27.

17. Ibid., 29.

18. For commentary on this image, see R. W. Scribner, *For the Sake of Simple Folk: Popular Propaganda for the German Reformation* (Cambridge and New York; Cambridge University Press, 1981), 172 – 73. My thanks to Jacques Revel for calling this fundamental study to my attention.

19. For a discussion of the images that illustrate this passage, see ibid., 170 – 77.

20. See ibid.

21. Martin Luther, quoted in Chastel, *Sac de Rome,* 106; quoted here from *Sack of Rome,* 78.

22. See Scribner, *For the Sake of Simple Folk,* 87.

23. On the Antichrist, see ibid., 150 – 55.

24. Chastel, *Sac de Rome,* 94 – 95; *Sack of Rome.* 78 – 83.

25. See Hans Preuss, *Die Vorstellung vom Antichrist im späteren Mittelalter, bei Luther und in der Konfessionellen Polemik* (Leipzig: Hinrichs, 1906), and Horst Dieter Rauh, *Das Bild des Antichrist im Mittelalter: Von Tyconius zum Deutschen Symbolismus* (Münster: Ascendorff, 1973). See also Aby Warburg, "Heidnisch-antike Weissagung im Wort und Bild zu Luthers Zeiten," in Warburg, *Gesammelte Schriften,* 2 vols. (Leipzig: Teubner, 1932), reprint (Berlin: Akademie Verlag, 1998 –), 2: 487 – 558. For a discussion of the Malanchthon-Cranach *Passional,* see Scribner, *For the Sake of Simple Folk,* 149 – 50.

26. Chastel, *Sac de Rome,* 109 – 10; *Sack of Rome.* 79, 82.

27. See Scribner, *For the Sake of Simple Folk,* 129 – 31.

28. See Natalie Zemon Davis, "Women on Top," in *Society and Culture in Early Modern France* (1965) (Stanford, Calif.: Stanford University Press, 1975), 124 – 51, in French translation as "La chevauchée des femmes," in *Les cultures du peuple; Rituels, pouvoir et résistances au XVIe siècle* (Paris, 1979), 216 – 50. For a positive perception of the hermaphrodite in Catholic juristic circles, see Valerio Marchetti, "Proposition de règlement juridique d'une troisième sexualité: Lorenzo Matheu y Sanz et les hermaphrodites (1663)," in *Droit, histoire et sexualité,* ed. Jacques Poumarède and Jean-Pierre Royer (Lille [Villeneuve-d'Ascq]: Espace Juridique; Paris: Distribution Distique, 1987), 131 – 43.

29. Michel de Montaigne, *Journal de voyage,* ed. Fausta Garavini and Jean Borie (Paris: Gallimard, 1983), 77 – 78; quoted from *The Complete Works of Montaigne,* trans. Donald M. Frame (Stanford: Stanford University Press, 1948, 1958), 869 – 70. See also Ambroise Paré, *On Monsters and Marvels,* trans., with introduction and notes, by Janis L. Pallister (Chicago and London: University of Chicago Press, 1982), 31 – 32.

30. Luther's statement is quoted in the preface to Martin Luther, *Propos de table,* ed. Louis Sauzin (Paris: Montaigne, 1932), 292, new ed. (Paris: Aubier, 1992).

31. Ibid., 292.

32. Chastel, *Sac de Rome,* 100 – 101; *Sack of Rome,* 72 – 74.

33. Preuss, *Die Vorstellung vom Antichrist,* 69.

34. Scribner, *For the Sake of Simple Folk,* 236 – 39.

35. For Thomas Murner, *Badenfahrt* (Strasbourg, 1514), see the edition by Ernst Martin (Strasbourg, 1887); for *Die Gäuchmatt* (Basel, 1519), see the edition by Wilhelm Uhl (Leipzig, 1896), 89 – 90.

36. These broadsides are now in Nuremberg, Berlin, and Munich; see Scribner, *For the Sake of Simple Folk,* 172, 273 n47.

37. John Bale, *Illustrium majoris Britanniae scriptores Summarium* (Basel, 1557), 118. This passage is given, in Italian translation, in Cesare D'Onofrio, *La Papessa Giovanna: Roma e papato tra storia e leggenda* (Rome: Romana Società Editrice, 1979), 114. See also Pier Paolo Vergerio, *Historia di papa Giovanni VIII che fu meretrice e strega* (1557).

38. Bale, *Illustrium majoris Britanniae scriptores*, 702; see D'Onofrio, *Papessa Giovanna*, 114–15.

39. See Pio Paschini, "P. P. Vergerio il giovane e la sua apostasia: Un episodio delle lotte religiose nel Cinquecento," *Lateranum* 788 (1925): 1–163, and Anne Jacobson Schutte, *Pier Paolo Vergerio: The Making of an Italian Reformer* (Geneva: Droz, 1977).

40. Vergerio, *Historia*, quoted in D'Onofrio, *Papessa Giovanna*, 117.

41. Vergerio, *Historia*, quoted in D'Onofrio, *Papessa Giovanna*, 117.

42. Vergerio, *Historia*, quoted in D'Onofrio, *Papessa Giovanna*, 118.

43. See D'Onofrio, *Papessa Giovanna*, 118–19.

44. Vergerio, *Historia*, quoted in ibid., 119.

45. D'Onofrio, *Papessa Giovanna*, 119–20.

46. Cyriacus Spangenberg, *Chronicon* (1614), quoted in Johannes Janssen, *L'Allemagne et la réforme*, translated from the German, vol. 5 (1899), 365–66.

47. Lucas Osiander, *Bedencken ob der newe päpstliche Kalender ein Nottdurfft bey der Christenheit seie* (Tübingen, 1583), 19.

48. *Ecclesiastica historia . . . congesta, per aliquot studiosos et pios viros in urbe Magdeburgica*, vol. 5 (Magdeburg, 1565), 333, 357ff.

49. Chastel, *Sac de Rome*, 106; *Sack of Rome*, 78.

50. Platina, *Le vite de' pontifici*, ed. Onofrio Panvinio (Vienna, 1663), 208–11.

51. Johannes Turmair (Aventinus), *Annalium Boiorum . . .* (Basel, 1580), a reprint of the 1554 edition, 368. See also Gerald Strauss, *Historian in an Age of Crisis: The Life and Work of Johannes Aventinus, 1477–1534* (Cambridge, Mass.: Harvard University Press, 1963).

52. Robert Bellarmine, *De romano pontifice*, in vol. 1 of Bellarmine, *De controversiis Christianae fidei adversus huius temporis haereticos*, bk. 3, chap. 24 (Rome, 1586).

53. For an accurate bibliography of Raemond, see Raymond Darricau, "La vie et l'oeuvre d'un parlementaire aquitain, Florimond de Raemond (1540–1601)," *Revue Française de l'Histoire du Livre* 1 (1971): 109–28.

54. Florimond de Raemond, *L'Anti-Christ et l'anti-papesse* 2d ed. (Paris, 1599), fol. 396r.

55. "In papatu nihil magis celebre ac tritum est quam futuri Antichristi adventus," quoted in Chastel, *Le sac de Rome*, 107.

56. Pierre Jurieu, *Histoire du Calvinisme et celle du pape . . .*, pt. 3, *Histoire du papisme*, chap. 2 (Rotterdam, 1683).

57. See Scribner, *For the Sake of Simple Folk*, 81, 82. On the carnality of the aggressive conviviality between Catholics and Lutherans, see Helena Schulz-Keil, "Le Christ phallophore," *Ornicar? Revue du Champ Freudien* 39 (1986 – 87): 51 – 90.

58. Gabriel Naudé, letter to Jacques Dupuy, in *Lettres de Gabriel Naudé à Jacques Dupuy: 1632–1653*, ed. Phillip Wolfe (Edmonton: Lealta/Alta, 1982), Letter 43, pp. 132 – 34. My thanks to Christian Jouhaud for pointing out this text to me.

59. Thomas Hobbes, *Leviathan*, ed. Edwin Curley (Indianapolis and Cambridge: Hackett, 1994).

60. Gottfried Wilhelm Leibniz, *Flores spersi in tumulum papissae*, in *Bibliotheca Historica Goettingensis*, ed. Christian Ludwig Scheidt (Göttingen, 1758), 297 – 392.

Chapter Seven

1. The edition of this text that I shall use is *Dietrich Schernbergs Spiel von Frau Jutten (1480) nach der einzingen Überlieferung im Druck des Hieronimus Tilesius (Eisleben 1565)*, ed. Edward Schröder (Bonn: A. Marcus und E. Weber, 1911).

2. Johann Christoph Gottsched, *Nöthiger Vorrath zur Geschichte der deutschen dramatischen Dichtkunst*, pt. 2 (Leipzig, 1765), 81 – 138.

3. Richard Haage, *Dietrich Schernberg un sein Spiel von Frau Jutten*, inaugural dissertation, University of Marburg, 1891.

4. Rutebeuf, *Miracle de Théophile*, in Rutebeuf, *Oeuvres complètes*, ed. Edmond Faral and Julie Bastin (1959 – 60), 2 vols. (Paris: Picard, 1977), 2: 167–203.

5. See Walter Benjamin, *Ursprung des deutschen Trauerspiels* (Frankfurt am Main: Suhrkamp, 1963, 1972), in French translation as *Les origines du drame baroque allemand*, trans. Sibylle Muller (Paris: Flammarion, 1985); in English translation as *The Origin of German Tragic Drama*, trans. John Osborne (London: NLB, 1977).

6. Hans Sachs, *Historia von Johanne Anglica, der bäpstin*, in vol. 8 of *Hans Sachs*, ed. Adelbert von Keller, Bibliothek des Litterarischer Vereins in Stuttgart, 121 (Stuttgart, 1874), 652 – 55.

7. *Encyclopédie, ou, Dictionnaire raisonné des sciences, des arts et des métiers*, ed. Denis Diderot and Jacques d'Alembert (Neuchâtel, 1765), s.v. "Papesse Jeanne."

8. Pierre Bayle, *Dictionnaire historique et critique* (Paris, 1695 – 97), s.v. "Papesse (Jeanne la)." There is a reprint edition of the Paris 1820 – 24 edition (Geneva: Slatkine, 1969). Bayle is quoted here from *The Dictionary Historical and Critical of Mr. Peter Bayle* (1737), reprint, 2d ed., 5 vols. (London: Routledge/Thoemmes Press, 1997), s.v. "Pope (Joan)."

9. Voltaire, *Essai sur les moeurs*, in *Oeuvres complètes* (Paris, 1878), 13: 196.

10. Voltaire, quoted in Frederick Hawkins, *The French Stage in the Eighteenth Century*, 2 vols. (London, 1888), 2: 339. Reprint (New York: Haskell House, 1969).

11. See Robert Darnton, *Bohême littéraire et Révolution: Le monde des livres au XVIIIe siècle* (Paris: Gallimard; Seuil, 1983).

12. Ibid., 173–74.

13. See *Dizionario biografico degli Italiani*, s.v. "Casti, Giambattista" (Salvatore S. Nigro).

14. I have used the bilingual edition of Giambattista Casti, *La Papesse* (Paris, 1878), 162–63.

15. Ibid., 134–37.

16. See Marvin A. Carlson, *The Theatre of the French Revolution* (Ithaca, N.Y.: Cornell University Press, 1966), in French translation as *Le théâtre de la Révolution française*, trans. J. and L. Bréant (Paris: Gallimard, 1970).

17. See Daniel Hamiche, *Le théâtre de la Révolution française: La lutte des classes au théâtre en 1789 et en 1793* (Paris: 10/18, 1973). The text of Maréchal's *Jugement dernier des rois* appears in appendix to this work, pp. 269–305.

18. Abraham Joseph Bénard Fleury, quoted from Carlson, *Theatre of the French Revolution*, 77; *Théâtre de la Révolution française*, 99.

19. On the circumstances of the performance of Maréchal's play, see Cleveland Moffett, *The Reign of Terror in the French Revolution* (New York: Ballentine, 1962), 143.

20. See Michel Vovelle, *Religion et Révolution: La déchristianisation de l'an II* (Paris: Hachette, 1976).

21. August Jean-Baptiste Defauconpret, *L'aînée des papesses*. This rare volume is held by the Bibliothèque de l'Arsenal, Paris, call number RF 18060.

22. Two copies of Pierre Léger, *La Papesse Jeanne* (Paris, 1793), are held by the Bibliothèque de l'Arsenal, call numbers RF 18535 and RF 8536.

23. Carlson, *Theatre of the French Revolution*, 116; *Théâtre de la Révolution française*, 141–42.

24. Carlson, *Theatre of the French Revolution*, 117–19; *Théâtre de la Révolution française*, 143–46.

25. Carlson, *Theatre of the French Revolution*, 144–45; *Théâtre de la Révolution française*, 172–74.

26. *Les Spectacles de Paris* (1793), 199, 211.

27. Defauconpret, *L'aînée des papesses*, preface.

28. Carlson, *Theatre of the French Revolution*, 229–30; *Théâtre de la Révolution française*, 269.

29. Chateaubriand, *Mémoires d'outre-tombe*, ed. Maurice Levaillant and Georges Moulinier, 2 vols. (Paris: Gallimard/Bibliothèque de la Pléiade, 1951), bk. 4, chap. 11, 1: 137–38, quoted from *The Memoirs of François René de Chateaubriand*, trans. Alexander Teizeira de Matos, 6 vols. (New York: G. P. Putnam's Sons, 1902), 1: 127–29.

30. Carbon Flins des Oliviers, *Les Voyages de l'Opinion dans les Quatre Parties du Monde*, issue 4 (n.p., 1790). This review is held by the Bibliothèque Nationale, Paris.

31. Carlson, *Theatre of the French Revolution*, 37, 57–58; *Théâtre de la Révolution française*, 50–51.

32. Michel Vovelle, *Théodore Desorgues, ou, La désorganisation: Aix-Paris, 1763–1808* (Paris: Seuil, 1985).

33. Théodore Desorgues, *Le Pape et le Mufti, ou, La réconciliation des cultes*, published in its entirety in Vovelle, *Théodore Desorgues*, 235–73. The passage quoted is on p. 242.

34. Desorgues, *Pape et le Mufti*, in Vovelle, *Théodore Desorgues*, 262.

35. Vovelle, *Théodore Desorgues*, 193.

36. Gottsched, *Nöthiger Vorrath*, pt. 2, 81–138.

37. Achim von Arnim, *Armut, Reichtum, Schuld und Busse der Gräfin Dolores* (1810), in *Sämtliche Romane und Erzählungen*, ed. Walter Migge (Munich: Hanser, 1962–65). The passage on Joan is pt. 4, chap. 6, pp. 348–63.

38. Ibid., 351.

39. Norbert Elias, *Über den Prozess der Zivilization* (1939), prologue to the French translation, *La civilisation des moeurs*, trans. Pierre Kamnitzer (Paris: Calmann-Lévy, 1973); the most recent English translation is *The Civilizing Process: The History of Manners and State Formation and Civilization*, trans. Edmund Jephcott, 3 vols. (Oxford and Cambridge, Mass.: Blackwell, 1994).

40. Jakob Grimm to Achim von Arnim, in *Achim von Arnim und die ihm nahe standen*, ed. Reinhold Steig and Herman Grimm, 3 vols. (Stuttgart: J. G. Cotta, 1894–1913), vol. 3 (1904), 78.

41. Achim von Arnim to Clemens von Brentano, in ibid., 240.

42. See Paul Merker, "Achim von Arnims 'Päpstin Johanne,'" in *Festschrift Theodor Siebs zum 70. Geburtstag*, ed. Walther Steller (Breslau: Marcus, 1933), 291–322.

43. Werner Kraft, *Die Päpstin Johanna: Motivgeschichtliche Untersuchung*, inaugural dissertation, Frankfurt, 1925.

44. Alfred Jarry, letter published in appendix to Alfred Jarry, *La Papesse Jeanne . . . suivi de Le Moutardier du pape*, ed. Marc Voline (Paris: Oswald-Neo, 1981), 253.

45. Bertholt Brecht, text published in Klaus Völker, *Päpstin Johanna: Ein Lesebuch* (Berlin: Klaus Wagenbach, 1977), 253.

46. My thanks to Daniel Milo for calling to my attention the importance of this theoretical notion among the Russian formalists.

47. See *Dietrich Schernbergs Spiel von Frau Jutten*, ed. Schröder, and Haage, *Dietrich Schernberg und sein Spiel*.

48. Max Weitemeyer, *Die Päpstin Johanna* (Erfurt: M. Luther, 1900); Adolf Bartels, *Die Päpstin Johanna*, in Bartels, *Römische Tragödien* (Munich: G. D. W. Callwey, 1905).

49. Rudolf Borchardt, *Die Päpstin Jutta: Ein dramatisches Gedicht*, part 1: *Verkündigung* (Berlin: E. Rohwohlt, 1920).

50. Ronald Firbank, *Concerning the Eccentricities of Cardinal Pirelli*, in Fir-

bank, *Works* (London: Duckworth, 1926; New York: Brentano's, 1929), vol. 5, in French translation as *Les excentricités du cardinal Pirelli,* trans. Patrick Reumaux (Paris: Rivages, 1987).

51. My thanks to Christian Jouhaud for bringing Taxil's text to my attention. For an excellent presentation of the personage of Léo Taxil, see Eugen Weber, *Satan franc-maçon* (Paris: Juillard, 1964).

52. Isaac Bashevis Singer, "Yentl," first published in *Commentary* (1962), available as *Yentle the Yeshiva Boy,* trans. Marion Magid and Elizabeth Pollett (New York: Farrar, Straus and Giroux, 1982), in French translation in Singer, *Yentl et autres nouvelles* (Paris: Laffont, 1965).

53. Georges Bernanos, *Un crime,* quoted here and below from *A Crime,* trans. Ann Green (New York: E. P. Dutton, 1936), 24, 22.

54. Bernanos, *A Crime,* 16, 20.

55. Ibid., 160, 63.

56. Ibid., 161, 139.

57. Ibid., 95, 161.

58. Ibid., 236, 36, 250.

CHAPTER EIGHT

1. Gottfried Wilhelm Leibniz, *Flores in tumulum papissae dispersi* (ca. 1695), in *Bibliotheca Historica Goettingensis* (Göttingen, 1758), 297.

2. Raymond Ruyer, *Homère au féminin: La jeune femme auteur de l'Odyssé* (Paris: Copernic, 1976).

3. Stendhal, *Promenades dans Rome,* in *Oeuvres complètes,* ed. Victor Del Litto (Geneva: Cercle du Bibliophile, 1974), 7: 241 – 46, quoted here from *A Roman Journal,* ed. and trans. Haakon Chevalier (New York: Orion Press, distributed by Crown, 1957), 196 – 98. My thanks to Bernard Guenée for pointing out this passage to me.

4. François Maximilien Misson, *Voyage d'Italie* (1691) (Paris, 1694), 2: 180 – 212.

5. Nicolaas Christiaan Kist, *De pausin Joanna (Eine sanwijzing, dat het onderzoek harer geschiedenis nog gunszins afgedaan of gesloten is),* appeared as an article in the *Zeitschrift für historische Theologie* 14, 2, 3 (1844); it was also reprinted separately in Leiden. Justus Henricus Wensing's response, *De verhandeling van N. C. Kist, over De Pausin Joanna, nagelezen en getoetst,* was published at The Hague in 1845. Ludwig Tross, *Een woord an Wensing over zijn geschrift wegens de pausin Joanna,* was published in Leiden in 1845.

6. See Henricus Guilielmus Wouters, *Dissertationes in selecta historiae ecclesiasticae capita* (Louvain, 1870), 3: 158; Cesare Baronio, *Annales ecclesiastici,* vol. 10 (1602); Angelo Mai, *Spicilegium Romanum* (Rome, 1823 – 38), quoted in *Pat. Graeca,* vol. 102 (Paris, 1860), col. 380 n85; Joseph Hergenroether, *Photius* (Regensburg, 1868), 2: 365; Karl Joseph von Hefele, *Conciliengeschichte* (Freiburg im

Breisgau, (1869 – 90), vol. 4 (1879), 458; Arthur Lapôtre, *L'Europe et le Saint-Siège à l'époque Carolingienne: Première partie, Le pape Jean VIII (872 – 882)* (Paris, 1895), 359 – 67; Onofrio Panvinio, *Historia B Platinae de vitis pontificum romanorum;* Florimond de Raemond, *L'Anti-Christ et l'anti-papesse* (Paris, 1599); Gaetano Moroni, *Dizionario di erudizione storico-ecclesiastica da S. Pietro sino ai nostri giorni,* 103 vols. (Venice, 1840 –), vol. 30 (1845), 279; *Dictionnaire apologétique de la foi catholique* (1911), s.v. "Jeanne (la papesse)" (Félix Vernet); Girolamo Arnaldi, introduction to Alain Boureau, "Un papa o piuttosto una papessa," *Storia e dossier* 1, 1 (1986): 26.

7. Leone Allacci (Allatius), *Confutatio fabulae de papissa Joanna ex monumentis graecis* (Rome, 1630); Alfonso Chacón (Ciaconius), *Vitae, et res gestae Pontificum Romanorum et S.R.E. Cardinalium,* 4 vols. (Rome, 1677), 1: 631 – 32; Théophile Reynaud, *Dissertatio de sobria alterius sexus frequentatione per sacros et religiosos homines* (Lyon, 1663), 465.

8. Pope Leo IX, letter to Michel Cerularius, patriarch of Constantinople, in *Pat. Latina,* vol. 143 (Paris, 1882), cols. 744 – 69, esp. col. 760.

9. Carlo Blasco, *Diatriba de Joanna papissa, sive de ejus fabulae origine* (Naples, 1778); Augustus Friedrich Gfrörer, *Geschichte der ost- und westfränkischen Carolinger, vom Tode Ludwigs der Frommen bis zum Ende Conrads I (840 – 918),* 2 vols. (Freiburg im Breisgau, 1848), 1: 288 – 93; Johann Joseph Ignaz von Döllinger, *Die Papst-Fabeln des Mittelalters: Ein Betrag zur Kirchengeschichte* (1863), 2d ed. (Stuttgart, 1890), available in English translation (of the first edition) as *Fables Respecting the Popes of the Middle Ages,* trans. Alfred Plummer (Oxford and Cambridge: Rivingtons, 1871).

10. For an analysis of another of these poles around which events move, see Alain Boureau, *L'aigle: Chronique politique d'un emblème* (Paris: Cerf, 1985).

CHAPTER NINE

1. Georges Bernanos, *Un crime* (Paris: Plon, 1935); quoted from *A Crime,* trans. Ann Green (New York: E. P. Dutton, 1936), 236, 239, 242.

INDEX

M8265-TX
95